Measuring Crime
&Criminality

Measuring Crime & Criminality

Advances in Criminological Theory

Volume 17

John MacDonald

editor

Routledge
Taylor & Francis Group

LONDON AND NEW YORK

First published 2011 by Transaction Publishers

2 Park Square, Milton Park, Abingdon, Oxfordshire OX14 4RN
711 Third Avenue, New York, NY 10017

Routledge is an imprint of the Taylor & Francis Group, an informa business

First issued in paperback 2017

Copyright © 2011 Taylor & Francis

ISBN 13: 978-1-4128-1481-2 (hbk)
ISBN 13: 978-1-138-51196-5 (pbk)
ISSN: 0894-2366

Contents

Introduction: The Measurement of Crime and Estimating Treatment Effects in Criminology

John M. MacDonald

In the early 1960s, Thorsten Sellin and Marvin Wolfgang set out on an ambitious research agenda to promote a more accurate measurement of the crime rate, culminating in a psychophysical scale for the seriousness of criminal offenses and their publication *The Measurement of Delinquency* (Sellin and Wolfgang, 1964). This pioneering work, along with Wolfgang and colleagues' subsequent *The National Survey of Crime Severity* (Wolfgang et al., 1985), provided the most comprehensive assessment of how to measure the severity of criminal offenses from normative ratings. Yet prominent scholars questioned the adequacy of this normative ranking approach for understanding the etiology of individual offending careers, its reliance on only official crime definitions, and the assumption that the seriousness scores could be added together.

Over the past four decades, criminology has adapted many other measurement approaches from the behavioral and social sciences in an attempt to gain greater theoretical leverage for understanding criminal behavior. Self-report survey methods are now commonly used to collect measures of crime perpetration and victimization. The self-report approach to measuring crime now plays a center stage in tests of criminological theory. Criminology has also advanced with the development of statistical models and methods of inference used to estimate various treatment effects.

The chapters in this volume were originally conceived through a series of meetings with Profs. William S. Laufer and Freda Adler. The preparation of these chapters has been supported by grants from a number of research agencies and foundations noted in the volume.

To introduce this volume, we need to first ask the following: How has our understanding of core issues of criminology changed from the various approaches to measuring crime and relevant theoretical constructs and tools of statistical inference? In this volume, scholars explore the potential benefits that different measurement and methods of statistical inference hold for understanding key criminological questions, examine what has been learned from the application of different approaches, and discuss other insights on how to improve measurement and methods for advancing core questions of criminological inquiry.

As the serving editor of this volume, it is my hope that these chapters help illustrate how understanding the measurement properties of criminal behavior and different approaches to estimating treatment effects is useful for developing theoretical insights on the "causes" of crime. There are plenty of excellent edited books and specialty journals that discuss issues of measurement and methods in other allied fields, but no thematic overview of these issues in criminology has been published for decades.

The purpose of criminological theories is to explain why some people engage in criminal behavior. Criminologists have adopted a wide range of theoretical perspectives—from genetic models that emphasize biosocial factors to more macro-sociological perspectives that examine neighborhood or societal factors—to address the core objective of explaining variation in crime between people and places. Criminological research has used a variety of research designs including the examination of administrative and self-report data, cross-sectional and longitudinal surveys, experimental designs, counterfactual approaches to causality, and the use of meta-analysis. These approaches are discussed in this volume. Before discussing these approaches, this volume focuses on the validity of the measurement of criminal behavior. Thornberry and Krohn's chapter explains how valid information on measuring criminal behavior is at the heart of how the science of criminology can progress, and the benefits of the self-report method. An often overlooked issue in the measurement of criminal behavior and related constructs is the effects of socially desirable response bias in the questions of surveys. MacDonald, Morral, and Piquero in their chapter discuss this problem for testing criminological theories with self-report surveys and provide a case study of socially desirable response bias in tests of Gottfredson and Hirschi's theory of self-control.

Beyond the issues of validity and reliability in the measurement of crime, there is also the need to have useful measures of crime severity and its social impact. Roman's chapter discusses the emerging literature developed in economics that estimates crime seriousness in monetized terms. In addition to providing an excellent summary of the economic approach to estimating crime severity and its logic, Roman provides a new method for estimating the severity of crimes using costs of criminal victimization. This entry is both novel and necessary if criminological theories are going to be advanced with any insight into practical value for public policy. I see this approach as a useful advancement of the normative ranking approaches developed in the 1960s by Sellin and Wolfgang.

Blending measurement and methods together, several chapters discuss issues that should be of fundamental interest to criminological endeavors. Taylor discusses why empirical tests of community-level theories of crime suffer from deficits in the conceptualization and measurement of key environmental constructs. Taylor provides a partial remedy for this problem by outlining an approach to construct validation of key measures of community-level attributes and their link to criminal behavior. Taylor suggests the use of a particular metamodel, a Boudon–Coleman diagram, capturing macro-to-micro, micro-to-micro, and micro-to-macro processes. Communities and crime scholars would be wise to read this chapter carefully for unique and important insights. Building on the issue of measurement and methods for testing core theories of criminology, Papachristos provides a thorough overview of the application of social network analysis to test criminological theories. In doing so, Papachristos provides a framework for how criminologists might conceptualize and employ social network analysis in their own work. Given the growing use of social network analysis in a variety of fields, this chapter is a welcome and necessary contribution. While criminologists may have "missed the boat" on the use of social network analysis, hopefully the field will embrace this approach where it is applicable and catch up with allied social sciences. Neuroscience is also playing an increasing role in all fields of study. Criminology is not immune to this trend. Odgers and Russell in their chapter note that genes play an important role in shaping human traits, including the propensity to commit antisocial behavior and crime. These authors provide a convincing review of the literature and suggested methodological approaches for gaining greater theoretical leverage on the gene–environment role in explaining criminal behavior. They are clear in noting that genetically informative research has yet to reach a point where it can be useful for prediction models. But they show how there are a number of important ways in which findings from gene–environment studies can be used in research designs to show the importance of environmental stimuli in the etiology of crime. This review chapter provides one with greater hope that biological measures can be integrated more clearly into models of crime and not be seen as competing explanations for criminal behavior derived from social or psychological theories.

In addition to issues of measurement, the importance of estimating various treatment effects is common in criminology, and many issues of criminological inquiry are at some level causal questions. What effect does gang membership have on delinquency? Does self-control cause criminal propensity? Does a good marriage cause desistance from crime? There is a growing appreciation in criminology for the role that causal inference has in answering our questions. The rigor of various methods of inference and research designs has a long tradition in the social sciences and criminological applications. There are a number of recent exchanges about experiments in criminology and other research designs using observational data for identifying treatment effects on crime or the desistance from it. More often than not criminological questions rely on statistical models that are based on probability distributions. A criminological question is addressed by examining a set of data presumed to represent a population. The key issue then becomes the appropriate probability distributions and the necessary parameters to approximate the population of interest. However, I would argue that even more fundamental than the appropriate reference probability distribution and method of approximation is our ability to identify an effect in the first place. After one has a good sense for identifying an effect, the search for the appropriate method of statistical approximation becomes more salient. As Manski (2007: 3) notes, "Studies of statistical inference seek to characterize the generally weaker conclusions that can be drawn from a finite number of observations. The study of identification logically comes first."

For better or worse, the literature in criminology is devoid of many succinct discussions of the role that identification strategies play in determining treatment effects or questions of causal relationships. The fields of economics, epidemiology, and statistics have spent considerable attention discussing theory and related methods for identifying causal effects, even in cases with ambiguous treatment assignment (see Manski and Nagin in the current volume). In these fields, causal inference is presumed to follow only after one has a reasonable strategy for identifying an effect on an outcome that is independent of differences in the units of observation. Estimation alone does not identify a treatment effect. Estimation provides approximations via a probability distribution to a reference population or group. A considerable amount of effort has been devoted in criminology over the past decade on estimation methods— typically focused on variance decomposition approaches and other extensions to the generalized linear model. Improvements in approximation are necessary and help advance science, but in the absence of transparent strategies for identification, these statistical models on their own do not provide us sound evidence of causal relationships.

Why has criminology become so fascinated with estimation over identification? While the answer to this question clearly varies within the population of criminologists and their academic orientation, a transparent discussion of identification strategies may provide some utility to our quest for a better understanding of the causes of crime and its consequences. Manski and Nagin provide an excellent overview of the problem of identification of treatment effects in criminology when there is uncertainty on the selection and outcomes. In Manski and Nagin's case study, the selection issue pertains to the assignment of juvenile delinquents to residential or nonresidential facilities. The outcome in their case study is recidivism. Manski and Nagin clearly show the tenuous assumption traditionally employed in criminology that once one includes observed covariates, the treatment selection is independent of the outcomes. Their chapter provides a compelling example developed from Manski's work on identification and estimation. Because much of the technical details of this literature are difficult to comprehend without requisite mathematical training, some fundamental issues of identification have not received enough attention in criminology. Identification strategies are, however, largely matters of logic and can be usefully discussed and applied to criminology. Manski and Nagin's illustration of the use of a bounding approach to identification is an important and overlooked contribution to criminology. I believe that criminology will face enduring problems of causal inference if the field remains focused on complicated methods of statistical estimation and ignores the importance of identification. After all, any situation in which one relies only on observable variables that have not been strictly subject to manipulation, a statistical model will invariably have more than one set of parameters that could generate the same distribution of criminal behavior.

Following on the issue of identification, Barnes and Hyatt provide an important chapter on the role of randomized experiments for testing core criminological theories. They show that the randomized experiment offers the best solution to clear conclusions about causality. True random assignment assures researchers that those groups receiving different treatments are equivalent on observable and unobservable features, thus assuring that the treatment effect of interest is exogenous to between-group differences. However, they also provide a clear discussion of why narrowly focused policy experiments provide fertile grounds for criticisms about the utility of the experimental design for testing core criminological theories. Barnes and Hyatt provide a review of the experiments that have been done in criminology and are quick to point out that experiments are often conducted for practical reasons and not in the interests of advancing theory. This fact, however, does not mean that experiments cannot be used to test theories of crime. Rather, the key issue to the use of randomized controlled trials (RCTs) in criminology is to design the experiments with a theory in mind and collect the necessary descriptive data.

Kirk's chapter can be viewed as a related discussion of the use of natural experiments as a method of improving on the identification of treatment effects in criminology. Kirk provides a nice illustration of the natural experiment methodology for testing criminological theories and how it can be used to overcome selection effects endemic in criminological research. Like the randomized experiment that by design creates independence between all variables apart from the assigned treatment and control conditions, the natural experiment mimics this design through the use of exogenous instrumental variables (IVs) that are induced by natures. Exogenous IVs by definition generate independence in observations that is separate from the features of individuals being studied. This approach to identification and generation of causal inference is a standard tool in economics, but has until recently had minimal application in criminology. Kirk relies on a real natural experiment—the August 2005 Hurricane Katrina natural disaster in the Gulf Coasts of Louisiana and Mississippi. The destruction from Hurricane Katrina is an exogenous source of variation that influences where people can reside upon release from prison that is separate from any observable feature of study subjects. Hurricane Katrina in effect operated like a randomized experiment in that individuals were sorted into different residential locations as a result of this disaster. Some share of this sorting mimics an RCT. Kirk provides an easy-to-read technical discussion of IV methods—the formulas and logic are accessible to criminologists with little statistical training. The use of IV methods in a natural experiment provides, like a true experiment, a remedy to the issue of selection bias by using only that portion of the variation in an independent variable that is generated from the randomness of nature. By design, then the IV provides the conditions under which individuals in the different groups are equivalent on all attributes except the treatment or control conditions.

Parting from the experimental design approach, the volume returns to the issue of estimation and methods used to test key questions of criminal careers, developmental, and life-course criminology. Sullivan and Piquero's chapter discusses the relative strengths of longitudinal growth models for improving the understanding of crime over the life course. These authors also compare and contrast latent class growth models typically used to study criminal careers with two conventional alternative approaches of growth mixture models and latent growth curves. Sullivan and Piquero focus on how these different model estimations converge and diverge, and the implications for theory and previous empirical findings. This chapter provides a clear illustration of statistical model comparisons and will be of interest to the growing number of criminologists conducting research using longitudinal data. Bushway and Paternoster's chapter departs a bit from a comparison of competing estimation models and propose a two-part methodological strategy to study desistance from crime over the life course—a growing interest among crime scholars. The first part of their approach is conceptual and involves thinking of longitudinal data as an individual time series. This permits the application of several statistical time series models developed from the fields of statistics and econometrics. Importantly, Bushway and Paternoster explicitly articulate their models of desistance from crime and how these fit with different time series models. These are welcome introductions because too often criminologists treat statistical models as interchangeable. All regression models and their variants won't produce useful estimates of treatment effects without a clear approach to identification. These entries highlight the need for criminology to first concentrate effort on identification models prior to estimation.

Wrapping up of this book is an important contribution by Mitchell on the use of meta-analysis for testing various criminological theories. Mitchell's chapter discusses the prospects, limitations, and challenges of using meta-analysis to gauge the empirical support of core criminological theories. He also provides a synopsis of the conventional practice and philosophy behind meta-analysis, or the formal quantification of research studies and their reported results to generate a weighted average effect size across studies. Mitchell discusses the benefits of meta-analysis for testing key hypotheses in criminological studies and why it is an imperfect but useful improvement over narrative reviews.

All the chapters written for this issue of Advances in Criminological Theory are from first-rate scholars. I am pleased with the cumulative knowledge this volume provides. I hope this volume will lead to further exchanges that help advance the field of criminology.

Conclusions

The desire to find ways to improve on the study of causal explanations for criminal behavior and its consequences is not unrealistic. There is a reasonable argument that many current approaches to measuring crime and methods for testing theories have stagnated. There are a myriad of opportunities to improve on conventional practice in criminology, and this should be a desire for any emerging field of science. The chapters in this volume provide some useful guidance for the field of criminology. The standard regression-based approach in criminology that attempts to correct the lack of comparability between the treatment and control conditions with a set of covariates, presumed to remove the difference between those exposed to the trait or treatment and those not exposed, is insufficient for the advancement of the field. In practice, it is very difficult in criminological applications to know when a regression model has been appropriately specified and adequately controlled for the differences between an observed treatment and the control state.

A key issue is for the advancement of criminological theories to conceptualize research designs that can be used to identify treatment effects. Understanding how to create or simulate a setting where the selection mechanism of treatment presumed to influence crime is independent of differences between observations in the treatment and control states. The use of experiments and quasi-experiments as identification approaches for estimating treatment effects fell out of favor among criminologists in the 1970s for more descriptive work on theory. I imagine that scholars with experience in the variety of traditions of urban research on crime and its control were a bit dismayed by the lack of evidence that emerged from a series of community- and employee-based interventions that were tied to experimental or quasi-experimental designs (e.g., the Chicago Area Project, Transitional Aid for Release Prisoners). Often these public policy interventions involved small dosage differences between treatment and control conditions, were delivered with little fidelity, or were fatally flawed in addressing larger systemic problems that affect people in high poverty–crime neighborhoods. A natural substitution has been the route of descriptive theories to form identification of parameters and the use of statistical models.

The shortcoming of past policy experiments as being too circumscribed or delivered with little fidelity or attention to theory shouldn't prevent us from pushing forward to advocate for experiments or quasi-experiments on important policy interventions complemented with population-based survey research to address larger structural questions. Health scientists often study population disparities on health outcomes as a method of identifying groups in need of greater health-care services, while medical research often relies on RCTs to study specific effects of medical treatments. It seems that criminology should be doing both, using observational research to study populations and subpopulations of people to look at systemic issues and experimental designs to figure out better methods to prevent crime (police deployment, arrest policies, neighborhood initiatives) or minimize the harm caused by crime (restorative justice conferences) (see Sampson, 2008, for related comments).

How can we make the response to crime more rational and just? Experiments, whether induced through an RCT or by nature, are helpful because they allow us to address at least incremental advancement with the strongest method for making observations comparable under treatment and control states and identify a treatment effect. At the same time, experiments will often identify only the causal effect for those eligible or most likely to receive treatment (Sampson, 2010). Cash payments may be a good use of public resources to encourage high school graduation for those at risk for prison, but they may make things worse for those already motivated to graduate from high school by encouraging the goal of graduation over the process of accumulating knowledge. The same issue applies to selection models for identification. It is important to not only get the selection model right but also figure out who is being compared. Is the comparison the average treatment effect on the treated or most likely to receive treatment? Is the comparison a local average treatment effect that applies to the entire population? Thinking carefully about the groups being compared is the first step needed before the computation.

Bibliography

Manski, Charles. *Identification for Prediction and Decision*. Cambridge, MA: Harvard University Press, 2007.

Sampson, Robert J. "Moving to Inequality: Neighborhood Effects and Experiments Meet Social Structure." *American Journal of Sociology* 114 (2008): 189–231.

————. "Gold Standard Myths: Observations on the Experimental Turn in Quantitative Criminology." *Journal of Quantitative Criminology* 26 (2010): 489–500.

Sellin, Thorsten and Marvin E. Wolfgang. *The Measurement of Delinquency*. New York: Wiley, 1964.

Wolfgang, Marvin E., Robert M. Figlio, Paul E. Tracy, and Simon I. Singer. *The National Survey of Crime Severity*. Washington, DC: U.S. Department of Justice, U.S. Government Printing Office, 1985.

1

The Self-Report Method and the Development of Criminological Theory

Terence P. Thornberry and Marvin D. Krohn

The core purpose of etiological theories of crime is to explain why some people engage in criminal behavior while others do not. There are many secondary purposes, for example, to explain why some people engage in more or less serious criminal behavior than others and why they do so at different rates and periodicities over their life course. There can, of course, be more refined or specialized questions; for example, why do some people commit certain types of offenses like violence or sex offenses, or how do certain contexts facilitate criminal behavior? But these specialized issues do not really alter the core issue—explaining why some people engage in criminal behaviors.

Criminologists have adopted a wide range of theoretical perspectives—from genetic models to broad macro-social perspectives—to address this core objective. They have also used a variety of research designs including the examination of official records, cross-sectional and longitudinal surveys, experimental designs, and, more recently, counterfactual approaches to causality. Indeed, many of these approaches are discussed in this volume. But whatever theory is adopted or research approach is taken, one central ingredient is required if we are to make progress in our scientific understanding of criminal behaviors: a valid measure of actual involvement in criminal behavior. That is, we need to know as accurately as possible whether each person in a study sample actually engaged in criminal behavior. Absent valid information on the behavior of interest, it is hard to see how science can progress.

Measuring actual involvement in crime is a difficult task. Crime, by its very nature, is a secretive and sensitive topic. Those who engage in crime are liable for punishment and not likely to broadcast their activities.

Thus, in criminology, the scientific need for full and accurate information to both describe and explain the phenomenon is hampered by the very characteristics of the behavior to be explained. This difficulty does not obviate the scientific necessity of generating valid and accurate measurement, however. It is a challenge that must be overcome if scientific knowledge is to advance.

Criminologists have adopted several approaches to the measurement of criminal behavior. They include the use of direct observation of criminal acts, life histories of criminals, the examination of official records such as arrest reports, self-report surveys, victimization surveys, biochemical assays such as urinalysis, and third-party reports, for example, from parents. The present chapter focuses on the self-report method and assesses its advantages for both informing and empirically assessing theories of criminal behavior. Although far from perfect, our core contention is that self-report data are currently the best single source of data to use in developing and testing etiological theories of crime.

We begin with a brief history of the self-report method and key requirements to generate a psychometrically acceptable measure. Following that, we return to an assessment of the advantages of the self-report measure for theoretical criminology.

Historical Overview

The development and widespread use of the self-report method of collecting data on delinquent and criminal behavior is one of the most important innovations in criminological research in the twentieth century. Initially, there was great skepticism about whether respondents would be willing to tell researchers about their participation in illegal behaviors. The earliest studies by Porterfield (1943) and by Wallerstein and Wylie (1947) found that not only were respondents willing to self-report their delinquency and criminal behavior, but also they did so in surprising numbers. Since those very early studies, the self-report methodology has become much more sophisticated in design, making it more reliable and valid, and extending its applicability to many criminological issues.

Although the self-report method began with the contributions of Porterfield (1943, 1946) and Wallerstein and Wylie (1947), Short and Nye (1957, 1958) "revolutionized ideas about the feasibility of using survey procedures with a hitherto taboo topic" and changed how the discipline thought about delinquent behavior itself (Hindelang et al., 1981: 23). Short and Nye's research is distinguished from previous self-report measures in its attention to methodological issues, such as scale construction, reliability and validity, and sampling, and their explicit focus on the substantive relationship between social class and delinquent behavior. Short and Nye did not find social class to be inversely related to delinquency based on their self-report scale. Other studies in the late 1950s and early 1960s also used self-reports to examine the relationship between social status and delinquent behavior (e.g., Reiss and Rhodes, 1959; Clark and Wenninger, 1962; Akers, 1964; Empey and Erickson, 1966; Gold, 1966; Voss, 1966). With few exceptions, these studies supported the general conclusion that if there were any statistically significant relationships between measures of social status and self-report delinquent behavior, they were weak and clearly did not mirror the findings of studies using official data sources. This failure to find a relationship between social status and delinquency served to question extant theories such as anomie theory (Merton, 1938) and social disorganization theory (Shaw and McKay, 1942) that were built on the assumption that crime was most prevalent among the lower class. It is the first clear example of how the self-report method changed the theoretical landscape.

The absence of a relationship between class and delinquency, especially when compared to the strength of the relationship using official data, raises fundamental questions about the operations of the juvenile and criminal justice systems. The contradictory findings from these two data sources were one of the primary factors in the development and prominence of labeling theory (e.g., Lemert, 1951; Becker, 1963) during the middle part of the twentieth century.

During this same period, researchers began to recognize the true potential of the self-report methodology. By including questions concerning other aspects of an adolescent's life, as well as a self-report delinquency scale on the same questionnaire, researchers could explore a host of etiological issues. Theoretically interesting issues concerning the family (Nye and Olson, 1958; Dentler and Monroe, 1961; Voss, 1964; Stanfield, 1966; Gold, 1970), peers (Short, 1957; Erickson and Empey, 1963; Reiss and Rhodes, 1964; Voss, 1964; Matthews, 1968; Gold, 1970) and the school (Reiss and Rhodes, 1963; Elliott, 1966; Polk, 1969; Gold, 1970; Kelly, 1974) emerged as the central focus of self-report studies. The results of these studies led to a shift in emphasis in theoretical criminology, away from macrolevel explanations for crime to more individual and family-based theories. The self-report method was used both to develop and to test social control theory (Hirschi, 1969; Hindelang, 1973; Conger, 1976), social learning theory (Akers et al., 1979), self-concept theory (Kaplan, 1972; Jensen, 1973), strain theory

(Elliott and Voss, 1974; Johnson, 1979), and deterrence theory (Waldo and Chiricos, 1972; Anderson et al., 1977; Jensen et al., 1978).

Most of these self-report studies were cross-sectional in design. The next major step in the development of this measurement approach, and its next major impact on theoretical criminology, came with the introduction of longitudinal self-report studies. The first major longitudinal self-report study is the National Youth Survey (NYS), conducted by Elliott et al. (1979). The NYS began in 1976 surveying a national probability sample of 1,725 youth aged eleven through seventeen and has followed them well into their thirties. The survey design was sensitive to a number of methodological deficiencies of prior self-report studies and has been greatly instrumental in improving the self-report method. Since that time, an increasing number of panel studies have collected self-report data from sample members over long portions of the life course. They include the three studies of the Program of Research on the Causes and Correlates of Delinquency conducted in Denver, Pittsburgh, and Rochester (Thornberry and Krohn, 2003) as well as similar studies conducted in Seattle (Hawkins et al., 2003), Montréal (Tremblay et al., 2003), and other cities.

Along with criminal career research based on official data (Wolfgang et al., 1972; Blumstein et al., 1986), these longitudinal self-report studies have changed our understanding of patterns of delinquency and reshaped theoretical criminology. Instead of focusing on static attributes of delinquency—for example, the level, variety, or seriousness of offending—longitudinal studies using the self-report method added a more dynamic orientation to the study of delinquency and crime. New descriptions of crime emerged including issues such as age of onset, the distribution of the age–crime curve, length of careers, trajectories or patterns of offending, intermittency, desistance, and so forth. Descriptions of these new and different aspects of offending careers required a shift in theoretical attention.

The application of the self-report method within longitudinal designs coupled with the conceptual framework developed by Glen Elder (1997) facilitated the emergence of life-course criminology as the dominant theoretical perspective in the latter part of the twentieth century (see, e.g., the summaries in Thornberry, 1997, and Farrington, 2005). Traditional theories had focused almost exclusively on between-individual explanations for offending, attempting to explain why delinquents differed from nondelinquents. Developmental theories, while interested in that issue, became increasingly focused on within-individual differences in attempting to explain changing patterns of offending over the life course. For example, there was an increased focus on explaining the link between early-onset offending and later criminal careers, explaining the notable level of continuity in offending over the life course, explaining different patterns of offending such as desistance and late bloomers, explaining the developmental consequences of involvement in delinquency, and so forth. Rather than focusing primarily on adolescent influences as traditional theories had, life-course explanations examine the origins and consequences of delinquency and crime over the full life course, from childhood through adulthood.

In sum, the advent and development of the self-report method has influenced the shape and development of theoretical criminology in several ways. The influence that the method had on changes in criminological theories was intimately linked to improvements in the scope and quality of self-report measures. We turn now to a discussion of how the self-report method itself developed over time.

Development of the Self-Report Method

Since the introduction of the self-report method by Short and Nye (1957), considerable attention has been paid to the development and improvement of the psychometric properties of self-report measures of delinquent behavior. The most sophisticated and influential work was done by Elliott and his colleagues (Elliott and Ageton, 1980; Elliott et al., 1985; Huizinga and Elliott, 1986) and by Hindelang et al. (1979, 1981). From their work, a set of characteristics for acceptable, that is, reasonably valid and reliable, self-report scales has emerged. Five of the most salient of these characteristics are the inclusion of (1) a wide array of offenses, including serious offenses; (2) frequency response sets; (3) screening for trivial behaviors; (4) application to a wider age range; and (5) the use of longitudinal designs. Each of these design features will be briefly discussed here; a fuller discussion can be found in Thornberry and Krohn (2001).

Inclusion of a Wide Array of Delinquency Items

The domain of crime covers a wide range of behaviors, from petty theft to aggravated assault and homicide. If the general domain of delinquent and criminal behavior is to be represented in a self-report scale, it is necessary for the scale to cover that same wide array of human activity. Simply asking about a handful of these behaviors does not accurately represent the theoretical construct of crime. In particular, it is essential that a general self-report delinquency index tap serious as well as less serious behaviors. Early self-report scales tended to ignore serious delinquent acts and concentrated almost exclusively on minor forms of delinquency. In part, this was due to concern about having a sufficient number of serious offenders in the sample to allow for reliable conclusions. With the increased concern for surveying adolescents at risk for serious and violent delinquency (see Thornberry and Krohn, 2003), more serious offenders could be included. Failure to include serious offenses misrepresents the full domain of delinquency, contaminates comparisons with other data sources, and impedes the testing of many delinquency theories that set out to explain serious, chronic delinquency.

Inclusion of Frequency Response Sets

Many early self-report studies relied on response sets with a relatively small number of categories that tend to censor high-frequency responses. For example, Short and Nye (1957) used a four-point response with the highest category being "often." Aggregated over many items, the use of limited response sets had the consequence of lumping together occasional and high-rate delinquents, rather than discriminating between these behaviorally different groups. Taking into account the full range of responses had implications for the relationship between demographic factors and delinquency (Elliott and Ageton, 1980) and, in turn, theories in which such factors play a significant role.

Inclusion of Screening for Trivial Behaviors

Self-report questions have a tendency to elicit reports of trivial acts that are very unlikely to elicit official reactions and even acts that are not violations of the law. This not only occurs more frequently with less serious offenses but also affects responses to serious offenses. For example, respondents have included such pranks like hiding a classmate's books in the respondent's locker between classes as theft, or events that are merely roughhousing between siblings as serious assault. Two strategies are generally available to address this issue. First, one can ask a series of follow-up questions designed to elicit more information about the event, such as the value of the property stolen, the extent of injury to the victim, and the like. Second, one can use an open-ended question asking the respondent to describe the event and then probe to obtain information necessary to classify the act. Both strategies have been used with some success.

Application to a Wider Age Range

With increasing emphasis on the study of crime across the entire life course, self-report surveys have had to be developed to take into account both the deviant behavior of very young children and the criminal behavior of older adults. The behavioral manifestations of illegal and antisocial behaviors can change, depending on the stage in the life course at which the assessment is taking place. For the very young child, measures have been developed that are administered to parents to assess antisocial behavior such as noncompliance, disobedience, and aggression (Achenbach, 1992). For the school-age child, Loeber et al. (1993) have developed a checklist that expands the range of antisocial behavior to include such behaviors as stubbornness, lying, bullying, and other externalizing problems. Unfortunately, there has not been as much development of instruments targeted specifically at adults (Weitekamp, 1989), and many studies simply use an upward extension of adolescent instruments.

Use of Longitudinal Designs

Perhaps the most significant development in the application of the self-report methodology is its use in following the same subjects over time in order to account for changes in their criminal behavior. This has enabled researchers to examine the effect of age of onset, to track the careers of offenders, to study desistance, and to apply developmental theories to study both the causes and the consequences of criminal behavior over the life course. While broadening the range of issues that can be examined, the use of the self-report technique in longitudinal panel designs introduces potential threats to the reliability and validity of the data. In addition to the concern over construct continuity in applying the technique to different aged respondents, the researcher needs to attend to the possibility of panel or testing effects in which the number of prior interviews can influence the individual's responses at the current interview (Thornberry, 1989; Lauritsen, 1998).

In sum, by adopting all or some of these five measurement characteristics, more recent self-report studies have been able to provide a better picture of involvement in criminal behavior. These characteristics should also improve validity and the reliability of self-report indexes since they improve our ability to identify delinquents and to discriminate among different types of delinquents. These are clearly desirable qualities, and we turn now to a brief discussion of the psychometric properties of self-report measures.

Reliability and Validity

For any measure to be scientifically worthwhile, it must possess both reliability and validity. Reliability is the extent to which a measuring procedure yields the same result on repeated trials. Validity is a more abstract notion. A measure is valid to the extent to which it measures the concept you set out to measure, and nothing else. While reliability focuses on a particular property of the measure—namely, its stability over repeated uses—validity concerns the crucial relationship between the theoretical concept one is attempting to measure and what one actually measures.

Assessing Reliability

There are two classic ways of assessing the reliability of social science measures: test–retest reliability and internal consistency. Huizinga and Elliott (1986) make a convincing case that the test–retest approach is fundamentally more appropriate for assessing self-report measures of delinquency, so we will focus our discussion on this approach. Test–retest is quite straightforward; a sample of respondents is administered a self-report delinquency inventory (the test), and then, after a short interval, the same inventory is re-administered (the retest). In doing this, the same questions and the same reference period should be used at both times.

A number of studies have assessed the test–retest reliability of self-report delinquency measures. In general, the results indicate that these measures are acceptably reliable. The reliability coefficients vary somewhat depending on the number and types of delinquent acts included in the index and the scoring procedures used—for example, simple frequencies or ever-variety scores—but scores well above .80 are common. In summarizing much of the previous literature in this area, Huizinga and Elliott state thus:

> Test–retest reliabilities in the 0.85–0.99 range were reported by several studies employing various scoring schemes and numbers of items and using test–retest intervals

of from less than one hour to over two months (Clark and Tifft, 1966; Belson, 1968; Kulik et al., 1968; Broder and Zimmerman, 1978; Braukmann et al., 1979; Hindelang et al., 1981; Skolnick et al., 1981; Patterson and Loeber, 1982). (1986: 300)

Perhaps the most comprehensive assessment of the psychometric properties of the self-report method was conducted by Hindelang et al. (1981). While mindful of the limitations of internal consistency approaches, Hindelang et al. (1981) report Cronbach's alpha coefficients for ever-variety, last-year variety, and last-year frequency scores for several demographic subgroups. The coefficients range from .76 to .93. Most of the coefficients are above .8, and eight of the eighteen coefficients are above .9. They also estimated test–retest reliabilities for these three self-report measures for each of the demographic subgroups; most of the test–retest correlations are above .9. Hindelang et al. point out that reliability scores of this magnitude are higher than those typically associated with many attitudinal measures and conclude that "the overall implication is that in many of the relations examined by researchers, the delinquency dimension is more reliably measured than are many of the attitudinal dimensions studied in the research" (1981: 82).

Huizinga and Elliott (1986) estimated test–retest reliability scores for a general delinquency index as well as a number of subindexes. The general delinquency index appears to have an acceptable level of reliability. The test–retest correlation for the frequency score is .75 and for the variety score it is .84. For the various subindexes—ranging from public disorder offenses to the much more serious index offenses—the reliabilities vary from a low score of .52 (for the frequency measure of felony theft) to a high score of .93 (for the frequency measure of illegal services). In total, Huizinga and Elliott (1986) report twenty-two estimates of test–retest reliability—across indexes and across frequency and variety scores—and the mean reliability coefficient is .74. Also Huizinga and Elliott did not find any consistent differences across sex, race, class, place of residence, or delinquency level in terms of test–retest reliabilities.

Assessing Validity

There are several ways of assessing validity. We will concentrate on three: content validity, construct validity, and criterion validity. Content validity is a subjective or logical assessment of the extent to which the measure adequately reflects the full domain, or the full content, that is contained in the concept being measured. A reasonable definition of delinquency and crime is the commission of behaviors that violate criminal law and that place the individual at some risk of arrest if the behavior were known to the police. Can we make a logical case that self-report measures of delinquency are valid in this respect?

As we noted above, the earlier self-report inventories contained relatively few items to measure the full range of delinquent behavior. For example, the Short and Nye (1957) inventory contains only twenty-one items, and most of their analysis was conducted with a seven-item index. Similarly, Hirschi's self-report measure (1969) is based only on six items. More importantly, the items that are included in these scales are clearly biased toward the minor or trivial end of the continuum.

The more recent self-report measures appear to be much better in this regard. For example, the Hindelang et al. (1981) index includes sixty-nine items that range from status offenses, such as skipping class, to violent crimes, like serious assault and armed robberies. The NYS index (Elliott et al., 1985) has forty-seven items designed to measure all but one (homicide) of the Uniform Crime Report Part I offenses, 60 percent of the Part II offenses, as well as offenses that juveniles are particularly likely to commit. The self-report inventory used by the three projects of the Program of Research on the Causes and Correlates of Delinquency has thirty-two items measuring delinquent behavior and twelve items measuring substance use.

These more recent measures, while not perfect, tap into a much broader range of delinquent and criminal behavior. As a result, they appear to have reasonable content validity.

Construct validity refers to the extent to which the measure being validated is related in theoretically expected ways to other concepts or constructs. In our case, the key question is: are measures of delinquency based on the self-report method correlated in expected ways with variables expected to be major risk factors for delinquency? In general, self-report measures of delinquency and crime, especially the more recent longer inventories, appear to have a high degree of construct validity. They are generally related in theoretically expected ways to basic demographic characteristics and to a host of theoretical variables drawn from various domains such as individual attributes, family structure and processes, school performance, peer relationships, neighborhood characteristics, and so forth. Hindelang et al. offer one of the clearer assessments of construct validity (1981: 127). They correlate a number of etiological variables with different self-report measures, collected under different conditions. With a few nonsystematic exceptions, the correlations are in the expected direction and of the expected magnitude.

Overall, construct validity may offer the strongest evidence for the validity of self-report measures of delinquency and crime. Indeed, if one examines the general literature on delinquent and criminal behavior, it is surprising how few theoretically expected relationships are not observed for self-report measures of delinquency and crime. It is unfortunate that this approach is not used to assess validity more formally and more systematically.

Criterion validity "... refers to the relationship between test scores and some known external criterion that adequately indicates the quantity being measured" (Huizinga and Elliott, 1986: 308). There is a fundamental difficulty in assessing the criterion validity of self-report measures of delinquency and crime and, for that matter, all measures of delinquency and crime. Namely, there is no "gold standard" against which to judge the self-report measure. That is, there is no fully accurate assessment that we can use as a benchmark. As a result, the best we can do is to compare different flawed measures of criminal involvement to see if we obtain similar responses and results. If so, the similarity across different measurement strategies heightens the probability that the various measures are tapping into the underlying concept of interest. While not ideal, this is the best that we can do in this area of inquiry.

We can begin by examining the correlation between self-report official contacts and official measures of delinquency. These correlations are quite high in the Hindelang et al. (1981) study, ranging from .70 to .83. Maxfield et al. (2000) report that the concordance between having an official arrest and self-reports of being arrested is quite high; of those arrested, 73 percent report an arrest.

It appears that survey respondents are quite willing to self-report their involvement with the juvenile and criminal justice systems. Are they also willing to self-report their involvement in undetected delinquent behavior? One way of examining this is to compare self-report delinquent behavior and official measures of delinquency. If these measures are valid, one would expect a reasonably large positive correlation between them.

Hindelang et al. (1981) present correlations using a number of different techniques for scoring the self-report measures. Overall, these correlations are reasonably high, somewhere around .60 for all subjects. For white and African American females and for white males, the correlations range from .58 to .65; for African American males, however, the correlations are low, ranging from .30 to .35. Huizinga and Elliott (1986) report that the majority of individuals who have been arrested do report their delinquent behavior and that the majority of offenses they commit are also reported. The reporting rates for gender, race, and social class groupings are quite comparable to the overall rates, with one exception. As was the case with the Hindelang et al. data, African American males substantially underreport their involvement in delinquency.

Farrington et al. (1996), using the Pittsburgh Youth Study data, suggest that there is a substantial degree of criterion validity for the self-report inventory used in the Program of Research on the Causes and Correlates of Delinquency. African American males are no more or less likely to self-report delinquent behavior than are white males. These researchers also compared the extent to which boys with official court petitions self-reported being apprehended by the police. Overall, about two-thirds of the boys with court petitions answered in the affirmative. Moreover, there was no evidence of differential validity by race.

In summary, we have examined three different approaches to assessing the validity of self-report measures of delinquency and crime: content, construct, and criterion validity. Overall, especially for the more recent self-report inventories, the self-report method for measuring criminal behavior appears to be reasonably valid. The content validity of the recent inventories is acceptable, the construct validity is quite high, and the criterion validity appears to be in the moderate to strong range.

Applying the Self-Report Method to Theoretical Criminology

Many years ago, Thorsten Sellin made the simple but critically important observation that "the value of a crime rate for index purposes decreases as the distance from the crime itself in terms of procedure increases" (1931: 337). The same can be said about its value for theoretical development. Since, as we noted in the introduction, the core objective of etiological theories of crime is to explain criminal behavior, the measure that most closely reflects actual behavior has the highest value. At the moment, that appears to be the self-report method, especially the more recent versions of this measurement approach that include the methodological advances summarized in previous sections.

The key advantage of the self-report method for testing criminological theory revolves around face validity. Self-reports simply map onto the key concept—a person's actual involvement in criminal behavior—better than any of the alternative sources of data. The self-report method asks the person most likely to know—the potential offender—if they engaged in the behavior. All other sources are more distant.

Official data, for example, are filtered through several gates. Typically someone other than the offender must be aware of the offense, they should decide to report it to the police, the police need to investigate, and then decide to record the event as a criminal act. At each gate, a nonrandom set of offenses are lost as decisions are influenced by offense, victim, and offender characteristics. Moreover, etiological research requires information, often detailed information, about offenders, and only a subset of officially recorded crimes have identified offenders. As a result, official data are likely to have a relatively small and nonrandom subset of the universe of criminals and of criminal behavior.

Descriptions of offending based on arrest or conviction data are likely to be biased, for example, overestimating relationships with demographic characteristics such as gender, race/ethnicity, and social class. To the extent to which they exist, such biases distort theories of crime and our efforts to empirically test those theories. These data, since they are collected for administrative purposes, also provide very little information about potential risk factors and causal risk factors.

Another major way of measuring crime is by victim surveys. Victim data, for example from the National Crime Victimization Survey, have many valuable uses such as measuring the overall crime rate and trends in criminal behavior. But for developing or testing etiological theories, they are severely limited. First, for obvious reasons they include only crimes with victims, which exclude large segments of the universe of crime thereby weakening the measure's content validity. Second, general samples tend to underestimate portions of the population that are at high risk for both victimization and offending—such as the homeless, institutionalized youth, and marginalized youth. Third, only the victim's perspective is available, and victims can only provide information about offenders—which is essential for theory development and testing—in a subset of the crimes in which they are involved. Victims are also not the most accurate reporters of offender characteristics and, at best, can provide relatively crude and categorical information. They also can provide no information about major risk factors, for example, family, peer, and school influences, for offending.

Direct observations of offending have similar problems. They only include a limited range of offenses—those that occur in public settings—and they can provide very little detailed information about the characteristics, behaviors, and attitudes of the offender, all of which are essential for theory development and theory testing.

More qualitative approaches to data collection, for example, ethnographic data and life histories of criminals, provide rich descriptions of offenders and their criminal behavior, and offer valuable insights into many of the processes that are related to offending. But they do so for very small and highly selected samples. As a result, it is not self-evident that the rich descriptions they provide apply to the entire population. Indeed, these studies typically select samples of offenders who differ from the general population on key dimensions such as the frequency, seriousness, or type of their criminality. It is essential that their results be validated on broad samples that represent the full population to which a theory applies. But that, of course, is not likely to be done with qualitative data, given the manner in which that type of data is typically collected.

This, of course, brings us back to self-report data as likely being the single best source of information for both developing and testing theories. First, recent self-report measures have demonstrated strong reliability and validity. Content validity is particularly important in this regard because, unlike the other measurement techniques, self-report inventories, if properly constructed, can cover the full range of criminal involvement from minor through serious offenses. Second, the self-report method can be and has been used with representative samples of the population to which general etiological theories are said to apply. These include nationally representative samples such as that in the NYS (Elliott et al., 1985) and samples representative of local communities such as those in the Program of Research on the Causes and Correlates of Delinquency (Thornberry and Krohn, 2003). Third, because self-report measures are collected in surveys, they can be directly linked to a host of risk factors and explanatory variables including the individual's own attitudes and perceptions. Those concepts form the heart of most theories of criminal behavior, and it is essential for data sets used to develop and test those theories to include measures of those concepts. No other method of measuring criminal involvement is able to meet all three of these criteria.

We do not mean to suggest that the self-report method is without its flaws when it comes to its utility for theoretical criminology. For example, while self-report inventories can and do include items measuring serious offenses, they often have very low frequencies, given the rare nature of those offenses. There does seem to be a tendency for self-report measures to elicit responses to more minor offenses. Nor do we mean to suggest that the other methods for measuring criminal involvement are without merit. Clearly, they are very valuable and have contributed to many different aspects of criminological study. Indeed, official and victim data are much more useful than self-reported data for estimating the overall crime rate and trends in offending. Our point is more focused: for the express purpose of developing and testing theories of crime, the self-report method has distinct advantages over the other methods. Finally, we note that there are many advantages to having multiple indicators of criminal involvement—self-report responses, official arrest histories, reports from other observers, and so forth. All available indicators of criminal involvement are flawed, and there is certainly no gold standard. Having multiple indicators is certainly wise. But for use in theory construction and testing, it is essential that one of those multiple indicators be self-report data. For all of the reasons enumerated above, the self-report method has unique and valuable qualities with respect to theoretical criminology.

Bibliography

Achenbach, T. M. *Manual for the Child Behavior Checklist/2–3 and 1992 Profile*. Burlington: University of Vermont, 1992.

Akers, Robert L. "Socio-Economic Status and Delinquent Behavior: A Retest." *Journal of Research in Crime and Delinquency* 1 (1964): 38–46.

Akers, Robert L., Marvin D. Krohn, L. Lanza-Kaduce, and M. Radosevich. "Social Learning and Deviant Behavior: A Specific Test of a General Theory." *American Sociological Review* 44 (1979): 636–55.

Anderson, Linda S., Theodore G. Chiricos, and Gordon P. Waldo. "Formal and Informal Sanctions: A Comparison of Deterrent Effects." *Social Problems* 25 (1977): 103–12.

Becker, Howard. *Outsiders: Studies in the Sociology of Deviance*. New York: Free Press, 1963.

Belson, W. A. "The Extent of Stealing by London Boys and Some of Its Origins." *Advancement of Science* 25 (1968): 171–84.

Blumstein, A., J. Cohen, J. A. Roth, and C. A. Visher. *Criminal Careers and Career Criminals*. Washington, DC: National Academy Press, 1986.

Braukmann, C. J., K. A. Kirigin, and M. M. Wolf. "Social Learning and Social Control Perspectives in Group Home Delinquency Treatment Research." *Paper Presented at the American Society of Criminology Meetings*, Philadelphia, 1979.

Broder, P. K. and J. Zimmerman. *Establishing the Reliability of Self-Reported Delinquency Data*. Williamsburg, VA: National Center for State Courts, 1978.

Clark, J. P. and L. L. Tifft. "Polygraph and Interview Validation of Self-Reported Delinquent Behavior." *American Sociological Review* 31 (1966): 516–23.

Clark, J. P. and E. P. Wenninger. "Socioeconomic Class and Area as Correlates of Illegal Behavior among Juveniles." *American Sociological Review* 28 (1962): 826–34.

Conger, Rand. "Social Control and Social Learning Models of Delinquency: A Synthesis." *Criminology* 14 (1976): 17–40.

Dentler, R. A. and L. J. Monroe. "Social Correlates of Early Adolescent Theft." *American Sociological Review* 26 (1961): 733–43.

Elder, G. H., Jr. "The Life Course and Human Development." In *Handbook of Child Psychology, Volume 1: Theoretical Models of Human Development*, edited by Richard M. Lerner, 939–91. New York: Wiley, 1997.

Elliott, Delbert S. "Delinquency, School Attendance and Dropout." *Social Problems* 13 (1966): 306–18.

———. "Serious Violent Offenders: Onset, Developmental Course, and Termination—The American Society of Criminology 1993 Presidential Address." *Criminology* 32, no. 1 (1994): 1–21.

Elliott, Delbert S. and S. S. Ageton. "Reconciling Race and Class Differences in Self-Reported and Official Estimates of Delinquency." *American Sociological Review* 45, no. 1 (1980): 95–110.

Elliott, Delbert S., S. S. Ageton, and R. Canter. "An Integrated Theoretical Perspective on Delinquent Behavior." *Journal of Research in Crime and Delinquency* 16 (1979): 3–27.

Elliott, Delbert S., D. Huizinga, and S. S. Ageton. *Explaining Delinquency and Drug Use.* Beverly Hills: Sage, 1985.

Elliott, Delbert S. and H. L. Voss. *Delinquency and Dropout.* Lexington, MA: D. C. Heath and Company, 1974.

Empey, LaMar T. and Maynard Erickson. "Hidden Delinquency and Social Status." *Social Forces* 44 (1966): 546–54.

Erickson, M. and L. T. Empey. "Court Records, Undetected Delinquency and Decision-Making." *Journal of Criminal Law Criminology, and Police Science* 54 (1963): 456–69.

Farrington, David P. "Conclusions about Developmental and Life-Course Theories." In *Integrated Development and Life-Course Theories of Offending*, 247–56. New Brunswick, NJ: Transaction Publishers, 2005.

Farrington, David P., Rolf Loeber, Magda Stouthamer-Loeber, Welmoet B. Van Kammen, and Laura Schmidt. "Self-Reported Delinquency and a Combined Delinquency Seriousness Scale Based on Boys, Mothers, and Teachers: Concurrent and Predictive Validity for African-American and Caucasians." *Criminology* 34 (1996): 493–517.

Gold, M. "Undetected Delinquent Behavior." *Journal of Research in Crime and Delinquency* 3 (1966): 27–46.

———. *Delinquent Behavior in an American City.* Belmont, CA: Brooks/Cole, 1970.

Hawkins, J. D., B. H. Smith, K. G. Hill, R. Kosterman, R. F. Catalano, and R. D. Abbott. "Understanding and Preventing Crime and Violence: Findings from the Seattle Social Development Project." In *Taking Stock of Delinquency: An Overview of Findings from Contemporary*

Longitudinal Studies, edited by Terence P. Thornberry and Marvin D. Krohn, 255–312. New York: Kluwer Academic/Plenum Publishers, 2003.

Hindelang, M. J. "Causes of Delinquency: A Partial Replication and Extension." *Social Problems* 20 (1973): 471–87.

Hindelang, M. J., T. Hirschi, and J. G. Weis. "Correlates of Delinquency: The Illusion of Discrepancy between Self-Report and Official Measures." *American Sociological Review* 44 (1979): 995–1014.

————. *Measuring Delinquency*. Beverly Hills: Sage, 1981.

Hirschi, T. *Causes of Delinquency*. Berkeley: University of California Press, 1969.

Huizinga, D. and D. S. Elliott. "Reassessing the Reliability and Validity of Self-Report Delinquent Measures." *Journal of Quantitative Criminology* 2, no. 4 (1986): 293–327.

Jensen, Gary F. "Inner Containment and Delinquency." *Journal of Criminal Law and Criminology* 64 (1973): 464–70.

Jensen, Gary F., Maynard L. Erickson, and Jack P. Gibbs. "Perceived Risk of Punishment and Self-Reported Delinquency." *Social Forces* 57 (1978): 57–78.

Johnson, R. E. *Juvenile Delinquency and Its Origins*. Cambridge, England: Cambridge University Press, 1979.

Kaplan, H. B. "Toward a General Theory of Psychosocial Deviance: The Case of Aggressive Behavior." *Social Science and Medicine* 6 (1972): 593–617.

Kelly, D. H. "Track Position and Delinquent Involvement: A Preliminary Analysis." *Sociology and Social Research* 58 (1974): 380–86.

Kulik, J. A., K. B. Stein, and T. R. Sarbin. "Disclosure of Delinquent Behavior under Conditions of Anonymity and Non-anonymity." *Journal of Consulting and Clinical Psychology* 32 (1968): 506–9.

Lauritsen, Janet L. "The Age-Crime Debate: Assessing the Limits of Longitudinal Self-Report Data." *Social Forces* 76, no. 4 (1998): 1–29.

Lemert, Edwin. *Social Pathology: A Systematic Approach to the Theory of Sociopathic Behavior*. New York: McGraw Hill, 1951.

Loeber, Rolf, P. Wung, K. Keenan, B. Giroux, and Magda Stouthamer-Loeber. "Development Pathways in Disruptive Child Behavior." *Development and Psychopathology* 5 (1993): 101–33.

Matthews, Victor M. "Differential Identification: An Empirical Note." *Social Problems* 14 (1968): 376–83.

Maxfield, Michael G., Barbara Luntz Weiler, and Cathy Spatz Widom. "Comparing Self-Reports and Official Records of Arrests." *Journal of Quantitative Criminology* 16, no. 1 (2000): 87–100.

Merton, R. K. "Social Structure and Anomie." *American Sociological Review* 3 (1938): 672–82.

Nye, F. I. and V. Olson. "Socio-Economic Status and Delinquent Behavior." *American Sociological Review* 22 (1958): 326–31.

Patterson, G. R. and R. Loeber. *The Understanding and Prediction of Delinquent Child Behavior*. Research proposal to NIMH. Eugene: Oregon Social Learning Center, 1982.

Polk, K. "Class Strain and Rebellion among Adolescents." *Social Problems* 17 (1969): 214–24.

Porterfield, Austin L. "Delinquency and Outcome in Court and College." *American Journal of Sociology* 49 (1943): 199–208.

———. *Youth in Trouble*. Fort Worth: Leo Potishman Foundation, 1946.

Reiss, Albert J., Jr. and A. L. Rhodes. *A Socio-Psychological Study of Adolescent Conformity and Deviation*. U.S. Office of Education Report, 1959.

———. "Status Deprivation and Delinquent Behavior." *Sociological Quarterly* 4 (1963): 135–49.

———. "An Empirical Test of Differential Association Theory." *Journal of Research in Crime and Delinquency* 1 (1964): 5–18.

Sellin, Thorsten. "The Basis of a Crime Index." *Journal of Criminal Law and Criminology* 22 (1931): 335–56.

Shaw, Clifford and Henry D. McKay. *Juvenile Delinquency and Urban Areas*. Chicago: University of Chicago Press, 1942.

Short, James F., Jr. "Differential Association and Delinquency." *Social Problems* 4 (1957): 233–39.

Short, James F., Jr. and F. I. Nye. "Reported Behavior as a Criterion of Deviant Behavior." *Social Problems* 5 (1957): 207–13.

———. "Extent of Unrecorded Juvenile Delinquency: Tentative Conclusions." *Journal of Criminal Law and Criminology* 49 (1958): 296–302.

Skolnick, J. V., C. J. Braukmann, M. M. Bedlington, K. A. Kirigin, and M. M. Wolf. "Parent-Youth Interaction and Delinquency in Group Homes." *Journal of Abnormal Child Psychology* 9 (1981): 107–19.

Stanfield, R. "The Interaction of Family Variables and Gang Variables in the Aetiology of Delinquency." *Social Problems* 13 (1966): 411–17.

Thornberry, Terence P. "Panel Effects and the Use of Self-Reported Measures of Delinquency in Longitudinal Studies." In *Cross-National Research in Self-Reported Crime and Delinquency*, 347–69. Los Angeles: Kluwer Academic Publishers, 1989.

———. *Developmental Theories of Crime and Delinquency*. New Brunswick, NJ: Transaction Publishers, 1997.

Thornberry, Terence P. and Marvin D. Krohn. "The Development of Delinquency: An Interactional Perspective." In *Handbook of Youth and Justice*, edited by S. O. White, 289–305. New York: Plenum, 2001.

———, eds. *Taking Stock of Delinquency: An Overview of Findings from Contemporary Longitudinal Studies*. New York: Kluwer Academic/Plenum Publishers, 2003.

Tremblay, R. E., F. Vitaro, D. Nagin, L. Pagani, and J. R. Séguin. "The Montreal Longitudinal and Experimental Study: Rediscovering the Power of Descriptions." In *Taking Stock of Delinquency: An Overview of Findings from Contemporary Longitudinal Studies*, edited by Terence P. Thornberry and Marvin D. Krohn, 205–54. New York: Kluwer Academic/Plenum Publishers, 2003.

Voss, H. L. "Differential Association and Reported Delinquent Behavior: A Replication." *Social Problems* 12 (1964): 78–85.

————. "Socio-Economic Status and Reported Delinquent Behavior." *Social Problems* 13 (1966): 314–24.

Waldo, Gordon P. and Theodore G. Chiricos. "Perceived Penal Sanction and Self-Reported Criminality: A Neglected Approach to Deterrence Research." *Social Problems* 19 (1972): 522–40.

Wallerstein, J. S. and C. J. Wylie. "Our Law-Abiding Law-Breakers." *Probation* 25 (1947): 107–12.

Weitekamp, Elmar. "Some Problems with the Use of Self-Reports in Longitudinal Research." In *Cross-National Research in Self-Reported Crime and Delinquency*, edited by M. W. Klein, 329–46. Los Angeles: Kluwer Academic Publishers, 1989.

Wolfgang, Marvin E., Robert M. Figlio, and Thorsten Sellin. *Delinquency in a Birth Cohort.* Chicago: University of Chicago Press, 1972.

2

Socially Desirable Response Bias in Criminology: An Example of Its Effect in Testing the Effects of Self-Control

John M. MacDonald, Andrew Morral, and Alex R. Piquero

Over the past two decades, there was a proliferation of research in criminology on the role of self-control in explaining criminal conduct. A meta-analysis of the criminological literature indicates that self-control is a significant predictor of both criminal and analogous behaviors (Pratt and Cullen, 2000). Much of this literature relies on cognitive measures of self-control, such as Grasmick et al.'s scale (1993), that require respondents to engage in a self-appraisal of the types of people they are, an activity that would be subject to a range of intentional or unintentional response biases. Hirschi and Gottfredson (1993) caution criminologists against using cognitive measures of self-control. Their line of reasoning is supported by research indicating that self-report criminal behavior is underreported among more serious delinquents (Hindelang et al., 1981). By extension, then, those with low self-control are either unwilling or unable to participate in surveys, thus attenuating the effects self-control on crime. Research has found that one's self-control influences survey responses, suggesting that external behavioral measures recorded from neutral observers may be more accurate for measuring self-control and predicting its influence on criminal behavior (Piquero et al., 2000).

This research was supported by a grant from the National Institute on Alcoholism and Alcohol Abuse (R01 AA12457) awarded to Andrew Morral, principal investigator. The opinions expressed in this chapter are those of the authors and do not represent the official positions of the NIAAA, the RAND Corporation, or any of its clients.

The ability to collect external indicators of self-control is costly and typically not undertaken in criminology. There are few examples of ways to control for the potential inadequacy of self-reports in examining the relationship between self-control and criminal behavior. This issue is particularly relevant to the use of cognitive measures of self-control that ask individuals to make assertions about their personality and preferences. In this chapter, we examine the extent to which socially desirable responding accounts for the relationship between self-control and criminal behavior. We also examine whether behavioral measures of self-control are better predictors of criminal offending than cognitive measures (Tittle et al., 2003), after taking into account the social desirability of answers. Importantly, this research offers an example of how criminologists can control for response bias in self-report measures of self-control and not overestimate their importance in explaining criminal offending. As such, it represents the first application of such an analysis to the self-control measurement issue—one that we believe is a relevant one.

Measuring Self-Control and Criminal Offending

According to the general theory of crime, self-control can best be measured through behavioral actions (e.g., reckless driving, excessive drinking of alcohol, sexual promiscuity) instead of cognitive measures (e.g., preferences and tendencies). Most studies examining the influence of self-control on criminal behavior, however, use the attitudinal scale developed by Grasmick et al. (1993). Hirschi and Gottfredson (1993) explicitly argue against the use of such an attitudinal scale and suggest that it is more akin to personality theories of psychological positivism than the self-control theory they developed (Hirschi, 2004). There also has been some disagreement on the psychometric properties of the Grasmick et al. scale. Longshore et al. (1996), for example, found among a sample of highly active drug-using offenders that lower order constructs of impulsivity and risk seeking were as good a set of predictors of criminal behavior as the higher order construct of self-control in the Grasmick et al. scale. Subsequent analysis of the data by Piquero and Rosay (1998), however, suggests that the higher order construct of self-control is the most predictive of criminal behavior.

A particular concern for self-report measures of self-control is that those with low self-control may produce less valid self-appraisals of their preferences and tendencies—thereby causing the scale to produce progressively more biased estimates of self-control as true self-control diminishes. Indeed, research applying item response theory to the

Grasmick et al. scale found that individuals scored differently on self-control, depending on "their level of intensity on the latent trait (e.g., their score on the self-control continuum)" (Piquero et al., 2000: 922). These results are consistent with Hirschi and Gottfredson's statement that "self-report measures whether dependent or independent variables, appear to be less valid the greater the delinquency of those to whom they are applied" (Hirschi and Gottfredson, 1993: 48). Thus, relying on self-appraisals to assess self-control may attenuate its true association with criminal offending.

Tittle et al. (2003) provide a thorough review of the literature comparing cognitive (attitudinal) and behavioral measures of self-control and criminal behavior, and suggest that both methods equally predict criminal behavior. They find that general deviance, a variety measure of crime, and specific criminal actions are equally predicted by behavioral and cognitive measures of self-control. For behavioral measures of self-control, they rely on self-report indicators of alcohol abuse, smoking, marital status, seat belt use, debt consumption, and willingness to take medication for a cold or minor ailment. This measure is consistent with Gottfredson and Hirschi's theory that suggests pursuits of immediate pleasure, such as smoking and drinking, reflect low self-control. They then compare their behavioral measure to the Grasmick et al. scale and find that both exhibit expected correlations with criminal behavior. They also find that the cognitive measures of self-control have higher reliability, suggesting that cognitive scales may have superior measurement properties.

If, however, people with low self-control provide less valid responses to self-appraisals of self-control, this could bias the association observed between cognitive measures and criminal behavior. Individuals with low self-control may also be more deceptive in responding to surveys (Hirschi and Gottfredson, 1993). If this is the case, then the association between self-control and criminal behavior in self-reports could merely reflect the fact that both the self-control measure and criminal behavior measure are subject to response bias.

One method of remedying the potential bias in survey responses is to rely on third party or external measures of self-control. There are a few studies that have included third-party behavioral indicators of self-control. Keane et al. (1993) assessed the relationship between self-control and driving under the influence of alcohol, relying on traffic stop data in Canada. Their study found that direct observations of self-control (e.g., not wearing a seat belt) were significantly related to blood alcohol concentration. Several longitudinal studies of adolescent development also have used external sources for assessing self-control. Studies have examined the issue of self-control and criminal behavior using data from the Cambridge Study of Delinquent Development (West and Farrington, 1973) and external sources to measure the construct. Polakowski (1994), for example, found that behavioral indicators of self-control reported from independent third parties (e.g., teachers, parent, and peers) were predictive of convictions during adulthood. Tremblay et al.'s (1995) longitudinal study of adolescents in Montreal also used measures of self-control ratings taken from teachers during early childhood and found that they were significant predictors of delinquent behavior and accidents during adolescence. Research from the Dunedin Multidisciplinary Health and Development Study also has used third-party (e.g., parent, teacher, and observer) reports of self-control and investigated their link to criminal behavior. Findings from these studies suggest that low self-control during early childhood is predictive of offending in adolescence and early adulthood and other negative life outcomes (Moffitt et al., 1996; Wright et al., 1999). In short, the results from the studies that employ direct observation or third-party indicators of self-control suggest that self-control is related to official and self-report criminal behaviors. Together, the literature indicates that various measures of self-control are predictive of criminal offending. Unfortunately, the time investment and expense required to collect external reports of self-control preclude most criminologists from using this method. As a result, self-report surveys remain the predominant method for testing the general theory of crime.

Socially Desirable Responding

Methods have been developed in social psychology that can help control for the potential response bias limitations related to self-assessments of self-control and crime. Socially desirable response bias refers to the tendency exhibited by some people to provide survey responses that are biased toward presenting an especially favorable self-impression (Paulhus, 1991). Early research in social psychology indicated that this type of response bias occurs in self-report measures of personality traits, attitudes, and psychopathology (Gough, 1952; Crowne and Marlowe, 1960; Arkin and Lake, 1983). Since then, socially desirable responding has been a continued concern with measuring self-report attitudes as well as other personality traits (Paulhus, 1991). Research, for example, indicates that people overestimate engaging in socially desirable behaviors like attending religious services (Hadaway et al., 1993) and underreport socially undesirable behaviors like drug use (Mensch and Kendel, 1988). However, the importance of measuring social desirable responding within the context of self-control as well as other criminological constructs is not well understood.

Typical methods for minimizing socially desirable response bias in criminology include only assurances of anonymity and factor analytic techniques. By contrast, social psychologists have developed measures of socially desirable response bias that can be used as control variables in analyses of interest (Paulhus, 1991). Edwards (1957), for example, created a social desirability scale from thirty-nine items in the MMPI that rank high or low on the social desirability of responses. Crowne and Marlowe (1960) similarly created a scale from the MMPI of thirty-three true–false items that measure rare but desirable behaviors or common but undesirable behaviors. More recently, social psychologists have created scales for social desirability that include items that measure self-deceptive (honest but overly positive self-presentation) and impression management (deliberate self-presentation) responses in attitude and opinion surveys (Schuessler et al., 1978; Paulhus, 1984).

Although a number of instruments have been developed to evaluate survey respondents' tendency to give socially desirable answers, the majority of these scales are lengthy, making it burdensome to incorporate them in surveys that already ask respondents a number of questions. As a result, assessments of social desirability are often missing from studies of high-risk persons along a number of issues including criminal behavior. To accommodate the difficulty in administering these lengthy instruments, a five-item social desirability response set (SDRS-5) was developed by Hays et al. (1989) for use in educational and psychological measurement. This five-item social desirability scale asks respondents to indicate (1) their level of courteousness to disagreeable people, (2) occasions when they have taken advantage of someone, (3) attempts to get even rather than forgive and forget, (4) feelings of resentment when they don't get their way, and (5) the extent to which they are a good listener. Results from an evaluation of the SDRS-5 on outpatients of medical providers indicate it is as internally consistent and reliable as lengthier instruments that measure social desirability (Hays et al., 1989).

There are clear theoretical reasons to suspect survey responses to self-control items would be susceptible to social desirability response bias. After all, cognitive measures of self-control ask individuals to make self-appraisals about sensitive personal characteristics. Individuals with low self-control may be less likely to provide uncomfortable information about themselves, either due to deception or due to impression management tendencies. Deception does not necessarily mean that respondents with low self-control are openly dishonest; rather, deception can occur because individuals with low self-control view themselves with an overly positive light (self-deception). When survey researchers query individuals on their tendency to be "impulsive, insensitive, physical (as opposed to mental), risk–taking, short-sighted, and nonverbal" (Gottfredson and Hirschi, 1990: 90), they are clearly asking respondents to make self-assessments. It is not unreasonable to suggest that individuals who exhibit low self-control will not understand that their actions are impulsive, risk-taking, and insensitive, especially if they have a tendency to justify their actions (Matza, 1964). According to Gottfredson and Hirschi, individuals with low self-control are more likely to be self-centered and uncaring. This trait may also make individuals with low self-control more inclined to respond with socially desirable answers because of their desire to create the most positive self-presentation (impression management).

Current Focus

Incorporating social desirability indicators into criminological studies may be fruitful for improving the mechanisms for assessing the relationship between self-control and criminal behavior in self-report survey methods. Herein, we rely on a widely used scale of social desirability (SDRS-5) to control for response bias in self-reports of self-control and criminal behaviors among a sample of repeat drinking and driving (DUI) offenders. Specifically, we examine if social desirability response patterns have a greater attenuating effect for cognitive compared to behavioral measures of low self-control on crime. Importantly, we apply the first application of social desirability to test the validity of the self-control/crime relationship. This application directly relates to Hirschi and Gottfredson's (1993) following suggestion: "[W]e would urge . . . differences among potential respondents be taken into account in research design and measurement. Unless this is done, apparently modest result may in fact be highly supportive of the validity of the theory" (48).

Methods

The sample for this study was drawn from baseline interviews conducted with 284 participants as part of an evaluation of an experimental therapeutic treatment court for DUI offenders. Face-to-face surveys were administered at the Rio Hondo Municipal Court in Los Angeles, California, to participants prior to sentencing for a DUI offense. All participants had a history of DUI convictions and multiple DUI and/or alcohol-related probation violations. The procedures for recruiting participants for the study were approved by an internal review board, as well as by the Rio Hondo presiding judge and the Los Angeles Public Defender's Office. Informed consent was obtained from all study participants. The majority of participants were Hispanic (84.5 percent) and male (93 percent). The survey administered was focused primarily on DUI behaviors. In addition, subjects were queried on a number of cognitive and behavioral patterns including consumption of alcohol, illicit drug use, stressful life events, criminal history, and cognitive indicators of self-control. The demographic and descriptive statistics for the measures used in the current study are included in Table 2.1.

This study sample has a unique advantage for testing self-control theory because all participants are chronic offenders with serious drinking-and-driving-related problems. Given that the distribution of self-control is highly skewed, this sample of DUI offenders corresponds closely with Hirschi and Gottfredson's (1993) suggestion that studies use "disproportionate sampling" procedures "to ensure sufficient numbers of low self-control subjects" (48). Moreover, this study design is consistent with Hirschi and Gottfredson's (2000) view that assessments and measurements of self-control can be taken using virtually any sampling frame.

Measures

Crime

Crime was assessed according to self-report crimes of force and fraud. Because the entire sample represents repeat DUI offenders, self-report offenses for DUI were excluded from the present analyses. To be consistent with Gottfredson and Hirschi's theory, this study focuses on crimes of force and fraud. Self-report crime was measured according to fourteen self-report (yes–no) items that asked participants to indicate whether they had engaged in these crimes of force and fraud in the previous two years. Respondents were asked if they had committed a number of personal and property offenses including credit or check fraud, larceny theft, burglary, motor vehicle theft, simple and aggravated assault, rape, robbery, gang fights, and murder. Together, 18.7 percent (see Table 2.1) of respondents indicated that they had engaged in at least one of these acts of force or fraud in the previous two years—the majority of those reported committing only one such criminal offense (68.5 percent) during this time period.

Table 2.1   Descriptive statistics for variables

Variables	Observations (N)	Mean	SD	Min	Max
Crimes of force or fraud	272	0.1875	0.391	0	1
Alcohol use (behavioral self-control 1)	284	2.849	5.561	0	54
Drug use (behavioral self-control 2)	273	1.186	4.743	0	34
Negative life events (behavioral self-control 3)	274	1.361	1.140	0	5
Self-control (cognitive)	267	28.603	7.425	12	53
Social desirability	270	9.237	3.068	5	21
Age	284	35.084	9.188	18	68
Female	284	0.0704	0.256	0	1
Hispanic	284	0.845	0.362	0	1

Self-Control

To assess the association between self-control and criminal offending, we used both cognitive and behavioral measures. To measure self-control cognitively, we used a twelve-item modified version of the Grasmick et al. scale (*cognitive self-control*) in which some wordings were changed to detect any bias due to "yea-saying" (see Longshore et al., 1996). All measures were based closely on the original Grasmick et al. scale, but the response options were changed from four- to five-point Likert scales: never (1), rarely (2), sometimes (3), often (4), always (5). Higher scores on this summed scale reflect increased levels of low self-control. The overall alpha reliability for this scale was .73, suggesting sufficient reliability in the present sample.[1]

To assess self-control along behavioral lines, we constructed several different self-report measures. Gottfredson and Hirschi (1990: 96) suggest that low self-control is not conducive to long-term goals and impedes educational, occupational, and interpersonal relationships. Accordingly, one can measure low self-control from a variety of indicators that reflect behavioral patterns exhibited by individuals with short-term orientation. Therefore, our attempt to measure self-control behaviorally fits closely with the idea that there may be "multidimensionality" in self-control "stemming from opportunity differences or situational factors" (Hirschi and Gottfredson, 1993: 50). The first behavioral measure of self-control represents an aggregate measure of six *negative life events* self-reported by the respondents. Specifically, respondents were asked if the following things had occurred for them in the preceding twelve months: (1) financial difficulties, (2) job loss, (3) problems at work or school, (4) conflict at home, (5) separate or divorce or breakup of a relationship, and (6) being an accident victim. The second behavioral measure of self-control relates to excessive *alcohol consumption*, and it is a measure of the alcohol quantity and intensity of drinking that represents the average daily consumption of alcohol over the past three months, expressed as standard drinks. For example, respondents were asked how often they generally drink alcohol beverages and then the number and type of alcohol beverages drank (e.g., beer, malt liquor, wine cooler, etc.) in a typical day. The measure reflects the product of typical drinking frequency and typical drinking quantity. The third behavioral measure of self-control is a measure of illegal *drug use*, and it represents the combined self-report drug use in the respondents' past two years and preceding thirty days. The measure represents the sum of the days of use of each type of illicit drug reportedly used.

Social Desirability

To measure the influence of social desirable responding, we utilize the five-item *social desirability* response set summed scale (SDRS-5) developed by Hays et al. (1989). The SDRS-5 asks respondents to indicate how often they are courteous to disagreeable people, take advantage of someone, try to get even rather than forgive and forget, feel resentful when they don't get their own way, and are always a good listener. Higher scores reflect increased levels of socially desirable responding (alpha = .59).

Control Variables

Research indicates that crime and self-control vary by age, gender, and ethnicity (Gottfredson and Hirschi, 1990). There are a variety of explanations for this, including maturational reform associated with aging and differences in supervision and socialization that occur between gender and ethnic groups. To control for the influence of gender on crime, we include a dichotomous measure indicating whether the subject was a female (=1). To control for the influence of age, we include a continuous measure of the age of the respondent (in years). Given that the majority of the sample is of Hispanic origin, we include a dichotomous measure indicating if the subject is Hispanic (=1).

Results

The outcome measures for crime we use in this study reflect the number of times someone self-reported or was arrested for a crime of force or fraud. The majority of the respondents (approximately 81.2 percent) report not committing a crime of force or fraud in the previous two years. Therefore, the majority of this sample of respondents is effectively censored at zero. To accommodate the left-hand censoring of the self-report criminal behavior, we estimated a logistic regression model (Long, 1997). Our analysis proceeds with two steps. First, we estimated several logistic regression models of crime on behavioral and cognitive measures of self-control separately before and after including the social desirability measure to assess whether it attenuates the influence of these measures of self-control. Second, we estimated logistic regression models that compare the simultaneous effects of the behavioral and cognitive measures of self-control before and after including the social desirability measure.

Table 2.2 displays the results from the logistic regression models in odds ratios (OR) on self-report participation in crimes of force and fraud. Consistent with the general theory of crime, across all models, age is negatively and significantly related to crime. Gender and ethnicity, however, do not have a statistically significant relationship with crime. This may be due to the relatively small number of females (7 percent) and non-Hispanics (15 percent) in the sample that diminish our ability to detect differences across groups.

The results displayed in column 1 indicate that the excessive alcohol consumption (OR = 1.091) and negative life events (OR = 1.596) are significantly related to participation in self-report crimes of force and fraud. Drug use is not significantly related to self-report crimes of force and fraud. The lack of a strong relationship between drug use and crime, however, may reflect the fact that the entire samples are repeat DUI offenders and lack sufficient variation compared to general population sample to detect the effects of these behavioral patterns of crime. Column 2 adds the measure of social desirability. The results from this model indicate that behavioral self-control (as measured by excessive alcohol use and negative life events) remains significant predictors of crimes of force and fraud. Consistent with Gottfredson and Hirschi (1990), social desirability is significantly related to self-report crime (OR = 1.219). A comparison of coefficients across these two models (see Z-test) (Clogg et al., 1995) indicates that the change in parameter estimates for the behavioral measures of self-control (alcohol use and negative life events) is not significantly different from zero. These findings suggest no attenuation on the effects of behavioral measures of self-control after the inclusion of a parameter for socially desirable responding.

Column 3 displays the results for the logistic regression model that includes only the modified cognitive Grasmick et al. self-control scale and the control variables. The results indicate that the cognitive measure of self-control (OR = 1.103) is significantly related to the participation in self-report crimes of force and fraud. Column 4 adds the measure of social desirability. The results indicate that self-control measured cognitively remains a statistically significant predictor of crime, but the overall effect diminishes slightly after including social desirability. A comparison of this self-control coefficient before and after including the parameter for social desirability indicates only a slight attenuation ($Z = .15$) that is not significantly different from zero.

Table 2.2   Estimated odds ratios of self-reported participation in crime on self-control ($n = 264$)

	(1)	(2)	(3)	(4)	(5)	(6)
Alcohol use (behavioral self-control 1)	1.091* (2.16)	1.074* (1.92)	–	–	1.068* (1.84)	1.067* (1.83)
Drug use (behavioral self-control 2)	1.052 (1.64)	1.048 (1.41)	–	–	1.039 (1.17)	1.041 (1.17)
Negative life events (behavioral self-control 3)	1.596** (2.81)	1.518** (2.37)	–	–	1.562** (2.54)	1.518** (2.33)
Self-control (cognitive)	–	–	1.103** (3.82)	1.064* (2.10)	1.077** (2.54)	1.045 (1.39)
Age	0.891** (4.15)	0.900** (3.76)	0.910** (3.75)	0.910** (3.65)	0.906** (3.56)	0.907** (3.51)
Female	2.962 (1.72)	2.192 (1.16)	2.862 (1.75)	2.260 (1.29)	2.545 (1.42)	2.162 (1.12)
Hispanic	1.023 (0.04)	1.316 (0.45)	0.742 (0.55)	0.970 (0.05)	0.946 (0.09)	1.173 (0.26)
Social desirability	–	1.219** (3.07)	–	1.187** (2.52)	–	1.162 (2.05)**
Pseudo R^2	.231	.270	.186	.212	.261	.278

Note: Z-values in parentheses.
*$p < .05$ (one-tail); **$p < .01$ (two-tailed).

Column 5 displays the results from the model that includes the behavioral measures of self-control and the cognitive measures simultaneously. The results from this model indicate that excessive alcohol use (OR = 1.068), negative life events (OR = 1.562), and the cognitive measures of self-control (OR = 1.077) are all statistically significant predictors of crimes of force and fraud. Column 6 adds the measure of social desirability to the simultaneous model. Consistent with Gottfredson and Hirschi, social desirability is significantly related to self-report crime (OR = 1.162), even after including both behavioral and cognitive measures of self-control. Importantly, including social desirability into the model diminishes the influence of the modified Grasmick et al. cognitive measure of self-control to a statistically insignificant level. A comparison of regression coefficients across models, however, indicates that the change in effect sizes is not significantly different from zero (Z =.12). The Grasmick et al. scale remains largely the same before and after controlling for socially desirable responding. These results, therefore, suggest that the relationship between self-report crime and self-control measured cognitively are only partially attenuated by socially desirable response bias.

Importantly, the results from these models suggest that individuals who report worse behavioral and cognitive measures of self-control are also more likely to report engaging in crimes of force and fraud. In short, the fact that the findings are consistent with the majority of other studies indicates that the Grasmick et al. cognitive measure of self-control as well as behavioral measures of self-control is significantly related to the participation in self-report crimes of force and fraud. The findings do not confirm Gottfredson and Hirschi's suspicions that the cognitive measures of self-control are measuring response bias in surveys. While people who are more likely to self-report crime also appear to be more inclined to give favorable responses to questions about their personality characteristics, the effects of this response bias pattern do not greatly attenuate the effects of self-control on crime.

Discussion

Since the publication of Gottfredson and Hirschi's theory, there has been contentious debate about how to best measure their concept of self-control. Despite Gottfredson and Hirschi's objections to using self-assessments to measure self-control, the Grasmick et al. self-report scale has become the most ubiquitous method for measuring this construct (Pratt and Cullen, 2000). While several studies have confirmed the measurement validity of this scale (Longshore et al., 1996; Piquero and

Rosay, 1998; Piquero et al., 2000; Tittle et al., 2003), little research has examined whether response bias impacts the relationship between this cognitive method of assessing self-control and crime (for exceptions, see Piquero et al., 2000).

This study provided the first test of the effects of social desirability in measuring the relationship between measures of self-control and crimes of force and fraud. The results suggest that social desirability is an important construct that should be measured in efforts to assess the relationship between measures of self-control and crime, but that the Grasmick et al. scale appears overall to be robust to the effects of socially desirable responding. While the Grasmick et al. scale asks respondents to make valid judgments about their personality traits and behavioral preferences (e.g., self-centeredness, present orientation) that are likely to be laden with problems of socially desirable responding, especially among samples of serious offenders, the findings from this study indicate that accounting for social desirability only marginally attenuates the relationship between the Grasmick et al. scale and crime. Our results, therefore, do not confirm strictly with Gottfredson and Hirschi's speculation that self-control is best measured through "operational" measures of the "propensity to offend" (Hirschi and Gottfredson, 1995: 134). While external reports may be the most preferable method for assessing behavioral problems related to self-control, few criminologists have the resources necessary to collect such data. Assessing social desirability provides an alternative cost-effective approach to controlling for response bias in self-reports.

There are several limitations to the current research that warrant mentioning. First, the measures used in this study are cross-sectional. In addition, one could argue that the behavioral measures of self-control may be tautological to the measures of crime (Akers, 1998). We have, however, attempted to resolve this issue—in part—by relying on measures of crimes (force and fraud) that are distinctly different from the self-control items (see Hirschi and Gottfredson, 1993). One may also question the sequence of these data because self-control was assessed according to both the respondents' current attitudes (e.g., cognitive scale of self-control) and their past behavior (e.g., excessive alcohol consumption), while the crime measures are based only on reported past behavior. Gottfredson and Hirschi state that self-control is established early in life (five to eight years of age) and is relatively time stable thereafter (Turner and Piquero, 2002). Therefore, measuring current levels of self-control should be consistent with relative differences between sample members in self-control in the past. On this score, Tittle et al. (2003) have shown that both cognitive and behavioral measures of self-control relate similarly to previous and future estimates of criminal activity. More importantly, the present study did not seek to test a causal model of self-control and crime. Rather, the emphasis was on the extent to which controlling for socially desirable responding attenuates the influence of different measures of self-control on crime.

The findings from this study have broader implications for criminology than resolving the debate over how to best measure self-control. We think these findings provide a useful illustration of why criminologists who are collecting self-report data should use methods for assessing socially desirable responding. There are a number of easy-to-use methods for assessing social desirability, including SDRS-5 used in the current study, that warrant its inclusion in most self-report studies that attempt to test criminological theories. Taking into account this form of response bias is particularly important, given that criminology is focused on asking respondents to report behaviors (e.g., crimes) that are not conventionally viewed as being socially desirable. Importantly, measuring socially desirable responding would provide a mechanism for controlling for response bias patterns in self-report data used to test a number of criminological theories. Future research, therefore, should examine how socially desirable response bias impacts the measurement of constructs from other criminological theories (e.g., strain) and their purported influence on criminal behavior.

Note

1. Specifically, we used four items to assess *impulsivity*: (1) "You act without stopping to think," (2) "You do what feels good now without thinking about the future," (3) "You focus on the short run rather than the long run," and (4) "You get restless when you spend too much time at home." Two items to assess *self-centeredness* are as follows: (1) "You try to get what you want even if it causes problems for other people" and (2) "There have been occasions when you took advantage of someone." Four items to assess *temper* are (1) "You lose your temper pretty easily," (2) "You feel that the best way to solve an argument is to sit down and talk it out," (3) "When you are really angry, other people better stay away from you," and (4) "When you have a serious disagreement with someone, it's hard for you to talk calmly about it without getting upset," and two items to assess *risk-seeking* are (1) "You would like to explore strange places" and (2) "You like to do scary things."

Bibliography

Akers, R. *Social Learning and Social Structure: A General Theory of Crime and Deviance*. Boston: Northeastern University Press, 1998.
Arkin, R. and E. Lake. "Plumbing the Depths of the Bogus Pipeline: A Reprise." *Journal of Research in Personality* 17 (1983): 81–88.

Clogg, C., E. Petkova, and A. Haritou. "Statistical Methods for Comparing the Regression Coefficients between Models." *American Journal of Sociology* 100 (1995): 1261–93.

Crowne, D. P. and D. Marlowe. "A New Scale of Social Desirability Independent of Psychopathology." *Journal of Consulting Psychology* 24 (1960): 349–54.

Edwards, A. L. *The Social Desirability Variable in Personality Assessment and Research.* New York: Dryden, 1957.

Gottfredson, M. R. and T. Hirschi. *A General Theory of Crime.* Palo Alto, CA: Stanford University Press, 1990.

Gough, H. G. "On Making a Good Impression." *Journal of Educational Research* 46 (1952): 33–42.

Grasmick, H. G., C. R. Tittle, R. J. Bursik, Jr., and B. K. Arneklev. "Testing the Core Empirical Implications of Gottfredson and Hirschi's General Theory of Crime." *Journal of Research in Crime and Delinquency* 30 (1993): 5–29.

Hadaway, C. K., P. L. Marler, and M. Chaves. "What the Polls Don't Show: A Closer Look at U.S. Church Attendance." *American Sociological Review* 58 (1993): 741–52.

Hays, R. D., T. Hayashi, and A. L. Stewart. "A Five-Item Measure of Socially Desirable Response Set." *Educational and Psychological Measurement* 49 (1989): 629–36.

Hindelang, M., T. Hirschi, and J. Weiss. *Measuring Delinquency.* Beverly Hills, CA: Sage, 1981.

Hirschi, T. "Self-Control and Crime." In *Handbook of Self-Regulation: Research, Theory, and Applications*, edited by R. F. Baumeister and K. D. Vohs. New York: Guilford Press, 2004.

Hirschi, T. and M. R. Gottfredson. "Commentary: Testing the General Theory of Crime." *Journal of Research in Crime and Delinquency* 30 (1993): 47–54.

———. "Control Theory and Life-Course Perspective." *Studies on Crime and Crime Prevention* 4 (1995): 131–42.

———. "In Defense of Self-Control." *Theoretical Criminology* 4 (2000): 55–69.

Keane, C., P. S. Maxim, and J. J. Teevan. "Drinking and Driving, Self-Control, and Gender: Testing a General Theory of Crime." *Journal of Research in Crime and Delinquency* 30 (1993): 30–46.

Long, S. *Regression Models for Categorical and Limited Dependent Variables.* Thousand Oaks, CA: Sage, 1997.

Longshore, D., J. A. Stein, and S. Turner. "Reliability and Validity of a Self-Control Measure: Rejoinder." *Criminology* 36 (1998): 175–82.

Longshore, D., S. Turner, and J. A. Stein. "Self-Control in a Criminal Sample: An Examination of Construct Validity." *Criminology* 34 (1996): 209–28.

Matza, D. *Delinquency and Drift.* New York: Wiley, 1964.

Mensch, B. S. and D. B. Kendel. "Underreporting of Substance Use in a National Longitudinal Youth Cohort: Individual and Interviewer Effects." *Public Opinion Quarterly* 52 (1988): 100–24.

Moffitt, T. E., A. Caspi, N. Dickson, P. Silva, and S. Warren. "Childhood-Onset versus Adolescent-Onset Antisocial Conduct Problems in Males: Natural History from Ages 3 to 18 Years." *Development and Psychopathology* 30 (1996): 235–60.

Paulhus, D. L. "Two-Component Models of Socially Desirable Responding." *Journal of Personality and Social Psychology* 46 (1984): 598–609.

———. "Measurement and Control of Response Bias." In *Measuring of Personality and Social Psychological Attitudes*, edited by J. P. Robinson, P. R. Shaver, and L. S. Wrightsman, vol. 1, 17–51. San Diego: Academic Press, Inc., 1991.

Piquero, A. R., R. MacIntosh, and M. Hickman. "Does Self-Control Affect Survey Responses? Applying Exploratory, Confirmatory, and Item Response Theory Analysis to Grasmick et al.'s Self-Control Scale." *Criminology* 38 (2000): 897–930.

Piquero, A. R. and A. B. Rosay. "The Reliability and Validity of Grasmick et al.'s Self Control Scale: A Comment on Longshore et al." *Criminology* 36 (1998): 157–74.

Polakowski, M. "Linking Self- and Social-Control with Deviance: Illuminating the Structure Underlying a General Theory of Crime and Its Relation to Deviant Activity." *Journal of Quantitative Criminology* 10 (1994): 41–78.

Pratt, T. C. and F. T. Cullen. "The Empirical Status of Gottfredson and Hirschi's General Theory of Crime: A Meta-analysis." *Criminology* 38 (2000): 931–64.

Schuessler, J., D. Hittle, and J. Cardascia. "Measuring Responding Desirably with Attitude-Opinion Items." *Social Psychology* 41 (1978): 224–35.

Tittle, C. R., D. A. Ward, and H. G. Grasmick. "Self-Control and Crime/Deviance: Cognitive vs. Behavioral Measures." *Journal of Quantitative Criminology* 19 (2003): 333–65.

Tremblay, R. E., B. Boulerice, L. Arseneault, and M. J. Niscale. "Does Low Self-Control during Childhood Explain the Association between Delinquency and Accidents in Early Adolescence?" *Criminal Behavior and Mental Health* 5 (1995): 439–51.

Turner, M. G. and A. R. Piquero. "The Stability of Self-Control." *Journal of Criminal Justice* 30 (2002): 457–71.

West, D. J. and D. P. Farrington. *Who Becomes Delinquent?* London: Heinemann, 1973.

Wright, B. R. E., A. Caspi, T. E. Moffitt, and P. A. Silva. "Low Self-Control, Social Bonds, and Crime: Social Causation, Social Selection, or Both?" *Criminology* 37 (1999): 479–514.

3

How Do We Measure the Severity of Crimes? New Estimates of the Cost of Criminal Victimization

John K. Roman

Criminology has a historic interest in measuring the severity of crimes. While normative rankings of the severity of crime have dominated criminology since the 1960s, a parallel interest in economics has developed crime severity measures on the basis of the costs crimes impose on victims or society. Robust estimates of the severity of crime, measured as the costs of crime to victims, inform a wide range of theory and policy interests. Prior studies of the price of crime, however, have been constrained by limited data that rely on indirect methods to estimate prices. As a result, these studies cannot adjust for sampling bias and do not account for uncertainty. This study demonstrates a more robust approach to estimating the severity of crimes that relies on individual-level data from two sources: jury award and injury data from the RAND Institute of Civil Justice (ICJ) and crime and injury data from the National Incident-Based Reporting System (NIBRS). Propensity score weights are developed to account for heterogeneity in jury awards. Data from the jury awards are interpolated onto the NIBRS data using the

I would like to thank Peter Reuter, Randi Hjalmarsson, Bill Sabol, Phil Cook, Ray Paternoster, Eric Grodsky, Adele Harrell, Avi Bhati, Aaron Chalfin, Bogdan Tereschenko, Caterina Gouvis Roman, and seminar participants at Cornell University and the University of Maryland for helpful comments on earlier drafts of this chapter. I wish also to thank Carly Knight for exceptional technical assistance, Nick Pace and the RAND Institute of Civil Justice for providing and interpreting the jury award data, and the National Institute of Justice for partially supporting this work (2005 TO 090). Despite their assistance, all errors, if any, are my own.

combination of attributes observable in both data sets. From the combined data, estimates are developed of the price of crime to victims for thirty-one crime categories.

Since social scientists started studying criminal behavior, there has been an interest in developing useful methods for measuring crime and its severity (see Ramchand et al., 2009 for a review). Sellin and Wolfgang's (1964) classic study on the measurement of delinquency pioneered the use of normative rankings in which respondents rank a set of offenses by their perceived severity as the conventional method for measuring the severity of crimes. A parallel interest in measuring the severity of crimes has been developed from the environmental economics literature. This research has rated crime severity on the basis of the costs crimes impose on victims or society. Monetizing the costs of victimization is becoming a conventional approach in criminology to measuring the severity of crimes (see Cohen, 1988a, 1988b). But there are only a handful of studies that have examined in any detail the cost to victims. Wolfgang et al. (1985) provided the most comprehensive normative measure of the severity of crime in their National Survey of Crime Severity study, a supplement to the National Crime Survey in 1977 that asked 51,623 household members to rate the severity of offenses against a reference crime (theft of a bicycle). A total of 204 criminal offenses were rated, and severity scores were developed from a regression-adjusted ratio to the crime of theft of $1 (values ranged from 0.2 to 72.1) (Wolfgang et al., 1985). While normative ratings provide a measure of crime severity, they do not provide an estimate that can inform social policy through standardized measures. Crime creates a substantial burden on society. Understanding the magnitude of the harms experienced by victims of crime is the key to determining the appropriate allocation of scarce crime control resources.

Harms from crime can be understood to include the direct losses to victims, the costs of crime control including prevention, and the losses to society from incapacitated offenders (Becker, 1968). Thus, a neoclassic view would suggest that society should invest in crime control up to the point that marginal crime prevention expenditures are equal to the marginal social costs from crime.[1] In order to calculate the optimal expenditure of crime prevention investment in society, a value must be placed on the cost of crime to victims, which is the product of the price and quantity of harms to victims. External costs to victims are the most difficult to quantify. While the amount of crimes can be directly estimated from self-report surveys and administrative data, the price of crime cannot be directly observed. Despite the importance of this measure in understanding the scale of the crime problem in society and determining the size of the response, most prior work on the costs of crime exclusively estimates the costs of the criminal justice system (Harwood et al., 1984; Rice et al., 1990). The challenge in measuring harms to victims is that there is no single data source that includes both the direct and indirect losses from crime and the type of criminal act that caused those losses. Thus, the most widely cited estimates of the social costs of crime rely on indirect methods that combine case-level civil jury award data with aggregate crime statistics (Miller et al., 1993b, 1996; Cohen et al., 1994; Rajkumar and French, 1997; Cohen and Miller, 1999) and, more recently, contingent valuation (Cohen et al., 2004).

Prior estimates using jury award data are now quite dated, but are still often cited in criminological research. In the interim, better data sources have become available that overcome some of the limitations faced by researchers in the past. The most critical limitation of prior studies was the forced reliance on aggregate crime data precluding those studies from incorporating uncertainty in their victimization prices. The result has been that only single-point estimates are available to estimate victim costs of different crimes, suggesting that the victimization is monolithic. Assuming monolithic severity of crime was a problem recognized in normative crime rankings and a justification for the Wolfgang et al. (1985) national study of crime severity. In estimating victim costs, there is the related need to recognize important heterogeneity in victim harms within and across crimes. Thus, studies that only estimate a mean price of specific crimes obscure important information about the distribution of harms.

This chapter develops new estimates of the price of crime to victims, measured as the willingness to accept (WTA) crime losses. These are estimated from individual-level administrative data from official crime statistics and jury award verdicts. Since there is no single source of data that includes both losses from victimization and type of crime, the estimate is generated by linking jury awards to crime data, using the common element of physical injury. Jury award data were collected from the RAND ICJ, and these data yield estimates of the average jury award by type of physical injury. These individual-level data are then linked with event-level crime data from the NIBRS to estimate harms for thirty-one types of criminal offenses.

There are five stages in the estimation process. First, four variables (with nineteen possible values) are identified that are observable in both the ICJ and NIBRS data, including age and gender of the crime victim, the type of injury resulting from victimization, and the region where the crime occurred. Second, a distribution of jury awards is estimated for each of the possible cross-combinations of those four variables in the ICJ data. For example, a distribution of awards is estimated for a male of thirty to thirty-nine age-group with a major injury from a crime occurring in the western United States, and a distribution of awards is estimated for a female of thirty to thirty-nine age-group with the same injury in the same region, etc. The process is repeated until distributions have been estimated for all possible combinations of the four variables. Next, the process is repeated in the NIBRS data to create cross-combinations in that data set.[2] Third, since it is often—but not always—difficult to determine whether the event in the ICJ data was criminal or not, three analytic data sets are created in the ICJ data set, including all observations in the ICJ data set (12,918), only those observations that can be affirmatively coded as crimes (895), and a subgroup of a propensity-weighted sample (5,415). All of the analytic data steps that follow are repeated for all three samples.

Fourth, the estimated mean award in ICJ data is interpolated onto the NIBRS data set for all 342 observations in NIBRS that have a cross-combination of attributes. The fifth step is to estimate prices of victimization for three different types of crimes: victims of serious person crimes who experience direct and indirect losses (such as pain and suffering); the victims of serious property crimes whose victims experience direct and indirect losses, but no physical injury; and victims of less serious crime who experience only pecuniary losses. Estimates for victims of serious person crimes are generated using the four steps described above. Estimates for victims of serious property crimes are estimated using observed losses in NIBRS weighted to include indirect losses derived from the ICJ data. Prices for victims of less serious property crimes are estimated directly from losses observed in the NIBRS data. Finally, to address the concern that those cases in NIBRS that are linked to a case in ICJ (about 1.4 million) are different from those cases in NIBRS that do not match to ICJ (about 400,000), statistical tests compare the mean property loss in Part I property crimes (burglary and robbery).[3]

The approach discussed in this study offers substantial advantages over extant estimates of the severity of crimes. Since the study uses more comprehensive data than what were available in previous research, the number and breadth of assumptions that must be made in the analysis are reduced. The use of individual data for both crime and victimization allows for estimates of the full distribution of possible harms within each crime type. In addition, the consistent use of individual-level data avoids problems associated with aggregation, and the use of a large data set improves power. The following sections describe a transparent method to aid replication and substantially expands the number of crimes for which an estimate could be developed.

Review of Prior Literature

There is a large literature describing the economic theory of criminal behavior. Economic analyses of crime control tend to focus on the relationship between policy and offending that are theoretically predictive of crime. For instance, the relationships between the incapacitation and deterrent effects of prison and crime and the value of human capital acquisition have been the topic of many studies (Becker, 1968; Ehrlich, 1973, 1981, 1996; Freeman, 1996; Levitt, 1996, 1998; Grogger, 1998; Raphael and Winter-Ebmer, 2001; Lochner and Moretti, 2004; Piehl and DiIulio, 1995). While the early literature in this area was mainly concerned with theory, more recent applied research has used estimates of the price of victimization to more precisely estimate the effect of changes in the scale of criminal justice institutions, such as the police and corrections (Levitt, 1996, 1998). Recently, applied studies of the economics of crime, in the form of cost–benefit modeling of anticrime interventions, have become more prevalent. These studies tend to link observational data on the local average treatment effect of a program and then use price data to convert those parameters into a standardized metric (usually dollars), which is interpreted as the program's economic effectiveness (Cartwright, 2000; Cohen, 2000).

The two key challenges in applied economic studies of crime are the resolution of identification problems that confound causal inference (Rubin, 1974; Rosenbaum and Rubin, 1983; LaLonde, 1986; Imbens and Angrist, 1994; Manski, 1995; Heckman et al., 1997, 1998, 2001; Dehejia and Wahba, 2002; Smith and Todd, 2005; Raphael and Stoll, 2006) and the development of robust estimates of prices of criminal victimization (Miller et al., 1993a, 1996; Cohen et al., 1994; Rajkumar and French, 1997; Cohen, 1998). The scholarly literature on problems in establishing causal inference with observational data is far more extensive than the literature on the price of crime to victims, and details of such issues are covered in this volume (see Manski and Nagin). The few studies that include victims' cost focus more on resolving identification problems than improving cost and benefits estimates (see, e.g.,

Levitt, 1996; Lochner and Moretti, 2004). Studies that focus on costs and benefits of crime control programs tend not to take identification issues seriously. Few—if any—studies give inference problems and pricing problems equal weight although the rigor of any economics of crime study depends on both.

Theoretically, the motivation for studying the costs of crime to victims is straightforward. Many neoclassic theories of crime, such as rational choice and routine activities theory, posit that potential offenders implicitly estimate the costs and benefits of committing a crime before acting. Costs of crime include the risk of detection and the severity of punishment, and criminal labor is supplied if the benefits outweigh the costs. While this supply model of offending is well developed, the demand side—where the crime victim appears—is less clearly articulated. Ehrlich (1996) proposes a model where demand for crime is derived from the supply of offenses function. Thus, the potential losses from crime determine the amount of public and private crime prevention. The amount of harm experienced by victims of crime therefore should be equivalent to the costs of detecting and responding to crime to make efficient allocations of scarce anticrime resources. More intuitively, this model posits that the costs of a program or policy designed to reduce crime should be less than the benefits that are measured as reductions in harm to society.

This model has been widely applied. Levitt (1996) compares the costs of deterrence from incarceration to the benefits of averted crimes from incarceration in evaluating the efficiency of prison. Lochner and Moretti (2004: 23) estimate "the social savings from crime reduction resulting from a 1 percent increase in high school graduation rates" using this approach. Lott and Mustard (1997) apply this theory to value the savings from increasing gun possession, and Ludwig and Cook (2001; Cook and Ludwig, 2000) use this theory to show the savings from decreasing gun ownership. More recently, a large literature has begun to emerge that measures the costs and benefits of various anticrime strategies where the benefits are understood in this way, such as the savings from early interventions with children (Schweinhart et al., 2005).

Estimating Harm to Victims of Crime

Two approaches are commonly used in neoclassic economics to value a policy change (Hicks, 1939). Compensating variation (willingness to pay or WTP) is the "the maximum amount of income that could be taken from someone who gains from a particular change while still leaving him no worse off than before the change." Equivalent variation (WTA) is the "the minimum amount that someone who gains from a particular change would be willing to accept to forego the change" (Pearce, 1992: 78, in Leung and Sproule, 2007). Each of the approaches described below relies on one or the other to justify the estimation strategy.

Hedonic Pricing

The first cost of crime to victims' studies used hedonic pricing to estimate market prices for crime. The studies observed revealed preferences for the components of crime, usually measured as heterogeneity in real estate prices or wages due to differential risk of victimization (Thaler and Rosen, 1975; Thaler, 1978; Clark and Cosgrove, 1990). The hedonic approach is strictly defined as a WTP method, using before the event measures of price to estimate equivalent variation (for instance, the amount an individual would have to be compensated to be indifferent between taking a higher wage job with a higher risk of criminal victimization and taking a lower risk, lower paying job). Thaler (1978) used a random sample of single-family homes from Rochester, New York, to estimate the price of property crime. Clark and Cosgrove (1990) use data on wages, structural features of homes, and individual attributes to estimate the relationship of rental values and safety. The hedonic pricing approach is criticized on the grounds that prices and crime are endogenously determined by Manski (1995: 6). The identification problem results from the fact that differential prices, for instance, for homes, are the result of both the consumers' demand for that goods (and its component parts such as crime riskiness) and the sellers' perception of the value of that goods. Thus, the difference in value between two otherwise identical homes is not the difference in the demand for crime. The other criticism is that results are aggregated individual estimates and not equivalent to social costs, and critics note that society's WTP for a policy is different from the sum of individual preferences, since an individual's WTP for a home is exclusively for their own benefit, while they may be willing to pay for crime reduction in the broader community.

Contingent Valuation

Recently, studies of the costs of crime to victims have estimated equivalent variation functions, which measure WTP to avoid crime using contingent valuation survey techniques (Cook and Ludwig, 2000; Cohen et al., 2004). The contingent valuation method uses stated preferences as the proxy for market behavior. A referendum-based approach that follows the recommendations of the NOAA Panel on Contingent Valuation is standard practice. Studies thus solicit prices that respondents would be willing to pay to reduce their (or their communities) risk of victimization policy (Arrow et al., 1995). While the Cohen studies cited above adhere closely to the NOAA recommendations, critics of the approach suggest that even those strict standards do not compensate for structural limitations in the method (Carson et al., 1999). Most importantly, the contingent valuation approach elicits stated preferences rather than observing behavior in a binding market transaction when individuals have to actually forgo money. Thus, contingent valuation tends to overestimate WTP (Diamond and Hausman, 1994; Portney, 1994; but see Schelling, 1968; Cook and Ludwig, 2000).

QALYs

A third approach, QALYs (quality-adjusted life years), has been used extensively among UK researchers to value the costs of crime to victims (DuBourg and Hamed, 2005) and internationally for the study of health interventions (Grossman, 1972). In health studies, the product of the sum of discounted health status over time and the value of a year of perfect health captures the trade-off between longer life and better health (Cutler and Richardson, 1998). In crime studies, the general strategy is to rank-order utility states anchored by high disutility from a criminal event to no disutility from a criminal event. These estimates, drawn from surveys or expert rankings of expectation of harm from crime, are then used to rank-order the harms from victimization across crime type (Dolan and Peasgood, 2005). Since the intangible costs of crime to be estimated are mainly psychic, a key disadvantage of this approach is that there are no extant estimates of QALYs in the presence of heterogeneity of mental health states (Zaric et al., 2000: 1104).

Jury Awards

The final approach values compensating variations to estimate WTA crime after the event by using the amount of compensation that would be necessary to return an individual to their original state before some event with negative consequences (Cohen, 2000). The approach has also been criticized, on the grounds that derived values are ex-post rather than ex-ante (and thus do not reflect how people would behave in a marketplace) and that the estimates are aggregated individual losses rather than social cost (Cook and Ludwig, 2000). However, the jury compensation strategy used in this analysis employs the same logic as equivalent variation, but instead of observing revealed preferences in a crime victimization market, the jury award is determined after a crime event by a third party. Thus, the jury compensation award is a proxy for ex-ante WTA, in a way that is less speculative than contingent valuation and more complete than a study that considers only costs of injury. Juries as a third party are setting the price for what they believe individuals should be compensated for being crime victims, thus providing a range of prices for different types of criminal victimizations that can be used to estimate the severity of crimes.

The general strategy in developing price estimates of victim harms is to observe the distribution of injuries in jury-adjudicated civil cases and use those data to estimate indirect costs of crime. Most of the jury studies use a blended approach linking jury compensation with cost of illness data, where the latter values harms from crime according to the medical expenses incurred by the victim (see Rajkumar and French, 1997). While the cost-of-illness approach is clearly estimated ex-post (harm values are assigned after a crime is committed), the jury compensation method seeks to approximate an ex-ante estimation of equivalent variation, by estimating the amount necessary to make an individual whole and thus return them to their pre-victimization state.

Prior Studies Estimating Crime Prices
Using Jury Award Data

Prior studies of the price of crime to victims have generally employed similar strategies. Data from multiple sources are mapped together to describe the relationship between jury awards and crime. As previously noted, many of these steps will use aggregate data. If aggregated data are combined with individual-level data, statements about the uncertainty of estimates can only be made with respect to the individual-level data. Nothing can be said about either the uncertainty around the aggregate data or the uncertainty about the combined data. While it is possible as some have recently proposed to use simulation models to estimate confidence intervals around point estimates derived from aggregate data, it is far more efficient to retain uncertainty through all iteration of data manipulation.

The Validity of Jury Awards

The logic behind the jury award approach is straightforward. Some victims of criminal acts will seek to have the costs of their harm internalized by the offender (or other liable party) and will use the tort system as the means of recovery. When plaintiffs win a case, civil juries compensate victims in two ways.[4] First, the jury may award damages for economic losses, including property loss, medical costs, and lost wages. Second, juries may award damages for noneconomic losses to compensate victim for indirect or intangible costs, including fear, lost or diminished quality of life, and pain and suffering and lost quality of life.

There are several threats to the validity of jury awards. In order for civil jury award data to provide reliable estimates of the true harms to victims, it must first be demonstrated that juries are capable of consistent and unbiased estimates of harms across heterogeneous civil cases. And since intentional torts (criminal acts) are a relatively small proportion of all civil claims, it must be the case that juries make awards based only on the harms suffered in the case and not the attributes of the victim or offender, whether it is an intentional tort, malpractice, or negligence. If the types of claim matters, for example, malpractice awards are different on average than tort awards for the same harms, then different types of claims cannot be combined, and small sample sizes will greatly limit any analysis of harms from crime.

The consistency of civil jury awards has been the subject of significant prior research. Critics assert that not only are juries unable to evaluate claims in complex cases, but they are not competent to evaluate claims in relatively simple cases as well (Sugarman, 1985; Vidmar, 1989). Jury awards have also been criticized on the grounds that juries make awards based on extra-legal information, and thus awards are not tied to harms, and that juries systematically use inappropriate criteria to make awards (Daniels, 1989: 280–81). These inappropriate criteria may include the perceived wealth of the defendant (which is hypothesized to lead to awards in excess of actual losses), smaller awards for female plaintiffs, higher awards (relative to actual losses) in certain time periods or in certain regions of the country, and awards in excess of actual losses in cases where the defendant is particularly reprehensible.

Notably, the overwhelming consensus in the scholarly literature is that civil juries are competent and allegations of award randomness are unfounded. The available evidence suggests that civil jury outcomes are not random lotteries. Although they are subject to substantial variation, awards "are nonetheless a function of variables we can specify" (Rodgers, 1993: 261). The overwhelming consensus in the literature contends awards that vary in a manner consistent with the expectations of economic and noneconomic loss (Viscusi, 1988). However, there are several potential sources of bias. Studies of award variation across case type suggest that work injury, malpractice, and product liability awards are higher than the awards in other types of cases (Peterson and Priest, 1982; Daniels and Martin, 1986; Goodman et al., 1989). Similarly, defendant wealth does not appear to be associated with higher awards, although the presence of a corporation as the defendant may (MacCoun, 1996). Moreover, geographic variations in legal culture and legal procedure account for the only non-extralegal impetus in award bias (Danzon, 1984; Peterson, 1984; Chin and Peterson, 1985; Hammit et al., 1985; Hans and Lofquist, 1992; Vidmar, 1993: 229; Tabarrok and Helland, 1999). Male defendants appear to receive higher awards than women, although the evidence is mixed (Goodman et al., 1989; Rodgers, 1993). And finally, the evidence indicates that the jury's perception of defendant culpability or reprehensibility may inflate compensatory awards, particularly when the jury does not have the option to assess punitive awards (Hans and Ermann, 1989; Horowitz and Bordens, 1990; MacCoun, 1996; Anderson and MacCoun, 1999; Wissler et al., 2001).

Overall, this literature suggests that it is reasonable to use jury award data linked to attributes of crime to estimate the severity of crimes. There are criticisms of the jury award/WTA approach, but the benefits outweigh the costs. The WTA approach is not as strong as the WTP approach in approximating societal benefits, but the use of actual awards is a substantial advantage over the hypothetical estimates from WTP. While jury awards are not a perfect approximation of victim losses, juries are generally unbiased observers of losses.

Data

Data to estimate the monetized harms to crime victims were developed from the RAND ICJ.[5] In total, there are 38,141 cases in the combined jury award database (Table 3.1). Data describe 38,141 civil cases with a disposition between 1985 and 1999. The data include all jury awards in California (14,803) and New York (10,416), and the cities and surrounding counties of Chicago, Illinois (4,332), Houston, Texas (4,410), Seattle, Washington (1,207), and St. Louis, Missouri (2,973). There is heterogeneity across places and times in the data. For instance, in 1998,

California verdicts account for 4.2 percent of all verdicts in the series, while in 1985 California accounted for only less than 2 percent. The number of cases increases gradually over time from 1,971 in 1985 to 2,723 in 1999, with a peak of 3,443 in 1997.

The plaintiff won in 47.5 percent of cases. There is substantial variation in awards in these cases, with a mean of $1.22 million and a median of $147,000 (Table 3.1). One percent of cases have an award greater than $10 million, and 1 percent has an award below $1,000. Data include awards for actual damages (including property loss, lost wages, and health-care costs), general damages (pain and suffering), and punitive damages (for specific and general deterrence). The data also include substantial information about both the plaintiff and the defendant (age and gender), the facts surrounding the criminal event and harms (injuries) inflicted on the victim.

The final data set contains 12,918 cases, and all observations have a valid award for damages. These cases are a stratified sample of all civil jury awards in the sampled jurisdictions between 1985 and 1999. Cases were dropped from the original sample of 26,000 for a variety of reasons, including missing data, but also in all cases where the plaintiff lost (about half the cases). Jury awards contain four components: an award for direct economic losses, including lost property, lost wages, and health-related costs; an award for indirect or noneconomic losses, which include fear, lost or diminished quality of life, and pain and suffering; punitive awards; and adjustments for shared negligence. In this analysis, punitive awards were not included, nor were the data adjusted for shared negligence.

As has been the case in prior jury award studies, the award amounts are highly skewed. The mean award ($1,328,677) is almost six times as

Table 3.1   Mean of total awards with and without outliers (unweighted)

Category	All cases		Crime cases only	
	Total	No outliers	Total	No outliers
Sample size	12,918	12,762	895	886
All observations (median) ($)	1,243,305 (202,615)	895,091 (194,479)	1,114,705 (111,628)	737,081 (117,491)

Note: All records include a non-missing value for total award. There are 12,918 in the full sample and 12,762 in the sample with the outliers removed. All values are adjusted for inflation and presented in 2003 dollars. The means and median values are after punitive awards have been removed, but do not include stratification weights. Median values are in parentheses.

large as the median award ($229,535). The data are in part skewed by a few outliers where the implied value of a life is in the tens or hundreds of millions, far outside the typical valuation (Viscusi, 1986). Thus, cases with an award *more* than three standard deviations from the mean were dropped from the analysis. Removing these 162 cases substantially reduced the mean by 33.9 percent for cases affirmatively coded as crime and 27.6 percent for cases that could not be coded as having resulted from a crime. The RAND data are a stratified probability sample with weights that approximate the population of jury awards. All analyses here employ those weights, and the weights are multiplied by the propensity score weight so that the estimates are weighted to the population and the different characteristics of crimes.

NIBRS

NIBRS data were developed by the FBI and the Bureau of Justice Statistics to detail characteristics of criminal events. NIBRS data are reported at the incident level. Data include information about the offense (type of weapon, completed or not), the offender (age, race, and gender), the victim (age, race, gender, ethnicity, and type of injury), type of property stolen or damage (including value), and arrestee data (age, race, gender, ethnicity, age, and type of arrest). Data in NIBRS are available for ten states[6] where more than half of the population in a given state is covered by NIBRS reporting.

Prior research often used data from the National Crime Victimization Survey (NCVS) to link jury awards to crime data, in part because NIBRS data were not yet available. NIBRS data offer some advantages over NCVS data. NIBRS includes far more observations, and thus more observations of the rarest, but most serious crime. Since the small number of serious person crimes explain most of the total cost of crime, access to these data is critical to the development of price estimates. It also includes data on "victimless" crime and crimes where a business but not a person was victimized that are not reported in NCVS.[7]

The NIBRS data for 2003 (the most recent data available at the time of the analysis) include 3.8 million observations for which data are not missing for the victim and the type of crime. Almost 97 percent of crimes in NIBRS were completed. The average direct loss from crime in NIBRS was $1,432 and the median loss was $100. Data are also available on recovered items for 325,000 cases (less than 10 percent of the sample), with an average recovery of $3,075 and a median recovery of

$90. Subtracting recovered losses from all losses does not substantively change the mean or median direct loss.

Analysis

The preferred estimation strategy is to predict the cost of crime to victims for different types of crimes by regressing jury awards on crimes, controlling for attributes of award size as in the following notation:

$$Jury\ award = b\left(crime_i\right) + Xi'q + e\left(1\right)$$

Here *jury award* is the total award for a case (including general awards, specials, and punitive damages), *crime* is a vector of criminal event types, and X is a vector of attributes associated with non-claimant-related jury awards. The parameter on *crime* is the average award for an additional crime of each type, which is interpreted as the cost to a victim of that type of crime.

This model cannot be directly estimated since there are too few observations for types of crime within the RAND ICJ data set that directly link a jury award to a criminal act. Only about 10 percent of the observations in the ICJ data are intentional tort cases, and while some other criminal victimizations can be identified by the type of injury suffered (sexual assault or gunshot, for instance), for most cases, the underlying criminality of the event that leads to the civil case is not observable. Thus, the ICJ jury award data alone are not sufficient to directly estimate the average costs of crime to victims.

This problem can be resolved by associating awards to victim injury and linking ICJ to NIBRS by type of injury. In the ICJ data, virtually all of the observations include some type of physical harm, and data are available to describe those harms. The ICJ data could be used to estimate direct costs of victimization and indirect damages such as the harms from pain and suffering as a function of different injuries. Since comparable victim injury data are available in both the ICJ and NIBRS data sets, the combined data set would contain information about both crime and damages. NIBRS data use eight relatively broad categories to describe injuries (broken bones, possible internal injury, severe laceration, apparent minor injury, loss of teeth, unconsciousness, other major injury, and no injury). RAND ICJ data include much finer injury descriptions that can be aggregated to match the NIBRS coding. Since awards are heterogeneous with respect to other attributes observable in both data (victim age and gender, and region), the means and distribution of each cross-combination of attributes can be estimated, and those values can be interpolated onto the NIBRS data to predict awards for criminal acts. These awards can then be interpreted as the distribution of expected costs of crime to victims.

The analysis was conducted using three samples developed from the RAND ICJ data. While many of these awards are for noncriminal events, juries are instructed to make awards based on the harms suffered, independent of the type of event that led to those harms. Thus, a rather strong assumption can be made that the awards from noncriminal events are appropriate proxies and, if anything, provide a lower bound since these injuries are not as likely to involve the psychological harm produced from a criminal victimization. A second data set was created that includes only those cases that can be affirmatively coded as having resulted from a criminal act. While this limits the number of different types of crime that can be used to interpolate the price for a much broader set of crimes, it is instructive to develop estimates of the price of crime that are limited to those observations that are known to result from a crime.

The third data set attempts to make use of only those noncrime civil cases that share attributes with the cases affirmatively coded as crime cases. Doing so somewhat relaxes the assumption that juries account for only the victims' harms in their deliberations. To address this potential selection problem, propensity score models will be used to model the likelihood that a noncrime case ($n = 12{,}023$) is similar in characteristics to a crime case ($n = 895$). The propensity score models thus produce a method for reducing the differences between the observed characteristics of noncrime and crime cases (Rosenbaum and Rubin, 1983).

In developing the propensity-weighted sample, I follow Heckman et al. (1998) and begin with a parsimonious model containing several theoretically important predictors of selection. The model includes all case attributes that can reasonably be expected to have an association with whether or not the case was a crime, variables common to both RAND ICJ and NIBRS, variables that are theoretically linked to bias jury awards—including a business as a defendant (and the type of business)—whether there was a punitive award, and whether there was shared negligence, and selected interaction terms were added to each model (age by gender and gender by region) to ensure that the functional form of the model is properly specified.

The initial propensity model did not adequately balance the sample using all observations in the RAND data. In a second iteration, only those observations with common attributes were retained.

Cross-combinations of all the covariates in the data were created, and only those cross-combinations that were observed in both groups were retained ($n = 5,403$). A total of 603 crime cases (weighted by the stratification weights to resemble 585 cases) and 4,800 noncrime cases (weighted to resemble 4,770 noncrime cases) were included. This approach substantially improved sample balance. In lay terms, this approach improves the equivalence of attributes between crime and noncrime samples. Before propensity score weighting, nineteen of twenty-three independent variables were significantly different between the noncrime and crime jury award samples compared to only three variables after weighting on the propensity score. The propensity weight is multiplied to ICJ stratified sample weights to adjust all observations for selection in subsequent analyses and to assure that the estimates of crime costs approximate the total jury award sample. Table 3.2 describes the jury awards for the eight categories of injury estimated by the three different samples.

Interpolation

Next, the estimates of harms in the ICJ data set were interpolated onto the NIBRS data. This approach requires two relatively strong assumptions. First, it must be assumed that the observed jury award associated with any injury in the ICJ data set would be the same as the harms for an identical injury observed in the NIBRS data. By relying on propensity score-weighted sample of jury awards to represent crime cases, this assumption is not unreasonable. Second, there is no geographic overlap between the two groups, and the time periods covered by the two data sets coincide only for two years. Since there are no common observations, the data cannot be simply merged. The two data sets do contain data on variables that are consistent across the two groups, and those similarities can be exploited to create a unified data set.

First, common elements are identified between the two sources. These include the following:

- Victim age (below twenty, twenty to twenty-nine, thirty to thirty-nine, forty to forty-nine, fifty, and older)
- Victim gender (male or female)
- Type of injury (broken bones, possible internal injury, severe laceration, apparent minor injury, loss of teeth, unconsciousness, other major injury, and no injury)
- Urban, rural, or suburban

Table 3.2 Award estimates by type of injury, RAND data only

Injury type	Costs by injury category ($)					
	Crime only (N = 886)		Propensity model (N = 5,403)		All cases (N = 12,756)	
	Mean	**Median**	**Mean**	**Median**	**Mean**	**Median**
None	368,823	31,876	423,460	114,421	356,614	100,330
Dead	1,985,398	911,261	1,854,949	1,146,531	1,645,356	879,604
Injuries/broken bones	358,638	74,154	708,886	222,316	585,164	165,076
Internal injuries	1,482,423	190,622	1,744,959	661,737	798,798	325,917
Severe lacerations	1,771,304	1,214,796	1,751,367	1,183,395	1,637,578	758,565
Apparent minor injuries	321,275	34,264	286,735	51,712	361,801	74,284
Other major injuries	844,058	139,350	1,143,109	197,595	1,065,753	216,282
Loss of teeth	386,382	63,604	423,308	100,968	472,747	104,966
Unconsciousness	313,047	101,532	381,595	90,148	497,094	77,747
Average award	737,251	110,827	981,600	197,423	895,401	194,479

Source: Analysis of data from the RAND Institute of Civil Justice, 12,918 cases from 1985 to 1999. Frequency weights are applied to all analyses. All dollars are calculated as 2003 dollars.

Next, a variable is created for each cross-combination of attributes, and a value is assigned to each observation in both data sets. That is, each time an award is observed for a male of thirty to thirty-nine age-group from an urban area with broken bones, that award is included in that cross-combination category. If there are multiple observations for a cross-combination, a mean and a distribution of awards are created. For each identical cross-combination in NIBRS, a random draw from that distribution is interpolated onto the first observation in NIBRS with that cross-combination of attributes. The process is repeated for all observations in NIBRS. Data in NIBRS are then re-sorted into crime categories so that the distribution of victim harms within each crime category can be observed. Since there is substantial variation in the types of victims within crimes, there is also substantial variation around the mean estimate. Estimates were generated for thirty-one crime categories (Table 3.3).

Table 3.3   Estimates of harms for serious injuries (RAND and NIBRS data)

| Crime type | Crimes with direct and indirect costs | | | | | |
| | Crime only | | Propensity model | | All cases | |
	Mean ($)	N	Mean ($)	N	Mean ($)	N
Murder/ nonnegligent manslaughter	1,532,342	1,146	1,445,463	818	1,466,160	2,369
Kidnapping/ abduction	64,358	6,117	140,697	6,115	161,433	9,565
Forcible rape	64,774	11,487	107,486	11,486	190,366	21,668
Forcible sodomy	103,359	1,456	425,168	1,456	229,024	4,207
Sexual assault with object	55,767	1,100	142,261	1,100	198,353	2,585
Forcible fondling	52,958	7,072	162,235	7,071	195,264	22,006
Robbery	197,741	31,542	279,085	31,524	236,487	45,458
Aggravated assault	223,180	76,256	283,793	76,114	307,768	120,148
Simple assault	77,008	342,201	101,624	342,201	127,356	501,645
Intimidation	57,850	137,362	117,625	137,362	151,726	175,605

Source: Analysis of data from the RAND Institute of Civil Justice, 12,918 cases from 1985 to 1999 and 2000 NIBRS data. Frequency weights are applied to all analyses. All dollars are calculated as 2003 dollars.

Two adjustments are then made to the above method. First, it should be noted that the ICJ and NIBRS do not perfectly overlap on all attributes. Thus, there are cross-combinations of attributes that are observable in NIBRS that are not observable in ICJ. To account for this, prior to running the propensity score models, only those observations that fall into a cross-combination that is observable in both data sets are selected. In practice, this has the effect of excluding almost one-third of NIBRS observations (about 29 percent) from the final analysis. As discussed below, this allows for a simple test of the assumption that awards for observations in ICJ are appropriate proxies for harms to victims in the NIBRS data. The analysis described above is performed only for serious crimes with a risk of victim injury, including the following:

- Murder/nonnegligent manslaughter
- Kidnapping/abduction
- Forcible rape
- Forcible sodomy
- Sexual assault with object
- Forcible fondling
- Robbery
- Aggravated assault
- Simple assault
- Intimidation

Since the link between the data is a measure of physical harm, it is only appropriate to use those data to interpolate harms where an injury could have occurred. However, the relationship between direct and indirect losses in the ICJ data can be used to make estimates about indirect losses to victims of serious property crimes, which has generally not been done in prior studies. While serious person crimes are often assigned both an indirect and a direct loss, many victims of serious property crimes experience harms as well. Past studies have routinely included estimates for indirect costs in addition to property loss in serious property crimes (Cohen, 1988a, b; Miller et al., 1995; Rajkumar and French, 1997; Cohen et al., 2004; McCollister, 2004). There is also empirical support for this assumption, as "theft/conversion" cases generally receive awards that include compensation for indirect losses. Serious property crimes include the following:

- Arson
- Extortion/blackmail

- Burglary/breaking and entering
- Motor vehicle theft
- Counterfeiting/forgery
- Swindle
- Credit card
- Impersonation

To estimate indirect harms in these cases, the logged jury award is regressed on direct losses and other covariates to predict the portion of the award that is from direct losses. From this, a ratio of direct to indirect losses is estimated from the ICJ data, which was estimated to be about 0.7, indicating that the indirect component of a jury award was 70 percent as large as the direct component. Again, a relatively strong assumption is required, which is that the ratio of indirect to direct losses experienced by civil litigants is the same as that experienced by the victims of a property crime. To mitigate this assumption, the regression described above included only observations for victims who experienced no injury or minor injuries. This multiplier is then used to inflate observed property losses from the NIBRS data in serious property crimes (those that are commonly considered felony offenses) to include indirect harms. For all other crimes, victim harms are calculated only as the property losses reported to police as described in the NIBRS data. These crimes include the following:

- Pocket-picking
- Purse snatching
- Shoplifting
- Theft from building
- Theft from coin-operated machine
- Theft of motor vehicle parts
- Theft from motor vehicle
- All other larceny
- Welfare fraud
- Wire fraud
- Embezzlement
- Stolen property offenses
- Destruction/vandalism

As noted, one important assumption of this study is that civil jury awards are an appropriate estimator of harms to victims of serious person crimes. A related assumption is that those cases that can be matched to ICJ (e.g., those cases with a cross-combination of attributes that exists in both data) are similar to those cases that cannot (about 29 percent of NIBRS observations). One way to test this assumption is to compare losses observable in both data, in this case property losses in robberies and burglaries. There are a total of 256,000 burglaries for which a property loss is observable in NIBRS. The mean loss is $2,613 for those that match to the ICJ data and $1,587 for those that do not match; however, the difference is not statistically significant ($p = .33$) in an independent samples t-test. Property loss is observable in about forty thousand robbery cases. The mean loss in those cases that are observable in both data sets is $1,510 and the mean loss in those cases observable only in NIBRS is $1,221, which is statistically significant at $p = .09$. This suggests that there is some upward bias when the cases that match to RAND ICJ data are used in the analysis; however, the hypothesis that there are no differences between the two groups cannot be rejected at conventional levels.

Results

Estimating Losses in Serious Person Crimes

Table 3.4 describes the estimated price of victimization in serious person crimes. Serious person crimes can result in economic losses of

Table 3.4   Price estimates for aggregated part one crimes, propensity score models

Crime type	Crimes with direct and indirect costs ($)					
	Mean	**90%**	**75%**	**Median**	**25%**	**10%**
Murder	1,445,463	2,838,800	1,782,500	1,380,246	848,183	272,169
Rape	149,542	238,395	214,449	18,908	3,524	1,393
Robbery	279,085	605,225	334,515	88,915	68,326	18,908
Assault	134,770	334,515	155,270	66,644	13,285	611
Aggravated assault	283,794	569,701	294,335	89,815	27,956	1,900
Simple assault	101,623	238,396	87,000	59,083	35,239	600

Source: All estimates are in 2008 dollars. The rape data in this study are a weighted average of forcible rape, forcible sodomy, and sexual assault with an object. The assault data from this study include a weighted average of aggravated assault and simple assault.

all three types: (direct (wages and health), direct (property), and indirect (fear, diminished value of life, and pain and suffering))

Overall, the propensity score results generally predict the highest awards, and the cases affirmatively coded as resulting from a crime produce the lowest awards. Crimes generally follow the expected pattern with respect to the ranking of crimes by severity. Homicides have the highest prices, and simple assaults and intimidation are the lowest. Not surprisingly, the least variation appears in the results for all jury award cases, and the greatest variation appears in the crime category, which has the smallest sample size.

The estimates in Table 3.4 suggest that there is a substantial skew in the price of serious crimes, where a small number of victimizations have exceptionally large awards. For every serious crime other than homicide, the mean award is substantially larger than the median, at least two to three times larger. It is also important to note that for these crimes it is common for a victim to suffer relatively small damages. In every crime but murder, the tenth percentile of cases experiences damages that are an order of magnitude smaller than the mean award.

Estimating Losses in Less Serious Property Crimes

As is the case for serious person crime, the estimates for serious property crimes are also highly skewed. For example, in counterfeiting and arson cases, the mean loss is greater than 90 percent of all losses, demonstrating that a very small number of cases have extreme harms. The mean harm estimate exceeds the seventy-fifth percentile of harms in every category but motor vehicle theft. And the median award is an order of magnitude smaller than the mean for most cases. It is also important to note that many cases result in no observable harm to the victim (Table 3.5).

Estimating Losses in the Least Serious Property Crimes

The losses reported in Table 3.6 are the mean and median losses in less serious crimes that are generated from the NIBRS data only. The assumption associated with these estimates is that there is no indirect loss from these crimes (and no direct losses other than property loss). To the extent that there are indirect losses, these estimates will tend to underestimate losses for those crimes.

Table 3.5 Price estimates for serious property crimes

Crime type	Crimes with direct and indirect costs ($)					
	Mean	90%	75%	Median	25%	10%
Arson ($N = 5,423$)	16,979	3,621	1,096	850	323	170
Extortion/blackmail (220)	3,498	7,700	1,700	170	0	0
Burglary/B & E (190,842)	4,444	5,279	2,210	782	222	12
Motor vehicle theft (135,685)	15,175	39,100	17,000	6,800	2,550	41
Counterfeiting/forgery (19,338)	8,208	1,870	459	34	0	0
Swindle (29,451)	4,389	7,990	1,771	170	2	0
Credit card (21,384)	973	1,820	617	37	0	0
Impersonation (19,817)	955	1,159	5	2	0	0

Source: Analysis of data from the RAND Institute of Civil Justice, 12,918 cases from 1985 to 1999 and 2000 NIBRS data. Frequency weights are applied to all analyses. All dollars are calculated as 2003 dollars.

Table 3.6 Estimates of harms for crimes with property losses only, plus indirect costs

Crime type (N)	Mean ($)	Median ($)
Pocket-picking (4,235)	408	90
Purse snatching (5,772)	447	72
Shoplifting (1,963)	459	60
Theft from building (125,141)	6,393	165
Theft from coin-operated machine (884)	532	140
Theft of motor vehicle parts (274,937)	408	210
Theft from motor vehicle (274,937)	990	100
All other larceny (367,978)	2,048	150
Welfare fraud (95)	461	47
Wire fraud (2,003)	1,930	275
Embezzlement (2,210)	9,781	1,633
Stolen property offenses (7,155)	3,341	500
Destruction/vandalism (460,629)	759	170

Source: Analysis of data from the RAND Institute of Civil Justice, 12,918 cases from 1985 to 1999 and 2000 NIBRS data. Frequency weights are applied to all analyses. All dollars are calculated as 2000 dollars.

Discussion

The discussion above focused mainly on the skew in the data, which raises questions about whether the mean or the median estimates should be used. As discussed above in the case of arson and counterfeiting, the mean estimate describes a high cost event that is rarely observed. For many crimes types, the mean (the average of all events) is an order of magnitude larger than the median (the typical event). This has important implications in using these estimates in other research, particularly cost–benefit analyses that seek to measure whether programs with significant effects on crime are cost-effective. Clearly, choosing the mean harm to victims instead of the median will have substantial consequences. One solution is to report both estimates.

The other important question is what to make of the magnitudes of the reported harm estimates, and that discussion also encounters problem due to the skewed data. When compared to other prices of victimization studies, the mean estimates reported here are higher than much of the published literature, while the medians are in line with the lowest estimates due to the skew in the price distribution. Table 3.7 compares the means and Table 3.8 compares the medians (it is important to point out that the other studies only report means and do not report measures of uncertainty).

Some of the differences are due to definitional issues. For instance, an assault in other studies may refer only to a simple assault, whereas in the present study, the assault price is an average weighted by the prevalence of both simple and aggravated assaults. This is the likely cause of differences with respect to theft, as I include thefts from businesses, which include relatively larger harms than other types of theft. There are two crimes for which the differences between my estimates and the prior literature are particularly notable: homicide and rape.

This study produces a lower homicide estimate than that appears in prior research. In part, this is because the price of homicide is directly estimated here, and most prior studies rely on an estimate of the statistical value of human life (VSL) that is usually estimated to be about $8 million or used the VSL as a weight to adjust for risk of death associated with other crimes. However, that strategy assumes no variation in the costs associated with homicide that is unlikely to be true from a social welfare perspective. While the approach used in this study does identify substantial variation in the costs of homicide, a substantial weakness of the approach with respect to homicide remains. That is,

Table 3.7 Comparison of new price estimates to extant estimates (mean)

| Crime type | | Jury award literature | | | CV | Roman |
| | | | | | | |
	Cohen (1988)	Miller et al. (1996)	Rajkumar and French (1997)	French and McCollister (2008)	Cohen et al. (2004)	Propensity model
Murder/nonnegligent manslaughter	2,842,242	4,178,096	7,772,054	9,322,054	10,825,622	1,564,186
Rape	102,218	129,629	74,271	219,566	264,502	156,295
Robbery	25,200	19,370	32,040	46,484	258,922	279,085
Assault	24,067	22,350	32,040	122,716	78,123	134,770
Burglary	2,745	2,235	1,909	4,362	27,901	4,444
Motor vehicle theft	6,257	5,960	1,666	9,141	5,412	15,175
Theft	362	551	1,067	1,475	819	2,655

The header spanning group above "Jury award literature", "CV", and "Roman": **Crimes with direct and indirect costs ($)**

Source: Each of the estimates is derived from the study cited. All estimates are presented in 2008 dollars (Cohen (1988) are estimated in 1985 dollars and Miller et al. (1996) are estimated in 1993 dollars). The rape data in Roman are a weighted average of forcible rape, forcible sodomy, and sexual assault with an object. The assault data from the Roman study include a weighted average of aggravated assault and simple assault and assault data from other studies may include aggravated or attempted assaults. The French and McCollister study presents estimates for aggravated assault only. The larceny/theft value in the Roman study is the weighted average mean of NIBRS categories: Theft from building, theft from coin-operated machine or device, theft from motor vehicle, theft of motor vehicle parts/accessories, and all other larceny.

Table 3.8 Comparison of new price estimates to extant estimates (median)

	Crimes with direct and indirect costs ($)					
	Jury award literature				CV	Roman
Crime type	Cohen (1988)	Miller et al. (1996)	Rajkumar and French (1997)	French and McCollister (2008)	Cohen et al. (2004)	Propensity model
Murder/nonnegligent manslaughter	2,842,242	4,178,096	7,772,054	9,322,054	10,825,622	1,380,246
Rape	102,218	129,629	74,271	219,566	264,502	18,908
Robbery	25,200	19,370	32,040	46,484	258,922	88,915
Assault	24,067	22,350	32,040	122,716	78,123	66,644
Burglary	2,745	2,235	1,909	4,362	27,901	782
Motor vehicle theft	6,257	5,960	1,666	9,141	5,412	6,800
Theft	362	551	1,067	1,475	819	192

Source: Each of the estimates is derived from the study cited. All estimates are presented in 2008 dollars (Cohen (1988) are estimated in 1985 dollars and Miller et al. (1996) are estimated in 1993 dollars). The rape data in Roman are a weighted average of forcible rape, forcible sodomy, and sexual assault with an object. The assault data from the Roman study include a weighted average of aggravated assault and simple assault and assault data from other studies may include aggravated or attempted assaults. The French and McCollister study presents estimates for aggravated assault only. The larceny/theft value in the Roman study is the weighted average mean of NIBRS categories: theft from building, theft from coin-operated machine or device, theft from motor vehicle, theft of motor vehicle parts/accessories, all other larceny.

unlike other categories of crime, the victim is not being compensated by the jury, and thus the estimate is not an ex-post proxy for WTA being the victim of a homicide.

The other estimate generated here that is inconsistent with prior estimates is the estimate for the price of rape. While the mean value for rape is in line with prior estimates, rape ($149,000) has a lower price in this study than robbery ($279,000), which reverses the usual ordering from other studies. In terms of injury, the profiles for rape and robbery look very similar, as about 70 percent of rape victims experience no injury or an apparently minor injury. However, severe lacerations, broken bones, and other internal injuries are reported more commonly in robbery cases than in rape cases, and as shown in Table 3.3, these kinds of injuries are associated with much larger awards. This difference in injuries leads to the higher price for robbery. It should be noted that the difference between robbery and rape exists in both the means reported above and the medians (about $100,000 for robberies compared to about $20,000 in rape cases).

Conclusions

Understanding the magnitude of the harms victims experience in a criminal event is a critical input for measuring the severity of crimes and informing investments in crime prevention policy. These data provide important information to inform a variety of important policy questions: How should scarce law enforcement resources be spread across crimes? How much should society spend as a whole to respond to and prevent crime? How long should sentences be for different types of crime? The advantage of the estimates developed here are that they incorporate data from a much richer data than that was available to researchers in the past, and thus prices of victimization can be estimated for more crimes, and uncertainty about those estimates can be incorporated into future analyses. One obvious conclusion is that there is tremendous variation in the harms experienced by victims and that future studies that use victim price data would be well-served to consider the impact of that variation within their analysis.

This chapter did not set out to directly contribute to the debate about the relative value of jury compensation studies compared to contingent valuation (WTP) studies. However, the skewness in the data seems to embolden the critics of WTP who have argued that respondents lack enough information to thoughtfully respond to WTP surveys. Clearly, a respondent needs to know whether a burglary will cost them $700 or more than $4,000 in formulating their WTP to avoid being burglarized. A similar critique has been made in normative valuations of the severity of crime (Wolfgang et al., 1985). Thus, it is far from certain that contingent valuation or normative ranking studies can be developed that create prices or severities for discrete types of crime rather than crime as a whole. Knowledge about the relative cost of crime by crime type is critical to policymaking on all but the broadest of social policy questions. In order to evaluate programs with defined objectives, such as desistance from domestic violence or drug use, or to make judgments about how police should respond to different kinds of crime, or to inform sentencing policy, prices must be available to describe the benefits of crime reductions. Thus, it is not clear that WTP studies are advantageous. This study also shows the advantage of economic approaches to measuring the severity of crimes that take into account the unique features of crimes in generating information on how much crimes cost victims.

Notes

1. For simplicity, I ignore issues of moral standing in the political economy of crime and thus do not differentiate between externalities and gains to the offender; External costs are generally defined as a cost imposed on individuals who are not party to a transaction, such as those who breathe air polluted in the production of some goods. Traditionally, costs to victim of a crime are considered external costs since the victim is an unwilling participant in the criminal transaction. However, since non-pecuniary losses from crime account for much of the harm, crime produces substantial negative externalities, and since public safety is a (quasi-) public good, the combination yields an underinvestment in private crime prevention (Samuelson, 1954; Tiebout, 1956).

2. Since the NIBRS data set includes more than one million observations and the RAND ICJ data set includes only about twenty-six thousand, it is not surprising that there are more cross-combinations observed in the NIBRS data (there are 1,213 valid combinations in NIBRS and fewer in RAND ICJ, yielding a total of 342 combinations that are available in both).

3. The cases in NIBRS that did not match to the ICJ data are those with a cross-combination of attributes that was observable in the NIBRS data but did not appear in the ICJ data.

4. Juries may also award punitive damages. However, punitive damages were excluded in this study on the grounds that they were not used to make a victim whole, but rather to deter future infractions.

5. RAND ICJ data were coded from trade publications (jury verdict reporters) that report the outcomes of civil proceedings. Cases in the file include any civil case resulting in a verdict that was adjudicated by a jury in the project period 1985–99. Cases closed by settlement, hung jury, or cases heard by a judge are not included in the data set.

6. Colorado, Idaho, Iowa, Massachusetts, Michigan, North Dakota, South Carolina, Utah, Vermont, Virginia.

7. In addition, some studies have shown that NIBRS data are more reliable on some measures than NCVS (Chilton and Jarvis, 1999). In addition, NIBRS includes

events linked to individuals excluded from NCVS, including military personnel, the homeless, the incarcerated, and itinerant guests, a group that likely includes many recently released ex-prisoners (Maxfield, 1999). And commercial businesses are excluded from NCVS, and thus some victims of "robbery, burglary, arson, larceny-theft, motor vehicle theft, and vandalism" may be excluded (Maxfield, 1999: 128). In addition, victimless crimes are not included in NCVS but are recorded in NIBRS. Finally, NCVS explicitly excludes victims below twelve years of age, who are included in the NIBRS data.

Bibliography

Anderson, Michelle Chernikoff and Robert J. MacCoun. "Goal Conflict in Juror Assessments of Compensatory and Punitive Damages." *Law and Human Behavior* 23, no. 2 (1999): 313–30.

Arrow, K., R. Solow, P. R. Portney, E. E. Leamer, R. Radner, and H. Schuman. "Report of the NOAA Panel on Contingent Valuation." *Federal Register* 58, no. 10 (1995): 4601–14.

Becker, Gary S. "Crime and Punishment: An Economic Approach." *Journal of Political Economy* 76, no. 2 (1968): 169–217.

Carson, R. T., W. M. Hanemann, R. J. Kopp, J. A. Krosnick, R. C. Mitchell, S. Presser, P. A. Ruud, V. K. Smith, M. Conaway, and K. Martin. "Referendum Design and Contingent Valuation: The NOAA Panel's No-Vote Recommendation." *The Review of Economics and Statistics* 80, no. 3 (1999): 484–87.

Cartwright, W. S. "Cost-Benefit Analysis of Drug Treatment Services: Review of the Literature." *The Journal of Mental Health Policy and Economics* 3 (2000): 11–26.

Chin, A. and M. A. Peterson. *Deep Pockets, Empty Pockets: Who Wins in Cook County Jury Trials.* Santa Monica, CA: RAND Corporation, 1985.

Clark, D. E. and J. C. Cosgrove. "Hedonic Prices, Identification, and the Demand for Public Safety." *Journal of Regional Science* 30, no. 10 (1990): 105–21.

Cohen, Mark A. "Pain, Suffering, and Jury Awards: A Study of the Cost of Crime to Victims." *Law and Society Review* 22, no. 3 (1988a): 537–56.

———. "Some New Evidence on the Seriousness of Crime." *Criminology* 26 (1988b): 343–53.

———. "A Note on the Cost of Crimes to Victims." *Urban Studies* 27, no. 1 (1990): 139–46.

———. "Measuring the Costs and Benefits of Crime and Justice." In *Measurement and Analysis of Crime and Justice. Criminal Justice 2000*, vol. 4, 263–316. National Institute of Justice, NCJ 182411, 2000.

———. *The Costs of Crime and Justice.* New York: Routledge, 2005.

Cohen, M. A. and T. R. Miller. "Willingness to Award Nonmonetary Damages and the Implied Value of Life from Jury Awards." *International Review of Law and Economics* 23 (2003): 165–81.

————. "Empirical Analysis of Civil Jury Awards." 1999. Unpublished.

————. "Pain and Suffering of Crime Victims: Evidence from Jury Verdicts." Working paper, Vanderbilt University, 1994.

Cohen, M. A., T. R. Miller, and S. B. Rossman. "The Cost and Consequences of Violent Behavior in the United States." *Understanding and Preventing Violence, Volume III: Social Influences and Volume IV: Consequences and Control*, edited by A. J. Reiss and J. A. Roth. Washington, DC: National Academy Press, National Research Council, 1994.

Cohen, M. A., R. T. Rust, and S. Steen. "Prevention, Crime Control or Cash? Public Preferences towards Criminal Justice Spending Priorities." *Justice Quarterly* 23, no. 3 (2006): 317.

Cohen, M. A., R. T. Rust, S. Steen, and S. Tidd. "Willingness-to-Pay for Crime Control Programs." *Criminology* 42, no. 1 (2004): 86–106.

Cook, Philip J. and Jens Ludwig. *Gun Violence: The Real Costs*. New York: Oxford University Press, 2000.

Cutler, D. M. and E. Richardson. "The Value of Health: 1970–1990." *The American Economic Review* 88, no. 2 (1998): 97–100.

Daniels, Stephen. "The Question of Jury Competence and the Politics of Civil Justice Reform: Symbols, Rhetoric and Agenda-Building." *Law and Contemporary Problems* 52, no. 4 (1989): 269–310.

Daniels, Stephen and Joanne Martin. "Jury Verdicts and the 'Crisis' in Civil Justice." *Justice Systems Journal* 11 (1986): 321–48.

Danzon, Patricia. "The Frequency and Severity of Medical Malpractice Claims." *Journal of Law and Economics* 27, no. 1 (1984): 115–48.

Dehejia, R. H. and S. Wahba. "Propensity Score-Matching Methods for Non-experimental Causal Studies." *The Review of Economics and Statistics* 84, no. 1 (2002): 151–61.

Diamond, P. A. and J. A. Hausman. "Contingent Valuation: Is Some Number Better Than No Number?" *Journal of Economic Perspectives* 8, no. 4 (1994): 45–64.

Dolan, P. and T. Peasgood. *British Journal of Criminology* 47, no. 1 (2005): 121–32.

Drazan, Dan. "The Case for Special Juries in Toxic Tort Litigation." *Judicature* 72 (1989): 292–98.

Dubourg, R. and J. Hamed. *Estimates of the Economic and Social Costs of Crime in England and Wales: Costs of Crime against Individuals and Households, 2003/04*. London: UK Home Office, 2005.

Ehrlich, Isaac. "Participation in Illegitimate Activities: A Theoretical and Empirical Investigation." *The Journal of Political Economy* 81, no. 3 (1973): 521–65.

————. "On the Usefulness of Controlling Individuals: An Economic Analysis of Rehabilitation, Incapacitation and Deterrence." *The American Economic Review* 71, no. 3 (1981): 307–22.

————. "Crime Punishment, and the Market for Offenses." *The Journal of Economic Perspectives* 10, no. 1 (1996): 43–67.

Freeman, R. "Why Do So Many Young American Men Commit Crimes and What Might We Do About it?" *Journal of Economic Perspectives* 10, no. 1 (1996): 25–42.

Goodman, Jane, Edith Greene, and Elizabeth F. Loftus. "Runaway Verdicts or Reasoned Determinations: Mock Juror Strategies in Awarding Damages." *Jurimetrics* 29 (1989): 285–310.

Grogger, J. "Market Wages and Youth Crime." *Journal of Labor Economics* 16, no. 4 (1998): 756–91.

Grossman, M. *The Demand for Health: A Theoretical and Empirical Investigation.* New York: Columbia University Press, 1972.

Hammitt, J. K., S. J. Carroll, and D. A. Relles. "Tort Standards and Jury Decisions." *The Journal of Legal Studies* 14, no. 3 (1985): 751–62.

Hans, Valerie P. and M. David Ermann. "Responses to Corporate versus Individual Wrongdoing." *Law and Human Behavior* 13, no. 2 (1989): 151–66.

Hans, Valerie P. and William S. Lofquist. "Jurors' Judgments of Business Liability in Tort Cases: Implications for the Litigation Explosion Debate." *Law and Society Review* 26, no. 1 (1992): 85–116.

Harwood, N. J., D. M. Napolitano, P. Kristiansen, and J. J. Collins. *Economic Costs to Society of Alcohol and Drug Abuse and Mental Illness: 1980.* Research Triangle Park, NC: Research Triangle Institute, 1984.

Heckman, J. J., H. Ichimura, J. Smith, and P. E. Todd. "Characterizing Selection Bias Using Experimental Data." *Econometrica* 66, no. 5 (1998): 1017–98.

Heckman, J. J., H. Ichimura, and P. E. Todd. "Matching as an Econometric Evaluation Estimator: Evidence from Evaluating a Job Training Programme." *The Review of Economic Studies* 64, no. 4 (1997): 605–54.

Heckman, J. J, J. L. Tobias, and E. Vytlacil. "Four Parameters of Interest in the Evaluation of Social Programs." *Southern Economic Journal* 68, no. 2 (2001): 210–23.

Hicks, J. R. *Value and Capital: An Inquiry into Some Fundamental Principles of Economic Theory.* Oxford: Clarendon Press, 1939.

Horowitz, Irwin A. and Kenneth S. Bordens. "An Experimental Investigation of Procedural Issues in Complex Tort Trials." *Law and Human Behavior* 14, no. 3 (1990): 269–85.

Imbens, G. W. and J. D. Angrist. "Identification and Estimation of Local Average Treatment Effects." *Econometrica* 62, no. 2 (1994): 467–75.

LaLonde, R. "Evaluating the Econometric Evaluations of Training Programs with Experimental Data." *American Economic Review* 76, no. 4 (1986): 604–20.

Leung, A. and R. Sproule. "Using the Compensating and Equivalent Variations to Define the Slutsky Equation under a Discrete Price Change." *Economics Bulletin* 4, no. 1 (2007): 1–9.

Levitt, Steven D. "The Effect of Prison Population Size on Crime Rates: Evidence from Prison Overcrowding Litigation." *The Quarterly Journal of Economics* 111, no. 2 (1996): 319–51.

―――. "Why Do Increased Arrest Rates Appear to Reduce Crime: Deterrence, Incapacitation, or Measurement Error?" *Economic Inquiry* 36 (1998): 353–72.

Lochner, L. and E. Moretti. "The Effect of Education on Crime: Evidence from Prison Inmates, Arrests, and Self-Reports." *American Economic Review* 94 (2004): 155–89.

Lott, Jr., John R. and David B. Mustard. "Crime, Deterrence, and Right-to-Carry Concealed Handguns." *The Journal of Legal Studies* 26, no. 1 (January 1997): 1–68.

Ludwig, Jens and Philip J. Cook. "The Benefits of Reducing Gun Violence: Evidence from Contingent-Valuation Survey Data." *Journal of Risk and Uncertainty* 22, no. 3 (2001): 207–26.

MacCoun, Robert J. "Differential Treatment of Corporate Defendants by Juries: An Examination of the 'Deep Pockets' Hypothesis." *Law and Society Review* 30, no. 1 (1996): 121–61.

Manski, C. F. *Identification Problems in the Social Sciences*. Cambridge, MA: Harvard University Press, 1995.

Miller, Ted R., P. Brigham, Mark A. Cohen, J. Douglass, M. Galbraith, D. Lestina, V. Nelkin, N. Pindus, and P. Regojo-Smith. "Estimating the Costs to Society of Cigarette Fire Injuries." In *Report to Congress in Response to the Fire Safe Cigarette Act of 1990*. Washington, DC: Consumer Product Safety Commission, 1993a.

Miller, Ted R., Mark A. Cohen, and S. B. Rossman. "Victim Costs of Violent Crime and Resulting Injuries." *Health Affairs* 12, no. 4 (1993b): 186–97.

Miller, Ted R., Mark A. Cohen, and Brian Wiersema. *Victim Costs and Consequences: A New Look*. National Institute of Justice Research Report, NCJ 155282, 1996.

Peterson, Mark A. *Compensation of Injuries: Civil Jury Verdicts in Cook County*. Santa Monica, CA: The RAND Institute for Civil Justice, 1984.

―――. *Civil Juries in the 1980s: Trends in Jury Trials and Verdicts in California and Cook County, Illinois*. Santa Monica, CA: The RAND Institute for Civil Justice, 1987.

Peterson, Mark A. and George L. Priest. *The Civil Jury: Trends in Trials and Verdicts, Cook County, Illinois, 1960–79*. Santa Monica, CA: The RAND Institute for Civil Justice, 1982.

Piehl, A. and J. DiIulio. "Does Prison Pay? Revisited." *The Brookings Review* (1995): 21–25.

Portney, P. R. "The Contingent Valuation Debate: Why Economists Should Care." *Journal of Economic Perspectives* 8, no. 4 (1994): 3–17.

Rajkumar, A. S. and M. T. French. "Drug Abuse, Crime Costs, and the Economic Benefits of Treatment." *Journal of Quantitative Criminology* 13, no. 3 (1997): 291–323.

Ramchand, Rajeev, John M. MacDonald, Amelia Haviland, and Andrew Morral. "A Developmental Approach for Measuring the Severity of Crimes." *Journal of Quantitative Criminology* 26 (2009): 129–53.

Raphael, S. and M. A. Stoll. "Evaluating the Effectiveness of the Massachusetts Workforce Development System Using No-Shows as a Non-experimental Comparison Group." *Evaluation Review* 30, no. 4 (2006): 379–429.

Raphael, S. and R. Winter-Ebmer. "Identifying the Effect of Unemployment on Crime." *Journal of Law and Economics* 44, no. 1 (2001): 259–84.

Rice, D. P., S. Kelman, L. S. Miller, and S. Dunmeyer. *The Economic Costs of Alcohol and Drug Abuse and Mental Illness: 1985*. DHHS Pub. No. (ADM) 90-1694. San Francisco: Institute for Health and Aging, University of California; Rockville, MD: Alcohol, Drug Abuse, and Mental Health Administration, 1990.

Rodgers, Gregory B. "Estimating Jury Compensation for Pain and Suffering in Product Liability Cases Involving Nonfatal Personal Injury." *Journal of Forensic Economics* 6, no. 3 (1993): 251–62.

Rosenbaum, P. R. and D. B. Rubin. "The Central Role of the Propensity Score in Observational Studies for Causal Effects." *Biometrika* 70, no. 1 (1983): 41–55.

Rubin, D. B. "Estimating Causal Effects of Treatments in Randomized and Nonrandomized Studies." *Journal of Education Psychology* 66, no. 5 (1974): 688–701.

Samuelson, P. A. "The Pure Theory of Public Expenditure." *The Review of Economics and Statistics* 36, no. 4 (1954): 387–89.

Schelling, Thomas C. "The Life You Save May Be Your Own." In *Problems in Public Expenditure Analysis,* edited by S. B. Chase, 127–62. Washington, DC: The Brookings Institution, 1968.

Schweinhart, Lawrence J., Jeanne Montie, Zongping Xiang, William S. Barnett, Clive R. Belfield, and Milagros Nores. *Lifetime Effects: The High/Scope Perry Preschool Study through Age 40*. (Monographs of the High/Scope Educational Research Foundation, 14). Ypsilanti, MI: High/Scope Press, 2005.

Sellin, T. and M. E. Wolfgang. *The Measurement of Delinquency*. New York: Wiley, 1964.

Smith, J. and P. E. Todd. "Does Matching Overcome Lalonde's Critique of Non-experimental Estimators?" *Journal of Econometrics* 125, nos. 1–2 (2005): 305–53.

Sugarman, S. D. "Doing Away with Tort Law." *California Law Review* 73, no. 3 (1985): 555–664.

Tabarrok, Alexander and Eric Helland. "Court Politics: The Political Economy of Tort Awards." *Journal of Law and Economics.* 42, no. 1 (1999): 157–88.

Thaler, Richard H. "A Note on the Value of Crime Control: Evidence from the Property Market." *Journal of Urban Economics* 5 (1978): 137–45.

Thaler, Richard H. and Sherwin Rosen. "The Value of Saving a Life: Evidence from The Labor Market." In *Household Production and Consumption*, edited by Nester Terleckyj. New York: National Bureau of Economic Research, 1975.

Tiebout, C. "A Pure Theory of Local Expenditures." *Journal of Political Economy* 64 (1956): 416–24.

Vidmar, Neil J. "Empirical Research and the Issue of Jury Competence." *Law and Contemporary Problems* 52, no. 4 (1989): 1–8.

———. "Empirical Evidence on the Deep Pockets Hypothesis: Jury Awards for Pain and Suffering in Medical Malpractice Cases." *Duke Law Journal* 43, no. 2 (1993): 217–66.

Viscusi, W. K. "The Risks and Rewards of Criminal Activity: A Comprehensive Test of Criminal Deterrence." *Journal of Labor Economics* 4, no. 3 (1986): 317–40.

———. "Pain and Suffering in Product Liability Cases: Systematic Compensation or Capricious Awards?" *International Review of Law and Economics* 8 (1988): 203–20.

Wissler, Roselle L., Katie A. Rector, and Michael J. Saks. "The Impact of Jury Instructions on the Fusion of Liability and Compensatory Damages." *Law and Human Behavior* 25, no. 2 (2001): 125–39.

Wolfgang, M. E., R. M. Figlio, P. E. Tracy, and S. I. Singer. *National Survey of Crime Severity*. Philadelphia: University of Pennsylvania, 1985.

Zaric, G. S., P. G. Barnett, and M. L. Brandeau. "HIV Transmission and the Cost-Effectiveness of Methadone Maintenance." *American Journal of Public Health* 90, no. 7 (2000): 1100–11.

4

Communities and Crime Theories: Construct Validation Deficits, a Paucity of Comparisons, and a Boudon–Coleman Metamodel Resolution

Ralph B. Taylor

Many ecologically oriented communities and crime theories discuss ecological processes or attributes that mediate between crime features and community structure. These models might be interested in crime or delinquency as an exogenous community attribute that over time alters fundamental neighborhood structural features like socioeconomic status (SES), housing quality, stability, or racial composition. These models are of the following form:

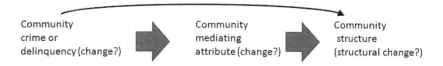

| Community crime or delinquency (change?) | Community mediating attribute (change?) | Community structure (structural change?) |

Topics pursued along these lines include changes in house value, changes in SES of residents, and out- and in-migration patterns (Taylor, 1995).

Acknowledgments. The author thanks Jaime Henderson for compiling and coding the studies described in the systematic review section. While working on this chapter, the author received support from the Office of the Provost, Temple University, for a research and study leave and from National Institute of Justice grant 2009-IJ-CX-0026. The content reflects neither the opinions nor the policies of Temple University, the National Institute of Justice, or the Department of Justice.

And more generally pursued by researchers in this area, there are models about

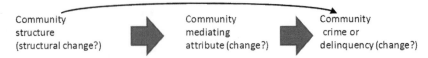

Community structure (structural change?) → Community mediating attribute (change?) → Community crime or delinquency (change?)

Of course well-known models such as social disorganization (SD), collective efficacy, or routine activities, as well as several others, address these matters. For example, Sampson and Wikstrom (2008) found somewhat comparable impacts of neighborhood-level collective efficacy on neighborhood-level violence in both Chicago and Stockholm neighborhoods. Neighborhood-concentrated disadvantage shaped collective efficacy at the neighborhood level and also had an independent impact on ecological violence levels.

The current chapter suggests that some portion of the *empirical tests* of some theories of either variety suffer from one or two deficits:

(1) Researchers confuse key mediating community attributes with demographic community setting conditions, treating the latter as an acceptable proxy for the former and/or

(2) researchers rarely conduct ecologically based comparisons of the relative merit of two or more alternate theories.

This chapter further contends that deficit (2) arises because of (1) and that (1) arises not only because of data limitations, but also because communities and crime theorists have not yet engaged in the needed construct validation activities. Researchers have not yet established the convergent *and* discriminant validities of indicators for mediating constructs from different conceptual frameworks using multiple methods to operationalize indicators from each key construct (Campbell and Fiske, 1959).

Because of the lack of systematic multimethod *ecological* construct validation, a situation of semantic ambiguity exists (Abbott, 2001: 69). It is not clear what constructs various indicators represent. Indicators thought by one researcher to reflect one concept (absence of SD) (Bursik, 1986) are thought by another researcher to reflect a different concept (sense of community) (Cantillon et al., 2003). If no one can agree which construct is reflected by which indicator, it is not possible to test one theory against another. Such comparison testing is important (Taylor and Wikstrom, 2009).

Finding empirical support for one theory does not promote that one theory over and above another theory, absent a test of the latter (Platt, 1964). Blalock has framed the issue as follows:

> Tests of the theories . . . will involve empirical tests of the derived theorems. Clearly if the theorems prove false the theory must be modified or the axioms of the theory even abandoned. But if they are true, one cannot claim that the theory has been "verified" unless all possible competing alternatives can be rejected. . . . Therefore we shall be in the unfortunate situation of having to proceed by eliminating inadequate theories, rather than ever really establishing any of them. This is of course a very general situation that is not peculiar to the social sciences. (Blalock, 1969: 11–12)

Resolution Challenges

An experienced ecological researcher is likely to contend that it is extremely difficult to establish community-level multimethod convergent and discriminant validities because of the well-known effects of aggregating by geographic proximity on relationships between variables (Hannan, 1991). What is going on behind the scenes *conceptually* as one aggregates is rather complicated (Blalock, 1964: 98–99). But the "bottom line" is that relations among indicators, even those from different concepts, are likely to tighten, making the establishment of multimethod discriminant validity all the more difficult.

There are two aspects of this deficit. Community structure and process cannot be differentiated. In addition, the impacts of a meditational process specified by one theory may not be distinguishable from the meditational process specified by a distinct but related theory.[1] Consider the challenge, for example, of separating willingness to intervene (WTI) indicators derived from SD/collective efficacy/informal social control theory, from capable guardianship (CG) indicators derived from routine activities theory (RAT).

If the establishment of discriminant validity, a key part of the construct validation process, is needed but challenging to accomplish with data aggregated by geographic proximity, what is to be done?

Outlines of a Solution

The suggested answer has two parts. The first is to move to a unified perspective (Messick, 1995) on the construct validation process. This opens up the range of empirical relationships that are relevant to establishing construct validity. The second is to carry out the activities associated with unified construct validation within a particular metamodel, a Boudon–Coleman diagram capturing macro-to-micro, micro-to-micro, and micro-to-macro processes (Boudon, 1986; Coleman, 1990). This moves the focus away from the macro-input → macro-output links that are the focus of the research with only community-level variables. Even if the study is multilevel with individuals or households grouped within communities, and an individual-level or household level outcome, the impact of community indicators are capturing only macrolevel ecological relationships (Taylor, 2010).[2]

Organization of Chapter

The next section documents the suggested semantic ambiguity in the area of SD. A few examples are described, and then the results of a more systematic review are reported. Messick's unified perspective on construct validation is introduced, and those ideas are then placed within a Boudon–Coleman diagram. A hypothetical example applying the unified perspective to construct validation is described.

Definitions

For a brief definition, crime means community-reported incidence or prevalence rates for adults and delinquents or reported resident victimization prevalence rates. Actions of local community justice agencies reflected in arrest, incarceration, return, and supervision rates contribute in important positive (Cousineau, 1973) and negative (Clear, 2007) ways to these crime rates.

Although some scholars argue and this author accepts that there are important differences between "community" and "neighborhood," these terms are used interchangeably here (Hunter, 1975; Brower, 1996: 57). Each of these two concepts has received scholarly attention for a century or more, has waxed and waned in that period as a topic of interest to both scholars and policymakers, and has been defined in numerous ways.

One publication that has appeared more than five decades ago listed more than ninety definitions of community tapping into sixteen different themes (Hillery, 1955). The concept of neighborhood is similarly diffuse, precluding scholarly consensus (Keller, 1968).[3] "There are many ways of defining neighborhood," and "different definitions serve different interests" (Brower, 1996: 17). At the core, however, all that can be really agreed upon *definitionally* is that neighborhood "is considered a social/spatial unit of social organization, and that it is larger than a household and smaller than a city. The problem with presenting a further list of definitive characteristics is that they often become normative rather than descriptive" (Hunter, 1979: 270). Hunter's minimalist but uncontroversial definition is accepted as a definition of both community and neighborhood, with two additions: the lower bound is set at the single streetblock—the two sides of the street bounded by cross streets at the ends—and the upper bound is sub-municipality areas, smaller than a jurisdiction. Spatially, communities are (1) imbricated and (2) nested arenas, as are the spatially delimited accompanying social patterns and dynamics (Suttles, 1972; Hunter, 1974; Taylor and Stough, 1978; Hunter, 1985, 2003). The imbricated nature of communities means that residents are members of multiple partially overlapping socio-spatial units, as well as progressively nested socio-spatial units (e.g., streetblocks (Taylor, 1997) within communities).

Semantic Ambiguity Examples: SD

When researchers fail to carry out the needed construct validation activities, key ideas in theories get operationalized in widely divergent and sometimes inappropriate ways. Abbott's (2001) semantic ambiguity surfaces. In SD, this ambiguity is reflected when researchers either equate demographic attributes of communities with SD processes or state that they know that demographic conditions are only proxies for the processes, but go ahead and use the one for the other anyway. Previous warnings against such practices for routine activity theorists (Sampson and Wooldredge, 1987), SD theorists (Bursik, 1986), and anomie theorists (Gordon, 1967) have gone unheeded by some.

The practice is incorrect for at least two reasons. Most obviously, demographics or land use is not the described conceptual processes. Second, community demographic structure or community land use patterns are broad setting conditions; each can set in motion any number of specific processes relevant to any number of theories. The range of processes that can be set in motion by something like variations in household SES or variations in the incidence of certain types of non-residential land uses is vast.[4] In Wikstrom's (2006) terminology, they are the "causes of causes" not the causes of crime.

The Concept

SD theory has, of course, a convoluted and controversial interpretive past. But there does seem to be agreement on key elements (Bursik, 1986):

[T]he current formulation of social disorganization assumes that the breadth and strength of local networks directly affect the effectiveness of two forms of community self regulation. The first reflects the ability of local neighborhoods to supervise the behavior of their residents . . . informal surveillance . . . movement governing rules . . . direct intervention . . . (p. 527). . . . [T]he second form of community self regulation implicit in the notion of social disorganization reflects the socializing, rather than supervisory, capability of a neighborhood. (p. 529)

Several of these elements were captured in one of the most widely cited SD articles that used having friends nearby, participation in local organizations, and perceptions of troublesome unsupervised teen groups, the latter reflecting an *in*ability to regulate the behavior of locals, to reflect SD processes (Sampson and Groves, 1989).

A couple of examples of indicator/concept slippage are presented in narrative form, followed by a more systematic review of empirical studies.

Select Examples

A study of 342 gang homicides in Newark (New Jersey) concluded (abstract) that "the SD measure did not predict gang homicide" (Pizarro and McGloin, 2006). At the census tract level, four demographic variables (e.g., percent unemployed) "conceptually tapped into the poverty dimension of social disorganization" and three demographic variables (number of racial/ethnic groups in tract, population size, percent living there less than five years) "addressed other dimensions, such as residential mobility, ethnic heterogeneity, and urbanization" (Pizarro and McGloin, 2006: 202). The study included no indicators of the intervening mechanisms described by SD theory (Bursik, 1986).

A study of violent and property crime rates in nonmetropolitan counties sought to test the idea "that predictors of crime from social disorganization theory exert different effects on violent and property crimes at different levels of population change in nonmetropolitan counties" (Barnett and Mencken, 2002: abstract). In some places, the authors preserved the distinction between setting conditions and mediating properties: "Conceptually, crime is indirectly a function of county structural characteristics (SES, residential mobility, population heterogeneity), and these measures affect crime indirectly through their impact on county social organization and social control" (Barnett and Mencken, 2002: 379). But they later maintained that the demographic setting conditions were relevant largely because of the unmeasured mediating properties: "We maintain that counties with high levels of poverty, income inequality, unemployment, and female-headed households suffer a structural disadvantage in the community resources needed to achieve formal and informal connections among members so as to realize common values and work toward solving or preventing social problems" (Barnett and Mencken, 2002: 380). No data relevant to this assertion were presented.

Researchers found a positive effect of resource *dis*advantage on crime rates, with more powerful impacts in counties losing populations and concluded "a model based on social disorganization is useful for explaining crime in rural America" (Barnett and Mencken, 2002: 390). No reference was made to potentially competing theoretical frameworks. The study included no SD variables (Bursik, 1986).

Jacob (2006: 37) used census demographic "structural factors, which represent the cohesiveness and informal social control of a community." These were linked to male and female youth crime rates. More specifically "in order to capture the level of SD in a community, five concepts were operationalized—SES, residential instability, urbanization, ethnic heterogeneity, and supervision" (p. 38). Percentage of single-parent families was used for the latter.

Mustaine and colleagues (2006) reported finding "RSOs (registered sex offenders) are likely to live in areas with greater social disorganization" (abstract) in census tracts in two Florida and Kentucky counties. "Based on the traditions of social disorganization theory . . . the following characteristics were assessed: the percent of households in the tract that are headed by females, the percent of the homes in the census tract that are owner occupied, the median household income, and the median housing value in the tract" (339–340). The study contained no indicators of SD processes as described by Bursik.

A number of studies do not completely downplay or overlook the differences between land use or structural setting conditions and intervening SD, but do skirt the issue. They do this by arguing that the impacts of demographic or land use setting conditions have strong implications for one particular theory, like SD (e.g., Osgood and Chambers, 2000: 86; Ouimet, 2000: 138; Kane, 2006: 197, 203). They fail to mention that these same setting conditions have strong implications for a number of other theories as well.

A More Systematic Consideration

To gain a more systematic picture, the following search was conducted. Using *Web of Science*, all publications from their social science database appearing between 1995 and January 21, 2010, with "social disorganization" (SD) appearing in the title were listed and reviewed. Fifty-four articles surfaced. Eleven were dropped from further analysis either because the outcome was not crime/victimization/delinquency or a reaction to crime (e.g., psychosocial adjustment, child maltreatment rates), or because they did not address SD theory. Of the remaining forty-three, forty were retained that provided empirical analyses, and three solely conceptual pieces were dropped from further consideration.

Of these forty studies, only eight (20 percent) included indicators clearly referencing SD-related processes and *only* referencing disorganization-related processes. An indicator was classified as reflecting SD if it captured one or more of the following attributes or processes: WTI, local organizational participation, features of local social networks, other features of local social climate, perceptions of disorderly conditions, or some indicator combining one or more of the above specific features. It seems that the instances where SD was operationalized in a manner theoretically misaligned with the underlying construct far outnumbered the instances that were theoretically congruent.

The empirical studies examined outcomes at a range of units of analysis from the individual (7 or 17 percent), to sub-city communities (24 or 60 percent) to cities or municipalities (2 or 5 percent) to larger entities such as states or metropolitan statistical areas (5 or 12 percent). (Two studies considered both individual- and community-level outcomes.)

In short, it appears that SD theory in the last fifteen years has addressed crime and related outcomes at a range of levels of analyses, with an apparent underlying presumption of comparable applicability across scales of analysis. It also appears that in about four out of five studies the content of the SD indicators is conceptually off target because those indicators include at least one element that is outside of core SD ideas. The semantic ambiguity appears to be widespread.

Messick's Unified Perspective on Construct Validation

Focusing solely on *ecological*, community-based multimethod patterns of convergent and discriminant validities for gauging the construct validity of SD mediators, or of mediators from other relevant communities and crime theoretical models (e.g., routine activities), faces several difficulties. Some of these arise from the nature of urban neighborhood-based samples and the attendant limitations including difficulties separating demographic structure from key mediating processes (Cook et al., 1997) and some from the conceptual challenges associated with aggregating by geographic proximity (Blalock, 1982). So pursuing standard construct validation procedures proves problematic.

Difficulties are reduced, however, if Messick's (1995) unified perspective on construct validation is adopted. It opens up a wider range of relevant empirical patterns for construct validity considerations.

Messick (1995) has argued that beyond links reflecting convergent and discriminant validities, and beyond criterion validities, how key indicators link to other parameters are relevant to construct validation. In a discussion in the context of test construction, he put the argument for a broader perspective this way:

> Historically, primary emphasis in construct validation has been placed on internal and external test structures—that is, on the appraisal of theoretically expected patterns of relationships among item scores or between test scores and other measures. Probably *even more illuminating in regard to score meaning* are studies of expected performance differences over time, across groups and settings, and in response to experimental treatments and manipulations. (Messick, 1995: 743; emphasis added)

Messick's (1995) updated unified perspective on construct validity argues that other types of validity, such as leave original content validities, are *themselves* part of construct validity. Investigations of these other validities could provide evidence relevant to the two major threats to construct validity:

> *construct underrepresentation* [where] the assessment is too narrow and fails to include important dimensions or facets of the construct [and] . . . *construct-irrelevant variance*, [where] the assessment is too broad, containing excess reliable variance associated with other distinct constructs as well as method variance. . . . Both threats are operative in all assessments. Hence a primary validation concern is the extent to which the same assessment might under-represent the focal construct while simultaneously contaminating the scores with construct-irrelevant variance. (Messick, 1995: 742; emphasis added)

Much of the construct validity discussion in psychology has centered on interpretations of individual-level test scores. Nevertheless, the same points pertain to interpretations of community-level indicators. For example, in a study of state-level ecological models of high school crime rates, Gary Gottfredson (1979: 316) applied the test of construct irrelevance. He found that the high school crime rate model predicted other outcomes conceptually unrelated to the intended outcome as well as it predicted the intended outcome. Introducing theoretically irrelevant outcomes is an important model-testing step.

Messick's expanded treatment of construct validation proposed six different aspects of the process and linked the *interpretation* of indicators to their consequences as well as to their correlates and criterion-related links.[5] The important point of Messick's work in the current context is that researchers seeking to establish the construct validity of particular indicators need to take a wide-ranging perspective and pay attention to a number of empirical patterns.

The Boudon–Coleman Metamodel

From the perspective of methodological individualism (Boudon, 1986: 29–32)—the view that the individual is the fundamental unit in analyses of social structures and changes, like community crime rates, changes in community crime rates, or community-level consequences of crime rates—a case can be made that ecological analyses based on community-sized areas and linking macrolevel inputs with macrolevel outputs are conceptually somewhat off the mark. Such analyses miss underlying dynamics (Liska, 1990). These dynamics include context effects, individual-level functioning, and agency.

Such a broad alternate view about the relevant dynamics can be called a metamodel. The Boudon–Coleman metamodel, also sometimes called a "boat" metamodel, is depicted in Figure 4.1 (Boudon, 1986; Coleman, 1990; Bunge, 2006). The presentation explicitly spatializes the macro-micro aspect of the model, and is thus just one specific way to interpret this type of metamodel.

Increasing spatial scale appears on the vertical axis. The passage of time is depicted moving left to right on the horizontal scale. Dynamics

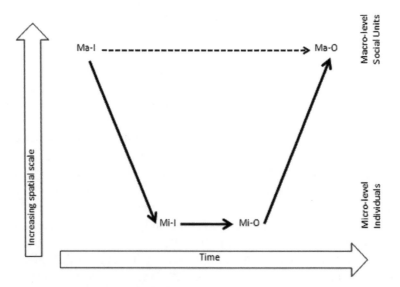

Figure 4.1   Boudon–Coleman metamodel

are depicted at two levels: the individual or microlevel and the community level or macrolevel. (Supra-macrolevel dynamics above the community level also are obviously relevant but are not depicted.) Such a model assumes that underlying a macrolevel relationship between an input and an output (the dashed Ma-I → Ma-O line—macrolevel inputs lead to macrolevel outputs) are three fundamental links: impacts of context on individuals (Ma-I → Mi-I—macrolevel inputs affect individual-level inputs), individual-level attributes that lead to individual-level outcomes (Mi-I → Mi-O), and ways that over time individual-level outcomes shape community features (Mi-O → Ma-O). The Ma-I → Mi-I link addresses the question: How does context affect individuals? The Mi-O → Ma-O link addresses the question: How does agency work?

The Boudon–Coleman "boat" metamodel is a particular way to organize a view toward human behavior called systemism, a view that assumes that "the constituents [i.e., individuals] interact both among themselves and with their environment" (Bunge, 2006: 13). Such a perspective concerns itself in part with linking microlevel and macrolevel theories, an area of perennial interest in sociology (Liska, 1990).

If one combines this type of metamodel with Hawley's (1950: 401–4) focus on change in the ecological sense (Bursik, 1986), then each input and output can be operationalized as an ecological or individual-level unexpected change (Δ).

Combining the Three Ideas

Messick's ideas about a unified perspective on construct validation can be combined with a dynamic Boudon–Coleman metamodel, and a focus on comparative theory tests, to suggest a construct validation research program for specific theories relevant to communities and crime. Putting aside for the moment extremely important questions about temporal and spatial scaling (Taylor, 2010), a hypothetical assessment program follows below. There are two parts: assessing convergent and discriminant validities of features at different levels in the model, and assessing additional links, as described by Messick. A longitudinal framework is assumed, with changes operationalized according to Hawley's ecological view. Each link in the boat metamodel (Ma-IΔ → Mi-IΔ; Mi-IΔ → Mi-OΔ; Mi-OΔ → Ma-OΔ) deserves attention as part of the *broader connections* of interest from a unified perspective on construct validation.

The suggested resolution involves a research program with the following features:

- Construct validation efforts are pursued by complementing a traditional focus on convergent and discriminant validities with Messick's unified perspective and attention to additional links.
- The investigation separately examines the attributes and links for each element in the appropriate boat metamodel that corresponds with the theory under consideration.
- Each link in the metamodel chain is investigated independently. Understanding how context or neighborhood effects work, and understanding the roles of agency, represents separate albeit related dynamics. And those context and agency dynamics are themselves separate from the within-person processes taking place over time (cf. Wikstrom's (2007) separation of developmental/situational/social mechanisms).
- Longitudinal data are used; all indicators are operationalized as unexpected changes (Bohrnstedt, 1969; Bursik, 1986). Not only is this appropriate given an ecological orientation, and not only is it the only appropriate test of a causal proposition (Lieberson, 1985: 180), it will help to uncouple aggregate-level variables. Of course, different patterns of results should be expected for longitudinal as compared to cross-sectional work (Lieberson, 1985: 181).
- For each link, the researcher examines the *relative* strength of indicators from *different* theories. Researchers in this arena need to move beyond just testing their preferred theory and instead start contrasting the strengths and weaknesses of complementary theories. For each of the three link types in the simplest boat metamodel, the key is to compare relative strengths of different theoretical approaches.

Working through an Example

This section illustrates a longitudinal approach to resolving the construct validation question relying on a dynamic boat metamodel. Two simplified models, one relying on a key construct in SD and the other on a key construct in RAT, will be considered.

Assumptions

1. The researcher has resolved questions about time horizons for theoretical cycles. He/she knows how long it takes for significant

shifts to appear on key indicators for a sufficient number of ecological units.

2. The range of competing theories within a particular arena yields
    just a relatively narrow set of theoretical alternatives.

3. And finally, perhaps most challenging of all, the researcher has
    requisite longitudinal data not only for the key theory of inter-
    est, but also for the alternative competing theories whose relative
    inferiority the researcher wishes to establish.

The Examination Framed in a Boat Metamodel

What is proposed next is a metamodel-based procedure for learning
about construct validity and simultaneously for gauging the differential
relevance of different theories.

The procedure is illustrated with reference to a specific two-level
dynamic example set within a metamodeling frame (see Figure 4.2).
The example is intended just to illustrate the key points deserving examination. More complex models of course will require more points of
examination.

In this example, the mesolevel reflects streetblocks. For simplicity of
exposition, impacts of neighborhood context on streetblocks are omitted.
A two-level example could instead have examined neighborhood effects
on individuals. The example here uses streetblocks and individuals because of the specific theoretical dynamics hypothesized to be relevant.

The microlevel reflects individuals on streetblocks. The model is pre-
sented in a longitudinal frame (e.g., $\text{Mi-I}_{(t-1)} \rightarrow \text{Mi-I}_{(t0)}$), which means that
each input and output in the metamodel chain of links actually reflects
unexpected change (Δ).

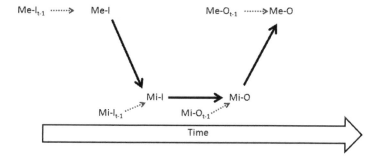

Figure 4.2   Generic two-level dynamic metamodel. Mesolevel represents streetblocks, microlevel represents individuals. Macrolevel inputs and outputs are not
shown for the purposes of simplifying the example

Theoretical Specifics

This section describes specific variables that would be of interest in a model that was predicting larcenies from motor vehicles. Two specific mediating processes, one from SD, and the other from RAT are described.

Model Setup

The outcome in question (Me-OΔ) is changes over time in the number of larcenies from motor vehicles while those vehicles are parked on respective streetblocks. Larcenies from motor vehicles owned by those living on the streetblock, as well as larcenies from motor vehicles whose owners do not live on the streetblock, for example, people going to a location nearby, or visiting friends or relatives on the block, are all of interest.

The mesolevel input (Me-IΔ) is changes in the percent of nonresidential land use on streetblocks. Imagine that the neighborhoods in which these streetblocks are located are experiencing significant demolition of some housing structures due to an ongoing, city-wide neighborhood transformation initiative and conversions of multifamily units into mixed commercial/residential land uses as part of recent zoning changes in the city (McGovern, 2006). Thus, over a two-year period, many blocks are seeing changes with increasing vacant lots and increasing small businesses on primarily residential blocks.

The microlevel input (Mi-IΔ) that is shifted because of the change in land use patterns (Me-IΔ) is local social legibility. Various environmental psychology and criminology models would anticipate reduced social legibility on the streetblock as a result of increases in nonresidential land uses like small commercial stores and their attendant increases in foot traffic (Baum et al., 1978). Depending on neighborhood context, the researcher also might anticipate decreased social legibility arising from demolition of abandoned structures and their replacements with vacant lots. Such lots might be widely used for things like car washing/waxing, kids playing games, or teens or adults hanging out and drinking (St. Jean, 2007). These activity shifts represent an associated mesolevel change that also could contribute to decreased social legibility at the individual level.

Note that the social construct is not about social ties, or cohesiveness, or perceived similarity with neighbors, or sense of community, or related social dynamics, although these undoubtedly also link to social legibility. At issue is the extent to which a resident householder on the streetblock knows or recognizes by face or name the people he/she sees there.

The researcher is interested in contrasting two elements of two different theories: the WTI component from SD/collective efficacy theory and the CG component from RAT.[6] It is hypothesized that both of these dynamics will be shifted due to the land use changes and the consequent shift in social legibility. Changes in WTI and CG, therefore, serve as individual-level changes (Mi-OΔ).

Following the strong inference guide (Platt, 1964), the researcher has set this up so that each theory makes a different prediction about the Mi-IΔ → Mi-OΔ link (impacts of changed social legibility on either changed WTI or changed CG). He/she expects that decreased social legibility will lead to a *weaker* WTI because of increased uncertainties about whether someone belongs on the streetblock—that is, lives there, has a relative or friend there, or is legitimately using a business on the streetblock—and heightened worries about not being backed up by other residents on the block. He/she also expects that decreased social legibility will lead to *stronger* CG. As a resident's neighbors become less familiar, the resident feels he/she must be more vigilant because of that increased uncertainty about whether the neighbors can be relied on to spot something amiss or to do something once they have seen something.

The researcher recognizes that numerous other dynamics relevant to other theoretical models also could be set in motion by the land use changes on streetblocks. Therefore, it is important, if the researcher wishes to present his/her research as a test of specific components of either SD/collective efficacy or RAT, that these theoretically irrelevant but plausibly related dynamics be controlled. After carefully considering theories that are outside of the two under consideration here, the researcher decided that the strongest competing theoretical framework was fear of crime/perception of risk (LaGrange and Ferraro, 1989, 1992; Ferraro, 1994). Indicators for those constructs will be included and controlled. Other potential competitors, like ecological strain theory (Agnew, 1999), although generally relevant given the predictors in the model, were deemed less applicable given the specific crime outcome under consideration.

The researcher has carefully considered and monitored additional ecological changes that, albeit outside the highlighted dynamics within each of the two central theories of interest, could prove relevant. For example, target attractiveness is a key component of routine activity theories. On a streetblock with a large number of home sales or apartment renovations, it is plausible that significant gentrification could take place in a short period. This could change the mix of vehicles parked on the streetblock and change offenders' linked perceptions that those vehicles either represent worthwhile theft targets or that they are alarmed. Such gentrification also could shift other local dynamics as well, including those involving local community groups' relations with police (Taylor, 2001: 346–54). Again, additional relevant indicators would be desirable for these ancillary dynamics.

Initial Construct Validation Assessment

For each of these two indicators, WTI and CG, the researcher has examined *individual-level* multi-construct, multimethod convergent and discriminant validities, *when focusing on changes taking place over a two-year period.*[7] Regardless of how satisfactory or unsatisfactory that pattern of results was, the researcher would want to investigate additional links, as recommended by the unified perspective on construct validation.

Additional Links from Unified Perspective

Following Messick's unified construct validation approach, and focusing on a model that links changes, the figure below describes the metamodel approach to ecological construct validation of relevant indicators. Δ indicates an unexpected change captured over a two-year period. Solid lines represent the metamodel links suggested by the theory in question, for example, SD. Dashed lines represent relevant links from other theoretical frameworks such as RAT (Figure 4.3).

More specifically, if the WTI component of SD is the primary focus and the CG portion of RAT the primary alternative framework under consideration, then indicators in the figure are as follows:

Me-IΔ: changes in land use patterns on the streetblock.

Mi-IΔ: individual-level changes in social legibility.

Mi-OΔ: individual-level changes in WTI.

Me-OΔ: streetblock changes in numbers of larcenies from parked vehicles.

Me-IΔ_{alt}: other potentially influential streetblock changes, for example, shifts in organizational climate or residential composition.

Mi-IΔ_{alt}: individual-level changes in fear/perception of risk if the alternate model is a fear/risk one. If the alternate model is RAT, the input is the same as under SD.

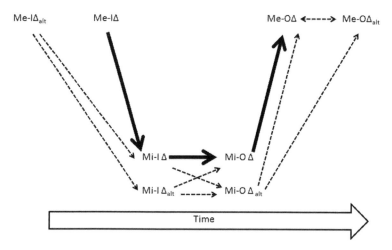

Figure 4.3   Metamodel links deserving attention as part of a unified construct validation effort investigating key indicators. *Solid arrows* indicate links of interest for the key theory being tested (SD). *Dashed arrows* indicate links involving indicators from alternate, potentially competing theories (e.g., RAT)

Mi-OΔ$_{alt}$: individual-level changes in CG.
Me-OΔ$_{alt}$: changes in alternate ecological outcomes.

Establishing such construct validity has implications for establishing the broader validity of the theory and its strength relative to competing theories.

In this instance, more specifically, for SD/collective efficacy theory, the core hypotheses to be examined include the following:

Me-IΔ → Mi-IΔ: Streetblock-level increases in nonresidential land uses link *negatively* to individual-level changes in local social legibility.

Mi-IΔ → Mi-OΔ: Individual-level changes in social legibility link *positively* to individual-level changes in WTI around incidents/scenarios plausibly related to larceny from motor vehicles (if social legibility declines, so too does WTI).

Mi-OΔ → Me-OΔ: Individual-level changes in WTI around incidents/scenarios plausibly related to larceny from motor vehicles link *negatively* with changes in rates or counts of larcenies from motor vehicles on the streetblock (if WTI declines, larcenies increase).

Suppose that all three hypothesized links receive empirical support in the direction expected for each. The researcher might be ready to conclude, especially if satisfactory convergent and discriminant validities were obtained, that the chosen theory has passed all tests and has been validated.

Such a conclusion, however, would be premature. Connections involving indicators from alternate theories are needed to gauge both the completeness of the key theory as specified and its merits relative to potential competitors. Some of the additional pieces of the pattern to be considered include the following:

Me-IΔ_{alt} <begin dashed arrow>= =><end dashed arrow> Mi-IΔ: This link describes the impact of *other* ongoing streetblock-level changes on changes in individual-level social legibility of the streetblock. Examples of changes from outside the theory might be as follows: changes in residential composition of the block due to any number of factors such as gentrification or a large similar-aged cohort of residents on a block moving away or passing away.

What is crucial is the strength of this link (Me-IΔ_{alt} <begin dashed arrow>= =><end dashed arrow> Mi-IΔ) *relative* to the Me-I$\Delta \rightarrow$ Mi-IΔ link. If one of the purposes of the version of SD/collective efficacy theory tested by the researcher was to deepen our understanding of SD/collective efficacy processes as shaped by key land use parameters, the theoretically central link ($\rightarrow$) should be much stronger than the link(s) from outside the theoretical domain (<begin dashed arrow>= =><end dashed arrow>). To the extent links from outside the domain prove equally strong or stronger, that would suggest the researcher needs to extend the theory. For example, broader consideration of stratification and political economy (Hunter, 1974; Logan and Molotch, 1987) might be merited. In other words, testing these alternative links provides a potential guide needed for further theoretical elaboration.[8]

Mi-IΔ <begin dashed arrow>= =><end dashed arrow> Mi-OΔ_{alt}: This link might address the impacts of changes in social legibility on changes in CG.

Suppose that the researcher finds that this link is statistically significant and in the anticipated direction. It would suggest some relevance for the element of RAT being investigated and would deepen our thinking about the relationship between CG and WTI. It would suggest that CG's strengthening is spurred by exactly the same social changes that weaken WTI. Perhaps the two dynamics, WTI and CG, each are "compensating" for each other at the individual level. Perhaps SD theory and routine activity theory, each provide an *incomplete* picture of the impacts of changing social legibility on dynamics key to this crime outcome.

But the broader significance and construct implications also depend on the *patterning* of links. For example, if the impacts of changes in CG on changes in larceny from motor vehicles (Mi-OΔ_{alt} <begin dashed arrow>= =><end dashed arrow> Me-OΔ) are stronger than the theoretically central link between changes in WTI and changes in larcenies from motor vehicles (Mi-OΔ → Me-OΔ), this would raise questions about the *relative* value of one theory versus another, at least for this outcome. This information is crucial from the unified construct validation perspective.

Mi-OΔ_{alt} <begin dashed arrow>= =><end dashed arrow> Me-OΔ_{alt}: Individual-level changes in CG link to ecological changes in an alternate ecological outcome.

For example, suppose that a noncrime ecological outcome is considered, such as some features of the overall pattern of streetblock activity. It might be the incidence of young children playing outside, unsupervised, on the streetblock at certain times of the day or week. Or it could be another crime outcome, but quite different in nature from larceny from motor vehicles. For example, it might be the presence of open air drug dealing on the streetblock.

The connection of the individual-level outcome from the alternate theory (e.g., CG from routine activity theory) with an alternate outcome, especially if that outcome indicator relies on a different data source than does the larceny from motor vehicle data, could be important. Suppose the link is strong. It speaks to whether the CG/routine activity dynamics are telling us about crime dynamics, or about broader residential dynamics, which just also happen to prove relevant to this crime. It speaks to the range of streetblock features shaped by individual agency, in this case changes in CG at the individual level.

Testing what happens with an alternate ecological outcome is especially important for the test of construct irrelevance. The theoretically key individual-level outcome changes should not link to ecological outcomes that could not possibly be linked theoretically to those same dynamics. If such connections were to emerge, that would suggest that some form of temporal spuriousness might be driving everything.

Suppose we were to now expand the thinking about additional alternate theories and allow "alt" to stand in for a third potentially relevant theory, such as perceptions of victimization risk, or fear of crime, and how they change. Presume that these were captured at the individual level and that indicators for this construct converge as expected and diverge as expected from indicators for WTI and CG changes. Consider the following two links:

Mi-IΔ_{alt} <begin dashed arrow>= =><end dashed arrow> Mi-OΔ: Individual-level changes in fear of crime/perceived risk link might link to WTI changes.

Suppose that the researcher finds this link is negative and significant. That would suggest expanding the SD framework to take safety concerns into consideration. Indeed, exactly this connection has been proposed (Bursik and Grasmick, 1993b: 103).

But again, the patterning across links is crucial as well. Are the effects of fear changes on WTI changes stronger than the effects of social legibility changes on WTI? Suppose that the effects of fear changes on CG changes also are strong and that they are stronger than the effects of social legibility changes on CG changes. Finally, suppose that changes in social legibility, WTI, and CG all demonstrate significant links of comparable strength to changes in larcenies from motor vehicles and that those links weaken when perception of risk/fear of crime is partialled.

If all the above points were observed, and ignoring for the moment the significant question of nonrecursive effects, it would argue in favor of thinking about how fear changes might be driving the social legibility, WTI, and CG dynamics. This might lead to an alternate type of modeling for the individual-level dynamics portion of the model. The alternate modeling is shown below in Figure 4.4.

If such alternate modeling were suggested by the links observed, there would be implications for the *meaning of the indicators* involved. *Ultimately, this is what construct validity is all about.*

In other words, even if all these indicators have excellent convergent and discriminant validities, the hypothetical pattern of links discussed

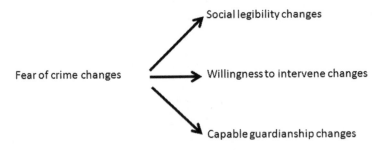

Figure 4.4   Potential alternate theoretical modeling of individual-level dynamics suggested by construct validation process

above is relevant to construct validity questions following the unified perspective. Fundamental rethinking would be needed about the relationships between the four constructs shown. Such a reexamination would require panel design data with at least three observation times to further unpack the relationships between the different changes and to better understand the ordering of the different changes.

Closing Comment, Including the Broader Agenda

This chapter draws attention to two limitations in current communities and crime research. At least in some theoretical frameworks, confusion abounds regarding key constructs. There is, to use Abbott's (2001) term, substantial semantic ambiguity. Further, there have been few systematic attempts to compare the relative adequacy of different theoretical perspectives (Taylor and Wikstrom, 2009). Such comparisons have been hampered in part because of semantic ambiguities. Both these matters can be resolved only by careful attention to construct validation efforts.

Of course, construct validation in the context of any ecological theory about community effects poses several challenges. These challenges are even more considerable for communities and crime models, given their heavy reliance of census and reported crime data.

A two-phase approach was recommended for pursuing construct validation. Both phases presume that the researcher has resolved temporal and spatial scaling concerns (Taylor, 2010); has indicators for each key construct derived from multiple data sources; and has data available that can be organized into a dynamic longitudinal boat metamodel as shown here. In the first phase, the researcher examines patterns of multimethod convergent and discriminant validities for key indicators in the theory of interest and preferably for competing theories as well. The investigation is conducted separately for each different segment of the metamodel (e.g., Ma-IΔ, Mi-IΔ, Mi-OΔ, and Ma-OΔ). Once these have been established, and in accord with suggestions from Messick's (1995) unified construct validation perspective, there is a second phase in which each of the links ($\rightarrow$) in the model is investigated both for the model of interest and for potential competing models with a similar metamodel structure. Then, as Cronbach (1970: 142) said "reasoning and imagination" come into play.

There is a broader and much more fundamental theoretical purpose at issue here: How do we integrate levels of explanation for crime across disparate levels of analysis such as individuals, situations, settings, and communities (Wikstrom and Sampson, 2003)? This will involve figuring out how different causal mechanisms—"developmental," "social," and "situational" (Wikstrom, 2007: 129–30)—operate, connect, and condition one another. Progress along these lines has been quite limited, perhaps in large part because "criminology lacks a developed theory of action through which causal mechanisms can be addressed and levels of explanation integrated . . . [the field lacks] a tool for integrating levels of explanation" (Wikstrom, 2004: 4). The types of investigations suggested here by the unified perspective on construct validation may help spur thinking along such integrative lines.

Notes

1. Cook et al. (1997: 116) described the situation as follows:

    The lack of clear discriminant validity within the process and demographic domains also has implications for testing neighborhood theories, the vast majority of which are couched in terms of specific, rather than global neighborhood attributes. The preference for such theory *implies that some neighborhood processes produce different consequences than do others* (emphasis added).

2. Although it sounds nonsensical at first to say that a cross-sectional, individuals-within-in-neighborhoods multilevel model with a community predictor and individual-level outcome is examining only an ecological relationship, this is what is happening, before or after conditioning on individual-level or other ecological predictors. The community predictor, if it yields a significant impact, does so because of connections with the between-community portion of the outcome variable.

3. Many of these definitions (Dahir, 1947; Mann, 1965; Keller, 1968; Suttles, 1972; Haney and Knowles, 1978; Crenson, 1983) highlight that (1) people live there, (2) it is more familiar or recognizable to its residents than locations farther away and that recognition may be externally recognized and politically represented, (3) within the neighborhood there may be some degree of social recognition or interaction among some fraction of the households living there, (4) nonresidential land uses and amenities contribute to or detract from the quality of neighborhood life, and (5) it is a geographically delimited locale, even though there may not be strong agreement among all residents about exactly where it begins and ends, depending on a range of housing, land use, and political factors (Firey, 1945; Taylor, 2001: 303–16).

4. More specifically, in the case of demographics, others have described the relevance of community SES (Sampson, 1985; Logan and Molotch, 1987; Bursik and Grasmick, 1993; Krivo and Peterson, 1996; Crutchfield and Pitchford, 1997), racial or ethnic composition (McDougall, 1993; Sampson and Wilson, 1995; Wilson, 1996; Peterson and Krivo, 2010), family composition (Sampson, 1987; Sampson and Lauritsen, 1994), and stability (Bursik and Webb, 1982; Bursik, 1988; Covington and Taylor, 1989; Bursik and Grasmick, 1993; Morenoff and Sampson, 1997) for a broad range of sociopolitical, cultural, social, psychological, and economic consequences, many of which may link to crime and/or delinquency and/or victimization. Given the multi-threaded impacts of each of these demographic components, each has been tied to a broad set of outcomes. Low community SES, for example, has been interpreted to generate, among other things, frustration (Gordon, 1967; Agnew,

1999; Maume and Lee, 2003), inability to access external resources (Morenoff and Sampson, 1997), inadequate internal social resources, the presence of large numbers of potential offenders (Cohen and Felson, 1979), or other aspects of routine activities (Sampson and Wooldredge, 1987; Osgood and Chambers, 2000), or institutional profiles (Peterson et al., 2000).

Land use patterns generally, including not only the patterning, density, and types of nonresidential land uses but also street traffic patterns and residential structure types, can influence a host of diverse processes (Harries, 1974, 1976, 1980; Brantingham and Brantingham, 1981, 1991, 1993) including but not limited to informal control (Kurtz et al., 1998), upkeep or lack thereof (Taylor et al., 1995), densities and patterns of guardians and potential victims (Roncek, 1981; Roncek and Bell, 1981; Roncek et al., 1981; Roncek and Lobosco, 1983; Roncek and Faggiani, 1985; Roncek and Pravatiner, 1989; Roncek and Maier, 1991), and neighboring and outsider space use patterns (Baum et al., 1978). Specific local land uses can interact with potential offenders' perceptions and behaviors in complex ways (St. Jean, 2007).

Given all these connections, it is easy to understand how these inappropriate conceptual substitutions arise. But it does not make them acceptable.

5. Those six aspects were content, substantive, structural, external, consequential, and generalizable (Messick, 1995).

6. Of course, each of these theories has a larger number of important theoretical threads. One thread of each is examined here in order to create a simple exposition.

7. For WTI, the researcher has surveyed residents with the usual items asking about hypothetical WTI in some manner if disorderly, mischievous, or criminal behaviors were witnessed. Several of these items focused on passersby looking into cars parked on the street, leaning on cars, and the like. Individual-level behavioral observation data were obtained as well. Trained research confederates traveling in pairs that were racially appropriate to the neighborhood moved through sampled streetblocks at times and under weather conditions when residents were likely to be home and outside, and they intentionally dropped litter directly in front of sampled households. They then moved on at a slow pace and waited to see if someone in the respondent household would respond. After dropping litter at all sampled households, they picked up all litter not previously drawn to their attention by someone in a sampled household. Being prompted to pick up the litter counted as being willing to intervene. Survey data from respondent households permitted controlling for household size and likelihood of someone being home at assessment times.

For CG, multiple methods also were used. Survey questions included those like the following: "Do you lock your car when it is parked out on the street in your neighborhood?"; "How important is it to be able to park your car right in front of your house?"; "How important is it to you to be able to park your car somewhere on the street where you can look out and see it?"; "On a typical weekday evening, if your car is parked in front of your house/apartment, how often do you look out to check on it?"; "How about on a typical weekend evening?"; "On a typical weekday evening, if your car is not parked on the street where you can see it from your house, say it is around the corner, how likely is it that you will go out and check on the car during the evening?"; "How about on a typical weekend evening?"; "If you were out of town for some reason, and you had to leave your car parked at home in front of your house, how likely would you be to ask a neighbor to check on it to be sure it was OK?"

Behavioral observation data collection for CG involved trained research confederates in pairs moving repeatedly through sampled streetblocks on randomly selected dates under specified weather conditions, which made it likely that residents would be outside. Following training, the groups moved slowly and acted rambunctious, veering close to and looking into cars as they moved along. If residents said something to the group, or if they perceived intentional surveillance from others on the block, they pressed a dedicated handheld device that noted the location where this occurred; the downloaded GPS information, accumulated over repeated trials on each study block, allowed the researcher to estimate how much surveillance existed near each sampled respondent's address. Since a large number of research confederates were trained and employed in the study, and the groups of confederates reconstituted, and the confederates adopted different clothing styles at different times, it seemed unlikely that residents' responses would be keyed to identification.

8.   Of course, in the case of SD theory, this is what Sampson and Grove did in the late 1980s with their systemic version (Sampson and Groves, 1989). That version, however, did not answer key questions about political economy/social control links, and this remains an area of some conceptual confusion in this theory.

Bibliography

Abbott, Andrew. *Time Matters: On Theory and Method*. Chicago: University of Chicago Press, 2001.

Agnew, R. "A General Strain Theory of Community Differences in Crime Rates." *Journal of Research in Crime and Delinquency* 36, no. 2 (1999): 123–55.

Barnett, C. and F. C. Mencken. "Social Disorganization Theory and the Contextual Nature of Crime in Nonmetropolitan Counties." *Rural Sociology* 67, no. 3 (2002): 372–93.

Baum, A., A. G. Davis, and J. R. Aiello. "Crowding and Neighborhood Mediation of Urban Density." *Journal of Population* 1 (1978): 266–79.

Blalock, Hubert M., Jr. *Causal Inferences in Non-experimental Research*. Chapel Hill: University of North Carolina Press, 1964.

———. *Theory Construction*. Englewood Cliffs, NJ: Prentice Hall, 1969.

———. *Conceptualization and Measurement in the Social Sciences*. Beverly Hills: Sage, 1982.

Bohrnstedt, George W. "Observation on the Measurement of Change." In *Sociological Methodology*, edited by E. F. Borgatta and G. W. Bohrnstedt. San Francisco: Jossey-Bass, 1969.

Boudon, Raymond. *Theories of Social Change*. Berkeley: University of California Press, 1986.

Brantingham, Patricia L. and Paul J. Brantingham. "Nodes, Paths, and Edges: Considerations on the Complexity of Crime and the Physical Environment." *Journal of Environmental Psychology* 13 (1993): 3–28.

Brantingham, Paul J. and Patricia L. Brantingham. *Environmental Criminology*. Beverly Hills, CA: Sage, 1981.

———. "Introduction: The Dimensions of Crime." In *Environmental Criminology*, edited by P. J. Brantingham and P. L. Brantingham. Prospect Heights, IL: Waveland Press, 1991.

Brower, S. *Good Neighborhoods*. Westport: Praeger, 1996.

Bunge, Mario. "A Systemic Perspective on Crime." In *The Explanation of Crime*, edited by P.-O. H. Wikstrom and R. J. Sampson. Cambridge, UK: Cambridge University Press, 2006.

Bursik, Robert J., Jr. "Delinquency Rates as Sources of Ecological Change." In *The Social Ecology of Crime*, edited by J. M. Byrne and R. J. Sampson. New York: Springer-Verlag, 1986.

————. "Social Disorganization and Theories of Crime and Delinquency: Problems and Prospects." *Criminology* 26, no. 4 (1988): 519–51.

Bursik, Robert J., Jr. and Harold G. Grasmick. "Economic Deprivation and Neighborhood Crime Rates, 1960–1980." *Law and Society Review* 27, no. 2 (1993a): 263–83.

————. *Neighborhoods and Crime*. Lexington, MA: Lexington Books, 1993b.

Bursik, Robert J., Jr. and Jim Webb. "Community Change and Patterns of Delinquency." *American Journal of Sociology* 88, no. 1 (1982): 24–42.

Campbell, D. and D. Fiske. "Convergent and Discriminant Validation by the Multitrait-multimethod Matrix." *Psychological Bulletin* 56, no. 2 (1959): 81–105.

Cantillon, D., W. S. Davidson, and J. H. Schweitzer. "Measuring Community Social Organization: Sense of Community as a Mediator in Social Disorganization Theory." *Journal of Criminal Justice* 31, no. 4 (2003): 321–39.

Clear, Todd R. *Imprisoning Communities: How Mass Incarceration Makes Disadvantaged Neighborhoods Worse*. Oxford: Oxford University Press, 2007.

Cohen, L. E. and M. Felson. "Social Change and Crime Rate Trends: A Routine Activity Approach." *American Sociological Review* 44 (1979): 588–608.

Coleman, James S. *Foundations of Social Theory*. Cambridge: Harvard University Press, 1990.

Cook, Thomas D., S. C. Shagle, and Serdar Degirmenciogly. "Capturing Social Process for Testing Mediational Models of Neighborhood Effects." In *Neighborhood Poverty, Volume II: Policy Implications in Studying Neighborhoods*, edited by J. Brooks-Gunn, G. J. Duncan, and L. Aber. New York: Russell Sage, 1997.

Cousineau, Douglas F. "A Critique of the Ecological Approach to the Study of Deterrence." *Social Science Quarterly* 54, no. 1 (1973): 152–57.

Covington, J. C. and R. B. Taylor. "Gentrification and Crime: Robbery and Larceny Changes in Appreciating Baltimore Neighborhoods in the 1970's." *Urban Affairs Quarterly* 25 (1989): 142–72.

Crenson, M. *Neighborhood Politics*. Cambridge: Harvard University Press, 1983.

Cronbach, L. J. *Essentials of Psychological Testing*. 3rd ed. New York: Harper and Row, 1970.

Cronbach, L. J. and P. E. Meehl. "Construct Validity in Personality Tests." *Psychological Bulletin* 52 (1955): 281–302.

Crutchfield, R. and S. R. Pitchford. "Work and Crime: The Effects of Labor Stratification." *Social Forces* 76 (1997): 93–118.

Dahir, J. *The Neighborhood Unit Plan: Its Spread and Acceptance.* New York: Russel Sage Foundation, 1947.

Ferraro, K. F. *Fear of Crime: Interpreting Victimization Risk.* Albany: SUNY Press, 1994.

Firey, W. "Sentiment and Symbolism as Ecological Variables." *American Sociological Review* 10 (1945): 140–48.

Gordon, Robert A. "Issues in the Ecological Study of Delinquency." *American Sociological Review* 32 (1967): 927–44.

Gottfredson, G. D. "Models and Muddles: An Ecological Examination of High School Crime Rates." *Journal of Research in Crime and Delinquency* 16 (1979): 307–31.

Haney, W. and E. S. Knowles. "Perception of Neighborhoods by City and Suburban Residents." *Human Ecology* 6 (1978): 201–14.

Hannan, Michael T. *Aggregation and Disaggregation in the Social Sciences.* Rev. ed. Lexington, MA: Lexington Books, 1991.

Harries, Keith. *The Geography of Crime and Justice.* New York: McGraw-Hill, 1974.

———. "Cities and Crime: A Geographic Model." *Criminology* 14 (1976): 369–86.

———. *Crime and the Environment.* Springfield: Charles C. Thomas, 1980.

Hawley, Amos H. *Human Ecology: A Theory of Community Structure.* New York City: Ronald Press, 1950.

Hillery, G. "Definitions of Community: Areas of Agreement." *Rural Sociology* 20 (1955): 111–23.

Hunter, A. *Symbolic Communities.* Chicago: University of Chicago Press, 1974.

———. "The Urban Neighborhood: Its Analytical and Social Contexts." *Urban Affairs Quarterly* 14 (1979): 267–88.

———. "Private, Parochial and Public School Orders: The Problem of Crime and Incivility in Urban Communities." In *The Challenge of Social Control, Citizenship and Institution Building in Modern Society,* edited by G. D. Suttles and M. N. Zald. Norwood, NJ: Ablex, 1985.

———. "Social Control." In *Encyclopedia of Community,* edited by K. Christensen and D. Levinson. Thousand Oaks: Sage, 2003.

Hunter, R. "The Loss of Community: An Empirical Test through Replication." *American Sociological Review* 40 (1975): 537–52.

Jacob, J. C. "Male and Female Youth Crime in Canadian Communities: Assessing the Applicability of Social Disorganization Theory." *Canadian Journal of Criminology and Criminal Justice* 48, no. 1 (2006): 31–60.

Kane, Robert J. "On the Limits of Social Control: Structural Deterrence and the Policing of 'Suppressible' Crimes." *Justice Quarterly* 23, no. 2 (2006): 186–213.

Keller, S. *The Urban Neighborhood*. New York: Random House, 1968.

Krivo, L. J. and R. D. Peterson. "Extremely Disadvantaged Neighborhoods and Urban Crime." *Social Forces* 75 (1996): 619–50.

Kurtz, Ellen M., Barbara A. Koons, and Ralph B. Taylor. "Land Use, Physical Deterioration, Resident-Based Control, and Calls for Service on Urban Streetblocks." *Justice Quarterly* 15, no. 1 (1998): 121–49.

LaGrange, R. L. and K. F. Ferraro. "Assessing Age and Gender Differences in Perceived Risk and Fear of Crime." *Criminology* 27, no. 4 (1989): 697–719.

———. "Perceived Risk and Fear of Crime: Role of Social and Physical Incivilities." *Journal of Research in Crime and Delinquency* 29 (1992): 311–34.

Lieberson, Stanley L. *Making It Count: The Improvement of Social Research and Theory*. Berkeley: University of California Press, 1985.

Liska, A. E. "The Significance of Aggregate Dependent Variables and Contextual Independent Variables for Linking Macro and Micro Theories." *Social Psychology Quarterly* 53, no. 4 (1990): 292–301.

Logan, John R. and Harvey Molotch. *Urban Fortunes*. Berkeley: University of California Press, 1987.

Mann, P. H. "The Neighborhood." In *An Approach to Urban Sociology*. New York: Humanities Press, 1965.

Maume, M. O. and M. R. Lee. "Social Institutions and Violence: A Sub-national Test of Institutional Anomie Theory." *Criminology* 41, no. 4 (2003): 1137–72.

McDougall, H. A. *Black Baltimore: A New Theory of Community*. Philadelphia: Temple University Press, 1993.

McGovern, Stephen J. "Philadelphia's Neighborhood Transformation Initiative: A Case Study of Mayoral Leadership, Bold Planning, and Conflict." *Housing Policy Debate* 17, no. 3 (2006): 529–70.

Messick, S. "Validity of Psychological Assessment: Validation of Inferences from Persons' Responses and Performances as Scientific Inquiry into Score Meaning." *American Psychologist* 50, no. 9 (1995): 741–49.

Morenoff, J. D. and R. J. Sampson. "Violent Crime and the Spatial Dynamics of Neighborhood Transition: Chicago, 1970–1990." *Social Forces* 76 (1997): 31–64.

Mustaine, E. E., R. Tewksbury, and K. M. Stengel. "Social Disorganization and Residential Locations of Registered Sex Offenders: Is This a Collateral Consequence?" *Deviant Behavior* 27, no. 3 (2006): 329–50.

Osgood, D. W. and J. M. Chambers. "Social Disorganization Outside the Metropolis: An Analysis of Rural Youth Violence." *Criminology* 38, no. 1 (2000): 81–115.

Ouimet, M. "Aggregation Bias in Ecological Research: How Social Disorganization and Criminal Opportunities Shape the Spatial

Distribution of Juvenile Delinquency in Montreal." *Canadian Review of Criminology* 42 (2000): 135–56.

Peterson, R. D. and L. J. Krivo. *Divergent Social Worlds: Neighborhood Crime and the Racial-Spatial Divide.* New York: Russell Sage, 2010.

Peterson, R. D., L. J. Krivo, and M. A. Harris. "Disadvantage and Neighborhood Violent Crime: Do Local Institutions Matter?" *Journal of Research in Crime and Delinquency* 37, no. 1 (2000): 31–63.

Pizarro, J. M. and J. M. McGloin. "Explaining Gang Homicides in Newark, New Jersey: Collective Behavior or Social Disorganization?" *Journal of Criminal Justice* 34, no. 2 (2006): 195–207.

Platt, J. R. "Strong Inference." *Science* 146, no. 3642 (1964): 347–53.

Roncek, D. W. "Dangerous Places: Crime and Residential Environment." *Social Forces* 60 (1981): 74–96.

Roncek, D. W. and R. Bell. "Bars, Blocks and Crime." *Journal of Environmental Systems* 11 (1981): 35–47.

Roncek, D. W., R. Bell, and J. M. A. Francik. "Housing Projects and Crime: Testing a Proximity Hypothesis." *Social Problems* 29 (1981): 151–66.

Roncek, D. W. and D. Faggiani. "High Schools and Crime: A Replication." *The Sociological Quarterly* 26 (1985): 491–505.

Roncek, D. W. and A. Lobosco. "The Effects of High Schools on Crime in Their Neighborhoods." *Social Science Quarterly* 64 (1983): 598–613.

Roncek, D. W. and P. Maier. "Bars, Blocks, and Crime Revisited: Linking the Theory of Routine Activities to the Empiricism of 'Hot Spots.'" *Criminology* 29 (1991): 725–53.

Roncek, D. W. and M. A. Pravatiner. "Additional Evidence That Taverns Enhance Nearby Crime." *Sociology and Social Research* 73 (1989): 185–88.

Sampson, R. J. "Neighborhood and Crime: The Structural Determinants of Personal Victimization." *Journal of Research in Crime and Delinquency* 22 (1985): 7–40.

————. "Urban Black Violence: The Effect of Male Joblessness and Family Disruption." *American Journal of Sociology* 93 (1987): 348–82.

Sampson, R. J. and W. Byron Groves. "Community Structure and Crime: Testing Social Disorganization Theory." *American Journal of Sociology* 94 (1989): 774–802.

Sampson, R. J. and J. L. Lauritsen. "Violent Victimization and Offending: Individual, Situational- and Community-Level Risk Factors." In *Understanding and Preventing Violence (Volume 3: Social Influences)*, edited by A. J. J. Reiss and J. A. Roth. Washington, DC: National Academy Press, 1994.

Sampson, R. J. and J. D. Wooldredge. "Linking the Micro- and Macro-Level Dimensions of Lifestyle-Routine Activity and Opportunity

Models of Predatory Victimization." *Journal of Quantitative Criminology* 3, no. 4 (1987): 371–93.

Sampson, R. J. and P.-O. H. Wikstrom. "The Social Order of Violence in Chicago and Stockholm Neighborhoods." In *Order, Conflict and Violence*, edited by I. Shapiro and S. Kalyvas. Cambridge: Cambridge University Press, 2008.

Sampson, R. J. and William Wilson. "Toward a Theory of Race, Crime, and Urban Inequality." In *Crime and Inequality*, edited by J. Hagan and R. Peterson. Stanford, CA: Stanford University Press, 1995.

St. Jean, Peter K. B. *Pockets of Crime: Broken Windows, Collective Efficacy, and the Criminal Point of View.* Chicago: University of Chicago Press, 2007.

Suttles, G. D. *The Social Construction of Communities.* Chicago: University of Chicago Press, 1972.

Taylor, R. B. "Impact of Crime on Communities." *Annals of the American Academy of Political and Social Science* 539 (1995): 28–45.

———. "Social Order and Disorder of Streetblocks and Neighborhoods: Ecology, Microecology and the Systemic Model of Social Disorganization." *Journal of Research in Crime and Delinquency* 33 (1997): 113–55.

———. *Breaking Away from Broken Windows: Evidence from Baltimore Neighborhoods and the Nationwide Fight Against Crime, Grime, Fear and Decline.* New York: Westview Press, 2001.

———. "Communities, Crime and Reactions to Crime Multilevel Models: Accomplishments and Meta-Challenges." *Journal of Quantitative Criminology* 26, no. 4 (2010): 455–66.

Taylor, R. B., B. Koons, E. Kurtz, J. Greene, and D. Perkins. "Streetblocks with More Nonresidential Landuse Have More Physical Deterioration: Evidence from Baltimore and Philadelphia." *Urban Affairs Review (formerly Urban Affairs Quarterly)* 30 (1995): 120–36.

Taylor, R. B. and R. R. Stough. "Territorial Cognition: Assessing Altman's Typology." *Journal of Personality and Social Psychology* 36 (1978): 418–22.

Taylor, R. B. and P.-O. H. Wikstrom. "Who Goes Where, Why, and Does What, for What Reason?: Disentangling the Influence of Settings and Selection on the Occurrence of Crime." *2009 Conference of the American Society of Criminology.* Philadelphia, PA, 2009.

Wikstrom, P.-O. H. "Crime as Alternative: Towards a Cross-Level Situational Action Theory of Crime Causation." In *Beyond Empiricism: Institutions and Intentions in the Study of Crime.* Advances in Criminological Theory, vol. 13, edited by J. McCord. New Brunswick, NJ: Transaction Publishers, 2004.

———. "Individuals, Settings, and Acts of Crime: Situational Mechanisms and the Explanation of Crime." In *The Explanation of Crime: Context, Mechanisms, and Development*, edited by P.-O. H.

Wikstrom and R. J. Sampson. Cambridge: Cambridge University Press, 2006.

————. "In Search of Causes and Explanations of Crime." In *Doing Research on Crime and Justice*, edited by R. D. King and E. Wincup. Oxford: Oxford University Press, 2007.

Wikstrom, P.-O. H. and R. J. Sampson. "Social Mechanisms of Community Influences on Crime and Pathways in Criminality." In *Causes of Conduct Disorder and Juvenile Delinquency*, edited by B. B. Lahey, T. E. Moffitt, and A. Caspi. New York: Guilford Press, 2003.

Wilson, W. J. *When Work Disappears: The World of the New Urban Poor*. New York: Knopf, 1996.

5

The Coming of a Networked Criminology?

Andrew V. Papachristos

To say that we live in a "connected world" is a bit cliché. Over the past decade, a new "network science" has emerged from its primordial origins in anthropology and sociology to overtake popular culture and the academy alike (Barabasi, 2003; Watts, 2003; Christakis and Fowler, 2009). From best sellers like Malcolm Gladwell's (2000) *Tipping Point* to revolutionary social media like Facebook, LinkedIn, and Twitter, the general populace wholeheartedly embraces the notion that social networks are key in understanding how the world works. *How* people are "linked" to other people makes a difference—it determines dating patterns, getting a job, shopping behaviors, health, and even the outcome of presidential elections. Within the academy, understanding the social relationships among people and organizations has been used to study problems as diverse as the diffusion of innovations and ideas (Burt, 1987; Chang and Harrington, 2005), the spread of public health epidemics (Eubank et al., 2004; Stoneburner and Low-Beer, 2004), processes of peer influence (Thompson, 1986; Watts et al., 2002; Gilbert et al., 2009), organizational and political behavior (Knoke, 1990; Burris, 2005; Baldassarri and Bearman, 2007), and even patterns of friendship and romantic relationships (Moody, 2001; Bearman et al., 2004). In short, the world—both in and beyond the academy—has come to an agreement that social networks matter.

Sadly, criminologists have largely missed the boat on this diffusion of social network analysis. Symptomatic of this point, very few papers published in criminology journals employ network analysis. Figure 5.1 illustrates this trend by plotting the annual number of articles published in top sociology, public health, and criminology journals that employed formal network analysis.[1] The dominance of sociology in publishing network-related articles is of little surprise as the discipline has been—and continues to be—at the forefront of this network revolution. Before 1990, public health and criminology show similar patterns of development: the occasional *single* paper talking about, or less often *measuring*, social networks, but with an overall modal count of zero network papers per year. After 1990, however, public health shows significant growth in this area. By contrast, the trend in criminology remains virtually flat with the exception of a few peaks (caused by one or two authors) and a small sign of hope with the slight uptick since 2005 (caused by the same one or two authors).

Criminology's neglect of social network analysis serves as a warning that the discipline is failing to keep up with important developments in scientific inquiry, not to mention the fact that criminology is missing an opportunity to test and expand upon some of its most treasured theories and concepts. Indeed, criminological theory oozes with network

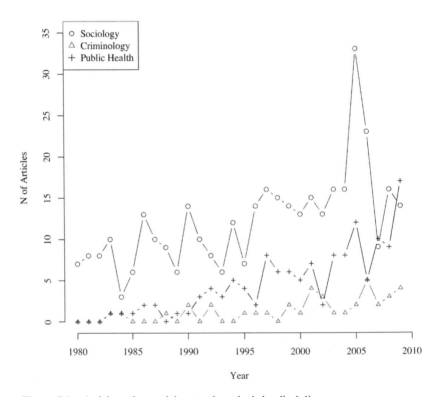

Figure 5.1   Articles using social network analysis by discipline

imagery and jargon. Ideas such as social bonding, cohesion and control, opportunity structures, diffusion, trust, and peer influence, just to name a few, now have methodological and statistical manifestations in social network analysis, which criminologists have only just begun to explore. Thus, the criminologist thinking outside of dominant methodological paradigms is in an excellent position to make a considerable contribution to our scientific understanding of crime, violence, and delinquent behavior. Such a rethinking of ideas and data could usher in a much-needed networked criminology.

This chapter is as much a polemic as it is an overview of the state of network research in criminology.[2] Rather than simply reviewing the past, my aim is to establish a basic framework for how criminologists might conceptualize and employ social network analysis in their work. To this end, this chapter is organized thematically. I begin with a (very) brief statement of what social network analysis is, some of its foundational principles, and how it relates to criminological theory. The remainder of the chapter is structured around how criminologists might conceive of social networks as either (a) *dependent* variables in their own right or else (b) *independent* variables essential in explaining specific patterns of crime and violence. The chapter concludes with some directed suggestions for the future of a networked criminology. The "literature review" happens along the way.

Social Network Analysis and Its Relevance for Criminology

Social network analysis encompasses both a theoretical perspective and a set of methodological techniques that cross disciplinary boundaries, ranging from field-driven anthropology (e.g., Bollig, 1998; Houseman and White, 1998) to theoretical physics (e.g., Barabasi et al., 2002; Dorogovtsev and Mendes, 2002). As a theoretical perspective, it stresses the *interdependence* among social actors, viewing the social world as patterns or regularities in relationships among interacting units (Wellman, 1983; Wasserman and Faust, 1994). More importantly, though the basic premise of social network analysis is that such interdependencies have important consequences for behavior. As a methodological approach, social network analysis refers to a catalog of techniques steeped in mathematical graph theory and that now extends to statistical, simulative, algebraic, and agent-based models (see Carrington et al., 2005). The portability of network analysis across areas of scientific inquiry has seen it employed to explain phenomenon such as how people get jobs (e.g., Fernandez and Sosa, 2005); the diffusion of technology, ideas, and disease (e.g., Christakis and Fowler, 2007); and even how political revolutions come to fruition (e.g., Gould, 1996).

Social networks are measured as a set of relationships on a bounded set of actors (Wasserman and Faust, 1994). *Actors* can be individuals, organizations, Web sites, cities, neighborhoods, or any "unit" of interest that can be considered to have relationships defined among the population.[3] A *relationship* refers to any type of tie or linkage between units—trading patterns, friendship, advice seeking, co-offending, sexual relationships, and so on. Formally, social networks are measured using *graph theory*, mathematical models that capture the pairwise relationships among a specified class of objects (ibid.). In graph theoretical terms, a network

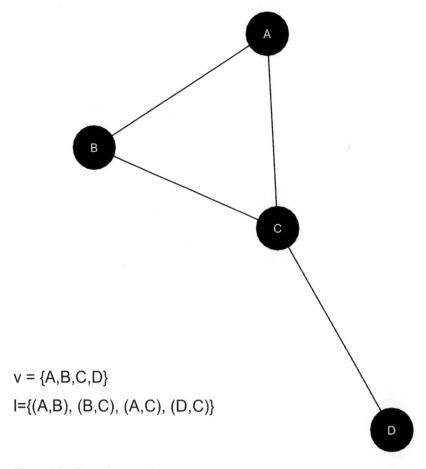

v = {A,B,C,D}

l={(A,B), (B,C), (A,C), (D,C)}

Figure 5.2   Example network

consists of a set of *vertices* or *nodes*, V, that represent the bounded set of actors or units and a set of *lines* or *edges*, E, that define the relationships among them. Figure 5.2 offers a simple example network consisting of a set of four vertices {A, B, C, D} and a set of four lines {(A,B), (B,C), (A,C), (D,C)}. The visual representation shows the basic structure of the network created by connecting the vertices with the lines between ordered pairs.

The same set of data could be conceived of as an *adjacency matrix*—a matrix in which the ordered rows and columns represent the vertices, and the cell values indicate the presence or absence of a tie.[4] Figure 5.3 shows the matrix associated with the example network given in Figure 5.2. In this case, the matrix shows the simple binary association of whether or not a tie exists between pairs. The diagonal—a self-tie—is most often excluded but may, in some cases, provide interesting informa-tion. Graphs (or their associated matrices) can also be *directed*; that is, the "sender" or "receiver" of the tie may be of relevance. For example, it might be important to know who sent a particular message or to use a criminological example, which gang shot a member of which other gang (Papachristos, 2009). In directed relationships, the order of the edgeset, E, matters, and the associated matrix would be asymmetric. Further-more, while in many cases networks are treated as binary (a tie exists or not), *values* may also be associated with relationships to indicate in-tensity of tie (e.g., strong versus weak ties), the number of interactions, or some other inherently interesting value (e.g., the amount of dollars traded between partners). Matrix transformations—such as the transpose of a matrix or the multiplication of different matrices—are often used to test for interaction effects and other network properties (Wasserman and Faust, 1994).

	A	B	C	D
A	-	1	1	0
B	1	-	1	0
C	1	1	-	1
D	0	0	1	-

Figure 5.3 Sociomatrix of example network

Social network thinking is often at odds with the dominant approaches to criminological inquiry. Borrowing a phrase from Abbott (1999), most contemporary social sciences (including criminology) adhere to a "variables paradigm" commonly associated with regression analysis (see also Emirbayer, 1997). From a regression-oriented perspective, theories are constructed based on abstractions such as "capitalism," "education," or "gender" that are measured as "variables" that capture some sort of central tendency. For example, our models often explain how education or poverty affects rates of crime and delinquency *net of other variables*. As a result, our theories assign much of the causal power to theoretical constructs captured by variables, rather than individuals, the interactions among them, or the interactions between categorical distinctions and social relationships. Roger Gould (2003) summarizes this situation quite nicely:

> [I]t is easy to forget that the collective relation is made of local interactions. Every time an employer fires a worker, lengthens work hours, or cuts wages, what is "really" happening according to this [variables-based] way of thinking is that capital is asserting its power over labor. Every time a white police officer uses a racial slur while questioning a black suspect, what is "really" going on is that whites are asserting their superiority over blacks as a race. And so on. It is easy to start believing that the abstract categories "capital and labor," "white" and "black," "male and female," are engaging in a battle of wills in which particular people are pawns. To think this way, however, is to mistake abstract categories for real things—to see them as agents rather than heuristic devices for classifying people and the things they do. . . . Capital has never in its history either hired or fired labor, although employers frequently hire and fire workers. They may even do so with the explicit thought that their actions could be subsumed under the broad rubric of power relations between capital and labor—but this does not change the fact that the actors in each instance are a particular worker and particular employer. (p. 32)

While the variables paradigm is indeed well suited to discuss findings pertaining to the generalizable "mean" across populations, it tends to obscure the simple fact that our theoretical constructs are just that—pedagogical devices to help us organize a complex world. Variables themselves do not act, people do.

Network analysis starts from a different position. In contrast to many (but not all) regression approaches, network analysis begins with the assumption that cases are *interdependent* and that such interdependences matter. There is no "net of other variables" caveat in the sense that the behaviors in the network—getting a job, starting a revolution, or committing a crime—are explicitly linked to the ways in which people are tied to each other. Standard "variables" can be included in network analysis, not simply to assess a "main effect," but more importantly, to determine how other social processes might be associated with such attributes. Thus, gender might exert a direct effect on crime simply because women commit less crime than men, but the network approach would also be interested in how gender influences patterns of social relationships that, in turn, are responsible for the gender effect in crime (e.g., Haynie and Payne, 2006). This approach differs from the variables approach in that "gender" is not doing something, but kids (with particular genders) are as they form friendships and commit delinquent acts together.

This distinction between assuming interdependence rather than independence is crucial. Stating that such interdependences between individuals are foundational—rather than simply error—violates the independence assumption at the foundation of most standard regression models that focus on causal analysis. The independence assumption is so strong in criminological thinking that we often take samples of individuals without even considering the ways in which they might be connected or how such interconnections might alter our understanding of what's "really" going on. In Figure 5.4, for example, I randomly selected twenty individuals who have been arrested in one Chicago neighborhood during the 2009 calendar year. These twenty individuals—the darker nodes, labeled as the "seeds"—are similar to a random sample of offenders that might be collected in a community-level study. The "alters" in Figure 5.4—the light gray nodes—are individuals with whom seeds have been arrested with over the prior three years with the act of "co-arrest" acting as the social tie.[5] The seed in "Group B" at the bottom of Figure 5.4, for example, was arrested with four different individuals, none of whom were arrested with each other. By contrast, the three seeds in "Group A" share many common "alters," some of whom have independent ties of their own.

Figure 5.4 tells us two important things that challenge the independence assumption of most classic regression approaches in criminology. First, even cases selected randomly from certain contexts may not be completely independent. In this case, eight out of the twenty cases—or roughly 40 percent of the sample—are in some way connected. Therefore, assuming independence among cases in samples such as these is simply wrong, especially if the interdependencies influence the *dependent variable*. Second, the variation in network structures seen in Figure 5.4, not to mention their potential effect on criminal behavior, cannot be adequately captured in standard survey measures, including the "number of delinquent friends" question that is a centerpiece in

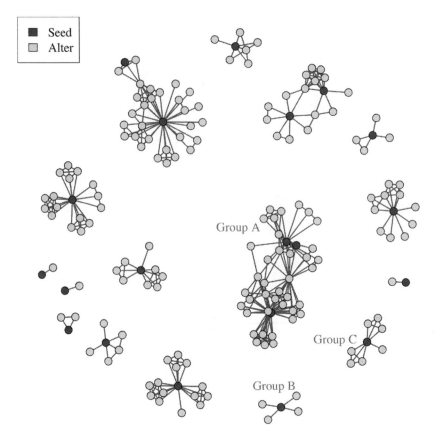

Figure 5.4 Example co-offending network, Chicago

much criminological research. Network research for more than two decades suggests that the *form* and *content* of networks matter in shaping behavior and not simply absolute size. Yet without considering the connections among the seeds in Figure 5.4—both the direct *and* indirect connections—such an approach would make the false assumption that cases are truly independent when, in fact, the interdependencies might be driving the behavior of interest or be a consequence of the behavior.

How might conceiving of the social world as points and lines like those depicted in Figures 5.2 and 5.4 benefit criminology? I argue that network analysis can help criminologists to refine concepts in our most prized theories by explicitly modeling the interdependencies among people, groups, institutions, and neighborhoods. In fact, the idea that "networks matter" is so omnipresent in criminology that we rarely give it much consideration. At its core, criminology is a "social" problem. People rob or steal from other people. Murders most often occur between "friends" or "acquaintances." Domestic violence takes place within a set of familial relationships that is highly contextualized. And outside of age and gender, the "number of delinquent friends" one has is perhaps one of criminology's most robust predictors of crime.

Thinking of the world in network terms, then, does not require a departure from current criminological thinking. Instead, it requires us to take stock of our discipline and engage in a candid discussion about how formal network methodologies might inform criminology and, conversely, how criminology might inform social network analysis. To do so, one must consider how the things criminologists care about—and measure—can be thought of in terms of relationships among actors. For example, the study of "group processes" and group influence can move past counting the "number of delinquent friends" one has and begin to measure the *content and form* of one's social network in more tangible and quantifiable ways: the composition of a network, a tendency toward homophily, a particular patterning of social ties (e.g., reciprocity), or the propensity to form or avoid ties with particular types of individuals.

Ideas such as these can find methodological and theoretical footing in social network analysis. Although the exact delineation of social network analysis with each of the criminological ideas just mentioned is well beyond the scope of this chapter, I hope to lay out a basic framework for how to approach this task. Such a framework involves two dimensions: conceiving of networks as *dependent variables* and conceiving of networks as having significant causal power as *independent* variables. As a dependent variable, social network analysis can be used to study the structure of peer influence (Haynie, 2001), organized crime syndicates (Morselli, 2003; Natarajan, 2006), street gangs (McGloin, 2005; Fleisher, 2006), and other group contexts in which crime and delinquency might occur. As independent variables, criminology would greatly benefit from understanding how the structure of networks and people's position in them relate to levels of criminality or victimization. The remainder of this chapter extends these two dimensions.

Networks as Dependent Variables: Finding and Describing the "Connected" World

One of the most common uses of social network analysis is to visualize and statistically summarize complex systems, organizations, and relationships. In such analyses, the network itself is the dependent variable, and network analysis is a powerful tool to describe the contours of the network and individual's position within it. Just like a spatial map provides powerful insight into how geography matters, social network analysis provides a similar map of the social topography of a group or system. Put another way, social network analysis describes the social landscape with all its contours, peaks, valleys, alleys, and boulevards.

The benefit of descriptive social network analysis for criminology comes from its ability to observe and measure "social structures"—regularities and patterns in the sets of ties and relationships among actors (Wellman, 1983; Wasserman and Faust, 1994). All too often, criminologists use some proxy to measure groups or structures—such as gang membership or the "number of delinquent friends" one has. What the structure of a group may look like—whether it is a cohesive group, for instance—is typically assumed rather than observed. The power of social network analysis, as Morselli (2009) aptly notes, is to "[s]eek, rather than assume, structure" (p. 18). And mapping groups, contexts, and relationships is a crucial first step in the advancement of a networked criminology.

To date, criminologists have most often employed formal social network analysis to describe the structure of street gangs (Tita et al., 2003, 2006; McGloin, 2005; Fleisher, 2006; Papachristos, 2009), organized crime syndicates (McIllwain, 2000; Klerks, 2001; Morselli, 2003), narcotics trafficking patterns (Natarajan, 2006), terrorist organizations (Xu and Chen, 2003; Pedahzur and Perliger, 2006), and white-collar conspiracies (Baker and Faulkner, 1993, 2003). For example, Natarajan (2006) uses data from 2,408 wiretapped conversations to recreate a heroin distribution organization in New York. Likewise, Morselli (2009) uses data from a long-term police investigation to analyze the organizational structure of the Hells Angels motorcycle club in Canada. Descriptive network techniques have also been used to uncover general properties of such groups that seem to distinguish criminal networks from noncriminal networks—an important way that criminology can also influence broader social network analysis. For instance, Baker and Faulkner's (1993) study of a price-fixing scheme in the heavy machining industry finds that whereas legitimate business networks organize in such a way to maximize efficiency, conspiratorial networks tend to develop a structure that maximizes concealment, even if this means sacrificing profits.

Descriptive social network techniques also provide a way to compare distinct theoretical conceptions of group structures with empirical data; and the robustness of various network measures affords an opportunity to compare measures across data and empirical contexts. Such an effort has been most fully realized in the study of street gangs. Research on gang organizational structures has produced numerous typologies and classification schemas of gang organizational forms and membership levels, most of which pivot around the familiar distinctions of hierarchical versus vertical forms of organization and core versus peripheral forms of participation (for a review, see Klein and Maxson, 2006). Such typologies are most often derived from surveys of law enforcement (and less often from gang members themselves) that ask respondents whether or not a gang has a set of formal organizational properties: written rules, weekly meetings, membership dues, and so on. In general, empirical research—but especially qualitative studies—concludes that gang structures tend to be much more amorphous and levels of gang participation tend to be dynamic than even the most comprehensive typologies would allow. Recent network studies of gang structures by McGloin (2007) and Fleisher (2005, 2006) have further questioned the utility of such distinctions by demonstrating that friendship, familial, and even criminal relationships among gang members can and frequently do transcend the classification silos of most gang typologies.[6]

This debate about gang structures provides an excellent opportunity to explore how social network analysis might guide the analysis of group structure and, more importantly, its relevance for criminological theorizing. To illustrate this point, Figure 5.5 displays the friendship networks derived from two gangs discussed in published ethnographies: The Erls gang as described in Suttles' (1968) *The Social Order of the Slum* and The Fremont Hustlers as described in Fleisher's (1998) *Dead End Kids*.[7] In both gang networks, each node represents a gang member and each tie represents a "friendship" as described in the ethnographic accounts.

Although these two gangs differ significantly in their social and historical contexts—the Erls are an all-male white gang during the late 1950s in Chicago, while the Fremont Hustlers are a mixed-race gang from Kansas City during the 1990s with a large number of female members—both groups display remarkably similar network characteristics. Most importantly, neither group shows a hierarchical pattern or any dramatic core versus periphery membership distinctions. Although three members of the Erls have only a single tie that might demark a small "periphery," the majority of members of the gang reside in larger clusters. In fact, *both* gangs display significant clustering. The Erls—a smaller gang in terms of the number of members—consists of two distinct clusters of members

(a) The Erls   (b) The Fremont Hustlers

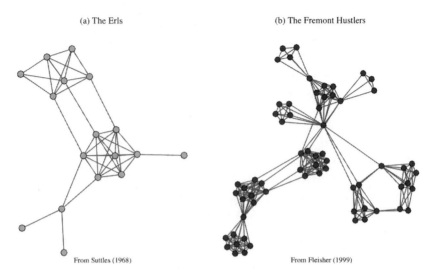

From Suttles (1968)   From Fleisher (1999)

Figure 5.5   The network structure of two gangs

held together by three ties between clusters. The Fremont Hustlers display greater clustering patterns that, in network parlance, might be considered a "caveman" graph—small pockets (or caves) that are bridged by one or two influential people (Watts and Strogatz, 1998; Watts, 1999).[8] While this type of clustering might be unfamiliar territory for gang research, it represents a quite familiar and robust area of research within the field of network analysis. In fact, the patterns of gang structure observed in Figure 5.5 are quite common in noncriminal social networks. A recent study even compared the social network patterns of gang members in Los Angeles with an online community of game users of *Worlds of Warcraft* and found that gang members and gamers display remarkably similar network patterns (Johnson et al., 2009).[9] Taken together, these findings suggest that future research on gang organization and structure would do well to conduct more structural analyses of gangs, comparing them with other types of delinquent groups and networks (see also Warr, 2002).

Using social network analysis to analyze the structure of criminal groups can (and should) move past the descriptive. In fact, a growing number of statistical models are being developed that help uncover the generative processes involved in the creation of social networks. This means that social network models can now offer us new directions in understanding the *etiology* of criminal groups, organizations, and contexts. In particular, the statistical properties of two classes of models—exponential random graph models (ERGMs) and dynamic actor-based models—are now well understood and gaining popularity in a number of empirical contexts.

ERGMs, also referred to as p* models, are a class of statistical models used to analyze the generative forces that give rise to an observed network structure.[10] The social networks—such as those in Figures 5.4 or 5.5—are considered the dependent variables where the predictors are properties of the network (e.g., reciprocity or transitivity), properties of the nodes themselves (e.g., main effects of gender or race), or other social processes such as assortative mixing and homophily. The most straightforward ERGMs take the form of a logistic regression model where the resulting coefficients represent the probability of a tie forming in the observed network conditioned on the specified model statistics.[11] Thus, ERGMs can be used to shed light on the precise processes used in the probability of the formation of ties in criminal networks.

Recent studies by Papachristos et al. (2010) and Young (forthcoming) have employed ERGMs to describe quite different networks. Studying networks of homicide and nonlethal shootings among gangs in Chicago and Boston, Papachristos and colleagues compare the influence of spatial proximity and social network distance on the probability of a negative tie forming between two groups—in this case, a shooting occurring between two gangs. Note that the outcome of interest is not the aggregate rates of gang violence, but rather the precise patterning of gang shootings—which gangs engage in shootings with particular other gangs (see also Papachristos, 2009). This study finds that while spatial proximity of gang turf is a positive predictor of a shooting occurring between any two groups, prior network connections have a larger effect on the probability of a shooting, even after controlling for racial composition of the gang, gang size, and city differences. Thus, it appears that while turf is a crucial element in shaping gang violence, prior network contact is a stronger predictor of any *specific* homicide or nonlethal shooting in cities with very different gang contexts.[12]

Using data from the National Longitudinal Survey of Adolescent Health (Add Health), Young (forthcoming) tests one of the basic premises of Gottfredson and Hirschi's (1990) "self-control" theory—that individuals with similar levels of self-control tend to sort themselves into different peer groups. This idea that similar individuals "end up together" drums up the adage of "birds of a feather flock together" and has received considerable attention in the network literature under the principle of *homophily*.[13] Although a long tradition of research clearly documents homophily with regard to levels of self-control in peer groups,

Young argues that previous research is unclear as to the actual *mechanism* underlying this sorting process. Using network data on sixty-three thousand adolescents from fifty-nine schools, Young finds little evidence that levels of self-control influence selection processes into peer groups. Rather, other underlying processes of friendship formation—such as assortative mixing by gender, grade in school, and simple triadic closure (or clique formation)—are better predictors of the observed homophily within peer groups with regard to levels of self-control. Although only a beginning, this study suggests a strong need for group-based criminological theories to expand their repertoire of statistical tests to include network-based data and models.

Recent developments in dynamic network modeling also hold considerable potential in criminological research, especially in understanding how criminal and delinquent networks evolve over time (Snijders, 2001; Heisman and Snijders, 2003). The basic premise of such models is that *network evolution* is represented as the result of many smaller (and typically unobserved) changes in the network that occur between observation points. The focus is on what factors contribute to tie formation and how such processes unfold over time. For example, such models might examine how friendship patterns contribute to the changing structure of delinquent groups over time. Dynamic network models, such as the actor-based SIENA approach (Snijders et al., 2010), also allow the modeling of specific network structural effects (e.g., reciprocity, transitivity, sender/receiver effects, and so on) as well as nodal characteristics (e.g., age, ethnicity, criminal propensity, etc.). Such models are/should be of particular interest to criminologists interested in the dynamics of delinquent and criminal groups as they are specifically geared toward uncovering the processes of network evolution.

Very few criminological studies have explored these dynamic models, but a recent study by Dukstra et al. (2010) illustrates their potential. Dukstra et al. examine weapon carrying among 167 school-aged youth from predominately Hispanic low social and economic status schools in the United States. Findings suggest that weapon carrying emerges from "a complex interplay between attraction of weapon carriers for affiliation, peer influence in friendship networks, and individual aggression" (p. 188). Weapon carrying, in fact, *increases* a youth's subsequent number of friendship ties in a network and the corollary social status associated with friendship nomination. In other words, particular criminal activities like carrying a gun can actually bolster the subsequent size and structure of one's social network. Such effects operate above the usual individual-level variables, such as aggression.

Whether studying informal friendship cliques in schools or sophisticated organized crime mafias, social network analysis can reveal the organizational subtitles of criminal and delinquent groups. Delinquent groups cease to become tallied by the size of its membership or by some checklist of organizational features. Instead, descriptive and statistical properties can be directly assessed using an array of network techniques. And in so doing, the contours of the criminal world might reveal something theoretical and empirically rewarding.

Networks as Independent Variables: How Do Connections Matter?

The real potential for social network analysis to influence criminology comes not simply from mapping the contours of delinquent groups, but also from the capacity to determine how specific network structures relate to criminal and delinquent behaviors. In other words, social network analysis can help unpack the black box often associated with ideas such as "peer influence," "group processes," or "facilitation effects." More to the empirical point, we can move past measuring concepts like peer influence merely as the number of delinquent friends one has and begin to uncover what type of network structures and group processes enhance or mitigate criminal behaviors.

Consider the two network structures depicted in Figure 5.6. These two networks provide straightforward examples of how understanding the actual structures of social networks might guide criminological theorizing and research. These two networks vary in the number of members, the number of ties, and the overall level of connectedness. Network (a), while larger in terms of membership and ties, is considerably less sparse than Network (b). Network (a) has a lower "density," defined as the proportion of all network ties that are present of all possible ties.[14] Furthermore, the distribution of ties in the networks—called the "degree distribution"—also differs between the two networks in Figure 5.6. In Network (a), Person 1 has the greatest number of ties with the number of ties diminishing the further out one goes from the center of the network. Such networks—often called "stars"—are highly centralized and are efficient structures for the diffusion of information and resources. Oftentimes, people who occupy the middle of starlike networks can wield considerable power and influence precisely because they bridge otherwise disconnected parts of the network (Burt, 1992). So for example, if Person 6 has information that might be of use to Person 4, that information *must* pass through Person 1 who can decide how (if at all) to pass along such information. Studies in formal and informal organizations continually suggest that "brokers do better," most often receiving higher economic and social returns to their behavior (Burt, 2004). Recent studies by Natarajan (2006) and Morselli (2003; Morselli and Roy, 2008) suggest that these same principles hold in criminal networks.

By contrast, Network (b) is a "closed" structure in which all of the members are linked to each other. Because of the high number of ties among members (greater density), networks like (b) are often considered to be "cohesive" subgroups similar to what one might find in friendship cliques, small working groups, or even street gangs such as those in Figure 5.5. Typically, dense networks are also associated with greater levels of social control as member behavior is more easily monitored (Coleman, 1988). As such, members in dense networks tend to exhibit strong tendencies toward homophily with regard to behaviors, attitudes, and opinions. Furthermore, learning and socialization can happen more quickly as there exist ample opportunities to learn from other members, and such processes are easily controlled. Principles such as these—as I discuss below—coincide with aspects of differential association and social learning theories.

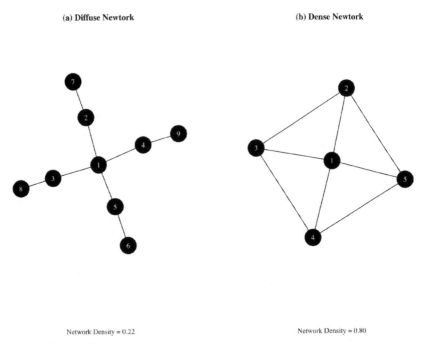

(a) Diffuse Newtork   **(b) Dense Newtork**

Network Density = 0.22   Network Density = 0.80

Figure 5.6   Comparison of diffuse and dense networks

A growing number of empirical studies have begun to consider the implications that network structures such as those in Figure 5.6 have on existing criminological theories. The most important steps in this direction have ensconced social network analysis within *social influence, opportunity,* and *self-control* theories. Since their creation, these three theoretical traditions have implicitly or explicitly invoked network thinking, especially the basic premise that the primary mechanism behind delinquency is the transmission of behaviors and beliefs between individuals who are closely associated with one another.[15]

Social influence theories, especially as formulated in differential social organization and learning theories, are based on the assumption that behavior is transmitted through processes of conformity in peer groups (Sutherland, 1947). As such, individuals are exposed to learn delinquent behaviors and norms as part of a complex interplay of forces that occur in groups such as socialization, fear of ridicule, status seeking, conformity, and so on (for a review, see Warr, 2002). Dense and cohesive networks, like Network (a), are precisely the types of structures hypothesized to be conducive to such processes. And the amount of time, involvement, and commitment (among other things) with delinquent peers increase delinquency. *Opportunity theories* posit that everyday life is structured by peer groups and the availability of behavioral options in the group (Cloward and Ohlin, 1960). Unstructured socialization thus provides ample opportunities for mischief, especially if the network contains illicit opportunities (drug use, graffiti prowess of members, the skills to pick a lock, the availability of drugs, etc.). Centralized networks (like Network (a)) may expose individuals to varying opportunities while other structures (like Network (b)) may close one off to opportunities. In contrast to social influence and opportunity theories, *self-control theory* suggests that criminal propensity is *exogenous* to exposure to the processes of peer influence found in delinquent groups—that is, that low social control individuals *select* into similar delinquent groups and, therefore, the observed peer effects are a product of selection into delinquent groups rather than facilitation by the group (Gottfredson and Hirschi, 1990). In other words, this theory suggests that the very formation of these networks is contingent on selection processes involving individual attributes rather than some underlying group effects.

Nearly all of the research connecting these theories with social network analysis has employed the school-based Add Health data. The Add Health data represent a unique opportunity in which traditional survey approaches are coupled with innovative sampling techniques and network methodologies with the end result of a nationally representative sample of adolescents and their social networks. This means, however, that most of our knowledge about social networks and delinquency is derived from a *school-based* population. To the best of my knowledge, no data of similar strength exist for nonschool samples or more serious adult offenders, although a few smaller scale network studies of adult criminal offenders have begun to emerge.

Still, studies using Add Health provide tremendous insight into how networks matter for criminal and delinquent behaviors. More specifically, five different types of network measurements have been marshaled to test these theories: (1) network density, (2) network centrality, (3) network involvement, (4) network selection, and (5) network composition.

As described above, *network density* refers to the overall connectedness or cohesion of a network.[16] Consistent with both prior network research and social influence theories, several network studies find a positive association between network density and delinquency: being in densely connected networks with a greater number of delinquent peers is associated with increased levels of self-report delinquency and violence (Haynie, 2001; McGloin and O'Neill Shermer, 2009). Furthermore, Kreager (2004) finds that network *isolation*—having few within school friendships—also increases self-report delinquency (also Haynie, 2001).[17] It is important to note that network density captures an aspect of one's social network above and beyond simply counting the number of one's "delinquent friends." For example, Person 1 in both Network (a) and Network (b) have exactly the same number of ties, but exist in quite different types of network *structures*. Simply counting the number of delinquent friends would discount the effect of the overall connectedness of one's friends, ignoring what we know to be a crucial aspect of one's social network. Moreover, network properties such as density are perhaps a more complete representation of our theoretical conceptions of differential association.

Network (degree) centrality refers to the number of "ties" an individual has in a group (see Wasserman and Faust, 1994).[18] Although dozens of measures of centrality exist in network research, perhaps the most common usage in criminological research is considered to be "popularity" or "prominence"—that is, the greater the number of ties one has in a network, ipso facto, the more involved, visible, or otherwise "embedded" one is in said network. In support of social influence and opportunity theories, network centrality appears to be positively correlated with delinquency: the more "connected" one is in a delinquent network, the greater one's self-report delinquency (Haynie, 2002; Haynie and Osgood, 2005; Haynie and Payne, 2006; McGloin and O'Neill Shermer, 2009). In some cases, network popularity is also related to delinquency in that certain delinquent acts (like carrying a gun) are related to subsequent friendship nominations (Dukstra et al., 2010). Furthermore, several studies on more organized criminal activities suggest that individuals more centralized in information flows—like Person 1 in Network (a)—experience greater returns to their criminal activities (e.g., higher criminal earnings) (Morselli, 2003; Morselli et al., 2007; Morselli and Roy, 2008).[19]

Studies by Haynie and Osgood (2005) and McGloin and O'Neill Shermer (2009) considered *network involvement* as the amount of time the named network associated "hung out" with each other outside of the school context during the past weekend.[20] Consistent with differential association and opportunity theories, increased involvement with network members is positively associated with self-report delinquency. Here, it is significant that involvement adds a level of complexity above and beyond the absolute number by speaking to the *content of the tie*. Involvement thereby signals the level of commitment one has to specific individuals or whether or not a specific set of ties could be consider "strong" or "weak" (Granovetter, 1973).[21] In a specific test of the effect of strong versus weak ties on delinquency, Weerman and Smeenk (2005) find that delinquency is more highly associated with stronger (best friend) ties than weaker (friend) ties. Bellair's (1997) study of sixty neighborhoods in three different states also suggests that weak ties—defined as meeting at least once a year with a neighbor—can mediate ecological factors associated with high rates of crime.

A few studies also consider how network selection influences levels of delinquency, mainly by examining individual's levels of "self-control." Here the evidence is less clear. In support of self-control theory, McGloin and O'Neill Shermer (2009) find that an individual's level of self-control is related to both the composition of one's network *and* subsequent levels of self-report delinquency; yet this study also finds that levels of self-control interact with other group processes and social influence indicators, thereby suggesting a perhaps more complex relationship between self-control and social influence theories than previously theorized. By contrast, Young (forthcoming) finds that the effect of an individual's level of self-control on friendship tie formation is trumped by other processes of tie formation. In other words, self-control may be less important in determining homophily than other "normal" (read nondelinquent) processes of tie formation. These disparate findings suggest that further research is needed to unpack other processes responsible for selection into delinquent networks.

Finally, studies on the effect of *network composition* have produced an impressive set of findings that suggest that in addition to understanding the *form* of an individual's network, it is also important to analyze *the content of the network*. Being part of a network in which members have been victims of violence increases one's self-report delinquency and self-report violence: in nearly all studies using Add Health, the mean level of delinquency and violence in one's social network is positively related to one's own delinquency and violence. The effect of such network exposure to delinquency also appears to hold for more distant friends (i.e., friends who are one or two handshakes away from the respondent), indicating that social influence operates above and beyond one's immediate social circle (Payne and Cornwell, 2007; Papachristos et al., 2010).[22] Outside of exposure to delinquency, recent studies also suggest that the racial composition of one's social network is associated with delinquency. Haynie and Payne (2006) find that racial heterogeneity in an adolescent's social network—especially, black youth—can have a mediating effect on self-report delinquency; in this case, having more white friends in one's networks reduce one's self-report delinquency. What is more, the effects of density and centrality described above may also be conditioned on racial and gender composition of one's network (Haynie and Payne, 2006; McGloin and O'Neill Shermer, 2009).[23]

The aforementioned studies illustrate effective ways that network thinking can be used to bolster criminological theory and empirical research. On the one hand, criminologists can—and perhaps should—delve into the more general research on social networks looking for ideas to poach. This approach to science views knowledge production as an act of arbitrage where the researcher (creatively) borrows ideas and methods form one discipline or area of research only to repackage and sell it in order to advance in their own area. This tried and true method of knowledge production is responsible for many advancements in the social sciences, the least of which are various regression techniques and path analysis. On the other hand, criminologists might also start by revisiting our theories with an eye toward *measuring* social networks in such a way that uncovers new and productive crime-inducing or crime-inhibiting mechanisms. Thus, we might associate network structures like those in Figure 5.6 with different social processes. Furthermore, those social processes might differ by the types of ties or types of actors. For example, while dense networks with a large number of delinquents may increase criminality, dense networks of nondelinquents may decrease criminality (Kreager, 2007). Same measurement, different network content.

To conclude this chapter, I advance this line of thinking by delving more deeply into two specific areas of criminological inquiry that might benefit from a more precise application of social network analysis: the study of crime epidemics and the study of neighborhood social organization. Both of these areas invoke network concepts—sometimes on purpose, sometimes not—and yet the use of formal network models has been limited at best.

Rethinking Crime Epidemics

When criminologists talk about "crime epidemics," they are typically referring to dramatic increases in crime and violence in specific locations over a short period of time (Cohen and Tita, 1999).[24] The focus of such research tends to be on (1) either the functional form of crime epidemics or else (2) the "risk factors" associated with the vanguard of crime rates. For example, the dramatic increase in violent crime during the 1980s and the early 1990s is often associated with the prevalence of crack cocaine, the increased availability of handguns, and the proliferation of street gangs as well as changes in the social, structural, and economic composition of urban neighborhoods (Blumstein and Wallman, 2000). And by and large, most criminological studies conceive of crime epidemics as being driven by corollary changes in such risk factors (Blumstein et al., 2000).

Such a risk factor approach to crime epidemics succeeds in explaining the correlates associated with the ebb and flow of crime rates. Yet from a true epidemiological perspective, the risk factor approach provides only a partial explanation of how changes in crime might be similar to (or different from) other types of health epidemics. In large part, the shortcomings of the criminological approach to crime epidemics stem from how we conceive of—and measure—*exposure*. In most cases, the rate of crime—and by extension any individual's risk of victimization—is directly related to the number of risk factors one has or the level of such risk factors in one's immediate social and physical environment. To summarize this research tradition, young minority men who live in socially and economically disadvantaged neighborhoods bereft of social and human capital are the most likely victims (and offenders) of crime.

Such a risk factor approach overlooks the deceivingly simple fact that the vast majority of individuals exposed to such risk factors—even at the most *severe* levels—never commit a crime. Exposure to risk factors, then, is in and of itself not sufficient to explain an individual's true risk of being a victim or offender of a crime. Here criminologists might learn from epidemiological studies of infectious disease. The rate of infectivity and timing of any health epidemic are related not only to disease-specific conditions but also to the *mode of transmission*. Airborne pathogens, like the recent H1N1 flu, require only modest levels of spatial proximity to reach epidemic proportions; people are at risk merely by proximate exposure to infected individuals as they go about everyday activities like riding a train, attending school, or going to work. Most criminological studies make a similar assumption where exposure to criminogenic risk factors increases one's likelihood of being a crime victim (or offender). Even spatial regression models, which provide perhaps the best explanations of the diffusion of crime epidemics, assume a world in which crime rates (in the aggregate) somehow spill across geopolitical boundaries of spatially proximate neighborhoods (Cohen and Tita, 1999; Morenoff et al., 2001). While many of these spatial analyses hypothesize that social networks are responsible for the transmission of crime across neighborhood boundaries, studies rarely measure said networks and, instead, model the airborne pathogen assumption.

However, even in the airborne pathogen example, the structure of social networks matters: the rate of infectivity will be higher in more densely connected networks and behavioral settings. For example, a recent study by Christakis and Fowler (2010) found that being a central actor in friendship network increases one's risk of getting the flu. In other words, those more active in social settings are at greater risk for exposure to airborne pathogens. It is the very same logic that warns parents to keep their kids home from the school when they display flu-like symptoms—not only to allow their child the chance to rest, but also to diminish exposure to other kids at school in the hectic and highly interactive classroom environment.[25]

Crime, I argue, is more like an infectious disease, especially blood-borne pathogens. Blood-borne pathogens, such as sexually transmitted diseases (STDs), require more active behavioral conditions to spread in a population. This means that the rate of infectivity is much more circumscribed in a population and can only "spread" through very *specific* and *identifiable behaviors* such as sharing drug needles or through certain types of sexual activities. Crime appears to precisely follow this type of distribution. Studies consistently demonstrate that crime—and especially violent crime—is highly concentrated within populations, even in neighborhoods otherwise characterized by multiple "risk factors."

For example, in Boston less than 3 percent of the adult male population is responsible for 75 percent of all fatal and nonfatal shootings (Braga et al., 2008). Likewise, other studies suggest that the majority of crime is concentrated in less than 10 percent of the adult population in several U.S. and European cities (Lipsey and Wilson, 1998). Thus, while the *distal* causes of high crime rates undoubtedly rest in this litany of risk factors, the *proximate* causes of crime can be found within such highly circumscribed populations. By comparison, while the abatement of STDs should include primary educational efforts in the general population (e.g., campaigns to increase the use of condoms), changing an immediate epidemic may require targeting particular populations at the core of infectivity (e.g., intravenous drug users, sex workers, or long-distance truck drives). Similarly, without denying the importance of reducing long-term risk factors such as poverty, these findings partially suggest that crime prevention efforts might be better served by focusing scarce resources on more precise populations and networks.

The network approach advanced here suggests that understanding social networks of the "riskiest" populations might help us better unravel the timing, duration, and even the mechanisms of diffusion of crime epidemics. Again, an example can help illuminate this point.

Approximately eighty thousand people live on the West Garfield Park and North Lawndale communities on the west side of Chicago. By any social and economic indicators, these two African American (>90 percent) communities are considered "high risk" for many social and health epidemics. Rates of poverty, unemployment, and overall morbidity are well above the city average, and these communities have some of the highest annual rates of homicide in the city with a staggering annual rate of fifty-six per one hundred thousand (as compared to the city's homicide rate that is about sixteen per one hundred thousand). This high homicide rate, not to mention the prominence of several highly organized street gangs and the prevalence of open-air drug markets, often ushers in descriptions of these communities as "war zones." Indeed, several highly publicized "stray bullet" murders of school-aged youth prompted local senators to (quite literally) petition the government to call in the National Guard to help abate the area's violence problem.

Yet even in this community, the majority of homicides are contained within small circumscribed social networks. Over the last five years, 191 homicides were committed in these two communities, of which *70 percent* occurred in a social network of only *sixteen hundred individuals* (see also Papachristos, 2011). This simple finding fundamentally changes the notion of risk in this community: the risk of homicides for those *inside* the network skyrockets to annual rate of *1,500 per 100,000*, while the risk in the general neighborhood population drops to *22.5 per 100,000*. While the homicide rate of the general (nonnetwork) population is still considerably high, it is less than half the rate when considering the high-risk network.

More than that, however, this network is easily identified using something as commonplace in criminological research as arrest records. Retrospectively, Figure 5.7 recreates the social network of homicide just described by creating a co-offending network of 119 homicide victims who were arrested at least one time between 2005 and 2010. Starting with the 119 homicide victims, I created a "two-degree" network. The

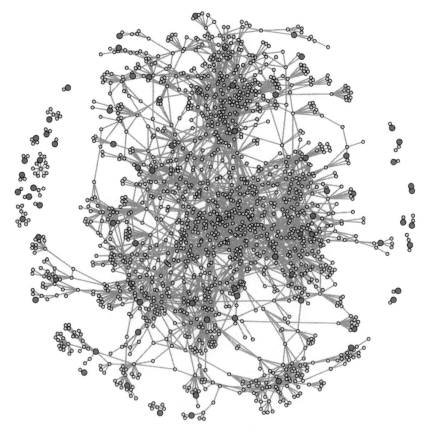

Figure 5.7   The two-degree arrest network of homicide victims on Chicago's westside, 2005–2010

"first degree" entailed extracting all known associates with whom a victim had been arrested during this time period. The simple assumption is that if two individuals are arrested together, they are likely to have some "association" or friendship. Thus, a tie exists when two (or more) individuals have been arrested together. The "two-degree" network emerges by repeating the first step for all of the associates of those from the first-degree networks.[26] This two-step process reveals the network structure in Figure 5.7, which began with 119 homicide victims and grew to a total number of 1,638 individuals—less than *2 percent* of the total population in these neighborhoods.

Even visually, Figure 5.7 shows several important factors that challenge prior thinking regarding crime epidemics. First, not only is the risk concentrated in a small portion of the population, but also this small segment of the population is virtually all connected: in this network, 1,507 of the 1,638 (92 percent) exist in a *single large network*. It thus appears that murder in these communities occurs in a very small world in which homicide victims are just a few handshakes away from each other. Second, while murder is spread out through this network, there are several points of clustering. Analyses such as those described throughout this chapter might be used to (1) determine the processes or attributes responsible for the observed clustering or (2) help identify others in this network that might be at increased risk. In other words, perhaps analyzing network patterns such as those in Figure 5.7 can help identify certain network signatures or positions that place people *within* this network at future risk. The forecasting of crime epidemics then shifts from a focus on risk factors to a more concrete focus of individuals who occupy particularly risky positions in social networks.

Advancing this networked study of crime epidemics also requires incorporating risk factors *and* social network approaches. Perhaps one of the most direct avenues for such an agenda, I believe, would be to consider incorporating spatial and social network models. Most spatial analyses of crime readily acknowledge that "networks" are the most likely mode of transmission of crime across neighborhood boundaries (Cohen and Tita, 1999; Morenoff et al., 2001). On a methodological level, spatial regression models share virtually all of the same assumptions of interdependency with network models, and, in fact, network and spatial autoregressive models share nearly the same functional form (Leenders, 2002). By incorporating both traditional risk factors that concentrate in geographic space (such as poverty and unemployment) with precise measures of network autocorrelation (such as co-offending or gang networks), one might successfully model both aggregate crime rates (Tita and Greenbaum, 2009) and individual risk (Papachristos et al., 2010). Recent studies by Tita and Greenbaum (2009) and Papachristos (2009; Papachristos et al., 2010) have incorporated both spatial and social network terms in models explaining gang violence, and both studies find that in all cases while geographic space matters in determining the diffusion of violence, social networks matter more. Thus, a small but growing number of studies are hinting at the utility of this very approach.

Neighborhoods and Social Networks

Yet another area of criminology particularly well suited for an advancing networked criminology is the study of neighborhood social organization. The "community question" in criminology has a long history rooted in the "Chicago School" of sociology (Sampson, 2000). Early Chicago studies equated crime and other social ills with the decline of small kin-based (gemeinschaft) societies and communities and the subsequent rise of non-kin (gesellschaft) communities based on impersonal ties (Thomas and Znaniecki, 1918–1920). In network terms, the decline of "strong ties" in a community hinders its capacity for social control—that is, the ability of a community to regulate itself according to desired goals and beliefs (Janowitz, 1975). The classic definition of social control and *social disorganization* considered the disruption of social networks as the result of population heterogeneity, high residential turnover, and impoverished social and economic conditions (Shaw and McKay, 1942). The Chicago School produced dozens of ecologically oriented studies—not to mention, dozens of maps—showing that socially disorganized areas of the city were correlated with high levels of vice, suicide, street gangs, and, of course, juvenile delinquency.

The idea that social disorganization referred to a lack of morality and social order was challenged early on by Whyte's (1943) class, *Street Corner Society*, which reveals the intricate social order and social institutions of a Boston slum. Whyte showed that while, from the outside, slum communities might be easily construed as "disorganized,' from the inside such communities have incredibly rich social networks. Kinship groups, social clubs, politicians, and street corner boys all played important roles in the social fabric of the community. Dozens of qualitative studies continue in this tradition documenting the intricate social networks that operate in disadvantaged communities (e.g., Suttles, 1968; Hannerz, 1969; Stack, 1970; Pattillo-McCoy, 1999; Venkatesh, 2006).

Most of these studies find that while poor communities are rich in dense kin and non-kin networks that provide social support, they lack networks that can access larger social, political, and economic resources (Wilson, 1987). Poverty, here, generates a sort of "network trap" by which poverty constrains the development of particular network forms that might help elevate the effects of poverty (see, e.g., Sampson and Graif, 2009).

While the qualitative research convincingly reveals the presence and importance of social networks in socially disadvantaged communities, this research also reveals a paradox of sorts. While, on the one hand, the presence of dense social networks is often equated with increased social capital and social support (Coleman, 1988), on the other hand, dense cohesive networks can also *constrain* the capacity of residents to intervene on the behalf of neighborhood social control. In part, this results from the fact that networks often form overlapping social webs where pro-social and deviant social networks can intermix and penetrate each other. For example, Venkatesh (2006) describes a situation in one Chicago neighborhood where formal resident organizations, religious institutions, and police all directly engage gang and drug-dealing networks in a complicated *pas de deux* in which each social group seeks to gain from its engagement with the other. Gang leaders promise not to deal drugs in a park, while at the same time extorting local businesses. Community leaders provide gang leaders information about the informal economic activities of residents in exchange for various services and favors. The end result is a situation in which networks that are often considered at odds with each other are, in fact, interwoven in complex and multifaceted ways.[27]

This research shows us that networks themselves are, in a sense, *value neutral*: in and of themselves, possessing dense social networks does not ensure effective community social control and, in some situations, may even hinder it (Browning et al., 2004; Sampson, 2004). Accordingly, social disorganization has been reformulated in *systematic* terms that focus on the ability of communities to "get things done" (Bursik and Grasmick, 1993). In contrast to the original Chicago School formulation—and borrowing from Granovetter's (1973) "Strength of Weak Ties" hypothesis—more recent conceptions of social disorganization theory do not assume that strong familial and friendship ties are necessary for the abatement of crime and delinquency. Rather, networks and community action can be *task specific* and need only be activated for particular tasks (Sampson et al., 1997). The idea of "collective efficacy" offered by Sampson and colleagues combines shared expectations, trust, and resident engagement in social control for task-specific objectives. And an impressive body of research has marshaled support for the effect of collective efficacy on a host of social behaviors, including crime and delinquency (for a review, see Sampson et al., 2002).

Despite the importance networks play in our theories and empirical research on neighborhood effects, very few quantitative studies of neighborhoods and crime employ formal network methodologies. Some creative research have used survey-based measures to extract measures of tie "strength" (Bellair, 1997) and "neighboring" (Hipp, 2010), but most quantitative studies simply lump "networks" into broader survey items pertaining to organizational capacity or trust. The main roadblocks keeping formal network analysis and the quantitative study of neighborhoods apart are both conceptual and methodological. Conceptually, where does one begin to measure networks and how do they fit into our existing theories of what constitutes a "neighborhood"?[28] Are neighborhood networks comprised only of interactions among residents, and if so, what *types* of interactions? What about networks between neighborhood residents and community or political institutions? What about relationships between organizations themselves? Are kin-based networks more important than non-kin networks? Can "neighborhoods" themselves the actors? In short, if neighborhood research were to take social network analysis seriously, what would constitute the vertices and what would constitute the ties?

The answer to the aforementioned questions are "all of the above" and "it depends." Network analysis can deal with networks on different levels of analysis—individual actors, relationships among organizations, and even networks between geopolitical entities. Without complex—and costly—sampling frames such as those found in Add Health and the Project on Human Development in Chicago Neighborhoods, what exactly constitutes a neighborhood "network" depends on the research question being asked. For example, a researcher interested in community-level crime control efforts might analyze the relationships between the police and community institutions. Or if the researcher is concerned with the effects of social networks on trust and informal social control, one might examine the networks created among important political and social leaders (e.g., Sampson and Graif, 2009). To cite a recent example that tackles the relationship between networks and geographic neighborhoods, Grannis (2009) goes so far to argue that the foundation of the idea of a "neighborhood" is directly linked to the formation of parenting networks between households and the role geography plays in shaping said networks.

All of this is to say that networks—be they in neighborhoods, countries, or other large social systems—have multiple meanings and operate at multiple levels. It is the analysts' job to decide on the unit of analysis without excluding the possibilities that networks can operate at levels not necessarily measured in any given study. In network oriented research, this entails circumscribing where networks begin and end, if only in the investigation of specific research questions.[29]

Methodologically, neighborhood research should consider new and creative ways to collect network-related data as well as think creatively about existing data. With regard to future data collection efforts, criminologists would do well to integrate various network sampling techniques to address questions that focus on individuals, organizations, and even neighborhood systems (Carrington et al., 2005). Survey-based measures of "ego-networks," for example, are one way to adequately capture the effect of local social support and are already often integrated into traditional social surveys (Marsden, 1987). Likewise, respondent-driven sampling methods have been developed that are especially helpful in revealing the network of "hidden populations," such as drug users and criminals (Heckathorn, 2007).[30] With regard to existing data, oftentimes all that is required is that criminologists open their eyes to the structure and meaning of data. For example, the data used in Figures 5.4 and 5.7 were derived from arrest records, while Figure 5.6 came from published ethnographies. Criminologists use these data regularly, often without considering their full potential. And if anything, the coming of a network criminology demands that we all take a step back and rethink our theories, methods, and data.

Coda

I began this chapter with a cautionary note that criminology appears to be falling behind other sciences in realizing the value of social network analysis. In part, criminology's tardiness to the network revolution is because of our overreliance on traditional regression-based frameworks and because of the usual navel-gazing found in any discipline. The main goal of this chapter was to drawn attention toward ways in which criminology can and should engage social network analysis in ways that both are consistent with and build upon our rich disciplinary traditions. The easiest way to move in such a direction is to (re)consider the ways that our most prized theories coincide or diverge from various network principles. To be sure, not all criminological theories may espouse a network approach. Yet the fact that criminology's so many central theories invoke network imagery or principles suggests that such a revisiting of network theory and methods is long overdue.

The recent growth of formal network analysis within criminology offers signs of hope. I firmly believe that criminology is ready to participate in the network revolution, not simply as a consumer of network methods and models, but also as a producer of scientific knowledge that can be exported to other disciplines. In so doing, the coming of a networked criminology may spark new and exciting areas of inquiry.

Notes

1. These data were captured by searching the terms "social network," "network analysis," "social networks," and "networks" in the top sociology journals (*American Journal of Sociology, American Sociological Review*, and *Social Forces*), public health journals (*American Journal of Public Health* and *American Journal of Epidemiology*), and criminology journals (*Criminology, Journal of Research in Crime and Delinquency*, and *Journal of Quantitative Criminology*).

2. For additional reviews of social network analysis, its applications in criminology, and an overview of methodologies and data collection strategies as they relate to criminology, see Carrington (2011), McGloin and Kirk (2010, forthcoming), and Papachristos (2006). In addition, a handful of articles have also been written about the practical applications of network analysis to criminal justice practice (Schwartz and Rouselle, 2009; van der Hulst, 2009).

3. While network analysis most often considers that actors are of single class (or mode), some network techniques are capable to handle two modes of data (see Wasserman and Faust, 1994).

4. The advantage of using adjacency matrices is that they enable one to view the entire set of ties, including ties that do not exist. The main drawback is that matrices can become unwieldy as the network increases in size.

5. See McGloin and Piquero (2010) for an excellent analysis of co-offending networks in Philadelphia.

6. These recent studies echo a similar finding based on sociometric data analyzed by Klein and Crawford (1967) nearly forty years before as well as the basic sociometric analyses found in ethnographies such as *Street Corner Society* (Whyte, 1943) and *The Social Order of the Slum* (Suttles, 1968).

7. Data on the Erls are described by Papachristos (2006). For the purposes of simplification, the present analyses deal only with *positive* ties in the Erls data. Data on the Fremont Hustlers were created by coding the ethnographic text itself where each "tie" is either (1) a reported incident of socialization or hanging out as described by the author or else (2) the reported socialization patterns of two key informants in a card-sorting exercise conducted by the author (Fleisher, 1998). The Fremont Hustler data were coded by a group of undergraduate students who coded the actual text of the ethnographer. Inter-coder reliability was high (0.78), and a "tie" was listed as present if at least two coders reported the same tie.

8. It is most likely those individuals who span the clusters—"brokers" in network jargon (Burt, 1992)—that could be considered "leaders" or "influentials" within the gang.

9. It is interesting to note that this study was published in a statistics journal and *not* a criminology journal. In fact, many of the other crime-related network studies referenced throughout this chapter seem to have greater appeal *outside* of criminology proper—yet another sign that criminology is losing ground in this area of science.

10. The general theory and methodologies of ERGMs have received considerable attention (Wasserman et al., 1999; Robbins et al., 2007).

11. When the proposed ERGM contains statistical terms pertaining to dyads and individual nodes, a normal logistic regression format suffices and maximum pseudolikelihood estimation is used to estimate the maximum likelihood (MLE) (Robbins et al., 2007). For models that include higher order terms—such as triadic effects or degree distribution—the maximum likelihood can be approximated using Markov Chain Monte Carlo simulation methods that generate a sample of possible networks to estimate test statistics and model fit.

12. A recent study of Tita and Greenbaum (2009) reaches a similar conclusion using network autocorrelation models to predict aggregate rates of crime in a Los Angeles neighborhood.

13. Homophily is perhaps one of the most robust social processes described in the social network analysis (see McPherson et al., 2001). Given that delinquent groups act like other human social groups, it is a wonder that it took criminologists so long to apply the network version of homophily to the study of delinquent groups.

14. Density is a basic network property that reflects the overall intensity of the connected actors (Wasserman and Faust, 1994). The more connected the network, the greater its density. Put another way, the more connected the network, the greater its network density.

15. Entire articles could—and *should*—be written that more fully delineate the implications of various network measures for specific criminological theories, including those mentioned here. For two exciting examples, see Matsueda (2006) for how networks might help understand social differentiation theory or Sampson and Graif (2009) for how the network structure of community leaders influence neighborhood levels of trust.

16. In a series of papers, Marvin Krohn (1986; Krohn et al., 1988) developed a network approach to delinquency that was based largely on the ideas of density and multiplexity. Well ahead of their time, these papers truly offered a concise theory of how certain network properties relate to delinquency.

17. A similar isolation effect also holds for the effect of network structure on suicide (Bearman and Moody, 2004).

18. The criminological literature here typically uses either the absolute number of ties of a respondent or the absolute number of ties "sent" or "received" (see Morselli, 2009). Yet as Morselli (2009) cautions it is important to understand the *content* of the tie when deciphering how network centrality should be interpreted. For instance, if arrest records or police observations are used to generate network ties, centrality may be best interpreted as "visibility" as opposed to "power" or "influence."

19. This notion of centrality entails a slightly different measure known as "betweenness" centrality (Wasserman and Faust, 1994).

20. Respondents were asked whether they had hung out during the past week or spent time with the friend during the past weekend (0 = no, 1 = yes). The measurement was created by summing all responses across friends and dividing by the square root of the total number of friends (see Haynie and Osgood, 2005).

21. Here again we can easily see how network theory can be further used to flush out additional aspects of differential association and social bonding theories. For an example of this line of theorizing, see Matsueda (2006).

22. Again, this finding is consistent with other developments in network analysis, and recent studies suggest that social influence of more distant people in one's social network can have an effect on behaviors such as obesity, smoking, and depression (e.g., Christakis and Fowler, 2007).

23. In a rather creative study, Kreager (2007) finds that young men who are on the football team or whose network is more saturated with football players are also more likely to get into fights. This suggests that other sorts of mixing or homophily tendencies within networks might also be related to delinquency and violence.

24. This, of course, sets aside moral or political reasons for invoking crime as "epidemic" that is often used in media accounts and sometimes, dare I say, even some academic accounts.

25. Eubank et al. (2004) have applied a similar logic to disease diffusion models in urban environments.

26. In theory, this process could continue to further steps, but prior research shows that much of what can be gained by social network sampling can be done within two or three steps of the foci individuals.

27. This idea dates back to Simmel's (1908 [1955]) idea of society as comprising a "web of group affiliations."

28. Questions such as these get layered in additional complexity since neighborhood research itself cannot necessarily agree on what constitutes a "neighborhood."

29. This is often referred to as the "boundary specification problem" in social network analysis (Laumann et al., 1983).

30. The sampling methods used in Figures 5.4 and 5.7 use such an approach.

Bibliography

Abbott, Andrew. *Department and Discipline: Chicago Sociology at One Hundred*. Chicago: University of Chicago Press, 1999.

Baker, Wayne E. and Robert R. Faulkner. "The Social Organization of Conspiracy: Illegal Networks in the Heavy Electrical Equipment Industry." *American Sociological Review* 58, no. 6 (1993): 837–60.

———. "Diffusion of Fraud: Intermediate Economic Crime and Investor Dynamics." *Criminology* 41, no. 4 (2003): 1173–206.

Baldassarri, Delia and Peter Bearman. "Dynamics of Political Polarization." *American Sociological Review* 72, no. 5 (2007): 784–811.

Barabasi, Albert-Laszlo. *Linked: How Everything Is Connected to Everything Else and What It Means*. New York: Plume, 2003.

Barabasi, Albert-Laszlo, H. Jeong, Z. Neda, E. Ravasaz, A. Schubert, and T. Vicsek. "Evolution of the Social Network of Scientific Collaborations." *Physica* 311 (2002): 590–614.

Bearman, Peter S. and James Moody. "Suicide and Friendships among American Adolescents." *American Journal of Public Health* 94, no. 1 (2004): 89–95.

Bearman, Peter S., James Moody, and Katherine Stovel. "Chains of Affection: The Structure of Adolescent Romantic and Sexual Networks." *American Journal of Sociology* 110, no. 1 (2004): 44–91.

Bellair, Paul E. "Social Interaction and Community Crime: Examining the Importance of Neighbor Networks." *Criminology* 35, no. 4 (1997): 677–703.

Blumstein, Alfred, Fredrick P. Rivara, and Richard Rosenfeld. "The Rise and Decline of Homicide—and Why." *Annual Review of Public Health* 21 (2000): 505–41.

Blumstein, Alfred and Joel Wallman. *The Crime Drop in America*. New York: Cambridge University Press, 2000.

Bollig, Michael. "Moral Economy and Self-Interest: Kinship, Friendship, and Exchange among the Pokot (N.W. Kenya)." In *Kinship, Networks, and Exchange*, edited by Thomas Schweizer and Douglas R. White. Cambridge: Cambridge University Press, 1998.

Braga, Anthony A. "Serious Youth Gun Offenders and the Epidemic of Youth Violence in Boston." *Journal of Quantitative Criminology* 19 (2003): 33–54.

Braga, Anthony A., David Hureau, and Christopher Winship. "Losing Faith? Police, Black Churches, and the Resurgence of Youth Violence in Boston." *Ohio State Journal of Criminal Law* 6 (2008): 141–72.

Browning, Christopher R., Seth L. Feinberg, and Robert D. Dietz. "The Paradox of Social Organization: Networks, Collective Efficacy, and Violent Crime in Urban Neighborhoods." *Social Forces* 83, no. 2 (2004): 503–34.

Burris, Val. "Interlocking Directorates and Political Cohesion among Corporate Elites." *American Journal of Sociology* 111, no. 1 (2005): 249–83.

Bursik, Robert and Harold G. Grasmick. *Neighborhoods and Crime: The Dimensions of Effective Community Control*. New York: Lexington Books, 1993.

Burt, Ronald S. "Social Contagion and Innovation: Cohesion versus Structural Equivalence." *American Journal of Sociology* 92, no. 6 (1987): 1287–335.

———. *Structural Holes*. Cambridge: Harvard University Press, 1992.

———. "Structural Holes and Good Ideas." *American Journal of Sociology* 110, no. 2 (2004): 349–99.

Carrington, Peter J. "Crime and Social Network Analysis." In *The SAGE Handbook of Social Network Analysis*. London: Sage, 2011.

Carrington, Peter J., John Scott, and Stanley Wasserman, eds. *Models and Methods in Social Network Analysis*. New York, NY: Cambridge University Press, 2005.

Chang, Myong-Hun and Joseph E. Harrington, Jr. "Discovery and Diffusion of Knowledge in an Endogenous Social Network." *American Journal of Sociology* 110, no. 4 (2005): 937–76.

Christakis, Nicholas A. and James H. Fowler. "The Spread of Obesity in a Large Social Network over 32 Years." *New England Journal of Medicine* 357 (2007): 370–79.

———. *Connected: The Surprising Power of Our Social Networks and How They Shape Our Lives*. New York: Little, Brown, and Co., 2009.

————. "Social Network Sensors for Early Detection of Contagious Outbreaks." *PLoS ONE* 5, no. 9 (2010): e12948. doi:10.1371/journal. pone.0012948.

Cloward, Richard A. and Lloyd Ohlin. *Delinquency and Opportunity: A Theory of Delinquent Gangs*. Glenco, IL: Free Press, 1960.

Cohen, Jacqueline and George Tita. "Diffusion in Homicide: Exploring a General Method for Detecting Spatial Diffusion Processes." *Journal of Quantitative Criminology* 15, no. 4 (1999): 451–93.

Coleman, James S. "Social Capital in the Creation of Human Capital." *American Journal of Sociology* 94, Supplement: Organizations and Institutions: Sociological and Economic Approaches to the Analysis of Social Structure (1988): S95–120.

Dorogovtsev, S. N. and J. F. F. Mendes. "Evolution of Networks." *Advanced Physics* 51, no. 4 (2002): 1079–187.

Dukstra, Jan Kornelis, Siegwart Lindenberg, Rene Beenstra, Christian Steglich, Jenny Issacs, Noel Card, and Ernest V. Hodges. "Influence and Selection Processes in Weapon Carrying During Adolescence: The Role of Status, Aggression, and Vulnerability." *Criminology* 48, no. 1 (2010): 187–220.

Emirbayer, Mustafa. "Manifesto for a Relational Sociology." *The American Journal of Sociology* 103, no. 2 (1997): 281.

Eubank, S., H. Guclu, V. S. A. Kumar, M. V. Marathe, A. Srinivasan, Z. Toroczkai, and N. Wang. "Modelling Disease Outbreaks in Realistic Urban Social Networks." *Nature* 429, no. 6988 (2004): 180–84.

Fernandez, Roberto M. and M. Lourdes Sosa. "Gendering the Job: Networks and Recruitment at a Call Center." *American Journal of Sociology* 111, no. 3 (2005): 859–904.

Fleisher, Mark S. *Dead End Kids: Gang Girls and the Boys They Know*. Madison, WI: University of Wisconsin Press, 1998.

————. "Fieldwork Research and Social Network Analysis: Different Methods Creating Complementary Perspectives." *Journal of Contemporary Criminal Justice* 21, no. 2 (2005): 120–34.

————. "Youth Gang Social Dynamics and Social Network Analysis: Applying Degree Centrality Measures to Assess the Nature of Gang Boundaries." In *Studying Youth Gangs*, edited by James F. Short, Jr. and Lorine A. Hughes. Lanham, MD: Alta Mira, 2006.

Gilbert, D. T., M. A. Killingsworth, R. N. Eyre, and T. D. Wilson. "The Surprising Power of Neighborly Advice." *Science* 323, no. 5921 (2009): 1617–19.

Gladwell, Malcolm. *Tipping Point: How Little Things Can Make a Big Difference*. New York: Little, Brown, and Co., 2000.

Gottfredson, Michael R. and Travis Hirschi. *A General Theory of Crime*. Stanford, CA: Stanford University Press, 1990.

Gould, Roger V. "Patron-Client Ties, State Centralization, and the Whiskey Rebellion." *American Journal of Sociology* 102, no. 2 (1996): 400–29.

———. *Collision of Wills: How Ambiguity about Social Rank Breeds Conflict*. Chicago: University Chicago Press, 2003.

Grannis, Rick. *From the Ground Up: Translating Geography into Community through Neighborhood Networks*. Princeton, NJ: Princeton University Press, 2009.

Granovetter, Mark S. "The Strength of Weak Ties." *American Journal of Sociology* 78, no. 6 (1973): 1360–80.

Hannerz, Ulf. *Soulside: Inquiries into Ghetto Culture and Community*. New York: Columbia University Press, 1969.

Haynie, Dana L. "Delinquent Peers Revisited: Does Network Structure Matter?" *American Journal of Sociology* 106, no. 4 (2001): 1013–57.

———. "Friendship Networks and Delinquency: The Relative Nature of Peer Delinquency." *Journal of Quantitative Criminology* 18 (2002): 99–134.

Haynie, Dana L. and D. Wayne Osgood. "Reconsidering Peers and Delinquency: How Do Peers Matter?" *Social Forces* 84, no. 2 (2005): 1109–30.

Haynie, Dana L. and Danielle C. Payne. "Race, Friendship Networks, and Violent Delinquency." *Criminology* 44, no. 4 (2006): 775–805.

Heckathorn, Douglas D. "Extensions of Respondent-Driven Sampling: Analyzing Continuous Variables and Controlling for Differential Recruitment." *Sociological Methodology* 37, no. 1 (2007): 151–207.

Heisman, M. and Tom Snijders. "Statistical Analysis of Longitudinal Network Data with Changing Composition." *Sociological Methods and Research* 32 (2003): 253–87.

Hipp, John R. "Micro-Structure in Micro-Neighborhoods: A New Social Distance Measure, and Its Effects on Individual and Aggregated Perceptions of Crime and Disorder." *Social Networks* 32, no. 2 (2010): 148–59.

Houseman, Michael and Douglas R. White. "Network Mediation of Exchange Structures: Ambilateral Sidedness and Property Flows in Pul Eliya (Sri Lanka)." In *Kinship, Networks, and Exchange*, edited by Thomas Schweizer and Douglas R. White. Cambridge: Cambridge University Press, 1998.

Janowitz, Morris. "Sociological Theory and Social Control." *American Journal of Sociology* 81 (1975): 82–108.

Johnson, Neil F., Chen Xu, Zhenyuan Zhao, Nicolas Ducheneaut, Nicholas Yee, George Tita, and Mak Ming Hui. "Human Group Formation in Online Guilds and Offline Gangs Driven by a Common Team Dynamic." *Physical Review E* 79 (2009): 1–11.

Klein, Malcolm W. and Lois Y. Crawford. "Groups, Gangs, and Cohesiveness." *Journal of Research in Crime and Delinquency* 4, no. 1 (1967): 63–75.

Klein, Malcolm W. and Cheryl L. Maxson. *Street Gang Patterns and Policies*. New York: Oxford University Press, 2006.

Klerks, Peter. "The Network Paradigm Applied to Criminal Organizations: Theoretical Nitpicking or a Relevant Doctrine for Investigators? Recent Developments in the Netherlands." *Connections* 24, no. 3 (2001): 53–65.

Knoke, David. "Networks of Political Action: Toward Theory Construction." *Social Forces* 68, no. 4 (1990): 1041–63.

Kreager, Derek A. "Strangers in the Halls: Isolation and Delinquency in School Networks." *Social Forces* 83, no. 1 (2004): 351–90.

———. "Unnecessary Roughness? School Sports, Peer Networks, and Male Adolescent Violence." *American Sociological Review* 72, no. 5 (2007): 705–24.

Krohn, Marvin D. "The Web of Conformity: A Network Approach to the Explanation of Delinquent Behavior." *Social Forces* 33, no. 6 (1986): 381–93.

Krohn, Marvin D., J. L. Massey, and M. Zielinski. "Role Overlap, Network Multiplexity, and Adolescent Deviant Behavior." *Social Psychological Quarterly* 51, no. 4 (1988): 346–56.

Laumann, Edward O., Peter V. Marsden, and David Prensky. "The Boundary Specification Problem in Network Analysis." In *Applied Network Analysis*, edited by Ronald S. Burt and Michael Minor. Beverly Hills, CA: Sage, 1983.

Leenders, Roger Th. A. J. "Modeling Social Influence through Network Autocorrelation: Constructing the Weight Matrix." *Social Networks* 24 (2002): 21–47.

Lipsey, M. W. and D. B. Wilson. "Effective Intervention for Serious Juvenile Offenders." In *Serious and Violent Juvenile Offenders: Risk Factors and Successful Interventions*, edited by Ralph Loeber and David P. Farrington, 248–83. Thousand Oaks, CA: Sage, 1998.

Marsden, Peter V. "Core Discussion Networks of Americans." *American Sociological Review* 52, no. 1 (1987): 122–31.

Matsueda, Ross L. "Differential Social Organization, Collective Action, and Crime." *Crime, Law, and Social Change* 46 (2006): 3–33.

McGloin, Jean Marie. "Policy Intervention Considerations of a Network Analysis of Street Gangs." *Criminology and Public Policy* 4, no. 3 (2005): 607.

———. "The Organizational Structure of Street Gangs in Newark, New Jersey: A Network Analysis of Methodology." *Journal of Gang Research* 15, no. 1 (2007): 1–34.

McGloin, Jean Marie and David S. Kirk. "Social Network Analysis." In *Handbook of Quantitative Criminology*, edited by David Weisburd and Alex R. Piquero, 209–24. New York: Springer, 2010.

———. "An Overview of Social Network Analysis." *Journal of Criminal Justice Education*, forthcoming.

McGloin, Jean Marie and Lauren O'Neill Shermer. "Self-Control and Deviant Peer Network Structure." *Journal of Research in Crime and Delinquency* 46, no. 1 (2009): 35–72.

McGloin, Jean Marie and A. R. Piquero. "On the Relationship between Co-offending Network Redundancy and Offending Versatility." *Journal of Research in Crime and Delinquency* 47 (2010): 63–90.

McGloin, Jean Marie, Christopher J. Sullivan, Alex R. Piquero, and Sarah Bacon. "Investigating the Stability of Co-offending and Co-offenders among a Sample of Youthful Offenders." *Criminology* 46, no. 1 (2008): 155–88.

McIllwain, Jeffrey Scott. "Organized Crime: A Social Network Approach." *Crime, Law, and Social Change* 32 (2000): 301–23.

McPherson, Miller, Lynn Smith-Lovin, and James M. Cook. "Birds of a Feather: Homophily in Social Networks." *Annual Review of Sociology* 27 (2001): 415–44.

Moody, James. "Race, School Integration, and Friendship Segregation in America." *American Journal of Sociology* 107, no. 3 (2001): 679–716.

Morenoff, Jeffrey D., Robert J. Sampson, and Stephen W. Raudenbush. "Neighborhood Inequality, Collective Efficacy, and the Spatial Dynamics of Urban Violence." *Criminology* 39, no. 3 (2001): 517–59.

Morselli, Carlo. "Career Opportunities and Network-Based Privileges in the Cosa Nostra." *Crime, Law, and Social Change* 39, no. 4 (2003): 383–418.

———. *Inside Criminal Networks*. New York: Springer, 2009.

Morselli, Carlo, Cynthia Giguere, and Katia Petit. "The Efficiency/Security Trade-off in Criminal Networks." *Social Networks* 29, no. 1 (2007): 143–53.

Morselli, Carlo and Julie Roy. "Brokerage Qualifications in Ringing Operations." *Criminology* 46, no. 1 (2008): 71–98.

Natarajan, Mangai. "Understanding the Structure of a Large Heroin Distribution Network: A Quantitative Analysis of Qualitative Data." *Journal of Quantitative Criminology* 22, no. 2 (2006): 171–92.

Papachristos, Andrew V. "Social Network Analysis and Gang Research: Theory and Methods." In *Studying Youth Gangs*, edited by James F. Short and Lorine A. Hughes. Lanham, MD: AltaMira Press, 2006.

———. "Murder by Structure: Dominance Relations and the Social Structure of Gang Homicide." *American Journal of Sociology* 115, no. 1 (2009): 74–128.

———. "The Small World of Murders." *Chicago Sun-Times*, January 28, 2011.

Papachristos, Andrew V., Anthony A. Braga, and David Hureau. "The Small World of Shootings: Violent Victimization in Risky Social Networks." Working paper, Harvard University, 2010.

Papachristos, Andrew V., David Hureau, and Anthony A. Braga. "Conflict and the Corner: The Impact of Intergroup Conflict and Geographic Turf on Gang Violence." Working paper, 2010. *Social Science*

Research Network. Available at SSRN: http://ssrn.com/abstract=1722329 (accessed December 20, 2010).

Pattillo-McCoy, Mary. *Black Picket Fences: Privilege and Peril among the Black Middle Class*. Chicago: University of Chicago Press, 1999.

Payne, Danielle C. and Benjamin Cornwell. "Reconsidering Peer Influences on Delinquency: Do Less Proximate Contacts Matter?" *Journal of Quantitative Criminology* 23 (2007): 127–49.

Pedahzur, Ami and Arie Perliger. "The Changing Nature of Suicide Attacks: A Social Network Perspective." *Social Forces* 84, no. 4 (2006): 1987–2008.

Robbins, Gary, Tom Snijders, P. Wang, Mark Handcock, and P. Pattison. "Recent Developments in Exponential Random Graph (p*) Models for Social Networks." *Social Networks* 29, no. 2 (2007): 192–215.

Sampson, Robert J. "Whither the Sociological Study of Crime?" *Annual Review of Sociology* 26 (2000): 711–14.

———. "Networks and Neighbourhoods: The Implications of Connectivity for Thinking about Crime in the Modern City." In *Network Logic: Who Governs in an Interconnected World?* edited by Helen McCarthy, Paul Miller, and Paul Skidmore, 157–66. London: Demos, 2004.

Sampson, Robert J. and Corina Graif. "Neighborhood Networks and Processes of Trust." In *Whom Can We Trust? How Groups, Networks, and Institutions Make Trust Possible*, edited by Karen S. Cook, Margaret Levi, and Russell Hardin. New York: Russell Sage Foundation, 2009.

Sampson, Robert J., Jeffrey D. Morenoff, and Thomas Gannon-Rowley. "Assessing 'Neighborhood Effects': Social Processes and New Directions in Research." *Annual Review of Sociology* 28 (2002): 443–78.

Sampson, Robert J., Stephen W. Raudenbush, and Felton Earls. "Neighborhoods and Violent Crime: A Multilevel Study of Collective Efficacy." *Science* 277 (1997): 918–24.

Schwartz, Daniel M. and Tony Rouselle. "Using Social Network Analysis to Target Criminal Networks." *Trends in Organized Crime* 12, no. 2 (2009): 188–207.

Shaw, Clifford R. and Henry D. McKay. *Juvenile Delinquency and Urban Areas*. Chicago: University of Chicago Press, 1942.

Simmel, Georg. *Conflict and the Web of Group Affiliations*. New York: The Free Press, 1908 [1955].

Snijders, T. A. B. "The Statistical Evaluation of Social Network Dynamics." *Sociological Methods* 31 (2001): 361–95.

Snijders, T. A. B., C. E. G. Steglich, and G. G. van de Bunt. "Introduction to Actor-based Models for Network Dynamics." *Social Networks* 32 (2010): 44–60.

Stack, Carol B. *All Our Kin: Strategies for Survival in a Black Community*. New York: Basic Books, 1970.

Stoneburner, R. L. and D. Low-Beer. "Population-level HIV Declines and Behavioral Risk Avoidance in Uganda." *Science* 304, no. 5671 (2004): 714–18.

Sutherland, Edwin H. *Principles of Criminology.* 4th ed. Philadelphia, PA: J.B. Lippincott, 1947.

Suttles, Gerald D. *The Social Order of the Slum; Ethnicity and Territory in the Inner City.* Chicago: University of Chicago Press, 1968.

Thomas, William I. and Florian Znaniecki. *The Polish Peasant in Europe and America.* Chicago: University of Chicago Press, 1918–1920.

Thompson, Maxine Seaborn. "The Influence of Supportive Relations on the Psychological Well-Being of Teenage Mothers." *Social Forces* 64, no. 4 (1986): 1006–24.

Tita, George, Kiminori Makamura, and David Krackhardt. "The Structure of Gang Rivalries: Using Balance Theory to Explore Patterns of Gang Violence." *Paper Presented at the Annual Meeting of the American Society of Criminology.* 1 November 2006, Los Angeles, CA.

Tita, George, K. Jack Riley, Greg Ridgeway, Clifford Crammich, Allan F. Abrahamse, and Peter W. Greenwood. *Reducing Gun Violence: Results from an Intervention in East Los Angeles.* Santa Monica, CA: RAND Corporation, 2003.

Tita, George and Robert Greenbaum. "Crime, Neighborhoods, and Units of Analysis: Putting Space in Its Place." In *Putting Crime in Its Place*, edited by David Weisburd, Wim Bernasco, and Gerben Bruinsma. New York: Springer, 2009.

van der Hulst, Renee C. "Introduction to Social Network Analysis (SNA) as an Investigative Tool." *Trends in Organized Crime* 12, no. 2 (2009): 101–21.

Venkatesh, Sudhir A. *Off the Books: The Underground Economy of the Urban Poor.* Cambridge, MA: Harvard University Press, 2006.

Warr, Mark. *Companions in Crime: The Social Aspects of Criminal Conduct.* New York: Cambridge University Press, 2002.

Wasserman, Stanley, Carolyn J. Anderson, and Bradley Crouch. "A p* Primer: Logit Models for Social Networks." *Social Networks* 21 (1999): 37–66.

Wasserman, Stanley and Katherine Faust. *Social Network Analysis: Methods and Applications.* Cambridge: Cambridge University Press, 1994.

Watts, Duncan J. "Networks, Dynamics, and the Small-World Phenomenon." *American Journal of Sociology* 105, no. 2 (1999): 493–527.

———. *Six Degrees: The Science of a Connected Age.* New York: W. W. Norton, 2003.

Watts, Duncan J., P. S. Dodds, and M. E. J. Newman. "Identity and Search in Social Networks." *Science* 296, no. 5571 (2002): 1302–5.

Watts, Duncan J. and S. H. Strogatz. "Collective Dynamics of 'Small-world' Networks." *Nature* 393, no. 6684 (1998): 440–42.

Weerman, Frank M. and Wilma H. Smeenk. "Peer Similarity in Delinquency for Different Types of Friends: A Comparison Using Two Measurement Methods." *Criminology* 43, no. 2 (2005): 499–524.

Wellman, Barry. "Network Analysis: Some Basic Principles." *Sociological Theory* 1 (1983): 155–200.

Whyte, William Foote. *Street Corner Society: The Social Structure of an Italian Slum*. Chicago: University of Chicago Press, 1943.

Wilson, William J. *The Truly Disadvantaged: The Inner City, the Underclass, and Public Policy*. Chicago: University of Chicago Press, 1987.

Xu, J. and H. C. Chen. "Untangling Criminal Networks: A Case Study." In *Intelligence and Security Informatics, Proceedings*, vol. 2665, 232–48. Berlin: Springer-Verlag, 2003. http://www.springerlink.com/content/4rn8l185w0rvl931/fulltext.pdf.

Young, Jacob T. N. "How Do They 'End Up Together'? A Social Network Analysis of Self-Control, Homophily, and Adolescent Relationships." *Journal of Quantitative Criminology*, forthcoming.

6

What Can Genetically Informed Research Tell Us about the Causes of Crime?

Candice L. Odgers and Michael A. Russell

Genes play an important role in shaping human traits. Reams of research now exist pointing to the influence of genes on a wide spectrum of traits and behaviors, ranging from susceptibility to mental disorders (Cannon et al., 1998; Hicks et al., 2004) and intelligence (Devlin et al., 1997) to whether an individual is more likely to turn out to vote in the next political election (Fowler et al., 2008). In fact, virtually every single behavior and trait studied to date has been shown to be under at least some genetic influence (Plomin et al., 2008). Thus, it comes as no surprise that genes are believed to explain at least a portion of the variation observed across individuals with respect to antisocial behavior and crime.

Meta-analytic work indicates that genes are responsible for approximately 50 percent of the variance in antisocial behavior and related outcomes, an estimate that places us squarely back in the middle of the centuries-old nature versus nurture debate. A nonzero estimate of the heritability coefficient for a trait lets us know that genes are involved (as they almost always are). However, heritability estimates are widely criticized as being prone to error, sensitive to methodological factors, and, perhaps most importantly, silent on the issue of *which* genes are involved. Rather than knowing whether a trait is heritable, most observers would like to know whether genetic information can be used to predict criminal behavior and related outcomes. At the risk of spoiling the plot of the chapter that follows, our answer to this question is "no" or at least "not yet." Simply put, genetically informative research has not yet reached the stage where it can reliably inform predictive models and practice in criminology. With that said, there are a number of exciting areas of research that are causing us to rethink how environmental factors may interact with genetic vulnerabilities to increase the likelihood of antisocial behavior. For example, emerging findings from gene-by-environment (G × E) studies, along with the use of genetically informed research designs to test whether proposed risk factors for crime are *environmentally mediated*, are providing new opportunities for discovery in criminological research. Our discussion will review the latest findings from genetically informed research designs related to antisocial behavior while considering whether "G" (genes) may eventually become a useful part of the crime equation. Throughout this review, we use the term "crime" and "criminality" to refer to a range of associated traits, including antisocial behavior, delinquency, aggression, and involvement in official offending.

The Crime Gene Does Not Exist

Let us begin our discussion with a simple assertion: *there are no genes for crime*. All of the single gene disorders have been identified (e.g., cystic fibrosis, hemophilia, Huntington disease, sickle-cell disease) and complex behaviors, such as criminality and antisocial behavior, are not among them. The most plausible view of genetic contributions to crime assumes that multiple genes are involved through their role in coding for enzymes and proteins that influence psychological processes that may make an individual more or less vulnerable to participation in antisocial behavior or crime. More recently, genetic contributions to complex behaviors have been conceptualized as being conditional on environmental risk factors, with epigenetic and gene expression studies challenging the idea that our genetic code is fixed. Within this framework, genes are not necessarily expected to exert a main effect on behavior but instead are assumed to create vulnerabilities that may be expressed *if* certain environmental conditions are present (see, e.g., work by Caspi et al., 2002). In addition, epigenetic research is providing compelling evidence that genes can be altered via environmental exposures (Meaney, 2010). This line of research has fundamentally changed our deterministic conceptualization of genes as fixed variables and raises the possibility that the expression of genes may vary across both context and development.

These conceptual shifts in understanding genetic contributions to criminality have left researchers with the daunting task of disentangling how complex systems of genes interact with each other—and the environment—to influence behavior. Genes have now become moving and dynamic targets within social science research, where linear and additive models of influence are no longer sufficient prerequisites for building explanatory models. To this end, genetically informed research is rapidly moving away from the estimation of heritability coefficients and toward approaches that can help to isolate the role of specific genetic *and* environmental factors in antisocial behavior. The following section briefly reviews what we have learned from classic twin studies of antisocial behavior and describes how researchers are moving beyond heritability in their search for genetic causes of crime. Throughout the review, we emphasize the point that, somewhat ironically, genetically informative research designs have become one of our most powerful tools for isolating *environmentally mediated* causes of crime.

Antisocial Behavior Is 50 Percent Heritable—So What?

Since the 1960s, hundreds of twin and adoption studies of antisocial behavior have been conducted (for a review see Slutske, 2001; Moffitt, 2005). These studies consistently show that antisocial behavior is at least partly heritable. Heritability estimates are typically derived based on studies of twins where the concordance of a given trait between monozygotic (MZ) twin pairs, who share 100 percent of their genes, and dizygotic (DZ) twin pairs, who share 50 percent of their genes, is compared. The primary objective of behavioral genetic analyses is to decompose the variance associated with a trait into its genetic and environmental components. Heritability estimates refer to the genetic effects and quantify the amount of variation in a behavior or trait that can be attributed to genetic factors.

Because the degree of environmental similarity is assumed to be equal for both MZ and DZ twin pairs reared together (known as the *equal environment assumption*), a higher trait correlation for MZ twins compared to DZ twins indicates a genetic effect. Although the equal environment assumption has been widely criticized, scholars have also argued that violations of this assumption are unlikely to significantly bias the heritability coefficients (for a more complete discussion, see Rutter, 2006). In the twin design, the observed trait correlation is assumed to be composed of the following constituent parts (see Rijsdijk & Sham, 2002 for a more complete decomposition of the twin model):

- *a*, which represents the additive effects of all alleles at all loci that influence the trait;
- *d*, which represents nonadditive genetic effects such as those resulting from allelic interactions at a single locus (dominance) or interactions between alleles at different loci (epistasis);

- *c*, which represents the effect of environmental experiences that are shared by twins (the common or shared environment); and
- *e*, which represents the effects of environmental experiences that are *not* shared by twins such as specific injury or trama that contribute to differences between them.

Each of these components is represented as a squared term, thus denoting its nature as a portion of variance. These components, when summed, make up the total phenotypic variation (P) observed for any given trait (Rijsdijk and Sham, 2002; Maes, 2005), such that $a^2 + d^2 + c^2 + e^2 = P$. The contribution of each of these variance components can be estimated in twin studies because MZ and DZ twins differ in their degree of genetic similarity. Members of MZ twin pairs have correlations of 1.0 for the a^2 and d^2 terms because they are assumed to share 100 percent of their genes, whereas DZ twins have correlations of 0.5 and 0.25 for these terms, respectively. Both MZ and DZ twins correlate 1.0 for c^2 and 0 for e^2, because the degree of environmental similarity is assumed not to differ between MZ and DZ twin pairs. Heritability (h^2) is calculated as the proportion of genetic variance to the total phenotypic variance, such that $h^2 = (a^2 + d^2)/P$ (Falconer and Mackay, 1996) and thus represents the total genotypic effect on the measured trait.

Results derived from twin studies have been challenging to synthesize, given the wide-ranging heritability estimates they report. For example, published estimates for antisocial behavior range from .00 to .98, or from nonexistent to explaining nearly all of the variance in the measured trait (Plomin et al., 1981; Baker et al., 2007). Moreover, methodological factors have been shown to partially explain the range of observed heritability estimates. To present an extreme example, one study that used multi-measure, multi-informant concurrent reports of antisocial behavior found a heritability of .98 among a sample of nine- to ten-year-old twins and triplets (Baker et al., 2007), whereas another study (Fu et al., 2007) found that 19 percent of the variance in conduct disorder (CD) was explained by genes among a sample of adult male twins who retrospectively reported childhood symptoms of CD.

Four meta-analytic reviews of twin and adoption studies on the heritability of crime and antisocial behavior have synthesized the often incongruent findings across studies (Walters, 1992; Mason and Frick, 1994; Miles and Carey, 1997; Rhee and Waldman, 2002). The first of these, Walters (1992), reported a moderate-to-low genetic influence on criminality (mostly official report), as evidenced by a mean unweighted phi coefficient of .25 and a mean weighted phi coefficient of .09 across eleven family, fourteen twin, and thirteen adoption studies. A meta-analysis conducted by Mason and Frick (1994) found an average heritability (h^2) coefficient of .48 across twelve twin and three adoption studies, suggesting that 48 percent of the variance in criminality, aggression, and antisocial personality can be explained by genetic factors. Similarly, Miles and Carey (1997) found that genes accounted for up to 50 percent of the variance in aggression across twenty twin and four adoption studies and reported a higher heritability estimate for aggression in males, although the effect was small.

The most comprehensive meta-analysis of the genetic and environmental effects on antisocial behavior to date was conducted by Rhee and Waldman (2002). They found that across forty-two independent twin and ten independent adoption samples, 41 percent of the variance in antisocial behavior was estimated to be explained by genetic factors whereas 59 percent of the variance was attributed to the environment. Heritability estimates were the highest in studies of criminality versus all other operationalizations ($h^2 = .69$ versus .50 to .36). Heritability was also higher in studies using other methods (including official report)— versus self-report assessment methods of antisocial behavior ($h^2 = .53$ versus .39) and in studies using only one type of zygosity determination method versus studies using a combination ($h^2 = .43$ to .47 versus .39). It is important to note that *all* of the studies assessing criminality included in Rhee and Waldman's (2002) meta-analysis used official report, leaving the possibility that the higher heritability estimate found in studies of criminality may be due to the assessment method. However, because the assessment method and the outcome were completely confounded in the case of criminality, the possibility of a methodologically driven effect could not be tested. Despite these limitations, the scope and rigor of Rhee and Waldman's (2002) meta-analysis help make a strong case that methodological factors are important to consider when interpreting heritability coefficients.

Taken together, these four meta-analyses suggest that approximately 50 percent of the variance between individuals in antisocial behavior and crime can be explained by genes and that the wide-ranging heritability estimates observed across studies can be, at least partially, explained by methodological factors. The fact that only one of the four meta-analyses reported a significant moderating effect for sex (Miles and Carey, 1997) suggests that although antisocial behavior is more *prevalent* among males than females (Moffitt et al., 2001), it may not be more *heritable*.

Has the Classic Twin Design Outlived Its Usefulness?

Twin-based studies and the behavioral genetic models used to derive heritability estimates have been heavily criticized due to the underlying assumptions and assumed values that are fed into the models, as well as their inability to identify specific genes that may be influencing a behavior. The list of criticisms waged against twin studies is lengthy, with some claiming that behavioral genetics is built on faulty (or muddled) mathematical models and may be best characterized as pseudoscience (Schonemann, 1997; Joseph, 2002). One of the main criticisms of the twin design is that the "equal environment assumption" for MZ and DZ twins may be unlikely to hold as the environments experienced by members of MZ twin pairs are likely to have a higher similarity than those experienced by DZ pairs. Critics also charge that measurement error is not taken into account when estimating the models and that twins are not representative of the larger population. With respect to the interpretation of the model estimates, the heritability coefficient is assumed to represent the additive genetic contribution to the trait or behavior. However, heritability estimates are likely to be inflated as they also capture $G \times E$ interactions that are influencing the trait. Perhaps most importantly, heritability estimates can inform questions related to *whether* genes contribute to behavior but are silent on the issue of *what* genes are involved.

Now that the mapping of the human genome is complete, and we have the ability to measure genes directly, many observers argue that twin studies are no longer useful. Instead the field has shifted toward the measurement of specific genes (candidate genes) that may play a functional role in biosocial models of criminal behavior. In this sense, twin studies are seen as one of the first stepping stones in the process of isolating genes that may be involved in antisocial behavior. Within this approach, heritability estimates are used to evaluate whether a given trait may be a good candidate for future studies involving molecular genetics. Despite the harsh criticism that twin studies have received, many believe that the twin study design has not outlived its usefulness. Advocates argue that twin designs continue to play a vital role in facilitating quasi-experimental tests of environmental explanations (Rutter et al., 2001; Johnson et al., 2009) and continue to provide appropriate genetic and environmental controls when estimating the effects of a wide range of risk factors on antisocial behavior (many of which are known to be subject to pervasive selection effects).

Leveraging the Classic Twin Design to Facilitate Causal Inference

Twin designs (and to a lesser extent sibling designs) offer the advantage of controlling for both genetic and environmental factors and can serve as quasi-experimental tests of environmental theories. While randomized experiments represent the gold standard with respect to testing causal theories, when the outcomes of interest are crime and antisocial behavior, it is often not feasible or ethical to design these types of studies. Although not perfect, twin designs provide a way of approximating the features of randomized studies and playing out the counterfactual scenarios required for testing whether effects may be environmentally mediated (see, e.g., McGue et al., 2010). Simply put, we want to estimate what the outcomes would have been among individuals exposed to a given risk factor if they had not been exposed (or vice versa). Because MZ twins share 100 percent of their genes, studies that include MZ twins provide a means of controlling for genetic factors when estimating environmental effects (in addition to offering controls for the shared environment). In other words, they provide an opportunity to approximate the counterfactual condition in situations where twin pairs are discordant for exposure. In this sense, the use of children from the same family can approximate experimental conditions and disentangle environmentally mediated effects from those attributable to selection and confounding factors.

Over the last decade, quasi-experimental and genetically informed studies have provided a means of testing whether exposures to some of the main social and familial risk factors for crime are environmentally mediated versus, for example, an artifact of shared propensity for antisocial behavior or selection into given environments (the largest confounds in developmental criminology). For example, Maughan and colleagues (2004) addressed whether maternal smoking during pregnancy exerts a causal effect on children's antisocial behavior. Although numerous studies had documented a prospective link between mother's smoking habits during pregnancy and child outcomes, questions remained as to whether this effect was due to other confounding factors, such as the fact women who smoke during pregnancy are also more likely to experience mental health problems, come from a disadvantaged background, and partner with antisocial men. By controlling for antisocial behavior in both parents, depression in mothers, family disadvantage, *and genetic influences*, estimates for the effects of prenatal smoking on antisocial behavior during childhood were greatly reduced—and in some cases eliminated (reductions in the effect size ranged from 75 to 100 percent across outcomes). These findings called into question the causal nature of the widely documented correlation between prenatal smoking and children's antisocial behavior and raise doubts regarding conclusions that are reached in the absence of strict controls.

Jaffee and colleagues (2004a, 2004b, 2005) have also tackled the issue of whether we can conduct more stringent tests of widely observed associations between early adversity and children's antisocial behavior. The authors used data from the Environmental-Risk (E-Risk) Longitudinal Study, a prospective study of 2,232 same-sex twins assessed starting at birth and followed through into early adolescence. Their findings supported the hypothesis that physical maltreatment plays a causal role in the development of children's antisocial behavior and exerts an effect that is, at least partially, environmentally mediated (versus the alternative explanation that the association between early maltreatment by caregivers and children's behavior problems can be attributed to a shared genetic propensity for antisocial outcomes). Using a similar research design, Kim-Cohen and colleagues (2005) found that although familial liability for antisocial behavior accounted for approximately one-third of the observed association between maternal depression and children's behavioral problems, maternal depression appeared to exert an effect on children's behavioral problems through a socially mediated risk process (an effect that was over and above the estimated shared genetic transmission of risk).

Wright and Beaver (2005) applied a similar twin difference model to test Gottfredson and Hirschi's theory of low self-control, one of the most influential theories within criminology. The authors brought a genetically informative research design to bear on the issue as the theory assumes that the development of low self-control can be attributed primarily to parenting factors, yet research consistently documents that low self-control is under substantial genetic influence. Their analyses suggest that, once genetic factors are accounted for, parenting measures have weak and inconsistent effects on low self-control. The implication of their findings is that causal attributions regarding the role of parents in the development of low self-control may be skewed due to the failure to recognize genetic influences on behavior.

Taken together, these findings illustrate the usefulness of the twin design to test the mechanisms through which some of the widely documented risk factors for the development of antisocial behavior operate, including exposure to toxins in utero, parental psychopathology, maltreatment, and the presence of low self-control. While prior research has acknowledged that selection issues may be confounding the association between these risk factors and outcomes, the use of twin difference score models provides the opportunity to introduce more stringent controls when testing for independent effects on antisocial behavior.

Moving Beyond Behavioral Genetics: Measured Genes and Antisocial Behavior

The mapping of the human genome and advances in molecular genetics over the last decade have spurred great interest in the identification of specific genes that may influence involvement in complex behaviors, such as criminality. Molecular genetics approaches include genome-wide association studies and candidate gene studies, where the objective is to identify specific genes that may be implicated in biological pathways involved in behaviors, as well as gene regulation and gene expression studies, where the goal is to understand which factors may restrict or promote transcription of DNA areas (epigenetics) and the quantification of how much mRNA is being transcribed (gene expression).

Early findings linking genes to psychiatric disorders fueled excitement in genetics research. However, this initial enthusiasm has been tempered by small effect sizes, non-replication of key findings, and the eventual acceptance that complex—and nonlinear—systems of genetic and environmental influence are likely involved. With respect to genome-wide analyses, only a handful of studies have located specific genes involved in antisocial behavior where the effects have reached genome-wide significance (for a review see Gunter et al., 2010). Moreover, genome-wide linkage studies of CD and related behaviors (e.g., Dick et al., 2004; Stallings et al., 2005; Kendler et al., 2006; Viding et al., 2010), for the most part, have not converged on the same chromosomal regions. Similarly, main effect studies using a candidate gene approach (where the genes of interest are identified a priori) have produced mixed and seemingly disappointing results (Craig and Halton, 2009).

The majority of genes that have been implicated in antisocial behavior (albeit with small effects) are located within the dopaminergic and serotonergic pathways. For example, candidate gene studies have reported a main effect association between polymorphisms in the serotonin transporter gene 5HTTLPR and conduct problems (Beitchman et al., 2006; Sakai et al., 2006). Genes in the dopamine neurotransmitter system that have been implicated in conduct problems include the dopamine receptor DRD4 and the dopamine transporter DAT1 (Holmes et al., 2002; Guo et al., 2007). However, not all replications of these findings have been positive (e.g., Schulz-Heik et al., 2008). In addition, the effects of specific genes are small and, in many cases, are conditional on environmental factors (Kendler, 2005; Moffitt, 2005).

Complex behaviors are often accounted for by tens or even hundreds of interacting genes that in the end only account for a fraction of the overall variance. Thus, the current working model for the field assumes that "many genes of small effect" are likely to underlie the majority of complex human behaviors and traits (Plomin et al., 2009). Although, to date, genetic research has disappointed many in search of genes that may be related to criminality, this line of inquiry has provided a unique window for understanding environmental causes of crime and the interplay between genes and environment. Thus, while the search continues for genes that predict antisocial behavior, a new field of research that is focused on the types of environments that may matter for gene expression and G × E interplay is exploding.

Studies That Include "G" Can Tell Us a Lot about "E"

Genetically informative research designs can often tell us as much, if not more, about how environmental factors shape the propensity for antisocial behavior and crime. In fact, some of the most exciting genetic discoveries in psychiatric and behavioral genetics over the last decade have *not* been about how genes cause behaviors or disorders; rather, the watershed moments in this field have focused on how the *environment* may act upon our genetic makeup to influence behavior. For example, Michael Meaney, a biologist at McGill University, opened up a new frontier in the nature versus nurture debate when he provided evidence that epigenetic changes (that is, factors that restrict or promote transcription of DNA areas, effectively switching gene expression "on or off") can occur as the result of experiences after birth. In a series of experiments, Meaney and his colleagues found evidence of distinct DNA methylation patterns in the hippocampus cells of infant rats who had randomly been assigned to a condition where they experienced grooming from their mother after birth versus those that were neglected. In addition to the differences at the genetic level, the well-groomed rats demonstrated better development in the hippocampi, released less of the stress hormone cortisol, and were calmer than their neglected counterparts when startled. The authors concluded that maternal behavior had literally helped to shape the brains of the rat pups (Weaver et al., 2004)! This was an extraordinary finding as it began to move us away from the idea that "genes are destiny" and provided evidence that interpersonal interactions and the social environment may be leading to epigenetic changes. Upon reflecting on advances in epigenetics and related research, Meaney (2010) has commented that it is a "rather arcane notion that we can partition the causes of individual differences into distinct genetic or environmental spheres of influence" (p. 41). More specifically, he argues that we need to abandon our additive models of influence (such as the equation detailed above for heritability) and respond to the demand of science in the postgenomic era by adopting models that are equipped to capture the complex interplay between genes and environment.

Avshalom Caspi and Terrie Moffitt's research team has responded to the demands of science in the postgenomic era by illustrating how environmental factors such as early abuse and life stressors can interact with a genetic vulnerability to increase the risk for future involvement in antisocial behavior and depression (Caspi et al., 2002, 2003). Caspi's seminal study in *Science* (2002) provided evidence that genetic variation in a promoter region polymorphism—in this case for the gene encoding monoamine oxidase A (MAOA), an enzyme that breaks down the neurotransmitters serotonin, dopamine, and norepinephrine—could help to explain why some children who are maltreated go on to become violent, while others do not. Their findings were based on data from the Dunedin Multi-disciplinary Health and Development Study, a prospective thirty-plus year study of one thousand individuals born in New Zealand and followed from birth into young adulthood. Although the MAOA genotype did not have a main effect on antisocial behavior, there was a significant interaction with a childhood history of maltreatment among males in the sample. Findings demonstrated that males in the Dunedin cohort who had experienced maltreatment, and who also possessed the low-activity MAOA allele, were more likely than high-activity MAOA allele carriers to engage in antisocial behavior and violence later in life: maltreated boys with the low- versus high-activity allele were twice as likely to be diagnosed with CD, three times more likely to be convicted of a violent crime, and were responsible for four times their share of violent crimes within the cohort (they were only 12 percent of the study group but they committed 44 percent of the crimes).

Caspi's study is important because it provides an example of how environmental factors can influence the expression of genes, and, perhaps most importantly, it illustrates that in the absence of environmental input a genetic predisposition may not be activated. Note that there was no main effect for MAOA on antisocial outcomes documented in this study. The risk allele conferred risk for antisocial behavior only when the adverse environmental conditions (e.g., maltreatment experiences) were present. A meta-analysis of seven studies testing this G × E interaction (Taylor and Kim-Cohen, 2007) supported these initial findings, with an estimated average correlation between maltreatment and conduct problems of .13 in high-activity genotype individuals, and .30 in low-activity genotype individuals.

Since these initial studies, there has been a rapid increase in the number of G × E interaction studies within psychology, psychiatry, and related disciplines. At last count, there have been over one hundred G × E interaction studies related to antisocial behavior published since Caspi's 2002 paper. However, while research is mounting in this area, biosocial interactions are notoriously difficult to replicate (Raine, 2002), and, as described below, we are still a long way from translating these findings into practice. The conditional nature of genetic effects, combined with individual differences in susceptibility to environmental exposures across contexts and the life span, has greatly complicated the task for those searching for causes of crime within biosocial frameworks.

Can Genetic Information Be Used in Practice?

A considerable amount of time and energy has now been devoted to identifying specific genetic factors that may contribute to the development of antisocial behavior. While evidence is building with respect to the genes-to-brain-to-behavior pathways in antisocial behavior (Raine, 2008), these efforts are yet to produce information that can be used to inform diagnosis or treatment. As Gottesman and Hanson (2005) remind us, there is a tremendous distance along the causal pathway from genes to any specific phenotype. As our explanatory models move from linear combinations of risk factors to complex interactions between genetic and environmental influences, the task of translating genetic findings into applied settings becomes increasingly daunting. As one example, Moffitt and colleagues (2008) recently evaluated whether there is sufficient evidence to integrate genetic markers to inform revisions to the CD diagnosis for the fifth version of the Diagnostic and Statistical Manual. The message from their review was clear: the body of research to date does not support the use of genetic markers within diagnostic protocols for CD. The authors based their conclusions on the facts that the associations between candidate genes and CD are weak and inconsistent; specificity in prediction is lacking, as the genes that have been shown to predict crime and antisocial behavior (albeit weakly) also predict disorders such as ADHD, depression, and psychosis; and there is no evidence that genetic information would improve the prediction of prognosis above conventional risk factors.

A review of the research converges on the message that there is much work to be done before findings related to genes can be translated into practice or policy. With these limitations in mind, there is emerging evidence suggesting that genetic factors may modify treatment responsivity and could be used to identify those who are most likely to benefit from a particular treatment or intervention (Beauchaine et al., 2008; Reiss, 2010). The most straightforward example of this idea comes from the field of medicine and psychiatry, where models of individualized medicine are being implemented in response to findings that genetic factors influence differences in the rates at which individuals metabolize or respond to medications (see, e.g., McGeary et al., 2006; McMahon et al., 2006). In these cases, genetic information may be used to inform decisions regarding the type or dosage of medication that is prescribed.

Extending this example into the realm of antisocial behavior, Bakermans-Kranenburg and colleagues (2008) have provided some of the first evidence that a measured gene (in this case the dopamine D4 receptor that is associated with motivation and reward systems) may moderate the effects of an intervention (a randomized controlled trial designed to decrease the effects of child externalizing behavior). These findings are unique in that they suggest that genetic information may help to explain heterogeneity in response to interventions targeting antisocial behavior and that, eventually, genetic information could be used to best allocate limited treatment resources or identify those most likely to response to a particular intervention. But again, research in this area is not at a point where it can be ethically used to inform decision-making within applied contexts. Moreover, it is likely that "many genes of small effect" are responsible for altering treatment responses for complex behaviors and mental health problems (e.g., for a review of the host of genetic moderators of treatment response in ADHD children, see Polanczyk et al., 2010).

Rethinking Genes as Destiny and the Future of Genetically Informed Research on Crime

Decades of research and hundreds of studies have now told us that both genes and the environment matter in the crime equation. Over the last decade, advances in molecular genetics have generated a great deal of excitement and opportunities for new discoveries. However, these advances are also complicating the story line with respect to the role that genetic factors play in criminal behavior. As we move beyond the false binaries and additive models of nature–nurture influence and toward more complex and dynamic models, skepticism is building with respect to whether we will one day be able to fill in the black box of genetic variance with measured genes and specific causal models.

Wright and Boisvert (2009) argue that biosocial approaches have the ability to transform criminological theory and research. In their writings, they encourage criminologists to break away from the institutionalization of many theories and methods in criminology and embrace the biosocial approach as it offers "intellectual excitement, new methodological techniques, increased theoretical specificity, a renewed look at individual differences, and suggestions for effective policies based on the scientific research on healthy human development" (p. 1229). Similarly, Beaver (2009) argues that criminologists have long ignored genes in G × E interactions, leading to overly simplistic causal models of the development of serious, violent conduct. Perhaps most damagingly, he charges that this omission has led those invested in the study of crime and deviance away from important findings from other disciplines. Criminologists such as Adriane Raine (1996, 2002, 2008) have also long advocated for a consideration of genetic factors in etiological models of antisocial behavior and for the adoption of biosocial models within criminological research and intervention.

While enthusiasm for the integration of genes into mainstream criminology appears to be building among a small minority of researchers, an institutionalized resistance and skepticism remains. The current state of the research resides somewhere between the enthusiastic endorsement for the embrace of biosocial research by Wright and colleagues and the skeptics that question what genetic research has to offer criminological theory and practice. Although the tools for mapping and studying genetic effects are evolving rapidly, effect sizes have been incredibly small, the field is plagued by a failure to replicate key findings, and the basic science is not yet in a position to inform practice or policy. At the same time, genetically informed designs appear to be generating some of the most exciting findings regarding the role of environmental exposures on antisocial behavior to date. Most notably, we are starting to understand how genes and environments may interact to influence behavior and how environmental exposures may "turn genes on and off" across development.

Epigenetic and gene expression studies are challenging the age-old idea that genes are destiny and are providing a more dynamic—and perhaps somewhat unwieldy—view of the interplay between nature and nurture with respect to crime. At the same time, genetically informed research designs are allowing us to address methodological issues that threaten many of the findings in the field of developmental criminology—that is, the possibility that hypothesized environmental effects (e.g., the effect of parenting on children's antisocial behavior) actually represent a shared genetic risk for antisocial behavior between the parent and child, (versus an effect of parenting per se). In fact, research in the postgenomic era appears to have just as much to say about environmental (versus genetic) determinants of crime and is quickly becoming one of our most powerful tools for isolating environmental effects on behavior. As new methodologies for examining genetic influences on complex behavior become available, it becomes more likely that genetic information could be used to inform our understanding of the etiology of antisocial behavior as well as the environmental conditions under which an individual may be most likely to engage in crime. The future of social science research and individualized medicine will almost invariably include measured genes; the question for the field of criminology is whether it is ready to embrace this new paradigm, and how much weight it is willing to give to "G" in the crime equation.

Bibliography

Baker, L. A., K. C. Jacobson, A. Raine, D. I. Lozano, and S. Bezdjian. "Genetic and Environmental Bases of Childhood Antisocial Behavior: A Multi-informant Twin Study." *Journal of Abnormal Psychology* 116, no. 2 (2007): 219–35.

Bakermans-Kranenburg, M. J., M. H. Van Hzendoorn, F. T. A. Pijlman, J. Mesman, and F. Juffer. "Experimental Evidence for Differential Susceptibility: Dopamine D4 Receptor Polymorphism (DRD4 VNTR) Moderates Intervention Effects on Toddlers' Externalizing Behavior in a Randomized Controlled Trial." *Developmental Psychology* 44, no. 1 (2008): 293–300.

Beauchaine, T. P., E. Neuhaus, S. L. Brenner, and L. Gatzke-Kopp. "Ten Good Reasons to Consider Biological Processes in Prevention and Intervention Research" [Review]. *Development and Psychopathology* 20, no. 3 (2008): 745–74.

Beaver, K. M. *Biosocial Criminology: A Primer.* Dubuque, IA: Kendall/Huent, 2009.

Beitchman, J. H., L. Baldassarra, H. Mik, V. De Luca, N. King, D. Bender, S. Ehtesham, and J. L. Kennedy. "Serotonin Transporter

Polymorphisms and Persistent, Pervasive Childhood Aggression." *American Journal of Psychiatry* 163, no. 6 (2006): 1103–5.

Cannon, T. D., J. Kaprio, J. Lonnqvist, M. Huttunen, and M. Koskenvuo. "The Genetic Epidemiology of Schizophrenia in a Finnish Twin Cohort—a Population-Based Modeling Study." *Archives of General Psychiatry* 55, no. 1 (1998): 67–74.

Caspi, A., J. McClay, T. E. Moffitt, J. Mill, J. Martin, I. W. Craig, A. Taylor, and R. Poulton. "Role of Genotype in the Cycle of Violence in Maltreated Children." *Science* 297, no. 5582 (2002): 851–54.

Caspi, A., K. Sugden, T. E. Moffitt, A. Taylor, I. W. Craig, H. Harrington, et al. "Influence of Life Stress on Depression: Moderation by a Polymorphism in the 5-HTT Gene." *Science* 301, no. 5631 (2003): 386–89.

Craig, I. W. and K. E. Halton. "Genetics of Human Aggressive Behaviour." *Human Genetics* 126, no. 1 (2009): 101–13.

Devlin, B., M. Daniels, and K. Roeder. "The Heritability of IQ." *Nature* 388, no. 6641 (1997): 468–71.

Dick, D. M., T. K. Li, H. J. Edenberg, V. Hesselbrock, J. Kramer, S. Kuperman, et al. "A Genome-wide Screen for Genes Influencing Conduct Disorder." *Molecular Psychiatry* 9, no. 1 (2004): 81–86.

Falconer, D. S. and T. F. C. Mackay. *Introduction to Quantitative Genetics*. New York: Pearson/Prentice Hall, 1996.

Fowler, J. H., L. A. Baker, and C. T. Dawes. "Genetic Variation in Political Participation." *American Political Science Review* 102, no. 2 (2008): 233–48.

Fu, Q., K. C. Koenen, M. W. Miller, A. C. Heath, K. K. Bucholz, M. J. Lyons, S. A. Eisen, W. R. True, J. Goldberg, and M. T. Tsuang. "Differential Etiology of Posttraumatic Stress Disorder with Conduct Disorder and Major Depression in Male Veterans." *Biological Psychiatry* 62, no. 10 (2007): 1088–94.

Gottesman, I. I. and D. R. Hanson. "Human Development: Biological and Genetic Processes" [Review]. *Annual Review of Psychology* 56 (2005): 263–86.

Gunter, T. D., M. G. Vaughn, and R. A. Philibert. "Behavioral Genetics in Antisocial Spectrum Disorders and Psychopathy: A Review of the Recent Literature." *Behavioral Sciences and the Law* 28, no. 2 (2010): 148–73.

Guo, G., M. E. Roettger, and J. C. Shih. "Contributions of the DAT1 and DRD2 Genes to Serious and Violent Delinquency among Adolescents and Young Adults" [Article]. *Human Genetics* 121, no. 1 (2007): 125–36.

Hicks, B. M., R. F. Krueger, W. G. Iacono, M. McGue, and C. J. Patrick. "Family Transmission and Heritability of Externalizing Disorders—a Twin-Family Study." *Archives of General Psychiatry* 61, no. 9 (2004): 922–28.

Holmes, J., A. Payton, J. Barrett, R. Harrington, P. McGuffin, M. Owen, et al. "Association of DRD4 in Children with ADHD and Comorbid

Conduct Problems." *American Journal of Medical Genetics* 114, no. 2 (2002): 150–53.

Jaffee, S. R., A. Caspi, T. E. Moffitt, K. A. Dodge, M. Rutter, A. Taylor, et al. "Nature × Nurture: Genetic Vulnerabilities Interact with Physical Maltreatment to Promote Conduct Problems." *Development and Psychopathology* 17, no. 1 (2005): 67–84.

Jaffee, S. R., A. Caspi, T. E. Moffitt, M. Polo-Tomas, T. S. Price, and A. Taylor. "The Limits of Child Effects: Evidence for Genetically Mediated Child Effects on Corporal Punishment but Not on Physical Maltreatment." *Developmental Psychology* 40, no. 6 (2004a): 1047–58.

Jaffee, S. R., A. Caspi, T. E. Moffitt, and A. Taylor. "Physical Maltreatment Victim to Antisocial Child: Evidence of an Environmentally Mediated Process." *Journal of Abnormal Psychology* 113, no. 1 (2004b): 44–55.

Johnson, W., E. Turkheimer, I. Gottesman, and T. J. Bouchard. "Beyond Heritability: Twin Studies in Behavioral Research." *Current Directions in Psychological Science* 18, no. 4 (2009): 217–20.

Joseph, J. "Twin Studies in Psychiatry and Psychology: Science or Pseudoscience?" *Psychiatric Quarterly* 73, no. 1 (2002): 71–82.

Kendler, K. S. "'A gene for . . .': The Nature of Gene Action in Psychiatric Disorders." *American Journal of Psychiatry* 162, no. 7 (2005): 1243–52.

Kendler, K. S., P. H. Kuo, B. T. Webb, G. Kalsi, M. C. Neale, P. F. Sullivan, D. Walsh, D. G. Patterson, B. Riley, and C. A. Prescott. "A Joint Genomewide Linkage Analysis of Symptoms of Alcohol Dependence and Conduct Disorder." *Alcoholism-Clinical and Experimental Research* 30, no. 12 (2006): 1972–77.

Kim-Cohen, J., T. E. Moffitt, A. Taylor, S. J. Pawlby, and A. Caspi. "Maternal Depression and Children's Antisocial Behavior—Nature and Nurture Effects." *Archives of General Psychiatry* 62, no. 2 (2005): 173–81.

Maes, H. H. "Ace Model." In *Encyclopedia of Statistics in Behavioral Science*, edited by B. S. Everitt and D. C. Howell, vol. 1, 5–10. Chichester: John Wiley & Sons, 2005.

Mason, D. and P. Frick. "The Heritability of Antisocial Behavior: A Meta-analysis of Twin and Adoption Studies." *Journal of Psychopathology and Behavioral Assessment* 16, no. 4 (1994): 301.

Maughan, B., A. Taylor, A. Caspi, and T. E. Moffitt. "Prenatal Smoking and Early Childhood Conduct Problems—Testing Genetic and Environmental Explanations of the Association." *Archives of General Psychiatry* 61, no. 8 (2004): 836–43.

McGeary, J. E., P. M. Monti, D. J. Rohsenow, J. Tidey, R. Swift, and R. Miranda. "Genetic Moderators of Naltrexone's Effects on Alcohol Cue Reactivity" [Article]. *Alcoholism-Clinical and Experimental Research* 30, no. 8 (2006): 1288–96.

McGue, M., M. Osler, and K. Christensen. "Causal Inference and Observational Research." *Perspectives on Psychological Science* 5, no. 5 (2010): 546–56.

McMahon, F. J., S. Buervenich, D. Charney, R. Lipsky, A. J. Rush, A. F. Wilson, et al. "Variation in the Gene Encoding the Serotonin 2a Receptor Is Associated with Outcome of Antidepressant Treatment" [Article]. *American Journal of Human Genetics* 78, no. 5 (2006): 804–14.

Meaney, M. J. "Epigenetics and the Biological Definition of Gene × Environment Interactions." *Child Development* 81, no. 1 (2010): 41–79.

Miles, D. R. and G. Carey. "Genetic and Environmental Architecture of Human Aggression." *Journal of Personality and Social Psychology* 72, no. 1 (1997): 207–17.

Moffitt, T. E. "The New Look of Behavioral Genetics in Developmental Psychopathology: Gene-Environment Interplay in Antisocial Behaviors." *Psychological Bulletin* 131, no. 4 (2005): 533–54.

Moffitt, T. E., L. Arseneault, S. R. Jaffee, J. Kim-Cohen, K. C. Koenen, C. L. Odgers, W. S. Slutske, and E. Viding. "Research Review: Dsm-v Conduct Disorder: Research Needs for an Evidence Base" [Review]. *Journal of Child Psychology and Psychiatry* 49, no. 1 (2008): 3–33.

Moffitt, T. E., A. Caspi, M. Rutter, and P. Silva. *Sex Differences in Antisocial Behavior*. Cambridge, UK: Cambridge University Press, 2001.

Plomin, R., J. C. DeFries, I. W. Craig, and P. McGuffin, eds. *Behavioral Genetics in the Postgenomic Era*. Washington, DC: American Psychological Association, 2008.

Plomin, R., T. T. Foch, and D. C. Rowe. "Bobo Clown Aggression in Childhood: Environment, Not Genes." *Journal of Research in Personality* 15, no. 3 (1981): 331–42.

Plomin, R., C. M. A. Haworth, and O. S. P. Davis. "Common Disorders are Quantitative Traits." *Nature Reviews Genetics* 10, no. 12 (2009): 872–78.

Polanczyk, G., M. P. Bigarella, M. H. Hutz, and L. A. Rohde. "Pharmacogenetic Approach for a Better Drug Treatment in Children" [Review]. *Current Pharmaceutical Design* 16, no. 22 (2010): 2462–73.

Raine, A. "Autonomic Nervous System Factors Underlying Disinhibited, Antisocial, and Violent Behavior—Biosocial Perspectives and Treatment Implications." In *Understanding Aggressive Behavior in Children*, edited by C. F. Ferris and T. Grisso, vol. 794, 46–59. New York: Annals of the New York Academy of Sciences, 1996.

———. "Biosocial Studies of Antisocial and Violent Behavior in Children and Adults: A Review" [Review]. *Journal of Abnormal Child Psychology* 30, no. 4 (2002): 311–26.

———. "From Genes to Brain to Antisocial Behavior" [Article]. *Current Directions in Psychological Science* 17, no. 5 (2008): 323–28.

Reiss, D. "Introduction to the Special Issue: Genetics, Personalized Medicine, and Behavioral Intervention—Can This Combination Improve Patient Care?" *Perspectives on Psychological Science* 5, no. 5 (2010): 499–501.

Rhee, S. H. and I. D. Waldman. "Genetic and Environmental Influences on Antisocial Behavior: A Meta-analysis of Twin and Adoption Studies." *Psychological Bulletin* 128, no. 3 (2002): 490–529.

Rijsdijk, F. V. and P. C. Sham. "Analytic Approaches to Twin Data Using Structural Equation Models." *Briefings in Bioinformatics* 3, no. 2 (2002): 119–33.

Rutter, M. *Genes and Behavior: Nature—Nurture Interplay Explained.* New York: Wiley-Blackwell, 2006.

Rutter, M., A. Pickles, R. Murray, and L. Eaves. "Testing Hypotheses on Specific Environmental Causal Effects on Behavior" [Review]. *Psychological Bulletin* 127, no. 3 (2001): 291–324.

Sakai, J. T., S. E. Young, M. C. Stallings, D. Timberlake, A. Smolen, G. L. Stetler, and T. J. Crowley. "Case-Control and Within-Family Tests for an Association between Conduct Disorder and 5HTTLPR." *American Journal of Medical Genetics Part B-Neuropsychiatric Genetics* 141B, no. 8 (2006): 825–32.

Schonemann, P. H. "On Models and Muddles of Heritability" [Proceedings Paper]. *Genetica* 99, no. 2–3 (1997): 97–108.

Schulz-Heik, R. J., S. K. Maentz, S. H. Rhee, H. L. Gelhorn, S. E. Young, D. S. Timberlake, A. Smolen, G. L. Stetler, J. T. Sakai, and T. J. Crowley. "Case-Control and Within-Family Tests for an Association between Conduct Disorder and DAT1" [Proceedings Paper]. *Psychiatric Genetics* 18, no. 1 (2008): 17–24.

Slutske, W. "The Genetics of Antisocial Behavior." *Current Psychiatry Reports* 3, no. 2 (2001): 158–62.

Stallings, M. C., R. P. Corley, B. Dennehey, J. K. Hewitt, K. S. Krauter, J. M. Lessem, et al. "A Genome-wide Search for Quantitative Trait Loci that Influence Antisocial Drug Dependence in Adolescence." *Archives of General Psychiatry* 62, no. 9 (2005): 1042–51.

Taylor, A. and J. Kim-Cohen. "Meta-analysis of Gene-Environment Interactions in Developmental Psychopathology." *Development and Psychopathology* 19, no. 4 (2007): 1029–37.

Viding, E., K. B. Hanscombe, C. J. C. Curtis, O. S. P. Davis, E. L. Meaburn, and R. Plomin. "In Search of Genes Associated with Risk for Psychopathic Tendencies in Children: A Two-Stage Genome-wide Association Study of Pooled DNA" [Article]. *Journal of Child Psychology and Psychiatry* 51, no. 7 (2010): 780–88.

Walters, G. D. "A Meta-analysis of the Gene-Crime Relationship." *Criminology* 30, no. 4 (1992): 595–613.

Weaver, I. C. G., N. Cervoni, F. A. Champagne, A. C. D'Alessio, S. Sharma, J. R. Seckl, S. Dymov, M. Szyf, and M. J. Meaney. "Epigenetic Programming by Maternal Behavior" [Article]. *Nature Neuroscience* 7, no. 8 (2004): 847–54.

Wright, J. P. and K. M. Beaver. "Do Parents Matter in Creating Self-Control in Their Children? A Genetically Informed Test of Gottfredson and Hirschi's Theory, of Low Self-Control." *Criminology* 43, no. 4 (2005): 1169–202.

Wright, J. P. and D. Boisvert. "What Biosocial Criminology Offers Criminology." *Criminal Justice and Behavior* 36, no. 11 (2009): 1228–40.

7

Bounding Disagreements about Treatment Effects with an Application to Criminology

Charles F. Manski and Daniel S. Nagin

Empirical inference on treatment effects is a core objective of social science research. All efforts to infer treatment effects, whether from observational or experimental data, must confront the fact that the data are inherently incomplete. Although it would be best to compare the outcomes of mutually exclusive treatments, each person being observed can experience at most only one of the treatments being compared.

Identification of treatment effects necessarily requires assumptions about the process determining treatment selection and outcomes. The most long-standing practice, and still the most prevalent one, is to assume that among those persons with specified observable covariates, treatment selection is statistically independent of outcomes. This assumption is variously called *random, exogenous,* or *ignorable* treatment selection. The specified covariates are often said to "control for" treatment assignment (see Maddala, 1983; Rosenbaum and Rubin, 1983).

The assumption of random treatment selection is appropriate in the analysis of data from classical randomized experiments, but it is suspected when observed treatments are self-selected or otherwise chosen purposefully. In the past twenty years, a variety of alternative assumptions have been proposed and applied to nonexperimental data. Parametric latent variable models specify the joint distribution of treatments and outcomes up to a finite set of parameters, while parametric instrumental variables approaches assume that treatment effects are constant across the population and that a specified covariate influences treatment selection but not outcomes. The development of parametric latent variable models and instrumental variables methods in the 1970s and early 1980s (e.g., Heckman, 1976, 1978; Maddala, 1983) was initially greeted with some enthusiasm as "solving" the problem of identifying treatment effects from nonexperimental data. It soon became apparent, however, that these approaches replace the suspect assumption of random treatment selection with alternative assumptions that are no less suspect (see Goldberger, 1983; LaLonde, 1986). More recent work on semi- and nonparametric latent variable models (e.g., Heckman and Honore, 1990; Ahn and Powell, 1993) and on nonparametric interpretations of instrumental variables methods (e.g., Imbens and Angrist, 1994) has deepened our understanding of the properties of these approaches, while retaining the conventional focus on exact identification of treatment effects.

The methodological research program initiated in Manski (1989, 1990) and carried forward in Manski (1993, 1994, 1995, 1996, 1997a, 1997b) moves away from the conventional focus of social science research on models that yield exact identification of treatment effects. This work shows that informative bounds may be obtained under various weak nonparametric assumptions. An important objective is to bound disagreements among researchers. Inferences predicated on weak assumptions can achieve wide consensus. Inferences that require strong assumptions almost inevitably are subject to sharp disagreements.

An early empirical case study applying the most basic elements of the approach was Manski et al. (1992), which examined the effect of family structure on children's outcomes. The present chapter uses a treatment question facing the juvenile justice system to more fully showcase the value of the new approach in empirical social science research. The question of how judges should sentence convicted juvenile offenders has long been of interest to policymakers, social scientists, and criminologists. Here we compare the impacts on recidivism of the two main sentencing options available to judges: confinement in residential treatment facilities and diversion to nonresidential treatment.

Our empirical analysis exploits the rich event history data on juvenile offenders collected by the state of Utah (National Juvenile Court Data Archive, 1992). We present several sets of findings and show how conclusions about treatment effects vary depending on the assumptions made. We begin by presenting estimates under the assumption of random treatment selection and bounds obtained without making any assumptions at all about the process determining treatment selection and outcomes. The assumption of random treatment selection is the traditional assumption made in tests of labeling and deterrence theories. We then present bounds obtained under two alternative models of judicial decision-making. The *outcome optimization model* assumes that judges make sentencing decisions that minimize the chance of recidivism. The *skimming model* assumes that judges classify offenders as "higher risk" or "lower risk," sentencing the former to residential treatment and the latter to nonresidential treatment. Each model expresses an easily understood hypothesis about judicial decision-making, and each has a potentially wide range of social science applications. Neither model imposes the poorly motivated functional-form and distributional assumptions that mar parametric latent variable models and instrumental variables methods. Our analysis of the outcome optimization model substantially generalizes work described in Manski (1990, 1995).

Finally, we bring to bear further prior information in the form of *exclusion restrictions*. We posit that specified subpopulations of offenders have the same response to treatment but face different treatment selection rules. The covariates defining these subpopulations have traditionally been called *instrumental variables* and have been used in a number of criminological studies (see Kirk in current volume).

The empirical findings depend critically on the assumptions imposed. With nothing assumed about treatment selection or outcomes, only weak conclusions can be drawn about the recidivism implications of the two sentencing options. With assumptions made about treatment selection, the results are far more informative. If we believe that Utah judges choose sentences in an effort to minimize recidivism, the empirical results point to the conclusion that residential treatment exacerbates criminality on average. If we believe that judges behave in accord with the skimming model, the results suggest the opposite conclusion—namely, that residential treatment has an ameliorative effect on average. Imposition of an exclusion restriction strengthens each of these opposing conclusions.

Abstracting from the specifics of our juvenile justice application, this chapter demonstrates the value for informed policy and scientific debate of analyzing treatment effects under a sequence of progressively stronger assumptions. We believe that reporting "layered" empirical findings in this manner improves upon the conventional practice of reporting only point estimates based on assumptions strong enough to identify treatment effects.

The chapter is organized as follows. The next section provides background on the juvenile justice application. We then use this application to motivate our description of the basic ideas underlying nonparametric bounding of treatment effects. This is followed by a presentation of the outcome optimization and skimming models and their implications for identification of treatment effects. We then explain the identifying power of exclusion restrictions. In each section, the empirical application follows presentation of the relevant theory. Finally, we sum up and provide a postscript to this earlier research originally published in 1998 with a discussion of more recent developments that are useful to consider for issues of theory and policy (see Manski and Nagin, 1998).

Background on the Application

The Impact of the Juvenile Justice System on Delinquency

From its inception, the juvenile justice system was philosophically different from the adult justice system (Schlossman, 1977; Rothman, 1980; Cullen et al., 1988; Bernard, 1992). Departing from the legal model of the adult system, with its principles of criminal responsibility, punishment, and deterrence, the juvenile justice system was predicated on a "medical model" of deviance. This model rejects notions of criminal responsibility in favor of the view that deviance/delinquency is merely symptomatic of an underlying pathology that requires treatment. Reflecting the different purposes of the two systems, the juvenile justice system abandoned the goal of separating the guilty from the innocent and punishing only the former, in favor of the goal of determining the "needs" of the child and directing the treatment resources of the state to ameliorating those needs.

Although the intention of juvenile justice has always been the provision of treatment and regenerative care for its clients rather than punishment, historically there has been a skepticism as to whether treatment was actually being delivered. Critics have contended that in spite of benevolent intentions and therapeutic rhetoric, the juvenile justice system delivered much the same kinds of punishment and coercion as did the adult system. This skepticism of the actual practices of the juvenile court was given theoretical guidance in the 1960s with the emergence of the labeling or social reaction school of deviance (Lemert, 1951; Kitsuse, 1962; Becker, 1963; Schur, 1971). More recently, the movement to waive juveniles charged with felonies to be tried in adult courts has led some to question the utility of the juvenile justice system in general. Feld (1999), for example, argues that children would be given more legal rights in the adult court setting and more fair treatment if age was used as an explicit mitigating factor in dispositions.

According to the labeling school of deviance, there is a constellation of negative consequences that may flow from official processing of an actor as deviant, even with a therapeutic intent. For example, confinement in a residential "treatment" facility may make it more likely that the actor thinks of himself as deviant, may exclude the actor from the "normal" routines of life and normal opportunities, or place the actor into closer affinity with deviant others who may reinforce negative feelings the actor has about himself.

Although the ultimate outcome is not deterministic (Paternoster and Iovanni, 1989), labeling theorists were instrumental in introducing the state and official processing as major causal elements in delinquency and crime (Matza, 1969). This prediction of labeling theory became referred to as the "secondary deviance" hypothesis: formal processing, even when performed for the purpose of treatment and remedy, is more likely to lead to additional deviance than is no processing or informal processing. Thus labeling theory was less a theory about the initial cause of deviance than a theory about its continuation once begun.

Although plausible, the secondary deviance hypothesis of labeling theory has not fared particularly well in the empirical literature. Extensive reviews of the research in the field of mental health by Gove (1980) and Tittle (1980) indicated that while many of the findings are ambiguous, most of the research is not consistent with the hypothesis of secondary deviance. The problem with this literature, critics have noted, is not its volume but its interpretation.

Tittle (1980: 259) concluded that "not a single good test of either of the major propositions of labeling theory exists in the literature." Researchers generally find that offenders who are subjected to formal judicial processing tend to have higher recidivism rates than those who are treated informally (Smith and Paternoster, 1990). While this finding accords with the prediction of labeling theory, it may also be an artifact of treatment selection. Smith and Paternoster (1990: 1111) observe: "High risk youth are more likely to receive more severe dispositions. Thus, those individuals assigned more severe sanctions would be more likely to commit new offenses whether or not any relationship existed between juvenile court disposition and future offending." They go on to argue that it is implausible to assume that treatment selection is random conditional on the covariates that researchers typically can measure.

Data

Our analysis is based on the data for male offenders born from 1970 to 1974, extracted from the state of Utah's extensive records on youth contacts with its juvenile justice system. The National Juvenile Court

Data Archive has organized these records into files, which, for each birth cohort from 1962 to 1974, record all delinquency, status offense, and abuse and neglect cases referred for court intake. The data for each case include the dates of referral and disposition and the reasons for and disposition of the referral. Also recorded are the age, race, sex, and number of prior referrals of the youth who is the subject of the case.

We restrict attention to referrals that are not ultimately dismissed and in which the most serious charge involves an act that would be criminal if committed by an adult. For this segment of the case population, we aggregate the many sentencing options available to juvenile court judges into two broad categories of treatments: placement in a residential facility or assignment to nonresidential treatment such as probation, restitution, or counseling.

The residential treatment alternative included confinement in a secure facility but more generally involved assignment to a nonsecure group home located in the individual's community. In early 1980, Utah adopted a policy of assigning juvenile offenders to the least intrusive treatment alternative (see Manski and Nagin, 1998, for more discussion of policy shifts).

We use the Utah data to bound the impact on recidivism of these two modalities of treatment. Recidivism is defined as the youth generating a subsequent referral that meets the above criteria for inclusion in the sample within the twenty-four-month period following the date of treatment. Referral is a filtered indicator of a return to offending—a referral occurs only when a youth is apprehended for an offense and the authorities deem it appropriate to refer the apprehended youth to the Utah juvenile justice system. Our analysis assumes that the probability that a new offense generates such a referral does not vary with the offender's prior treatment by the juvenile justice system.

The date of treatment is defined as the date of disposition, and the date of recidivism as the date of referral of the subsequent qualifying case. Because the age of majority in Utah is eighteen, we consider only those cases in which the offender was aged less than sixteen at the date of treatment. After culling the data of cases in which it was not possible to determine an individual's age, treatment, offense, or exposure period following treatment, 13,197 cases were available for analysis.

The twenty-four-month exposure period includes the time that an offender sentenced to residential treatment is detained in the residential facility. In principle, residential treatment affects recidivism through two channels: (1) by incapacitating the offender while detained and (2) by deterring or stigmatizing the offender after the sentence is completed. In practice, the incapacitative effect is limited by the nonsecure nature of some residential facilities, which allows juveniles some access to the outside or crimes committed in facilities, and by the short duration of juvenile residential sentences, which usually are less than six months in length.

Basic Analysis

The Classical and Status Quo Treatment Effects

There are many different ways to formalize the loose idea of a "treatment effect," and we shall be concerned with two of these. First, we examine the *classical treatment effect* (CTE) that has long been the focus of empirical research—namely, the expected value of the population difference in the outcomes of two mandated treatments. In our juvenile justice application, the CTE is the difference in the recidivism rate of juvenile offenders under two extreme treatment selection rules. One extreme is residential treatment of all juvenile offenders with specified covariates and the other is nonresidential treatment of all such offenders.

In practice, judges generally apply neither of these extreme treatment selection rules. The norm is for a judge to sentence some offenders to a residential program and others to nonresidential treatment. Policymakers may be more interested in assessing changes from this status quo than that in the CTE. Many such changes are of potential interest. We examine one that is easily described and analyzed: the expected difference in recidivism if the treatment selection rules actually used by judges were replaced by one mandating residential treatment of all juvenile offenders. We refer to this as a *status quo treatment effect* (STE).

Definition of treatment effects requires specification of a population of interest. Here this is the population of male offenders who are aged sixteen or less at the time of treatment. For various reasons, we might be interested in treatment effects within an identifiable subset of the population, characterized by specified covariates, rather than the entire population. For example, we might want to focus on juveniles convicted of committing a felony and ask how their recidivism would change if the status quo were replaced by mandatory residential treatment. Clearly, the problem of inferring treatment effects on identifiable subpopulations is no different conceptually from that of inferring treatment effects on the entire population. One simply redefines the "population" to include only the subpopulation of interest.

It is important for the reader to understand that our use of covariates to specify a subpopulation of interest differs fundamentally from the common use of covariates to control for treatment assignment. When we present estimates of, or bounds on, CTEs conditioning on specified covariates, we seek to answer this question:

> Among persons with the specified covariates, what would be the difference in recidivism rate if all such persons were assigned one treatment rather than the other?

This question is well-posed; however, the covariates are specified. In this chapter, for example, we present treatment effects within subpopulations defined by the offender's gender, age, and number of prior referrals. Researchers commonly assert that there is some minimal set of "correct" covariates to use in the analysis of treatment effects and that "omitted variable bias" may occur if one conditions on only a subset of these covariates. These statements relate to the use of covariates to control for treatment assignment. A set of covariates is said to be "correct" if treatment assignment is random conditional on these covariates; "omitted variable bias" is said to occur if one conditions only on a subset of these covariates and if treatment assignment is not random conditional on this subset. We do not assume that treatment assignment is random conditional on gender, age, and number of prior referrals or any other set of covariates. Hence, the concepts of "correct" covariates and "omitted variable bias" are not germane to our analysis.

Throughout this chapter, we reluctantly maintain the standard assumption of "individualistic treatment" made routinely, albeit often only implicitly, in analyses of treatment effects. Individualistic treatment means that each person's outcome may depend on the treatment received but not on the treatments received by other persons. In our application, individualistic treatment means an absence of general deterrence effects wherein the expectations that an offender holds for his own future residential confinement, should he commit a subsequent crime, depend on the frequency with which judges currently sentence offenders to residential confinement. Individualistic treatment also means an absence of social norm effects in which the stigma of being labeled a delinquent decreases with the prevalence of delinquency in the population. General deterrence, social norm effects, and other "macro effects" may well be important in practice, but their complexity has long led researchers analyzing treatment effects to abstract from them (see Garfinkel et al., 1992).

The Problem of Identifying Treatment Effects

Estimation of treatment effects requires consideration of two distinct issues: identification and sampling variability. Identification concerns the conclusions that could be drawn if one could observe the treatments received and outcomes experienced by everyone in the population. Sampling variability arises when these data are available for only a sample of the population. Here our central concern is identification. To ease exposition, the discussion in this section makes no distinction between sample and population quantities. We shall, however, consider the question of sampling variability when we present our empirical analysis.

The present discussion also supposes, in order to ease exposition, that the objective is to infer treatment effects on the entire population. Treatment effects on identifiable subpopulations will be estimated in our empirical application.

What quantities do the data reveal? To be concrete, consider the data set that we analyze, assembled from the records of the Utah juvenile justice system. For each juvenile offender, we know (1) the treatment received, residential or nonresidential, and (2) whether the offender recidivated and, if so, how long after treatment. The Utah data also report various characteristics of each case (e.g., felony or not) and the offender (e.g., prior record) that may be used to define identifiable subsets of the population of offenders.

Three features of the population (or of a subpopulation of interest) are revealed by the data: (1) the probability that an offender is sentenced to residential treatment, (2) the probability of recidivism among offenders who are residentially treated, and (3) the probability of recidivism among offenders who are nonresidentially treated. Definition of recidivism requires specification of an exposure period (i.e., period at risk of failure) of interest. We might, for example, want to know about recidivism during the one-year, two-year, or five-year period following conviction. Our notation leaves the exposure period implicit, in order to simplify the presentation of basic ideas.

The data reveal some but not all of the information necessary for estimating treatment effects. Two vital counterfactuals are missing. One is the probability of recidivism among offenders sentenced to residential treatment had they instead been sentenced to nonresidential treatment. The other is the probability of recidivism among offenders sentenced to nonresidential treatment had they instead been sentenced to residential treatment.

Let us formalize how these counterfactuals combine with the measurable quantities to determine treatment effects. Let $t = 1$ denote residential treatment and $t = 0$ denote nonresidential treatment. Let $y(t) = 1$ if an offender would recidivate during the exposure period if that offender were to receive treatment t, and let $y(t) = 0$ if the offender would not recidivate. Let $z = 1$ if an offender is actually sentenced to residential treatment and $z = 0$ if the offender is sentenced to nonresidential treatment. Three quantities are revealed by the data:

1. $P(z = 1)$—This is the probability of residential treatment, which can be measured directly from the data by the fraction of offenders who are sentenced to residential facilities.
2. $P[y(1) = 1|z = 1]$—This is the probability of recidivism under treatment 1, among those offenders who actually receive treatment 1. This quantity can be measured directly from the data by the rate of recidivism among offenders sentenced to residential treatment.
3. $P[y(0) = 1|z = 0]$—This is the probability of recidivism under treatment 0, among those offenders who actually receive treatment 0. This quantity can be measured directly from the data by the rate of recidivism among offenders sentenced to nonresidential treatment.

Two counterfactual quantities are not revealed by the data:

1. $P[y(1) = 1|z = 0]$—This is the probability of recidivism under treatment 1, among those offenders who actually receive treatment 0.
2. $P[y(0) = 1|z = 1]$—This is the probability of recidivism under treatment 0, among those offenders who actually receive treatment 1.

With this background, we can now define formally the CTEs and STEs and pinpoint the problem of identifying each. The CTE is the difference between the recidivism probabilities that would occur under mandatory residential treatment of all juvenile offenders and mandatory nonresidential treatment of all offenders. Thus

$$\text{CTE} \equiv P\big[y(1)=1\big] - P\big[y(0)=1\big]. \quad (7.1)$$

The first element of the CTE measures the probability of recidivism if all offenders were sentenced to residential treatment; the second element measures the probability of recidivism if all were sentenced to nonresidential treatment.

The STE examined here is the difference between the recidivism probability that would occur under mandatory residential treatment of all juvenile offenders and the one that is observed under the actual sentencing rules used by judges. Thus

$$\text{STE} \equiv P\big[y(1)=1\big] - P\big[y(z)=1\big]. \quad (7.2)$$

Observe that the STE has the same first element as the CTE but a different second element. The quantity $y(z)$ is the recidivism outcome experienced by an offender under the treatment that this offender actually receives. So $P[y(z) = 1]$ measures the probability of recidivism under the status quo sentencing rules used by judges. We could analogously compare the recidivism probability that would occur under mandatory nonresidential treatment with the one that is observed under the actual sentencing rules used by judges. This STE is $P[y(0) = 1] - P[y(z) = 1]$. The identification problem is that, of all the elements of the CTE and STE, the only one fully revealed by the data is $P[y(z) = 1]$. To see this, we use the law of total probability to write the three recidivism probabilities as follows:

The recidivism probability under mandatory residential treatment is

$$P\big[y(1)=1\big]$$
$$= P\big[y(1)=1 \,|\, z=1\big]P(z=1) + P\big[y(1)=1 \,|\, z=0\big] \cdot P(z=0). \quad (7.3)$$

The recidivism probability under mandatory nonresidential treatment is

$$P\big[y(0)=1\big]$$
$$= P\big[y(0)=1 \,|\, z=1\big] \cdot P(z=1) + P\big[y(0)=1 \,|\, z=0\big] \cdot P(z=0). \quad (7.4)$$

The recidivism probability under the status quo is

$$P\big[y(z)=1\big]$$
$$= P\big[y(1)=1 \,|\, z=1\big] \cdot P(z=1) + P\big[y(0)=1 \,|\, z=0\big] \cdot P(z=0). \quad (7.5)$$

Consider equation (7.3). The missing quantity needed to identify the recidivism probability under mandatory residential treatment is the counterfactual probability $P[y(1) = 1|z = 0]$; all other quantities are revealed by the data. Similarly, in equation (7.4), the missing quantity is the counterfactual probability $P[y(0) = 1|z = 1]$. Only in equation (7.5) do the data reveal all the quantities needed to identify the recidivism probability of interest.

Bounds on Treatment Effects Using the Data Alone

If our data were obtained from a classical randomized experiment, or if we could argue convincingly that treatment selection was effectively random, then it would still be the case that the counterfactual probabilities in equations (7.3) and (7.4) would not be revealed by the data. But random selection of treatment implies that the counterfactual probability $P[y(1) = 1|z = 0]$ equals the measured recidivism probability $P[y(1) = 1|z = 1]$ of those offenders who actually receive residential treatment. Similarly, randomization implies that $P[y(0) = 1|z = 1] = P[y(0) = 1|z = 0]$. Hence, the CTEs and STEs under the assumption of random treatment selection are

$$\text{CTE} \equiv P\big[\,y(1) = 1\,|\,z = 1\big] - P\big[\,y(0) = 1\,|\,z = 0\big] \quad (7.6)$$

and

$$\text{STE} \equiv P\big[\,y(1) = 1\,|\,z = 1\big] - P\big[\,y(z) = 1\big]. \quad (7.7)$$

Thus the assumption of random treatment selection identifies both treatment effects.

Our data are not the product of a randomized experiment, and we cannot argue convincingly that judges effectively sentence in a random manner. How should we proceed then?

A logical starting point is to assume nothing at all about the counterfactual probabilities. Even if no assumptions are made, we can still make progress toward identifying treatment effects. We know that each counterfactual probability must be no smaller than zero and no larger than one. This simple fact implies bounds on the recidivism probability under mandatory residential treatment.

The lower bound on $P[y(1) = 1]$ is derived by assuming that none of the offenders who receive nonresidential treatment would have recidivated had they received residential treatment. Thus we set $P[y(1) = 1|z = 0] = 0$ in equation (7.3) to obtain the lower bound. The upper bound is derived by assuming that all of the offenders who receive nonresidential treatment would have recidivated had they received residential treatment. Thus we set $P[y(1) = 1|z = 0] = 1$ in equation (7.3) to obtain the upper bound. Analogous reasoning applies to the recidivism probability under mandatory nonresidential treatment. We can summarize as follows:

The no-assumptions bound on recidivism probability under mandatory residential treatment is

$$P\left[y(1)=1\,|\,z=1\right]\cdot P(z=1)\le P\left[y(1)=1\right]$$
$$\le P\left[y(1)=1\,|\,z=1\right]\cdot P(z=1)+P(z=0). \quad (7.8)$$

The no-assumptions bound on recidivism probability under mandatory nonresidential treatment is

$$P\left[y(0)=1\,|\,z=0\right]\cdot P(z=0)\le P\left[y(0)=1\right]$$
$$\le P\left[y(0)=1\,|\,z=0\right]\cdot P(z=0)+P(z=1). \quad (7.9)$$

As used here and elsewhere in the chapter, the phrase "no-assumptions bound" should not be taken to mean that our analysis makes no assumptions at all. We do, after all, maintain various assumptions—treatment is individualistic, outcomes and treatments are correctly measured, and so on. The phrase only means that no assumptions are made that restrict the values of the counterfactual probabilities.

Observe that the bound on $P[y(1) = 1]$ has width $P(z = 0)$, the fraction of the population who receive treatment 0. Symmetrically, the bound on $P[y(0) = 1]$ has width $P(z = 1)$. These bounds on recidivism probabilities imply bounds on the CTEs and STEs. Consider the CTE. The lower bound on this quantity is the lower bound on $P[y(1) = 1]$ minus the upper bound on $P[y(0) = 1]$. The upper bound on the CTE is the upper bound on $P[y(1) = 1]$ minus the lower bound on $P[y(0) = 1]$. Hence we have the following:

The no-assumptions bound on the CTE

$$\left\{ P\left[y(1)=1 \,|\, z=1 \right] \cdot P(z=1) \right\}$$
$$-\left\{ P\left[y(0)=1 \,|\, z=0 \right] \cdot P(z=0) + P(z=1) \right\} \leq \text{CTE}$$
$$\leq \left\{ P\left[y(1)=1 \,|\, z=1 \right] \cdot P(z=1) + P(z=0) \right\} \qquad (7.10)$$
$$-\left\{ P\left[y(0)=1 \,|\, z=0 \right] \cdot P(z=0) \right\}.$$

The bound on the CTE has width $P(z=1) + P(z=0) = 1$. If no data were available, we would be able to make only the trivial statement that the CTE must be no smaller than -1 and no larger than 1. The data allow us to narrow this interval of width 2 to one of width 1. In a very real sense then, the data move us halfway toward identification of the CTE. Unfortunately, the data alone are not sufficiently informative to identify the sign of the CTE. Having width 1, the bound on the CTE always contains the value zero. Thus identification of the sign of the CTE necessarily requires assumptions about the treatment selection and outcome process.

We must now consider the STE. The lower bound on this quantity is the lower bound on $P[y(1) = 1]$ minus the known value of $P[y(z) = 1]$, given in equation (7.5). The upper bound on the STE is the upper bound on $P[y(1) = 1]$ minus the known value of $P[y(z) = 1]$. Hence we have the following:

No-assumptions bound on the STE

$$-P\left[y(0)=1 \,|\, z=0 \right] P(z=0) \leq \text{STE}$$
$$\leq P\left[y(0)=0 \,|\, z=0 \right] P(z=0). \qquad (7.11)$$

The width of this bound is $P(z = 0)$, which is less than the width of the bound on the CTE. Nevertheless this bound, like the earlier one, always contains the value zero. This means that the sign of the STE is not identified using the data alone.

The bounding argument presented in this section was introduced in Manski (1989, 1990) and developed further in Manski (1994). The broad idea of using no-assumptions bounds to express the possible effects of missing data has a much longer history. Frechet (1951) developed no-assumptions bounds to determine the possible joint distributions of data that are compatible with specified marginal distributions. Cochran et al. (1954), in their study of statistical problems of the Kinsey report on sexual behavior, used no-assumptions bounds of the specific form of equation (7.8) to express the possible effects of missing outcome data due to nonresponse in the Kinsey survey. Unfortunately, the subsequent literature on survey nonresponse did not pursue the idea.

Application

Table 7.1 derives the no-assumptions bounds on the CTE and STE for the combined 1970–1974 Utah cohorts. As described in section *Data*, these individuals generated 13,197 cases meeting our screening criteria. The bounds are computed for an exposure period of twenty-four months.

The data reveal that 11 percent of the offenders are sentenced to residential treatment; the remaining 89 percent are sentenced to non-residential treatment. Recidivism rates are high regardless of treatment, with 77 percent of the offenders sentenced to residential treatment re-cidivating within twenty-four months, and 59 percent of those sentenced to nonresidential treatment. Thus, abstracting from sampling variability, $P(z = 1) = 0.11$, $P[y(1) = 1 | z = 1] = 0.77$, and $P[y(0) = 1 | z = 0] = 0.59$.

Table 7.1   Basic analysis (all cases, twenty-four-month exposure period)

Probability of residential treatment: $P(z = 1) = 0.11$

Status quo recidivism probability: $P[y(z) = 1] = 0.61$

Recidivism probability in subpopulation receiving residential treatment:

   $P[y(1) = 1 | z = 1] = 0.77$

Recidivism probability in subpopulation receiving nonresidential treatment:

   $P[y(0) = 1 | z = 0] = 0.59$

Classical treatment effect assuming random treatment selection: $0.77 - 0.59 = 0.18$

Bound on recidivism probability under mandatory residential treatment:

   $0.08 = (0.77) \times (0.11) \leq P[y(1) = 1] \leq (0.77) \times (0.11) + 0.89 = 0.97$

Bound on recidivism probability under mandatory nonresidential treatment:

   $0.53 = (0.59) \times (0.89) \leq P[y(0) = 1] \leq (0.59) \times (0.89) + 0.11 = 0.64$

No-assumptions bound on CTE:

   $-0.56 = 0.08 - 0.64 \leq CTE \leq 0.97 - 0.53 = 0.44$

No-assumptions bound on STE:

   $-0.53 = 0.08 - 0.61 \leq STE \leq 0.97 - 0.61 = 0.36$

Sample size: $N = 13,197$

Because only 11 percent of offenders are sentenced to residential treatment, the bound on the recidivism probability under mandatory residential treatment, $P[y(1) = 1]$, is very wide—at least 0.08 and no more than 0.97. With 89 percent of the population receiving nonresidential sentences, the bound under mandatory nonresidential treatment is quite narrow—$P[y(0) = 1]$ must lie between 0.53 and 0.64. These bounds on the recidivism probabilities under the two mandatory sentencing regimes imply that the CTE is at least −0.56 but no more than 0.44. The STE is at least −0.53 but no more than 0.36.

The bounds in Table 7.1 pertain to the population of all cases. It is of interest to examine whether treatment effects vary with case characteristics. Labeling theory, for example, suggests that the adverse impact of contact with the juvenile justice system may diminish with the number of contacts because the stigmatization that triggers "secondary deviance" may be completed within the first few contacts. Indeed, once the initial stigmatization occurs, subsequent contact might have a deterrent effect. If this were found to be so, there would be reason to make treatment policy vary with the number of prior referrals of the offender.

Table 7.2 reports no-assumptions bounds on the CTE conditioned on the number of prior referrals of the offender, and 90 percent confidence intervals around the estimated bounds. The confidence intervals, which are computed using the bootstrap method described in Manski et al. (1992), measure sampling precision under the assumption that our data on Utah juvenile offenders are a random sample from a population of potential offenders. Observe that the widths of the confidence intervals are only slightly larger than the widths of the estimated bounds. Whereas the estimated bounds necessarily have width 1, their confidence intervals

Table 7.2   **No-assumptions bound on classical treatment effect, by number of prior referrals**

Priors	Sample size	Fraction residential treatment	CTE assuming random treatment selection	CTE		90 percent confidence interval	
				Lower bound	Upper bound	Lower bound	Upper bound
0	7,406	0.04	0.09	-0.48	0.52	-0.49	0.53
1	2,719	0.11	0.07	-0.65	0.35	-0.67	0.36
2+	3,072	0.27	0.02	-0.65	0.35	-0.66	0.37

have widths 1.02 or 1.03. Thus identification is the dominant problem in inference on these treatment effects; sampling variation is no more than a second-order concern.

Sampling variation would be a more consequential matter if the Utah data set were smaller in size or if we were to seek to infer treatment effects within smaller subpopulations than those defined by gender, age, and number of prior referrals. Holding fixed the specification of the subpopulations of interest, identification would remain the major problem even if the size of the Utah data set were quite small.

Refining the subpopulations of interest by conditioning on covariates other than gender, age, and number of prior referrals would inevitably decrease the sampling precision of the estimates. That sampling precision tends to fall as one conditions on more covariates is a generic attribute of all statistical analysis, whether parametric or nonparametric, but it is particularly acute in nonparametric analysis, where the problem is often referred to as "the curse of dimensionality" (see Manski (1991) for a discussion).

The curse of dimensionality is sometimes cited as a reason for researchers to prefer parametric analysis to nonparametric analysis. It should be kept in mind, however, that a parametric statistical analysis is meaningful only to the extent that the assumed parametric model correctly describes the probabilistic process under study. Furthermore, as discussed above, our analysis does not assume that treatment selection is random conditional on the specified covariates and, hence, is not susceptible to conventional criticisms of "omitted variable bias." Thus there is no specific need for us to condition on a long list of covariates. The bounds on CTEs reported in Table 7.2 are unambiguously interpretable as comparisons of the recidivism rates that would be observed if all offenders with the specified covariates (gender, age, and number of prior referral) were sentenced to residential treatment or, alternatively, to nonresidential treatment.

Table 7.2 also reports nonparametric point estimates of the CTE obtained under the assumption that treatment selection is random conditional on gender, age, and number of prior referrals. The fact that these point estimates always lie within the no-assumptions bounds is not happenstance. If we do not make any assumptions, we obviously cannot reject the hypothesis that treatment selection is random.

All the estimates assuming random treatment selection turn out to be positive, implying that residential treatment increases recidivism probability for each number of prior referrals, but the magnitude of the estimates declines with the number of prior referrals. This pattern is consistent with the aforementioned prediction of labeling theory. Of course, this interpretation of the pattern of estimates collapses if one is unwilling to maintain the assumption that treatment selection is random.

In empirical studies, researchers have typically assumed not only that treatment selection is random but also that recidivism probabilities follow some parametric model. They might, for example, specify the logit model $P[y(t) = 1|x] = \exp(a + bx + ct)/[1 + \exp(a + bx + ct)]$, where t denotes the treatment, x denotes the number of prior referrals, and (a, b, c) are parameters. Maximum likelihood estimation on the Utah data set yields $(0.021, 0.552, 0.242)$ as the estimates for (a, b, c). The implied parametric estimates of the CTEs for offenders with 0, 1, and 2 prior referrals are, respectively, 0.06, 0.05, and 0.04. As was the case with the nonparametric estimates presented in Table 7.2, these parametric estimates are positive and their magnitudes decline with the number of prior referrals.

Given that the assumption of random treatment selection alone suffices to identify CTEs, we must ask what is to be gained by also assuming that recidivism probabilities follow the logit model or some other model. This question has two standard answers. First, the model permits us to extrapolate off the support of the data; in the present case, to estimate treatment effects for hypothetical offenders who have values of x that are not observed in the Utah data. Second, estimates of CTEs obtained using the assumed model may be more precise than the nonparametric estimates available when only random treatment selection is assumed. However, these potential positive features of modeling the recidivism probabilities are realized only to the extent that the assumed model accurately describes reality. Criminological theory provides no basis for thinking that recidivism probabilities should follow the logit model or any other specific model. So the potential benefits of modeling the recidivism probabilities come at the cost of lessened credibility for the reported findings.

Two Models of Treatment Selection

Although the logical starting point for the analysis of treatment effects is to assume nothing about the counterfactual probabilities, researchers ordinarily want to make sharper inferences than those implied by the data alone. The price of sharper inferences is the loss of credibility associated with the imposition of untestable assumptions. Methodological research cannot determine when this price is worth paying, but it can assist empirical research by clarifying the identifying power of alternative assumptions.

The analysis in this section examines the identifying power of two alternative assumptions about treatment selection. The literature on the analysis of treatment effects makes substantial use of assumptions about treatment selection. The classical assumption, of course, is that treatment selection is random conditional on specified covariates. Here we examine the identifying power of two behaviorally motivated treatment selection assumptions. These are the *outcome optimization model* and the *skimming model.* These models are intended to capture two pervasive themes in the literature on juvenile sentencing: whether the objective of sentencing should be (1) to reduce crime by juveniles or (2) to punish a dangerous criminal, who also happens to be young (Bernard, 1992; Sanbor, 1996; Singer, 1996).

Although the models differ in important respects, they share some critical simplifying assumptions. Both assume that judges are concerned only with recidivism, not with the cost of a treatment or with its normative appropriateness as a "punishment fitting the crime" except insofar as "blameworthiness" is defined by recidivism probability. Moreover, both assume that judges correctly perceive how treatment affects recidivism.

The outcome optimization model operationalizes the economist's standard assumption that decisions under uncertainty are made to minimize expected loss or, equivalently, to maximize expected utility. Given the available information, the decision-maker chooses the treatment that yields the better expected outcome. The outcome optimization model has an enormous range of possible applications, from selection of educational and training treatments, to family planning, to disease prevention. In our juvenile justice application, we assume that the judge selects the sentencing alternative, residential or nonresidential treatment that minimizes recidivism probability. A sizable contingent of scholars and policymakers have long held that the objective of the juvenile justice system should be to reform juvenile offenders, not to punish them (Cullen et al., 1988; Bernard, 1992). Sanbor's (1996) survey of juvenile court workers on their judgments about factors that should affect disposition reflects this view. Asking respondents to rank order the importance of seven dispositional goals, he found that rehabilitation received the top ranking. The outcome optimization model assumes that judges actually sentence in accord with this normative view.

The outcome optimization model is also consistent with sentencing strategies designed to reduce crime through incapacitation of high-rate offenders rather than by their rehabilitation. Going back at least to the 1970s, critics of a treatment-oriented perspective on sentencing have argued that confinement should focus on the punishment of the most active juvenile offenders. For example, Van den Haag (1975: 174) argues that whether the perpetrator is a "twenty-year-old mugger" or a "fourteen-year-old murderer or rapist," "the need for social defense or protection is the same." More recently, Singer (1996: 15) observes that "within the various governmental courtrooms, there is a bottom-line concern with making decisions to best control the delinquent or violent behavior of juveniles. Officials want to identify the serious delinquent and prevent his or her repeated criminal behavior."

The skimming model operationalizes the idea that program administrators may act to maximize the apparent rather than the actual effectiveness of their programs. In the simple form discussed here, the model assumes that judges assign only high-risk offenders to residential treatment and only low-risk offenders to nonresidential treatment, regardless of which treatment is more effective in reducing recidivism. In educational and training programs, for example, it is sometimes hypothesized that administrators select participants whom they expect will be most successful following completion of the program, regardless of how this success is influenced by the program. By "skimming" or "creaming" the applicants with the best prospects, administrators seek to maximize the apparent effectiveness of their programs.

In our juvenile justice application, the skimming model assumes that the population of offenders can be decomposed into "higher risk" and "lower risk" individuals. Higher risk individuals (type A) have higher probabilities of recidivism under both residential and nonresidential treatment than do lower risk individuals (type B). (The population does not contain persons who are at higher risk under one treatment but at lower risk under the other.) The model assumes that judges sentence all type A persons to residential treatment and type B to nonresidential treatment.

Why might judges sentence in accord with the skimming model? One possibility is that judges, like the administrators of educational and training programs, act to maximize the apparent rather than the actual effectiveness of their sentencing decisions. Alternatively, if the public blames the judicial system when offenders given "light" sentences commit subsequent crimes, then judges have an incentive to give light sentences only to type B persons, regardless of how sentencing actually affects recidivism.

Still another possibility is that judges act in accord with the normative view that the objective of the juvenile justice system should be to "punish the bad and forgive the good," where bad and good are interpreted as higher risk and lower risk, respectively. Under this view, high-risk individuals are perceived to be more blameworthy or culpable and thus are confined for retributive purposes. Singer (1996: 15) observes thus: "George Herbert Mead clearly saw the difficulty that was in store for the traditional juvenile justice courts in their attempt to pursue the 'best interests' of juveniles and society." In many ways it is easier simply to satisfy society's need to punish the offender. According to Mead (1961: 882), it is impossible "to hate the sin and love the sinner."

The outcome optimization model and the skimming model both assume that the dominant concern of judges in sentencing is recidivism, albeit for different reasons. How then do the predictions of these models differ? In some circumstances they do not. If the high-rate offenders are also the most amenable to treatment, both models predict that residential confinement will be focused on this group. However if the low-rate offenders are most susceptible to rehabilitative treatment, the models make opposing predictions. In this circumstance, the outcome optimization model predicts that the lower rate group will be sentenced to residential confinement, whereas the skimming model predicts that the high-rate group will still be sentenced to residential treatment and the low-rate offenders diverted. We formally demonstrate these divergent predictions in the section *Skimming* below.

In posing the outcome optimization model and the skimming model, we assert only that these models capture two competing and enduring tensions on the purpose of sentencing in the juvenile justice system, not that they are used in their pure form by any single judge or jurisdiction. Sanbor's (1996) survey suggests considerable variation across jurisdictions in perceptions of the emphasis that should be placed on these competing sentencing objectives. In one jurisdiction, for example, 66.7 percent of respondents believed that treatment needs should affect disposition, whereas in another only 21.5 percent cited treatment needs as a priority consideration. Thus in the former jurisdiction, the outcome minimization model may reasonably approximate the dominant objective of sentencing whereas in the latter it might be a poor approximation.

Qualitative studies (e.g., Cicourel, 1968; Emerson, 1969; Eisenstein and Jacob, 1977) may provide insightful subjective impressions of what transpires in isolated judicial proceedings, but they do not offer data that can be subjected to formal statistical analysis. The available statistical studies of sentencing decisions (e.g., Klepper et al., 1983; Peterson and Hagan, 1984; Albonetti, 1991) often begin by posing some verbal theory of judicial behavior but then do not go on to formalize this theory. The statistical analysis typically reported is a set of regressions of sentences on covariates such as race, gender, number of prior referrals, and severity of the crime. Such regressions may reveal that certain covariates predict observed sentences, but they do not explicitly model the process by which judges use these covariates or other available case information to reach decisions. In particular, the available statistical studies generally do not seek to analyze judges' perceptions of recidivism probabilities and the manner in which these perceptions affect sentencing decisions. A partial exception is Drass and Spencer (1987), which seeks to determine covariates that predict the probation risk assessments that probation officers report in their evaluations of defendants during presentencing processes.

In the course of writing this chapter, we have found that, in the absence of compelling empirical evidence, thoughtful criminologists are able to hold widely divergent views on the reality of judicial decision-making.

An anonymous reviewer of this chapter has asserted that in his or her experience, a judge's behavior cannot be explained by the skimming model. Yet other criminologists have stated to us that the skimming model does approximate the way that judges behave, while the outcome optimization model does not. Still others have emphasized that judges are heterogeneous, some behaving in a manner close to one model, some in a manner close to the other, and some basing their decisions primarily on ethical considerations of retribution or treatment rather than on practical considerations of recidivism.

The wide divergence in views on the reality of judicial decision-making makes it critical for social scientists to understand how inferences on treatment effects depend on the treatment selection assumptions imposed. Our objective in this section is to shed some light on this matter as it applies to an important theoretical question of the effect of treatment in the juvenile justice system on subsequent offending.

Outcome Optimization

Let s denote all the characteristics of the offender and environment that may be associated with treatment selection in a given case. That is, s

is a vector of variables measuring the information available to the judge at the time of sentencing. We do not need to specify what this information is, and we do not need to assume that different judges handling different cases possess the same types of information about those cases. The variable s simply symbolizes the information available to a judge handling a case, and so the treatment z chosen by the judge necessarily is a function of s. The outcome optimization model makes two assumptions. First, the judge knows the probabilities $P[y(1) = 1|s]$ and $P[y(0) = 1|s]$ of recidivism under the two possible treatments. Economists refer to this as the *rational expectations assumption.* Second, the judge selects the sentence yielding the smaller probability of recidivism. Thus,

$$P\left[y(1)=1|s\right]<P\left[y(0)=1|s\right]\Rightarrow z=1, \quad (7.12a)$$

$$P\left[y(0)=1|s\right]<P\left[y(1)=1|s\right]\Rightarrow z=0. \quad (7.12b)$$

Given these assumptions, judges are already acting to minimize recidivism. Hence changing from the status quo to mandatory residential treatment cannot lower the recidivism probability. Thus the status quo recidivism probability $P[y(z) = 1]$ is the lower bound on the recidivism probability $P[y(1) = 1]$ under mandatory residential treatment. The same reasoning applies to the policy of mandatory nonresidential treatment. Hence we have the following:

The bound on recidivism probability under mandatory residential treatment, assuming outcome optimization is

$$P\left[y(z)=1\right]\leq P\left[y(1)=1\right]$$
$$\leq P\left[y(1)=1|z=1\right]{\cdot}P(z=1)+P(z=0).$$
$$(7.13)$$

The bound on recidivism probability under mandatory nonresidential treatment, assuming outcome optimization is

$$P\left[y(z)=1\right]\leq P\left[y(0)=1\right]$$
$$\leq P\left[y(0)=1|z=0\right]{\cdot}P(z=0)+P(z=1).$$
$$(7.14)$$

Bounds (13) and (14) generalize to problems of decisions under uncertainty an earlier finding for problems of deterministic choice reported in Manski (1990, 1995). There, bounds (13) and (14) were shown to hold under a special case of the outcome optimization model, wherein the person selecting treatments knows the outcomes [$y(1)$, $y(0)$] and selects the treatment yielding the better outcome. That is, the information s was assumed to be so extensive that the probabilities $P[y(1) = 1|s]$ and $P[y(0) = 1|s]$ take the extreme values zero or one. In the literature on labor economics, this special case is sometimes referred to as the Roy model after Roy (1951), who applied it to the study of occupation choice. In the literature on survival analysis, this case is commonly known as the competing risks model (e.g., Kalbfleisch and Prentice, 1980).

Bounds on the CTEs and STEs are computed in the same fashion as in the no-assumptions case:

The bound on the CTE, assuming outcome optimization is

$$-P\big[y(1)=0\,|\,z=1\big]\cdot P(z=1)\le \text{CTE} \atop \le P\big[y(0)=0\,|\,z=0\big]\cdot P(z=0).$$ (7.15)

The bound on the STE, assuming outcome optimization is

$$0 \le \text{STE} \le P\big[y(0)=0\,|\,z=0\big]\cdot P(z=0).$$ (7.16)

The new bound on the CTE is narrower than the no-assumptions bound derived earlier, but the new lower bound is still non-positive and the new upper bound is still nonnegative. Thus combining the data with the outcome optimization assumption still does not suffice to identify the sign of the CTE.

The new lower bound on the STE is zero. This provides an ironic reminder that under the outcome optimization model, judges are already acting to minimize recidivism. Under this model, changing from the status quo to mandatory residential treatment cannot possibly lower the recidivism rate.

Skimming

Again let s denote all the characteristics of the offender and environment that may be associated with treatment selection and assume that the judge knows the probabilities $P[y(1) = 1|s]$ and $P[y(0) = 1|s]$ of recidivism under treatments 1 and 0. Type A and type B offenders are distinguished by their values of these probabilities. In particular, there exist thresholds Π_1 and Π_0 such that

Type A offenders:

$$P[y(1)=1|s]\geq \Pi_1 \quad \text{and} \quad P[y(0)=1|s]\geq \Pi_0, \quad (7.17a)$$

Type B offenders:

$$P[y(1)=1|s]<\Pi_1 \quad \text{and} \quad P[y(0)=1|s]<\Pi_0. \quad (7.17b)$$

Thus, for each treatment, type A offenders have higher recidivism probabilities than do type B offenders.

The skimming model assumes that judges assign residential treatment to the higher risk, type A offenders, and nonresidential treatment to the lower risk, type B offenders. Thus,

$$\begin{aligned} &P[y(1)=1|s]\geq \Pi_1 \quad \text{and} \\ &P[y(0)=1|s]\geq \Pi_0 \Rightarrow z=1, \end{aligned} \quad (7.18a)$$

$$\begin{aligned} &P[y(1)=1|s]<\Pi_1 \quad \text{and} \\ &P[y(0)=1|s]<\Pi_0 \Rightarrow z=0. \end{aligned} \quad (7.18b)$$

When these assumptions hold, the observed recidivism rate among the type A offenders sentenced to residential treatment forms an upper bound on the recidivism rate that would occur if residential treatment were made mandatory for offenders of both types. Analogously, the observed recidivism rate among the type B offenders sentenced to nonresidential treatment forms a lower bound on the recidivism rate that would occur if nonresidential treatment were made mandatory for offenders of both types. Hence we have the following:

Bound on recidivism probability under mandatory residential treatment, assuming skimming

$$\begin{aligned} &P[y(1)=1|z=1]\cdot P(z=1) \\ &\leq P[y(1)=1]\leq P[y(1)=1|z=1]. \end{aligned} \quad (7.19)$$

Bound on recidivism probability under mandatory nonresidential treatment, assuming skimming

$$\begin{aligned} &P[y(0)=1|z=0]\leq P[y(0)=1] \\ &\leq P[y(0)=1|z=0]\cdot P(z=0)+P(z=1). \end{aligned} \quad (7.20)$$

Manski and Nagin (1998) provide a full detailed derivation of these bounds.

It is important to understand that, although the outcome optimization model and the skimming model pose distinct decision rules, they need not yield different sentencing decisions. In principle, the skimming rule can result in exactly the same or entirely opposite treatment assignments as the outcome optimization rule. To illustrate, let the two thresholds be the same, with $\Pi_1 = \Pi_0 = \Pi$, and consider two special cases of equations (7.18). In one case, the recidivism probabilities satisfy

Type A offenders : $P\big[y(0)=1\,|\,s\big] > P\big[y(1)=1\,|\,s\big] \geq \Pi$

and

Type B offenders : $P[y(0)=1\,|\,s] < P[y(1)=1\,|\,s] < \Pi.$

In the other case, they satisfy

Type A offenders : $P[y(1)=1\,|\,s] > P[y(0)=1\,|\,s] \geq \Pi$

and

Type B offenders : $P[y(1)=1\,|\,s] < P[y(0)=1\,|\,s] < \Pi.$

In the first case, outcome minimization and skimming yield the same treatment decisions—type A offenders are sentenced to residential treatment and type B offenders to nonresidential treatment. In the second case, the two models imply contrary decisions. Under the outcome optimization rule, all of the type Bs are sentenced to residential treatment and all of the type As to nonresidential treatment. Under the skimming rule, the opposite occurs.

Bounds on the CTEs and STEs under the skimming model are computed in the same fashion as in the no-assumptions case. The results are as follows:

Bound on the CTE, assuming skimming

$$P[y(1)=1\,|\,z=1] \bullet P(z=1) -$$
$$\big\{ P[y(0)=1\,|\,z=0] \bullet P(z=0) + P(z=1) \big\} \leq \text{CTE} \qquad (7.21)$$
$$\leq P[y(1)=1\,|\,z=1] - P[y(0)=1\,|\,z=0].$$

Bound on the STE, assuming skimming

$$-P[y(0)=1 \mid z=0] \cdot P(z=0) \leq \text{STE} \tag{7.22}$$
$$\leq \{P[y(1)=1 \mid z=1] - P[y(0)=1 \mid z=0]\} \cdot P(z=0).$$

The new lower bounds on both treatment effects are the same as their respective no-assumptions lower bounds, and so they are necessarily non-positive. The new upper bounds are both less than their respective no-assumptions upper bounds and can, in principle, be either negative or positive. If the quantity $P[y(1) = 1 \mid z = 1] - P[y(0) = 1 \mid z = 0]$ appearing in both upper bounds is negative, then the skimming model implies that the CTEs and the STEs are both negative. If this quantity is positive, then the signs of these treatment effects are not identified.

In section *Bounds on Treatment Effects Using the Data Alone*, we showed that $P[y(1) = 1 \mid z = 1] - P[y(0) = 1 \mid z = 0]$ is the CTE under the assumption that treatment selection is random. Here we find that this quantity has an alternative interpretation as the upper bound on the CTE under the skimming model.

Application

Table 7.3 reports bounds on the CTE under the two alternative models of treatment selection. Inspection of the table reveals that these two models imply distinctly different conclusions. Assuming that judges select treatments to minimize the probability of recidivism, the results point strongly, although not definitively, to the conclusion that the CTE is positive—that is, mandatory residential treatment yields a higher rate of recidivism than mandatory nonresidential treatment. Consider, for

Table 7.3 **Bound on classical treatment effect under alternative models of treatment selection, by number of prior referrals**

| | Treatment selection model | | | | | |
| | No assumptions | | Outcome optimization | | Skimming | |
Priors	Lower bound	Upper bound	Lower bound	Upper bound	Lower bound	Upper bound
0	−0.48	0.52	−0.02	0.50	−0.48	0.09
1	−0.65	0.35	−0.03	0.26	−0.65	0.07
2+	−0.65	0.35	−0.04	0.13	−0.65	0.02

example, the subpopulation of cases where the offender has one prior. Here we find that $-0.03 \leq \text{CTE} \leq 0.26$. Thus mandatory residential treatment can at most be marginally beneficial (the lower bound of -0.03) but might be substantially harmful (the upper bound of 0.26).

Assuming that judges use skimming rules to select treatments, the evidence points more to the efficacy of residential treatment. Consider again the subpopulation of cases where the offender has one prior. Now we find that $-0.65 \leq \text{CTE} \leq 0.07$. Thus mandatory residential treatment might be substantially beneficial (the lower bound of -0.65) but can be no more than moderately harmful (the upper bound of 0.07).

Table 7.4 reports bounds on the STE, which measures the change in recidivism probability that would occur if mandatory residential treatment were to replace the existing treatment rules used by judges. The STE may be of greater interest to policymakers than the CTE.

Consider in particular the subpopulation of cases in which the offender has two or more prior referrals—these offenders being the most likely target of a policy of mandatory residential treatment. The results offer a potent reminder of the sensitivity of conclusions to the assumed model of treatment assignment. Under the skimming model, the results imply that mandatory residential treatment at most marginally increases recidivism (the upper bound of 0.02) and may greatly decrease recidivism (the lower bound of -0.61). Under the outcome optimization model, we reach the opposite conclusion. Here the best possible outcome of mandatory residential treatment is no increase in recidivism. This conclusion follows directly from the model's defining supposition that juvenile court judges are already assigning the recidivism-minimizing treatment.

Table 7.4   Bound on status quo treatment effect under alternative models of treatment selection, by number of prior referrals

	Treatment selection model					
	No assumptions		Outcome optimization		Skimming	
Priors	Lower bound	Upper bound	Lower bound	Upper bound	Lower bound	Upper bound
0	−0.46	0.50	0	0.50	−0.46	0.09
1	−0.62	0.26	0	0.26	−0.62	0.07
2+	−0.61	0.13	0	0.13	−0.61	0.02

Exclusion Restrictions

Theory

The analysis of the two sections above may be applied to any identifiable subpopulation of offenders. Our notation has not explicitly denoted the subpopulation of interest, but this is easily done. A subpopulation is composed of those offenders with specified covariates x. The subpopulation is identifiable if x is observed by the researcher.

With this notation, we can explicitly make our analysis subpopulation-specific by everywhere conditioning on x. Thus $P[y(1) = 1|x]$ and $P[y(0) = 1|x]$ are the recidivism probabilities in the subpopulation with covariates x under mandatory residential and nonresidential treatment respectively, $P[y(z) = 1|x]$ is the status quo recidivism probability, and $P(z = 1|x)$ is the probability of receiving treatment 1 in this subpopulation. In the outcome optimization and the skimming models, we need to assume that the information s available to judges includes knowledge of the covariates x. In the skimming model, the thresholds used to define type A and B offenders may now vary with x.

In principle, each identifiable subpopulation may have a distinct treatment selection and outcome process, implying distinct values of the treatment effects. An exclusion restriction assumes that the recidivism probabilities under mandatory treatments do not vary with x. Formally, let $x = 1, \ldots, K$ denote K different subpopulations comprising a larger population of interest. Then x is "excluded" from the determination of recidivism under mandatory treatments if

$$P[y(1) = 1\,|\,x] = P[y(1) = 1], \quad \text{all } x = 1,\ldots,K \quad (7.23a)$$

and

$$P[y(0) = 1\,|\,x] = P[y(0) = 1], \quad \text{all } x = 1,\ldots,K \quad (7.23b)$$

An exclusion restriction does not state that the subpopulations are identical in all respects. The treatment selection process may vary across subpopulations. For example, it may be that skimming takes place in some subpopulations, outcome optimization in others, and yet other treatment rules elsewhere.

An exclusion restriction can be imposed alone or it can be layered on top of other assumptions (e.g., outcome optimization or skimming) that restrict the values of the recidivism probabilities in each subpopulation separately. Whatever other assumptions may be imposed, an exclusion restriction is used in the same way, which we now describe.

Consider the problem of inference on $P[y(1) = 1]$; the case of $P[y(0) = 1]$ is analogous. We first ignore the exclusion restriction and determine what can be learned about $P[y(1) = 1|x]$ in each subpopulation x using the other assumptions imposed. If no other assumptions are imposed, we compute the no-assumptions bound in each subpopulation. If outcome optimization or skimming is assumed in a given subpopulation, we compute the bound given in section *Outcome Optimization* or *Skimming*, as appropriate.

Let $B_{1.x}$ denote the bound on $P[y(1) = 1|x]$ thus obtained in subpopulation x. The exclusion restriction implies, by equation (7.23a), that the population-wide recidivism probability $P[y(1) = 1]$ must lie within all of the bounds $B_{1.x}$, $x = 1, \ldots, K$. That is,

$$P[y(1) = 1] \in B_{1.x}, \quad \text{all } x = 1, \ldots, K. \quad (7.24)$$

Equation (7.24) expresses the identifying power of an exclusion restriction. Whereas the analysis of the previous two sections placed $P[y(1) = 1]$ within one population-wide bound, imposition of an exclusion restriction places $P[y(1) = 1]$ within the intersection of K subpopulation-specific bounds. The basic bounding argument just given was introduced independently by Manski (1990) and Robins (1989), and developed further in Manski (1994). Distinct bounds that apply under a stronger form of the exclusion restriction have been developed by Balke and Pearl (1997).

Application

The bounds obtained under the outcome optimization model and the skimming model are much narrower than the no-assumptions bounds but do not sign the CTE. We next examine whether the addition of an exclusion restriction narrows the bounds sufficiently to identify the sign of the effect.

In particular, we suppose that treatment selection may vary geographically within the state of Utah but that treatment response does not vary across the state. The Utah juvenile justice system is divided into eight districts composed of geographically contiguous counties. Four districts are relatively small and so we aggregate them into a single "mega-district." There is reason to think that treatment selection varies from district to district, each district having different judges and, perhaps, different sentencing norms. The critical feature of the exclusion restriction is that treatment response is assumed not to vary from district to district. That is, we assume that if all districts were to have policies of mandatory residential (or nonresidential) treatment, all districts would experience the same recidivism probability. This assumption may or may not be realistic. Our objective is simply to illustrate the identifying power of an exclusion restriction. This approach could be applied to a number of tests of sentencing that seek to examine the influence of geographic disparities in judicial philosophies.

Table 7.5 reports on bounds on the CTE using the district exclusion restriction. Panel A reports the estimated bounds and Panel B reports companion 90 percent confidence intervals. The results are striking. Under the outcome optimization model, the estimated bounds are strictly positive for each number of prior referrals, which implies that residential treatment exacerbates recidivism. Under the skimming model, the bounds are strictly negative for offenders with one or more prior referrals, which implies that residential treatment has an ameliorative effect. Finally, if no assumptions are made about the treatment selection process, imposition of the district exclusion does little to narrow the no-assumptions bounds reported in section *Basic Analysis*.

Table 7.5   Bound on classical treatment effects under alternative models of treatment selection, by priors, using district as exclusion restriction

Priors	No assumptions		Outcome optimization		Skimming	
	Lower bound	Upper bound	Lower bound	Upper bound	Lower bound	Upper bound
A. Estimated bounds						
0	−0.43	0.48	0.06	0.46	−0.43	0.03
1	−0.59	0.27	0.07	0.19	−0.59	−0.08
2+	−0.62	0.28	0.02	0.06	−0.62	−0.11
B. 90 percent confidence interval						
0	−0.45	0.50	0.04	0.47	−0.45	0.05
1	−0.62	0.31	0.03	0.20	−0.62	−0.00
2+	−0.64	0.32	−0.01	0.07	−0.64	−0.04

Conclusion

This chapter has sought to demonstrate the usefulness of a research approach that differs from the conventional practice of the social sciences. It is conventional to make assumptions strong enough to yield point identification and then argue the merits of those assumptions relative to alternatives. We seek instead to bound disagreements among researchers by examining what can be learned about treatment effects under alternative models of treatment selection and by layering progressively stronger assumptions about which there is likely to be less consensus.

In this spirit, what conclusions can be drawn from our empirical findings? The answer plainly depends on the assumptions one is willing to make. If no assumptions are made about the treatment selection process, the results mostly provide guidance in the negative. The bounds on the treatment effects do not identify their signs and place relatively weak restrictions on their magnitudes. However, for those who have a favored model of treatment selection, the results are far more informative. If one's favored model of judicial sentencing behavior is outcome optimization, the results suggest that residential treatment exacerbates recidivism. If one favors the skimming model, the results suggest that residential treatment has an ameliorative effect on recidivism. Imposition of the district exclusion restriction strengthens each of these opposing conclusions. Thus our empirical research implies fairly strong conclusions provided that there is a consensus favoring either the outcome optimization model or the skimming model.

That said, we do not see such a consensus among criminologists. In the absence of consensus, our empirical analysis remains instructive. The opposing conclusions arising from the two models of treatment selection demonstrate the value for informed scientific discourse of identifying zones of agreement and disagreement among researchers, as well as the reasons for such agreements and disagreements. In this application, unless researchers can agree on the treatment selection process, analysis of observed sentences and recidivism can do little to settle the question of the sign of treatment effects.

Our work clearly points to the need for further research analyzing how judges actually make sentencing decisions. Although the outcome optimization model and the skimming model differ from one another, they share critical simplifying assumptions—namely, that judges are concerned only with recidivism and that judges have rational expectations about recidivism. It may be that these shared assumptions are unrealistic. To make further progress in the analysis of recidivism using observational data, we need to better understand how sentencing decisions actually are made.

The results also illustrate the value of layering assumptions based on consensus about their validity. Suppose, for example, that one believes the skimming model to be a realistic depiction of the actual treatment selection process. This model alone does not provide a firm basis for signing treatment effects. Only with the additional imposition of the district exclusion restriction were we able to sign treatment effects with full confidence. It should, moreover, be kept in mind that all of the conclusions drawn in this chapter rest on the maintained assumptions that treatment is individualistic and that outcomes and treatments are correctly measured.

Postscript to "Bounding Disagreements about Treatment Effects"

The work reported in our chapter was performed in the mid-1990s. Readers interested in the themes of the chapter may be curious about developments since then. This postscript calls attention to some of them. We focus on identification of treatment response and the closely related problem of treatment choice. Other developments that are more distant from our chapter are exposited in the research monograph of Manski (2003), the graduate textbook of Manski (2007), and the review article of Tamer (2010).

Identification of Treatment Response

First consider the use of weak assumptions to bound treatment effects in observational studies, as performed in our chapter. Manski and Pepper (2000) introduced the idea of *monotone instrumental variables* (MIVs). These assumptions weaken traditional exclusion restrictions. Instead of assuming that mean treatment response is the same in different groups, MIVs assume that mean response weakly increases across specified groups. Manski and Pepper used the idea to bound the returns to schooling. Subsequent applications are described in Manski and Pepper (2009).

Next consider the use of experimental data to analyze treatment response. The classical literature presumes complete compliance and no missing data on outcomes or covariates. However, these assumptions are often violated in practice. Hence, analysis of experimental data faces identification problems similar to those occurring with observational data.

Horowitz and Manski (2000) and Scharfstein et al. (2004) report bounds on treatment effects when subjects may exit from an experiment before their outcomes are recorded. The former article also studies identification of treatment effects conditional on covariates, when some covariate data are missing. Manski (2007, Chapter 7) describes a spectrum of approaches to the analysis of experiments with imperfect compliance.

Manski (1997a) introduced and studied the *mixing problem*, an unappreciated problem in the analysis of experimental data. The mixing problem arises when data from experiments are used to predict the outcomes of policies that offer but do not mandate treatments. Choice among alternative preschool policies was used to illustrate findings. Randomized experiments with preschool interventions have sought to learn the outcomes that occur when members of treatment and control groups are required to enroll or not enroll in a proposed program. The mixing problem occurs when one wants to use such experimental data to forecast outcomes under a policy that makes the program available, but does not mandate participation.

Treatment Choice under Ambiguity

An important objective of research analyzing treatment response is to provide information useful in choosing treatment policy. Economists and other analysts have long asked how a policymaker, or *planner*, should act. A standard exercise specifies a set of feasible treatment policies and a welfare function. The planner is presumed to know how persons respond to treatment. The goal is to characterize the optimal policy.

The practical relevance of the standard exercise is limited by the fact that, as described in our chapter, research typically yields only partial knowledge of treatment response. Hence, planners cannot determine optimal policies. Instead, they must choose treatments under ambiguity.

Treatment under ambiguity is common when setting criminal justice policy. Judicial sentencing is one important example. Another is choice of policies that aim to deter crime. Researchers have long sought to learn the deterrent effect of punishment on criminality. Yet progress has been slow and public debates about the deterrent effect of alternative policies are frequent.

Identification problems were first connected with treatment choice under ambiguity in Manski (2000, 2002). The work has since advanced through Manski (2005, 2006, 2007, 2009, 2010). Manski (2006) may be of particular interest to criminologists, studying the policing problem of setting a rate of search for evidence of crime, when the deterrent effect of search is not known.

A broad theme of this research is that diversified treatment may be appealing when the optimal policy is unknown. The minimax regret criterion, a venerable idea in decision theory, can be applied to choose a diversified policy. *Adaptive diversification* can reduce ambiguity over time. See Manski (2009).

Bibliography

Ahn, Hyungtaik and James L. Powell. "Semiparametric Estimation of Censored Selection Models with a Nonparametric Selection Mechanism." *Journal of Econometrics* 58 (1993): 3–29.

Albonetti, Celesta A. "An Integration of Theories to Explain Judicial Discretion." *Social Problems* 38 (1991): 247–66.

Andrews, D., I. Zinger, R. Hoge, J. Bonta, P. Gendreau, and F. Cullen. "Does Correctional Treatment Work? A Clinically Relevant and Psychologically Informed Meta-analysis." *Criminology* 28 (1990): 369–404.

Balke, Alexander and Judea Pearl. "Bounds on Treatment Effects from Studies with Imperfect Compliance." *Journal of the American Statistical Association* 92 (1997): 1171–77.

Becker, Howard. *Outsiders*. New York: Free Press, 1963.

Bernard, Thomas. *Cycles of Juvenile Justice*. New York: Oxford University Press, 1992.

Cicourel, Aaron V. *The Social Organization of Juvenile Justice*. New York: Wiley, 1968.

Cochran, William, Frederick Mosteller, and John Tukey. *Statistical Problems of the Kinsey Report on Sexual Behavior in the Human Male*. Washington, DC: American Statistical Association, 1954.

Cullen, F., J. Cullen, and J. Woznick. "Is Rehabilitation Dead? The Myth of the Punitive Public." *Journal of Criminal Justice* 16 (1988): 303–17.

Drass, Kriss A. and J. William Spencer. "Accounting for Pre-sentencing Recommendations: Typologies and Probations Officers' Theory of Office." *Social Problems* 34 (1987): 277–93.

Eisenstein, James and Herbert Jacob. *Felony Justice*. Boston: Little, Brown, 1977.

Emerson, Robert. *Judging Delinquents*. Chicago, IL: Aldine, 1969.

Feld, Barry. *Bad Kids*. New York, NY: Oxford University Press, 1999.

Frechet, Maurice. "Sur les Tableaux de Correlation dont les Marges Sont Donnees." *Annales de Universite de Lyon A* 14, no. 3 (1951): 53–77.

Garfinkel, Irwin, Charles F. Manski, and Charles Michalopolous. "Micro-Experiments and Macro Effects." In *Evaluating Welfare and Training Programs*, edited by Charles F. Manski and Irwin Garfinkel, 253–73. Cambridge, MA: Harvard University Press, 1992.

Goldberger, Arthur S. "Abnormal Selection Bias." In *Studies in Econometrics, Time Series, and Multivariate Statistics*, edited by Samuel Karlin, Takeshi Amemiya, and Leo Goodman, 67–84. New York: Academic Press, 1983.

Gove, Walter. "Labelling and Mental Illness: A Critique." In *The Labeling of Deviance*, edited by W. Gove, 2nd ed. Beverly Hills, CA: Sage, 1980.

Heckman, James J. "The Common Structure of Statistical Models of Truncation, Sample Selection, and Limited Dependent Variables and a Simple Estimator for Such Models." *Annals of Economic and Social Measurement* 5 (1976): 479–92.

———. "Dummy Endogenous Variables in a Simultaneous Equation System." *Econometrica* 46 (1978): 931–59.

Heckman, James J. and Bo Honore. "The Empirical Content of the Roy Model." *Econometrica* 58 (1990): 1121–49.

Horowitz, Joel L. and Charles F. Manski. "Nonparametric Analysis of Randomized Experiments with Missing Covariate and Outcome Data." *Journal of the American Statistical Association* 95 (2000): 77–84.

Imbens, Guido and Joshua Angrist. "Identification and Estimation of Local Average Treatment Effects." *Econometrica* 62 (1994): 467–76.

Kalbfleisch, John D. and Ross L. Prentice. *The Statistical Analysis of Failure Time Data*. New York: Wiley, 1980.

Kitsuse, J. "Societal Reaction to Deviant Behavior: Problems of Theory and Method." *Social Problems* 9 (1962): 247–57.

Klepper, Steven, Daniel L. Nagin, and Luke-Jon Tierney. "Discrimination in the Criminal Justice System: A Critical Appraisal of the Literature." In *Research on Sentencing: The Search for Reform*, edited by Alfred Blumstein, Jacqueline Cohen, Susan Martin, and Michael Tonry, vol. 2, 55–128. Washington, DC: National Academy Press, 1983.

LaLonde, Robert. "Evaluating the Econometric Evaluations of Training Programs with Experimental Data." *American Economic Review* 76 (1986): 604–20.

Lemert, Edwin M. *Social Pathology*. New York: McGraw-Hill, 1951.

Maddala, G. S. *Qualitative and Limited Dependent Variable Models in Econometrics*. Cambridge, England: Cambridge University Press, 1983.

Manski, Charles F. "Anatomy of the Selection Problem." *Journal of Human Resources* 24 (1989): 343–60.

———. "Nonparametric Bounds on Treatment Effects." *American Economic Review Papers and Proceedings* 80 (1990): 319–23.

———. "Regression." *Journal of Economic Literature* 29 (1991): 34–50.

———. "Identification Problems in the Social Sciences." In *Sociological Methodology 1993*, edited by Peter V. Marsden, 1–56. Cambridge, MA: Blackwell Publishers, 1993.

———. "The Selection Problem." In *Advances in Econometrics, Sixth World Congress*, edited by Christopher Sims, 143–70. Cambridge, England: Cambridge University Press, 1994.

———. *Identification Problems in the Social Sciences*. Cambridge, MA: Harvard University Press, 1995.

———. "Learning about Treatment Effects from Experiments with Random Assignment of Treatments." *Journal of Human Resources* 31 (1996): 707–33.

———. "The Mixing Problem in Programme Evaluation." *Review of Economic Studies* 64 (1997): 537–53.

———. Partial Identification of Probability Distributions, New York: Springer, 2003.

———. *Social Choice with Partial Knowledge of Treatment Response*. Princeton: Princeton University Press, 2005.

———. "Search Profiling with Partial Knowledge of Deterrence." *The Economic Journal* 116 (2006): F385–401.

———. *Identification for Prediction and Decision*. Cambridge: Harvard University Press, 2007.

Manski, Charles F. "Diversified Treatment under Ambiguity," *International Economic Review* 50 (2009): 1013–1041.

Manski, Charles F. "Vaccination with Partial Knowledge of External Effectiveness," Proceedings of the *National Academy of Sciences* 107 (2010): 3953–3960.

Manski, Charles F. and Daniel Nagin. "Bounding Disagreements about Treatment Effects: A Case Study of Sentencing and Recidivism." *Sociological Methodology* 28 (1998): 99–137.

Manski, Charles F. and John Pepper. "Monotone Instrumental Variables: With an Application to the Returns to Schooling." *Econometrica* 68 (2000): 997–1010.

Manski, Charles F. and John Pepper. "More on Monotone Instrumental Variables," *The Econometrics Journal* 12 (2009): S200–S216.

Manski, Charles F., Gary Sandefur, Sara McLanahan, and Daniel Power. "Alternative Estimates of the Effect of Family Structure During Adolescence on High School Graduation." *Journal of the American Statistical Association* 87 (1992): 25–37.

Matza, David. *Becoming Deviant*. Englewood Cliffs, NJ: Prentice-Hall, 1969.

National Juvenile Court Data Archive. *Users Guide to Utah Juvenile Court Case Records, 1962–1972 Birth Cohort.* Pittsburgh, PA: National Center for Juvenile Justice, 1992.

Paternoster, Raymond and Leeann Iovanni. "The Labeling Perspective and Delinquency: An Elaboration of the Theory and Assessment of the Evidence." *Justice Quarterly* 6 (1989): 359–94.

Peterson, Ruth D. and John Hagan. "Changing Conceptions of Race: Towards an Account of Anomalous Findings of Sentencing Research." *American Sociological Review* 49 (1984): 56–70.

Robins, James. "The Analysis of Randomized and Non-Randomized AIDS Treatment Trials Using a New Approach to Causal Inference in Longitudinal Studies." In *Health Service Research Methodology: A Focus on AIDS*, edited by L. Sechrest, H. Freeman, and A. Mulley, 112–59. Rockville, MD: National Center for Health Services Research, U.S. Public Health Service, 1989.

Rosenbaum, Paul and Donald Rubin. "The Central Role of the Propensity Score in Observational Studies for Causal Effects." *Biometrika* 70 (1983): 41–55.

Rothman, David J. *Conscience and Convenience: The Asylum and Its Alternative in Progressive America.* Boston, MA: Little, Brown, 1980.

Roy, A. "Some Thoughts on the Distribution of Earnings." *Oxford Economic Papers* 3 (1951): 135–46.

Sanbor, J. "Factors Perceived to Affect Delinquent Dispositions in Juvenile Court: Putting the Sentencing Decision in Context." *Crime and Delinquency* 42 (1996): 99–113.

Scharfstein, Daniel, Charles Manski, and James Anthony. "On the Construction of Bounds in Prospective Studies with Missing Ordinal Outcomes: Application to the Good Behavior Game Trial." *Biometrics* 60 (2004): 154–64.

Schlossman, Steven L. *Love and the American Delinquent.* Chicago, IL: University of Chicago Press, 1977.

Schur, Edwin M. *Labeling Deviant Behavior: Its Sociological Implications.* New York: Harper and Row, 1971.

Sechrist, Lee, Susan White, and Elizabeth D. Brown. *The Rehabilitation of Criminal Offenders: Problems and Prospects.* Washington, DC: National Academy Press, 1979.

Singer, Simon I. *Recriminalizing Delinquency.* New York: Cambridge University Press, 1996.

Smith, Douglas A. and Raymond Paternoster. "Formal Processing and Future Delinquency: Deviance Amplification as Selection Artifact." *Law and Society Review* 24 (1990): 1109–31.

Tamer, Elie. "Partial Identification in Econometrics." *Annual Review of Economics* 2 (2010): 167–95.

Tittle, Charles. "Labelling and Crime: An Empirical Evaluation." In The Labelling of Deviance, edited by W. Gove, 2nd ed. Beverly Hills, CA: Sage Publications, 1980.

Van den Haag, Ernest. *Punishing Criminals: Concerning a Very Old and Painful Question.* New York: Basic Books, 1975.

Whitehead, J. and S. Lab. "A Meta-analysis of Juvenile Correctional Treatment." *Journal of Research in Crime and Delinquency* 26 (1989): 276–95.

Willis, Robert and Sherwin Rosen. "Education and Self-Selection." *Journal of Political Economy* 87 (1979): S7–36.

8

Randomized Experiments and the Advancement of Criminological Theory

Geoffrey C. Barnes and Jordan M. Hyatt

Randomized experiments can be typecast as a means of program evaluation, feeding the deceptive perception that they are more useful for testing specific policy options than they are for building criminological theory. The history of science, however, is marked by "crucial experiments." These key turning points have occurred when theoretical principles were either confirmed or disproven, and our knowledge of the world suddenly sprinted forward. There is no reason why this pattern of advancement should be any less applicable to criminology than it is to other scientific disciplines. What remains unclear are the features of an experimental research design that can make it most useful for playing this leading role.

The power of experimental trials to do certain things very well is fairly well established. While the label may be something of a misnomer (Berk, 2005), randomized experiments are often referred to as the "gold standard" of research methods within criminology (Sherman et al., 1998), as well as in medicine (Meldrum, 2000), education (Mosteller, 2002), and other scientific disciplines. The primary, and well-known, justification for randomized trials is their ability to draw clear conclusions about causality. Through random assignment—and, ultimately, only through random assignment—researchers can create equivalent groups of participants, and then allow some of these groups to receive a treatment intervention, while others do not (Sherman, 2009). Any

This work was supported by a grant from the Smith Richardson Foundation and by Grant 2008-IJ-CX-0024 from the National Institute of Justice. The findings and conclusions are those of the authors and do not necessarily reflect the official position or policies of the U.S. Department of Justice.

subsequent differences between these formerly equivalent groups can be safely seen as true effects that were caused by the intervention. Though other methods may attempt to mimic this ability, Farrington (2003: 218–19) warns of their shortcomings:

> A randomized experiment can establish the effect of an intervention more convincingly than alternative quasi-experimental evaluation methods that involve matched intervention and control groups, the comparison of predicted and actual outcomes in each group, or statistical adjustment for preexisting differences between groups. Basically, statistical control is not as good as experimental control.

This is not to say, however, that randomized trials are the only method through which valid evidence can be obtained. Experiments are narrowly focused instruments, with particular skill at revealing causal effects. While this focus is the source of their power, it also leaves them subject to both practical burdens and a healthy amount of criticism. Nonexperimental and observational studies most certainly have a role to play. They can be particularly effective at revealing the underlying patterns within human behavior that often form the basis of criminological theory. They may also be the only option available when ethical, practical, and political hurdles make the use of a randomized controlled trial (RCT) impossible (Weisburd, 2000). Nevertheless, there comes a time when the need to demonstrate clear and unambiguous causal effects becomes crucially important. In these situations, designing and implementing a randomized experiment may be challenging, controversial, and even imperfect, while still remaining the best option available to advance our understanding of criminal behavior.

Randomized experiments and the progression of criminological theory, therefore, go hand in hand. Theory can be developed without testing its causal predictions, but it cannot be refined. Refinement takes evidence, and more specifically evidence that can be widely accepted as accurate, and not simply ignored due to perceived methodological shortcomings. Our goal in this chapter is to address how randomized trials can play this crucial role in the development of theory and to demonstrate which features of RCT design are needed to have this impact. We begin this process by examining some of the more potent criticisms of experiments that have appeared in the literature in recent times.

Contemporary Criticisms of Randomized Experimentation

Despite their oft-cited benefits, the use of randomized trials in criminological settings has lately become the target of some wide-ranging skepticism. As both Berk (2005) and Hough (2010) suggest, criminology seems to be caught in ever-widening swings between advocacy for and criticism of this particular form of research, and we face some danger that the rhetoric—on both sides—will soon surpass realistic boundaries. In this section, we attempt to address some of the more recent criticisms of experiments in criminology and to assess what alternative methodologies, if any, could best address these concerns.

Testing the "Soil" Instead of the "Crop"

One fundamental question about randomized trials—and perhaps particularly those that focus upon the "intention-to-treat" (ITT) as the tested intervention—is what kind of treatment is really being tested. An ITT analysis sticks resolvedly to the experimental dictum to "analyze as you randomize," regardless of what treatment was ultimately delivered to, or received by, the individual participants in the research. A participant who was randomly assigned to attend a community-based drug treatment program, but who quit the program when they were rearrested and sent to prison, would nevertheless be analyzed as a member of their assigned treatment group. By focusing on the intention to provide treatment, instead of the successful delivery of it, the benefits of random assignment are preserved and the ability to demonstrate causation is maintained, but at a potentially significant cost. If the number of treatment failures grows too large, the ITT becomes essentially meaningless, and the findings produced by the experiment can quickly suffer the same fate.

While clearly defined and strongly enforced eligibility rules can prevent untreatable participants from being randomly assigned in the first place, some degree of treatment failure is inevitable in almost every RCT. Researchers who manage most experiments, therefore, end up devoting much of their time and effort to ensuring that these failures are kept to a minimum and that most participants receive the treatment to which they were randomly assigned. The complication here is that certain types of participants will be inherently more likely to become treatment failures than others. Although these participants will be present in both the treatment and the untreated control groups, they will be detectable only among those who were offered the treatment. Thus the central research focus in many RCTs ultimately becomes a two-stage question. First, which kinds of participants are most likely to be treatable, and only then—once they have been treated—how will they respond to the treatment that they have received?

Hope (2009: 129) provides an excellent illustration of this problem, using Neighborhood Watch as an example of the inferential difficulty that it creates:

> [S]ince [Neighborhood] Watch (NW) groups are unlikely to germinate in communities that lack the appropriate social soil (Hope and Trickett, 2004), a field experiment that sought to evaluate NW by creating exchangeable treatment groups would only be evaluating the effectiveness of implementing NW (i.e., the method of planting the crop) and not the effectiveness of NW per se (i.e., whether NW was a better strain of crop than another) (Hope, 2005), and would not therefore solve the crop planting problem (is it the crop or is it the soil?) that is central to community crime prevention. (Rosenbaum, D. P.: 1987)

What Hope is missing here, however, is any suggestion of what method or methods would constitute a better approach. There are numerous theoretical reasons to propose that an organized and functioning Neighborhood Watch could reduce crime in certain kinds of neighborhoods (Bennett et al., 2006). There is also an extensive literature that suggests which kinds of neighborhoods have the fertile soil that will allow Neighborhood Watch to thrive, and which other kinds of neighborhoods are likely to see these efforts wither on the vine (Bennett, 1990).

Assuming that one wished to test the effects of Neighborhood Watch, one possible method would be the type of RCT that Hope (2009) describes. A full range of neighborhoods—both fertile and non-fertile—could be randomly allocated so that half of them received some kind of Neighborhood Watch organizing effort. In the experimental treatment group, many of the fertile neighborhoods would bear fruit, and watch efforts would be established within them. Meanwhile, similar fertile areas that were assigned to the control group would go without the benefits of outside organizing efforts. This absence of treatment, however, would not preclude the establishment of organic, homegrown programs that were very much like Neighborhood Watch in everything but name.

In both treatment groups, however, the non-fertile neighborhoods would not probably develop any kind of watch program. Most non-fertile areas assigned to the experimental group would not respond to the treatment program, and the residents in the non-fertile control areas would be unlikely to come up with such an idea on their own. As Hope warns us, we would be left with an RCT that was more of a test of the soil than of the crop.

But what alternatives do we have? First, we could forego random assignment and simply compare the (largely fertile) neighborhoods that, on their own, seek out this assistance and establish a Neighborhood

Watch program with other (largely non-fertile) neighborhoods that do not. A second option would be to limit the sample to only those areas that ask for and receive organizing assistance and then compare those where a watch program successfully develops to those where the effort falters.

A third possibility would employ a time series design, comparing the period immediately before the installation of Neighborhood Watch—presumably, the point of peak fertility of the area's social soil—to what happens afterward. This kind of analysis, however, would be strongest if we were able to use other neighborhoods (most likely less fertile) to serve as a comparison group (Bennett et al., 2006). Finally, more complicated designs could, using available data, somehow quantify this fertility and rank-order a list of known neighborhood areas on their calculated receptiveness to Neighborhood Watch. Every area that was above a certain level of fertility could then be provided with standardized Neighborhood Watch organizing efforts, while those below this threshold would not. Assuming that our fertility measure was valid, a nonexperimental regression discontinuity design (Berk et al., 2010) could detect the difference in subsequent crime between the neighborhoods on both sides of the threshold.

Once again, however, we are left with designs that are more focused on the fertility of soil than the crop that grows in it and cannot tell us very much about the effects of Neighborhood Watch itself. Even when the research design attempts to match areas that have a watch program with similar ones that do not, the fact remains that the nonexperimental comparison neighborhoods are ones that are potentially—perhaps even probably—less fertile than those that successfully implemented the program. No matter how we attempt to statistically control for this problem, the most complex nonexperimental design cannot force Neighborhood Watch to develop in non-fertile areas that are simply not receptive to it. Any nonexperimental comparison of neighborhoods with and without a watch program must, therefore, also be a comparison of fertile and non-fertile neighborhoods, and the impact of this confounding variable—one that is likely to be complexly correlated with each neighborhood's level of crime and social disorder (Bennett, 1990)—will be just as destructive to nonexperimental approaches as Hope (2009) contends it would be to an RCT.

Thus while a broad-spectrum RCT of this sort does face difficulty in separating the crop from the soil, so do all of the alternative approaches. These other methods, moreover, also lack the ability to make clear causal inferences from their results. Even if we ignore what a Neighborhood Watch RCT could teach us about which kinds of locations really are the most fertile for the development of an effective program, random assignment would also allow us to unambiguously determine the policy effects of *offering* such a program to a set of neighborhoods (i.e., the same "ITT" test described earlier).

In addition, consider what we have already learned from existing, nonexperimental research on Neighborhood Watch. Since so many of these studies have required the use of matched comparison neighborhoods (Bennett et al., 2006), we have some rather strong indications about what kinds of neighborhoods are and are not fertile for the development of these programs. We also have developed the ability, at least to a certain extent, to measure this fertility. If it's possible for nonrandomized studies to match one neighborhood with others that are similarly fertile, then a comparable process should also be possible within an experiment. If we were truly limited to the broad-based RCT that Hope (2009) proposes, with a wide range of both fertile and non-fertile areas in our sample, we could use this knowledge to conduct a subgroup analysis of the results. Such an analysis would look only at those areas—in both the experimental and control groups—whose characteristics would seem to make them receptive to Neighborhood Watch.

While this approach would allow us to hold constant the perceived level of fertility in each neighborhood's social soil, it is also clearly less than ideal. The debate about whether subgroup analysis is permissible, in what circumstances it should be allowed, and how to attenuate its many potential drawbacks remains both ongoing and impassioned (Rothwell, 2005). Nevertheless, even a potentially flawed experimental subgroup analysis of Neighborhood Watch would be a valuable addition to the literature, which currently consists, perhaps even exclusively, of quasi-experimental and observational results (Bennett et al., 2006).

Even more importantly, subgroup analysis could be avoided altogether if this hypothetical Neighborhood Watch RCT was designed somewhat differently. Instead of randomly assigning a wide range of both fertile and non-fertile neighborhoods, we could use the same techniques employed in nonexperimental research to identify a sample that contained only areas that were thought to be fertile ground for Neighborhood Watch. These areas would then be placed into a separate block of cases, which would use a random assignment process that was completely separate and independent from that applied to less fertile neighborhoods. Assuming that our fertility measure had any real validity, most of the neighborhoods in the treatment group would go on to embrace the efforts to organize a watch program, while most of those in the control group would go forward without such a program.

This kind of an RCT would certainly be difficult to conduct. The small number of fertile areas in any given city would have a huge impact on the available sample size, perhaps necessitating the broadening of the sample to other cities. Since these cities would have different policing strategies and different methods for organizing Neighborhood Watch, an additional source of variation would need to be measured and taken into account. Travel and coordination between the research sites would be complicated and expensive, but it is also certainly possible. While arduous to perform, this kind of block-randomized RCT would provide us with clear evidence about the crop that we are really interested in and would do so with far less ambiguity than the existing nonexperimental techniques in our methodological tool kit.

Violations of Stable Unit Treatment Value Assumption

The idea behind "stable unit treatment value assumption" (SUTVA) is fairly simple. The assumption requires that the outcome for any given participant in an experiment, while dependent on their own randomly assigned treatment, is independent of all the other random assignments made for other participants (Berk, 2005; Sampson, 2010). This assumption is therefore violated if the randomly assigned treatment for one participant influences the outcomes of any other participants.

From Sampson's (2010) perspective, SUTVA is the core assumption that underlies all randomized experiments. To illustrate the danger that SUTVA violations pose to RCTs, Berk (2005) provides a hypothetical example of an in-custody juvenile drug treatment program, in which some inmates are randomly assigned to receive the treatment, while the others are placed into an untreated control group. The effects of this treatment, however, could very well depend on the unique blend of juveniles who were randomly assigned into the treatment classroom. Peer pressures will form within the treatment group that—depending on the nature of the young people in the class—could either enhance or detract from the desired treatment effect. Even worse, if the treatment group juveniles return to their living areas and mix with those assigned to the control group, they could pass along some of what they are learning in the classroom and thus violate SUTVA in a way that could attenuate the treatment differences between the two assigned groups.

Sampson (2010) provides his own example of potential SUTVA violations in the Moving to Opportunity experiments, which randomly assigned residents of public housing to either receive, or not receive, vouchers that would enable them to move to non-poverty neighborhoods (Clampet-Lundquist and Massey, 2008; Ludwig et al., 2008; Sampson, 2008). Those who were given these vouchers (and who also chose to use them) almost certainly retained some ties with friends in their old neighborhoods. Some of these acquaintances were also, in all likelihood, participants in the experiment. As these treatment group compliers shared stories about how difficult it was to move, or how nice their new neighborhoods were, they may have influenced the feelings and decisions of those participants who had not (yet) made a move of their own. This influence violates SUTVA, creates an "interference" term that cannot be corrected for statistically (Berk, 2005), and renders causal inference— the central reason for doing an RCT in the first place—difficult, if not impossible (Sampson, 2010).

One core element in these discussions of how SUTVA applies to the social sciences, and criminology in particular, is the heightened ability of the participants in our RCTs to interact with and influence one another. Hope states this concern quite elegantly:

> Unlike natural science, our own quanta think and act on the basis of their thoughts (including what they think about experiments upon them). Such inter-subjectivity— between the observer and the subject, and among the subjects themselves—has a fundamental impact on our ability to attach certainty to our observation of our subjects' action. (2009: 126)

This quote also features a recurring theme in the literature, focusing upon how SUTVA violations are more problematic for social experiments than they are in other fields of study. Maintaining the SUTVA may be easy for the natural sciences, where fertilizer is applied to plants or medications are given to patients (Hough, 2010), but seemingly impossible when we are seeking to test social treatments with participants who can easily—and perhaps are even required to—talk to and influence one another (Tilley, 2009; Sampson, 2010).

Botany, medicine, and other "hard" natural sciences, however, are far from immune to SUTVA violations within their randomized trials. Consider, for example, a hypothetical clinical trial of a new antibiotic for the treatment of postoperative infection. Assuming that this new medication is effective, the potential for SUTVA to be violated could depend on how the RCT is designed, managed, and implemented. The control patients could still benefit from the experimental medication, even after receiving only a placebo, if their hospital beds were in close proximity to members of the treatment group. The overall bacterial load in their immediate environment could be lower, and the chance of infection being spread by well-intentioned caregivers would therefore be reduced. On the other hand, if participating patients are kept isolated from one another, it's possible for SUTVA to be violated in other ways, such as by the differences in nursing care on different floors of the hospital.

Violations of SUTVA would also seem to have varying degrees of effect on different outcome measures. When measuring the benefits of our example antibiotic, the fact that control and treatment group patients were often roommates could be a legitimate SUTVA concern. When looking for adverse reactions to this medication, on the other hand, this violation of experimental assumptions may not be as important. Thus even if SUTVA is violated in some manner, it is certainly possible that some outcome measures remain unaffected by it.

As was true in the earlier discussion of Neighborhood Watch, however, it is important to ask what methodological alternatives are available that can avoid (or at least mitigate) the influence of SUTVA violations, especially when we are seeking to determine causal effects. The Moving to Opportunity experiments, in light of Sampson's (2008, 2010) arguments, certainly do seem to have great potential for this particular assumption to be violated, at least among some participants in the research. But assuming that we want to know what effects are caused by making housing vouchers available to residents of public housing, how can we avoid violating SUTVA? We could, for example, make a fixed number of such vouchers available to everyone, on a nonrandom, first-come-first-served basis, and then observe those families who do and do not receive them. Even here, however, the same violations of SUTVA are likely to occur, since our nonexperimental participants will continue to interact with one another. Another option would be to offer these vouchers in some neighborhoods but not others, but SUTVA would still remain a real concern. The departure of residents from one neighborhood could open up housing units that the residents of the non-voucher neighborhoods may then decide to move into.

In short, nonexperimental "observational" approaches can easily face the same SUTVA concerns that affect randomized trials (Berk, 2005), while still failing to support the clear causal inferences that experimentation can help produce. Violations of this particular assumption would seem to affect all kinds of research, both inside and outside of the social science sphere, and our approaches to dealing with this problem will continue to evolve over time. RCTs, however, would not seem to be any more reliant upon, or subject to the limitations of, the SUTVA than any other method of studying causal effects.

The Difficulty of Doing Experiments

Part of the folklore surrounding the use of RCTs in criminal justice settings is that they are very difficult to do (Lum and Yang, 2005; Weisburd, 2010), and even harder to do well (Berk, 2005). All experimental criminologists have an unending set of war stories about their RCTs, and indeed there are a multitude of things that can go wrong. Painfully divisive negotiations with participating agencies, hostile reporting by the local press, anemic referral rates of eligible cases, sudden changes in treatment delivery, attempts to put an end to random assignment, and participants who refuse to fit neatly into their assigned treatment groups are all part of experimental criminology and have been extensively reported in the literature (Sherman et al., 1992a; Feder et al., 2000).

In some ways, one wonders whether the difficulties of doing RCTs in criminology may not have been a bit overstated by those who have been on the front lines. Random assignment, in and of itself, does not necessarily make research any more difficult to conduct. Any form of prospective causal analysis, in which cases must be identified prior to the start of a treatment program and then followed for a period of time afterward, will involve many of the same difficulties. The central question is what unique difficulties are presented by randomized trials, and how these problems might affect the findings drawn from them.

Berk (2005) sets forward a number of other ways in which experiments can prove difficult to conduct successfully. For example, the actual flow of eligible cases into the randomly assigned sample is often far less than expected. At least in some circumstances, it is fair to suppose that the use of random assignment itself may play a role in limiting case intake. In a number of field experiments, for instance, practitioners were told to refer cases to the RCT only when they were relatively agnostic about how the cases should handled, and would be willing to accept any of the randomly assigned treatment outcomes (Sherman et al., 1992a; Barnes, 1999). These experiments clearly lost some potentially eligible cases when the referring practitioners felt strongly about employing a specific kind of response. In other instances, some practitioners may have felt uneasy about the use of random assignment itself, or have had such strong doubts about the usefulness of the experimental treatment, that they simply refused to send any cases into the RCT. With enough resources to do so, lower-than-expected case flow can be compensated for by simply extending the period of new case enrollment, but that option is not always available. When it isn't, researchers face an unhappy choice between either loosening their eligibility criteria for random assignment or accepting a smaller sample size; both of these options are likely to reduce statistical power (Weisburd et al., 1993).

Another concern is sample attrition, which can come about in two rather different ways (Berk, 2005). The first form, which we will refer to as "primary attrition," occurs when cases are completely removed from the sample. In a properly designed experiment, this should almost never be allowed to occur, particularly when cases are more likely to be eliminated from some treatment groups but not others. Investigators conducting experiments are usually bound to retain every case that was randomly assigned—including those that were enrolled in error or that failed to complete their assigned treatment—within the analysis sample. Thus primary attrition seems more of a concern for nonexperimental research, which may present more flexibility in defining the final sample, than it is for randomized trials. When it does occur within an RCT, it could very well mean that benefits of random assignment have been lost and that the resulting analysis is little different from a nonexperimental one.[1]

The second form of attrition could perhaps best be referred to as "treatment attrition" and occurs when participants fail to experience part—or perhaps even any—of the treatment they were randomly assigned to receive. Randomized trials can, in theory, get around this problem by presenting their results as an ITT analysis (Berk, 2005). In other words, the experiment can randomly assign participants onto a path that is designed to lead to the experimental treatment, instead of assigning them to the treatment itself. This approach can be satisfactory (to a certain degree) when the goal is to the test the effects of implementing the treatment in the real world, where some participants will always drop out. It can become deeply unsatisfactory, however, when too many of these intentions to treat never come to fruition.

An ITT analysis therefore requires that the exact amount of treatment delivered to the participants be measured, provided in the published results, and substantial enough to warrant pursuing any further comparisons between the treatment groups. It can be very difficult to know how much treatment delivery is "enough," and much may depend on the nature of the treatment itself. In the end, the best that experimental researchers may be able to offer is to rigorously report the degree of treatment as delivered and allow their readers to make their own determinations.

A related problem within some RCTs concerns unanticipated, midstream changes to the experimental treatment itself. Feder and colleagues (2000), for example, describe a police-led domestic violence initiative that became so labor intensive and costly that the senior officer in charge of the effort unilaterally decided to implement a less demanding version of the treatment. In other experiments, some adjustments to the treatment protocol became necessary, after random assignment began, to prevent an excessive number of treatment group cases from going untreated (Barnes, 1999). The only real defense against this type of problem—and it is far from perfect—is to run both the treatment and the random assignment through a kind of "pilot phase" prior to the beginning of the "real" experiment. With luck, most of the treatment delivery problems will be discovered and addressed during this phase, and the treatment can be delivered consistently once the actual experiment begins.

While there certainly are problems and difficulties associated with randomized experimentation, the central question remains whether RCTs are substantially more problematic and difficult than the available alternatives. If our goal is to determine the effects of a particular intervention, it is not clear that they truly are. For example, if one wanted to nonexperimentally observe offenders who voluntarily participated in restorative justice conferencing, and then measure their subsequent criminal behavior, most of these same issues would still be real concerns. This hypothetical evaluation would still face difficulties if the agency handling the conferences was resistant, if the flow of new cases was too low, if offenders had to be dropped from the sample, if too many offenders failed to complete the conferences, or if the nature of the conferences themselves changed substantially over the course of the research.

In short, it's simply not clear that the addition of a single research element—namely, the random assignment of participants into different treatment groups—makes randomized trials much more difficult to perform than other methods, at least when we are seeking to measure the effects of a treatment intervention. That is not to say that random assignment, in and of itself, cannot be a real burden. It provides a point of obvious objection for those who are resistant to the research, and it requires the ongoing oversight and measurement of treatment to ensure that it gets delivered as assigned. But with time, experience, and the availability of new technology, even this element of randomized experimentation has gotten progressively easier to accomplish. As we have seen before, neither quasi- nor nonexperimental approaches avoid any of the difficulties presented by RCTs and clearly lack the equivalent ability of randomized trials to demonstrate causation.

External Validity and the Ability to Generalize

As Berk (2005) correctly notes, RCTs are not pursued just for the sake of performing them, publishing the results, and moving on to the next study. No matter how well they demonstrate causation, experiments are not worth doing unless their results can be applied to other settings and can be used to inform future decisions. Ideally, experimental findings would be applicable not only to the sample that was used in the RCT, but also to other types of participants, other locations, other times, other interventions that are reasonably similar to one that was randomly assigned, and to other types of outcomes. No matter how strong an experiment is at producing internal validity, a lack of external validity[2] will prevent an experiment's findings from being generalized and can cripple its utility.

The conventional wisdom about randomized experimentation is that it has exceptional internal validity, but is weak when it comes to external validity (Hough, 2010; Sampson, 2010; Weisburd, 2010). There seem to be four primary ways in which the external validity of RCTs is thought to be inadequate. First, experiments can obviously take place only in settings where the treatment providers (e.g., police, probation, and correction officials) are willing to accept the use of random assignment (Eck, 2002). Second, the eligibility criteria used to limit entry of participants into the experiment can make the randomly assigned sample substantially different from the general population. Third, even within the eligible subset of the population, the participants in most RCTs are usually not drawn from a probability sample, but come instead from a convenience sample of whichever eligible participants happened to be around at the time (Berk, 2005). Finally, randomly assigned participants are likely to be more aggressively tracked during the treatment phase of an experiment, in order to ensure high rates of treatment compliance, than they would be if the experiment were not taking place. As a result, they may be more likely to both begin and complete their assigned treatment than they would be if they did not have researchers pushing them (and their practitioners) to do so.

As in earlier discussions, many of these external validity concerns would seem to apply equally to both experimental and nonexperimental approaches. All real-world research efforts, for example, are limited to settings where the practitioners will allow researchers to operate. What isn't clear is whether any sizable number of these research-friendly settings would permit only nonexperimental studies to proceed and would refuse to allow the use of random assignment (Weisburd, 2010). It is certainly clear that the random assignment of participants has been a tough sell in some research settings and that the controversy over its use has caused the near-collapse of some RCTs (Feder et al., 2000). In our own research, both authors have encountered a number of instances in which we suggested the use of a randomized trial and were immediately told that such an approach would not be possible in that particular instance. At times, practitioners and agencies have proven willing to entertain random assignment for some types of interventions, but not others.

Anecdotally, one gets the feeling that criminal justice practitioners are growing more comfortable with the use of random assignment. Much of the controversy about the ethics of random assignment seems, at this stage, to be behind us (Weisburd, 2010). In addition, preferences by funding agencies for randomized trials—which can obviously be a big factor in determining a research design (Lum and Yang, 2005)—would seem to be growing more common. Nevertheless, there likely remain an almost limitless number of instances in which practitioners will refuse to permit the use of an RCT, even after several decades of successful experimentation in the criminal justice system. Today's refusals to permit random assignment, however, may have more to do with the intervention being studied, and the types of offenders who will participate in the treatment, than they do with an overall bias against the RCT method itself. As best we can tell, any agency that would be willing to permit other kinds of research would also be likely—depending on the nature of the intervention and a few other factors—to allow an RCT.

The second concern about external validity would also seem to apply equally to both experimental and nonexperimental research. Any effort to discover the causal effects of an intervention will necessarily employ some rules to determine which types of cases should appear in analysis data. Regardless of methodology, one would not include patients suffering from low blood pressure in an evaluation of a new drug to treat hypertension. Nevertheless, the eligibility rules employed in randomized trials may have a slightly different focus when compared to those used in quasi-experimental or observational analyses. During the design of an RCT, particular care is usually taken to ensure that participants who will have difficultly completing the treatment are excluded from random assignment. Offenders with outstanding warrants, for example, could be declared ineligible for an experiment that was testing the use of arrest by the police. Ideally, nonexperimental studies would take similar care in constructing their samples, but data on all potential exclusionary conditions may not be available retrospectively. Moreover, randomized experiments—with their need to both measure and maximize the treatment delivered to their appropriately assigned participants—have a special motivation to keep untreatable cases out of their samples. Treatment eligibility is a central concern when conducting an RCT. In quasi- or nonexperimental studies, however, this issue is either not addressed, ignored, or corrected for through the statistical modeling of treatment eligibility. Whether this focus on treatable participants is any more detrimental to external validity than the eligibility rules that are used (or should be used) in other forms of analysis, however, is highly debatable.

The third worry surrounding the external validity of RCTs is the (quite frequent) absence of probability sampling prior to random assignment (Berk, 2005). This kind of sample would be built in a three-stage process. First, the full population of eligible cases would be defined. Next, a random sample would be drawn from that population and could therefore be assumed to be fully representative (within known limits) of that population. Finally, all the members of this probability sample would be randomly assigned into the appropriate number of experimental treatment groups. The advantage would be that the results of the experiment could be instantly generalized to the entire population.

Most randomized experiments, including those conducted in criminology, simply do not build their samples this way. Sampson (2010: 491) notes that he is ". . . hard pressed to think of many experiments in criminology either with multiple stage randomization . . . or where the selection mechanisms into the convenience samples are fully known." We must confess that no such examples of multistage randomization within an experiment come to our minds, either.[3] At the same time, most observational studies in criminology also don't rely on probability samples, including some of the most widely cited studies of criminal behavior over the life course (Farrington, 1986; Sampson and Laub, 1993).

In many experiments, however, it would be unreasonable to draw a smaller probability sample from what is already a very small population of eligible cases. Randomized trials, as we have already seen, have historically had issues with low case flow, particularly when they rely on practitioners to refer new cases into the experiment. Most RCTs therefore take pains to enroll *every* eligible case that comes to their attention. In many ways, one could argue that these studies don't need to generalize to some larger population of eligible cases, because the entire population of such cases is already enrolled and has been randomly assigned. The "sample" is the population, and the sample estimates produced by the analysis are exactly the same as the population parameters.

Much of this argument, however, turns on the question of how potential cases into an experiment and how one chooses to define the term "eligible." In the Australian Reintegrative Shaming Experiments' (RISE) drunk driving trial, for example (Strang et al., 1999), intoxicated drivers were referred to the research team by their arresting officers. Out of more than 600 sworn police officers in Canberra, 244 enrolled at least one eligible case into the experiment, which would seem to account for a healthy proportion of the line patrol officers who were most likely to make these kinds of arrests. During a single year of the RCT's case intake, however, an analysis of the case enrollment "pipeline" showed that only 56 percent of all apparently eligible, territory-wide arrests for intoxicated driving were placed into the experiment. Moreover, the cases that were ultimately referred into the randomized trial were significantly different in many ways from those that were not (Barnes, 1999). Thus even with a large percentage of all known arrests placed in the experiment, it is clear that the RISE sample is not representative of Canberra's intoxicated driving arrests generally, or even of those that appeared to be eligible for random assignment.

This pipeline analysis, however, could not shed light on each and every one of the eligibility restrictions that governed an offender's entry into RISE. One eligibility criterion that was missing from the data was the willingness of the arresting officer to accept the randomly assigned treatment outcome, regardless of the result. If an officer was unwilling to cede this authority to random assignment, the case was not eligible for RISE, and there was no reason for the officer to refer it to the RCT. From this perspective, nearly all of the offenders who were *not* referred to the experiment could therefore be seen as ineligible, simply because their arresting officers were not willing to enroll them.

Even without this tortured definition of eligibility, however, the case flow implications are clear. RISE took nearly two-and-a-half years to enroll every eligible intoxicated driver that came to the research team's attention. In doing so, it accounted for more than half of the known potentially eligible cases across the entire Australian Capital Territory. While the result was not anything close to a probability sample of the population, it is not clear how a multistage randomization process would have functioned here. To create a probability sample from this population, the experiment would have needed to both accept some offenders who were unlikely to complete the experimental treatment (e.g., those whose arresting officers were unwilling to abide by random assignment), and leave a number of otherwise treatable offenders out of the sample. These steps would have increased heterogeneity, reduced treatment integrity, required a longer period of case intake, and generally weakened the ability of the experiment to produce a coherent result.

In the end, the RISE results are not generalizable to every intoxicated driver who was arrested during the course of study, but they may be sufficiently representative of those who were willing and able to complete the experimental treatment. There seems little point in demonstrating the effect of a treatment intervention on participants who are ineligible or unable to receive it. Given what most criminological experiments set out to do, and the types of interventions that they test, the treatable population may be the only one that really matters. As long as the results can be extended to the population of eligible and treatable participants, an experiment may have all the external validity that it needs.

The final concern about external validity, however, is not so easily explained away. It seems quite likely that randomized trials—with researchers continually looking at treatment delivery and constantly pushing to maximize treatment integrity—do a better job at getting participants into, and all the way through, their assigned treatments than would occur if everyone was left to their own devices. Even when researchers have no contact at all with the participants, they can (and indeed, probably should) exert pressure on the practitioners who are managing and delivering the experimental treatment, in an effort to get the right participants into the right treatments. This issue is, and will long remain, a difficult balancing act for experimental researchers. On the one hand, tracking treatment delivery is essential if the experiment is to be a valid test of anything; nobody wants to read the results from an experiment that utterly failed to deliver its treatments as assigned. On the other hand, these efforts can also undermine external validity and make the results much harder to replicate in an operational non-research environment.

In his own effort to help dampen the widening pendulum swings between overstated advocacy and inflated criticism surrounding RCTs in criminology, Berk (2005: 430) reached the following conclusion:

Perhaps the key retort to individuals who claim randomized experiments are undesirable is to ask, "compared to what?" Quasi-experiments, such as the generalized
regression discontinuity design (Berk and de Leeuw, 1999) have many of the same
implementation problems as randomized experiments, and more. . . . If the alternative
to a randomized experiment is an observational study, the difficulties are likely to be
even worse. There are a host of potential implementation problems, and the modeling
required can be highly suspect. (Rosenbaum, P. R., 2002; Berk, 2003)

Similar conclusions have been reached here. None of the arguments
presented above, however, should be perceived in a manner that deni-
grates the overall utility of quasi-experimental or observational research.
All forms of well-conducted research and analysis have their place in
the investigation of social and criminological problems, and there are
indeed many times, places, and treatment interventions where random
assignment would be massively difficult, and even truly impossible, to
carry out. Moreover, as we will see, observational methods can easily
be applied in concert with randomized experimentation, and are likely
necessary to address what is perhaps the deepest and most penetrating
criticism of RCTs in criminology.

Making Experiments Useful to Criminological Theory

In some ways, today's debate over randomized experimentation could
be seen as beginning with a similar round of consternation in the early
1970s over the role of foundational theory (Carr, 2010). At that time,
criminology was, according to its critics, too focused upon theories
concerning the causes of crime, especially at the societal level. Those
theories tended to focus attention upon aspects of society and human
nature that policymakers had little power to change, and away from the
things that governmental policy could control, such as the allocation
of police resources and the sentencing of convicted offenders (Wilson,
1974). This argument was followed by a gradual shift away from the
construction and testing of grand theories of crime, and toward the examination of governmental responses to crime and the effects they produce.
With an increased focus on cause and effect, and upon narrow questions
surrounding individual policy options, randomized experimentation on
issues of crime and justice was both natural and inevitable.

Perhaps as a result of these roots, randomized experimentation can
often be portrayed as atheoretical and far more relevant to questions of
policy than it is to the development of criminological theory (Hough,
2010; Sampson, 2010). Criminology's current divide concerning the use
and promotion of RCTs is mirrored by the well-established polarization

between the empirical examination of policy and the development of criminological theory. In Hough's (2010) assessment, this polarization has become as firmly entrenched in our field as ever, regardless of how unnecessary this distinction may be. As in politics, however, polarization has an unpleasant tendency to demand the placement of everything and everyone at one end of the spectrum or the other. Investigators who conduct experiments tend to study the effects of policy, and government officials tend to give great weight to conclusions drawn from RCTs, so it logically follows that randomized experiments are narrowly focused on the practical question of applied research and have less relevance to theory.

In reality, of course, theory and research—even randomized trials— are inextricably linked. Policies are not (or at least not always) created in a theoretical vacuum, and thus tests of policies are often also tests of applied theory. Moreover, when these evaluations are complete, even the strong causal inferences made possible by randomized experimentation are not enough by themselves. To fully understand what the results mean and how they came about, theory is still required. As Sampson (2010: 491–92) clearly teaches us, even "*randomistas*" need theory to explain their results:

> Causal inference is ultimately tied up with causal explanation, which resides at a theoretical level and is not something that comes directly from the data. Data never "speak for themselves"—making sense of causal patterns requires theoretical claims about unobserved mechanisms and social processes no matter what the experiment or statistical method employed (Wickström and Sampson, 2006). Causal explanation requires theory, in other words, not a particular method. (Heckman, 2005)

In this section, we hope to illustrate the important connection between theory and randomized experimentation, using our own experiences with three different RCTs to highlight what each can do to advance the other.

The Reintegrative Shaming Experiments (RISE)

The RISE studies consisted of four different RCTs, conducted in Canberra, Australia, during the late 1990s. In total, 1,286 criminal incidents were enrolled into the experiments, involving 1,375 different arrestees. Of particular interest for the present discussion are the 900 intoxicated driving arrests that were enrolled into the largest of the four RCTs, which involved 896 different offenders. Each incident was randomly assigned to either be handled by the courts in the traditional manner (control) or be referred to a special diversionary program that offered accused offenders the chance to have the matter dealt with at a restorative justice conference. RISE was set up as an ITT experiment, since the very design of the diversionary conferences required that offenders be sent to court if they failed to cooperate. Overall, however, treatment integrity in the intoxicated driving experiment was very strong; more than 99 percent of those assigned to court and 95 percent of those assigned to conference were treated in their randomly assigned manner (Barnes, 1999).

Theoretical Foundation

As its very name suggests, the RISE program was conceived, designed, and managed—from the ground up—as a test of a Braithwaite's (1989) theory of reintegrative shaming. Based on earlier experiences in New Zealand and Australia, the restorative justice conferences were thought to present an ideal opportunity to deliver a reintegrative form of shaming (i.e., shame that acknowledges the harm done by the offender's actions, while seeking ways to reconnect them to conventional society) and to minimize stigmatizing shaming (i.e., shame that attaches to the offender as a person and pushes them away from conventional society). Special care was taken to train the police facilitators who led the conferences, so that the treatment they provided would closely align with the theory being tested, and a measurement strategy (described below) was devised to capture all of the elements outlined in Braithwaite's presentation of his theory.

Method of Random Assignment

All four RISE experiments used rolling enrollment, where new cases were randomly assigned as they occurred, came to the research team's attention, and successfully passed the eligibility screening. For the intoxicated driving experiment, this process took twenty-nine months to complete.[4] Case enrollment began when the arresting officer decided to refer the case and placed a telephone call to a member of the research team. All eligible cases were enrolled into the experiment. The random assignment for each case was predetermined, but kept sealed in an envelope and not revealed until the moment of case enrollment. Once this assignment took place, however, it was impossible to blind either the offenders or the police to its outcome, since both parties were involved in the delivery of the treatment.

Measurements Employed

In addition to measures drawn from official records, a very large set of observational and interview data were gathered during RISE. Whenever the offenders appeared at either court or conference, the research team sought to observe these treatment events and record what transpired. After the matter had been resolved (in either venue), the offenders were asked to participate in a structured interview to measure their reactions to their experience. Next, after two years had passed, the offenders were contacted again for a follow-up interview, which measured both their longer term reactions to treatment and their subsequent self-reported behavior. Questionnaires were also completed by the arresting officers, the conference facilitators, and the community representatives who participated in the conferences.[5] While these wide-ranging instruments were specifically designed to measure all of the elements important to reintegrative shaming theory, they also contained a large number of items that were designed to shed light on other theoretical approaches (Strang et al., 1999).

Effects on Offending

At least within the intoxicated driving experiment, there was no apparent difference in the subsequent offending of the two randomly assigned treatment groups.[6] Roughly 16 percent of both treatment groups were rearrested within one year of random assignment, and 22 percent were rearrested within two years. If these figures are limited to only new arrests for intoxicated driving, the corresponding values were 6 percent and 8 percent. In their two-year follow-up interviews, 42 percent of both treatment groups reported having driven while intoxicated during a single post-treatment year. The only notable difference between the two groups comes in the frequency of their self-report drunk driving. Those assigned to court reported committing this offense, on average, 5.1 times during the targeted year, while those in the conference group reported just 3.6 offenses. This difference, however, was not statistically significant.

The Philadelphia Low-Intensity Community Supervision Experiment

This experiment began in October 2007 and continued for exactly one year. A total of 1,559 probationers were enrolled into the study, after having been identified as low risk,[7] using a statistical forecasting model (Berk et al., 2009) that predicted their offending over the next two years. Of these eligible offenders, eight hundred were to be assigned to just two probation officers, increasing the size of the officers' caseloads and reducing the intensity of the supervision that they could provide.

The remaining 759 offenders were supervised in the usual manner, by officers whose caseloads contained fewer than 150 offenders. Like RISE, the experiment was designed to test the intention to treat rather than the treatment itself. The low-intensity protocol deliberately removed some offenders from the experimental caseloads under a variety of circumstances, including the commission of new offenses. The goal was therefore to give these offenders the opportunity to experience low-intensity supervision, and not necessarily to retain them under these conditions for the entire length of the experiment. More than 89 percent of those assigned to the experimental treatment group, however, experienced at least thirty days of low-intensity supervision, and 61 percent were in these caseloads for 180 days or more (Barnes et al., 2010).

Theoretical Foundation

At its conception, the experiment was almost purely a policy evaluation, and theory was not much of a consideration in determining the RCT's design. Instead, Philadelphia's Adult Probation and Parole Department set out to test the safety of a proposed reorganization plan that would eventually stratify its entire caseload into different levels of risk, based on the offenders' forecasted level of future offending. The primary reason for the experiment was to determine if it was possible to safely supervise a large number of lower risk offenders with just a few officers, thereby freeing up other officers to concentrate on higher risk offenders. Despite these atheoretical beginnings, the treatment being tested did present some elements of a variety of different theories, including some which presented contradictory predictions about how probationers would react to having less supervision (Barnes et al., 2010). Thus while the experiment was not designed with any specific criminological theories in mind, the results still had some utility in testing a number of competing premises.

Method of Random Assignment

Unlike RISE and many other criminological RCTs, the experiment did not rely on rolling enrollment and instead used a batch method of random assignment. The sample was identified by screening the agency's entire active caseload for forecasted level of risk. Those whose forecasts indicated a lower level of risk were then further screened for eligibility, leading to the final sample of 1,559 offenders. This entire sample was randomly assigned at one time, and the transfers of the treatment group offenders into the low-intensity caseloads were largely complete within two weeks of the RCT's start.

This use of batch random assignment had two important consequences. First, every offender in the sample came from the agency's standing caseload and therefore had some existing experience on supervision before the experiment began. Second, it required—like so many other criminological experiments—that every single eligible case be randomly assigned, and no probability sampling from a larger population was possible.

Another very important element to this experiment was its ability to partially blind some participants and practitioners to the randomly assigned treatment. Those offenders assigned to the control condition did not need to be transferred to a new officer and experienced no change in their pre-existing supervision requirements. There was therefore no reason for either these offenders or their supervising officers to know that they were part of an experiment or even that the offenders had been forecasted as low risk in the first place.

Measures Employed

Only official sources of information, including the agency's own case management system and court data on new arrests and charges, were available for analysis. No attempt was made to interview the offenders or their supervising officers, and no direct observations were made of how they interacted with one another.

Effects on Offending

There were no significant differences between the two randomly assigned groups in the prevalence, frequency, or seriousness of offending during the first year after random assignment. At the operational level, this result had been both predicted and eagerly anticipated by the agency's senior staff, since it allowed them to go forward with their planned reorganization.

The Philadelphia High-Risk Supervision Experiment

This experiment is currently underway within the same agency that hosted the low-intensity supervision experiment described above, and therefore has yet to produce any results. Nevertheless, its features help illustrate the connection between randomized trials and the development of theory. By the time that enrollment is completed, approximately 1,300 probationers—all forecasted to commit a new serious offense within two years of random assignment, using an updated version of the agency's risk prediction model—will be randomly assigned into three different treatment groups. One group will be supervised in a manner that largely mirrors the agency's traditional methods, while offenders in the second group will be assigned to high-risk officers who have sharply reduced caseloads. The third group will experience the same high-risk supervision protocol as the second, but will also be offered the opportunity to attend a fourteen-week, classroom-style program of cognitive behavioral therapy (CBT). This three-way assignment was designed to demonstrate the unique effects of both high-intensity supervision alone and the additive impact of the CBT treatment.

Theoretical Foundation

In part, the high-risk experiment—like the low-intensity research that preceded it—is a test of operational policy. Now that the agency has access to risk-forecasting results on its entire population of offenders, it needs to develop some means to manage those who are predicted to commit serious crimes. But particularly within the group slated to receive CBT, there is a clear set of theories being tested by this randomized trial. The basic theoretical tenets of CBT, found in Ellis's (1973) rational emotive theory, suggest that negative attitudes and beliefs play a central role in the expression of psychological stress through behavior. In practice, CBT programs also borrow from social learning theory (Bandura, 1977), employing strategies including modeling, role-playing, performance feedback, generalization training, and self-reinforcement to aid in the reshaping of the decision-making processes. Within an offender population, the attention is focused on criminal orientations including blaming of the victim, entitlement, harm to others, a lack of empathy, refusal to accept responsibility, and grandiosity (Yochelson, 1976). In Philadelphia, specially assigned probation officers have been trained by a clinical psychologist in both the theoretical foundations and the necessary techniques of CBT. They are now using a prepared curriculum to apply these principles in a classroom environment to the randomly assigned probationers.

Method of Random Assignment

As with RISE, and unlike the low-intensity experiment, the high-risk experiment employs a rolling enrollment strategy. All offenders who begin a new term of supervision at the participating agency are run through a computerized risk-forecasting process. This same forecasting system handles all of the eligibility screening and random assignment for the RCT, which eliminates the reliance on willing practitioners to refer cases into the experiment. Every high-risk offender who meets the computer-assessed eligibility criteria is randomly assigned into one of the three treatment groups. Similar to the low-intensity study, this new experiment employs a form of partial blinding; those assigned to the traditionally managed control group are not aware that they are enrolled in the RCT, and neither they nor those who manage their cases are aware that these offenders have been forecasted as high risk.

The (Potential) Impact of Three Experiments on Theory

Of the three experiments presented above, it seems clear that RISE has made—and is likely to continue to make—the largest contribution to criminological theory. For example, an analysis of the data from its intoxicated driving experiment formed a key part of Braithwaite's effort to significantly revise his own theory of reintegrative shaming (Ahmed et al., 2001). These same data have also contributed to our knowledge on procedural justice (Barnes, 1999; Tyler et al., 2007), restorative justice (Woods, 2009), and numerous theories within the field of victimology (Strang, 2002; Strang et al., 2006).

This influence is not simply the result of the RISE experiments' age. While there certainly has been a great deal of time for the RISE results to be repeatedly analyzed, disseminated, and reacted to by interested theoreticians, the other two experiments simply seem less capable of making this same impact. Even if we allowed the two probation experiments the same number of years in which to do so, it seems very unlikely that either could shed as much light on as many theories as RISE has. Nor is it a function of the strength of the RISE treatment effects, which were as close to perfectly null in the drunk driving RCT as experimental findings could possibly be. Instead, the power of an experiment to shape theory seems to hinge upon two very important aspects of its design—the extent to which theory is considered while the research is still being planned, and the depth of the measurement that it can make available for analysis.

The Canberra RISE experiments combined both of these elements. They were built, from the very beginning, as a means of testing a known and coherent theory of criminal sanctioning. They also produced an immense volume of data—gathered using a variety of methods from a diverse set of respondents—that is still difficult to conceive of. To be sure, the primary result from the intoxicated driving experiment presented problems for any number of the theories that could be applied to restorative justice conferencing. The experiment was well-run, achieved unmatched treatment integrity, clearly delivered the desired theoretical elements (e.g., fairness, shaming, restoration) to the offenders in the conferencing treatment group, and yet still failed to produce even the slightest effect on their subsequent offending.

Two different things occurred when these results became clear. First, the findings were presented to a ready audience of theoreticians and researchers, some of whom were seeing their very own ideas being put to the test, who immediately had to ask themselves just what had gone "wrong" in the RISE intoxicated driving experiment. Second, analysts were able to tap into the rich data made available by RISE to address that very important question. Over the next few years, these efforts led to a number of discoveries, both about the nature of the treatment produced in the Canberra conferences and about the limitations of existing theory. Ahmed and colleagues (2001), for example, found that the courtroom experiences of the control group were not nearly as stigmatizing as had been expected, and indeed did not seem to produce any real emotional impact of any kind when compared to conferences. At the same time, they also discovered that the two different forms of shame (i.e., stigmatizing and reintegrative) described in Braithwaite's (1989) original theory were not mutually exclusive, and that an offender's opportunities to acknowledge and deal with their feelings of shame were far more important than that had been previously hypothesized. The result was a revision to reintegrative shaming theory, and a substantial advancement in our understanding of the effects produced by legal sanctioning.

It is questionable whether this same kind of effort and discovery could ever flow from the findings of the other two experiments. The low-intensity probation RCT, for example, has already published its findings (Barnes et al., 2010), demonstrating the same sort of null findings as the RISE intoxicated driving experiment. As yet, however, there have been no major efforts to determine what caused the offenders who were receiving less supervision to have the same rate of offending as their more intensely supervised counterparts. To some extent, it does not matter why the levels of offending remained the same; it only matters that they did. While portions of deterrence, defiance, and deviant peer contagion theories were all seemingly falsified by these results, the experiment was never designed as a direct test of these theories, and it would be unreasonable to see the RCT as anything more than (at best) a weak and secondary test of hypotheses derived from them.

Because it has a stronger theoretical foundation, the high-risk experiment may have some greater potential to shape theory once its findings become available. Compared to the low-intensity experiment, it will be much more difficult to claim that the high-risk study constitutes a weak test of CBT, since so much of the study—from the random assignment method to the creation of the classroom materials—has been built around the very notion of testing this approach to behavior modification. If the experiment shows a benefit from CBT, there seems little doubt that the theorists behind this method will trumpet it as a success. If the experiment finds a null or even backfiring effect, on the other hand, these same theorists will almost certainly want to know what went "wrong" in Philadelphia.

Sadly, however, there will be little or no data available to answer this kind of question. In both of the probation experiments, there is (and will remain) so much that we simply will never know. We can't know how the offenders perceived the probation officers who were supervising them, how likely they thought it was that they would be detained following a new arrest or positive drug test, the degree to which they felt fairly treated by the agency, how much their supervision appointments affected their ability to maintain a job, or even their self-reported criminal offending after random assignment. Even if the resources were available to conduct over twenty-four hundred interviews with the offenders, the experiment's use of blinding would add a substantial complication. Any attempt to interview the control offenders would essentially alert them and their officers to the fact that they were part of the research program and therefore unblind them to their enrollment, random assignment, and high-risk forecast. With only official data to work from, we can answer the question about whether these experimental treatments worked, but we can never find out how this effect came about.

It is also important to note how useful a well-measured randomized experiment can be to the production of quasi- and nonexperimental research. Many of the analyses undertaken with the RISE data were not experimental in form, in that they did not use the randomly assigned treatment as the key explanatory variable to account for the outcomes. Tyler and colleagues (Tyler et al., 2007), to cite just one example, after demonstrating that assigned treatment was irrelevant to subsequent offending, proceeded to show that experiencing fairness—regardless of which venue it occurred in—was associated with later beliefs concerning the legitimacy of the law and a lower prevalence of subsequent offending. Similarly, Strang and coauthors (Strang et al., 2006) were able to use victim interview data from RISE to do a quasi-experimental analysis of how restorative justice conferencing affected their fear of crime and sympathy for their offenders.

Randomized experiments can be enormously useful to both test *and* develop theory. This power comes not just from their ability to directly test the causal predictions of theories, but from the reaction that a scientific community must have to the emergence of new evidence as well. If new findings run in contradiction to existing theory, a common reaction can be to find methodological fault with the research that produced them, and hang on to the status quo. When these findings come from a randomized trial—especially an experiment that was custom-designed around a specific theoretical framework—they become much harder to ignore. Solid results can spur us to do the hard, but necessary, work of adapting theory around empirical discoveries. If the experiment in question also provides a rich array of observations, interviews, and other data, this process of adaptation will occur faster, more comprehensively, and with a firmer degree of confidence than that would otherwise be possible.

It seems clear that experiments by themselves are powerful, but that theoretically grounded experiments with rich sources of data can multiply this power greatly. In the next section, we attempt to determine how often these kinds of experiments are reported in the literature.

Theory and Measurement in Criminological Experiments

While identifying every randomized experiment in criminology is beyond the scope of this chapter, we are fortunate that the recent review provided by Farrington and Welsh (2005) has already defined a list of RCTs from which to work from. In their original review, the authors identified eighty-three separate randomized trials, all reported between 1982 and 2004, that featured offending-based outcomes and reasonably large sample sizes. From this list, we were able to obtain copies of the identified publication for sixty-three of them. Though not exhaustive, our available sample of RCTs captures the breadth, nature, and variety of experiments in criminology and allows us to estimate how often these studies combined a focus on theory with the types of measurement needed to understand the causal process.

For each source we located, we examined the cited publication for any indications of each experiment's theoretical justification. We sought out any in-depth explanations that provided insight into *why* the theory, as embodied by the intervention, could explain behavioral outcomes. We then looked to the outcome data for each project, and the methods used for its collection, to determine whether responses were gathered directly from offenders (or potential offenders) after the delivery of the randomly assigned treatment. Our goal was to find any data that measured the offenders' experiences with the intervention and their reactions to it. Interviews regarding self-report criminality—while valuable in determining treatment effects—were not considered useful here, since they cannot shed light on the degree to which the key elements of theory were put into practice.

To be sure, our review is imperfect. The fact that theory is not discussed in the cited publication, for example, does not mean that theory was not considered when the experiment was initially designed. Indeed, the same researchers may very well have gone into great detail about the links between theory and their experimental intervention in other sources that were not cited in Farrington and Welsh's (2005) review. At the same time, even a detailed discussion of theory, written after an experiment has been completed, does not guarantee that theory was a fundamental consideration in the study's early days.

Of the sixty-three studies considered, only fourteen (22 percent) both presented a clear theoretical framework and also collected feedback from participants to assess the subjective impact of the assigned treatment. The distribution of study designs can be seen in Table 8.1. In total, twenty-four (38 percent) of the publications included some discussion of theory, while twenty-three (37 percent) employed some measurement of how participants reacted to their assigned treatment. Just under half (48 percent) of the cited publications, however, did neither of these things. Many of the studies we reviewed seemed to have little or no contact with their participants after random assignment had taken place, and collected their outcome data using government records alone. These figures suggest that, although they can be used to advance theoretical understanding, many experiments in criminology are simply not designed for this purpose.

The inclusion and testing of theory were, using the categories provided in the initial review (Farrington and Welsh, 2005), more prevalent in some topical areas than others. For example, studies focusing on court-based interventions relied much more heavily on post-treatment offender interviews, with nine of sixteen (56 percent) experiments employing them in some capacity. Many of these studies—which included the four RISE experiments described above—were evaluations of restorative justice initiatives, a unique intervention designed to actualize a theoretical framework (Strang and Sherman, 2005). The universal

Table 8.1   Theoretical discussion and measurements employed in presentations of criminological experiments

	Study Categorization					
Elements Observed	Policing	Prevention	Corrections	Court	Community	Total	Percent
Discussion of theory	4	–	1	–	5	10	16%
Participant reactions to treatment	–	5	2	2	–	9	14%
Both theory and treatment reactions	–	4	2	7	1	14	22%
Neither	6	–	6	7	11	30	48%
Total	**10**	**9**	**11**	**16**	**17**	**63**	**100%**

application of post-treatment participant measures in the prevention literature, meanwhile, likely came about due to the disciplinary focus of the researchers. As psychologists publishing in psychological journals, it is inevitable that their designs would feature a wide variety of well-defined and rigorously tested assessment measures. Thus while our overall review is already somewhat disappointing, suggesting a rarity of the strongest experimental designs, this shortage becomes even more acute if we shift our focus to only criminological publications.

Randomized trials, of any kind, are still relatively rare in criminology. Visher (2003) showed that of 320 crime-control evaluations reviewed in 1997, only 13.1 percent of them were field experiments, and the proportion remains strikingly low today (Garner and Visher, 2003; Weisburd, 2010). Within this small population of randomized trials, experiments designed with theory testing in mind—or even those whose results can be used to this end—remain even more exceptional. Our review suggests that perhaps less than a quarter of this 13 percent, amounting to under 3 percent of the research on controlling crime, combines a randomized experimental design with a strong foundation in theory and a measurement strategy designed to examine the entire chain of causal effects. Despite their potential, experimental methods remain largely untapped resources for the development and refinement of theories of crime.

Conclusion

The separation of criminological research findings into two groups— those based on randomized experiments and those that are not—is in many ways a false dichotomy. Unfortunately, it is also a distinction that has led to an increasingly divisive debate, which has only served to polarize the issue further. RCTs have some distinct advantages. They also present some real challenges, including many of the same problems inherent in nonexperimental research designs. Randomized experiments cannot solve every methodological shortcoming of social research, and it would be unfair to expect them to do so.

Criminological experiments are often necessarily focused on the effects of different policy options, which can lead to a perception that they are better used for answering practical questions than theoretical ones. Again, this seems an unnecessary distinction. The testing of a policy does not necessarily imply that the results are devoid of theoretical interest. It seems clear, however, that experiments—indeed, like any type of research—can have the most impact on theory when theory is built into their design from the very beginning. It is unclear how often this happens, but the fact that theory is only rarely presented as part of experimental findings suggests that it should take place far more frequently that it has in the past.

In order for an experiment to have substantial impact on theory, it must also measure something other than mere outcomes. Outcome measures—in our field, usually some quantification of recidivism—are obviously crucial, but they are not sufficient. They may be enough to answer the key policy questions concerning an intervention, but they lack the ability to shine a light inside the black box and tell us *why* the treatment produced the effects that it did.

It is perhaps on this point that the false divisions between experimental and observational research, and between theory and policy, become most dangerous. Only randomized experimentation can demonstrate clear and unambiguous causal effects. Only descriptive research, meanwhile, can tell us how offenders react to society's efforts to change their behavior. Observing, recording, and analyzing these reactions is the key to understanding why similar interventions work in one context, but fail in another (Hough, 2010). The key is not for researchers to do more of one kind of research than the other, or to focus more on either theory or policy-related questions. The key, instead, is to do all of these things at once. By combining randomized experimentation with strong theoretical foundations and rich observational measurement of treatment and its effects, we have the best chance possible to push our knowledge forward.

Appendix

Review of Theory Specification and Offender Reaction Data

Policing

Abrahamse et al. (1991): No discussion of theory; no offender interviews conducted.

Berk et al. (1992): No discussion of theory with respect to instant experiment (some discussion of theory applied to other experiments); no offender interviews conducted (victims were interviewed).

Dunford (1990): Some discussion of theory; no offender interviews conducted (victims were interviewed).

Dunford et al. (1990): No substantive discussion of theory; no offender interviews conducted (victims were interviewed).

Hirschel et al. (1992): No substantive discussion of theory; no offender interviews conducted (victims were interviewed).

Pate and Hamilton (1992): Substantial discussion of theory; no offender interviews conducted.

Sherman and Berk (1984): Substantial discussion of theory; no offender interviews conducted (victims were interviewed).

Sherman et al. (1992b): No substantive discussion of theory; partial offender interviews[8] conducted (victims were interviewed).

Location-Based Experiments

Sherman and Rogan (1995): Substantial discussion of theory; no interviews conducted.

Sherman and Weisburd (1995): Some discussion of theory; no interviews conducted.

Prevention

Borduin et al. (1995): No substantive discussion of theory; extensive offender and family member interviews conducted.

Campbell et al. (2002): Substantial discussion of theory; extensive participant interviews conducted.

Harrell et al. (1999): No discussion of theory; extensive participant and caregiver interviews conducted.

Henggeler et al. (2002): No discussion of theory; extensive offender interviews conducted.

Henggeler et al. (1997): Substantial discussion of theory; extensive offender and caregiver interviews conducted.

Leschied and Cunningham (2002): Some discussion of theory; self-completion data gathered from offenders, caregivers, and teachers.

Mills et al. (2002): Some discussion of theory;[9] extensive participant interviews and self-completion data.

Olds et al. (1998): No substantive discussion of theory; extensive participant and caregiver interviews conducted.

Schochet et al. (2008): No discussion of theory; extensive participant interviews conducted.

Correctional Experiments

Armstrong (2003): No discussion of theory as it applies to the intervention (some discussion of general theory); no offender interviews conducted.

Dugan and Everett (1998): Some discussion of theory; no offender outcome interviews (preinterviews used for screening) conducted.

Greenwood and Turner (1993): No discussion of theory; offender interviews limited to self-report criminal behavior.

Inciardi (1997): No discussion of theory; offender interviews limited to self-report criminal behavior.

Lewis (1983): Substantial discussion of theory; offenders interviewed.

Marques (1994): No discussion of theory; no offender interviews conducted.

Ortmann (2000): Some discussion of theory; offenders interviewed.

Robinson (1995): No discussion of theory; no offender interviews conducted.

Wexler (1999): No discussion of theory; no offender outcome interviews (preinterviews used for screening) conducted.

Peters (1997): No discussion of theory; no offender interviews conducted.

Court Experiments

Davis (2000): Substantial discussion of theory; both offenders and victims were interviewed.

Deschenes (1995a): No discussion of theory; no offender interviews conducted.

Feder and Dugan (2002): No discussion of theory; both offenders and victims were interviewed.

Goldkamp (1992): No discussion of theory; no offender interviews conducted.

Gottfredson (2003): No discussion of theory; no offender interviews conducted.

Klein (1986): Substantial discussion of theory; extensive offender interviews conducted.

Marlowe (2003): No discussion of theory; offenders were interviewed regularly.

McCold and Wachtel (1998): Substantial discussion of theory; extensive offender interviews conducted.

McGarrell (2000): Substantial discussion of theory; extensive offender interviews conducted.

Schneider (1986): No discussion of theory; no offender interviews conducted.

Strang and Sherman (2005): Substantial discussion of theory; extensive offender interviews conducted.

Community Experiments

van Voorhis (2004): Substantial discussion of theory; no offender interviews conducted.

Petersilia and Turner (1993): No discussion of theory; no offender interviews conducted.

Deschenes (1995a): No discussion of theory; no offender interviews conducted.

Deschenes (1995b): No discussion of theory; no offender interviews conducted.

Barton (1990): No discussion of theory; no offender interviews conducted.

Fagan (1990): Some discussion of theory; no offender interviews conducted.

Sontheimer and Goodstein (1993): Some discussion of new theory; no offender interviews conducted.

Swanson (2001): Some discussion of theory; offenders interviewed conducted.

Latessa (1992): No discussion of theory; no offender interviews conducted.

Kling (2005): Some discussion of multiple theories; no offender interviews conducted.

Killias (2000): No discussion of theory; offender interviews conducted with questionnaires.

Notes

1. The one possible exception to this rule would be the removal of cases that were grossly ineligible for the experiment, but only when the disqualifying condition would be equally obvious across all randomly assigned treatment groups. For example, if a record mix-up resulted in the enrollment of a participant who was deceased, we could safely assume that this condition would be just as apparent in the control group as it would be in any of the experimental treatment groups. Even here, however, any form of primary attrition in a randomized trial should be regarded with a certain degree of suspicion and must be accompanied by a very thorough and convincing explanation.
2. Internal validity refers to an evaluation's ability to determine whether the treatment intervention caused certain effects to occur. External validity, on the other hand,

is the ability of the evaluation's findings to be applied to other settings (Shadish et al., 2002).

3. In our own work, however, we would point out that we have always taken great pains to illustrate exactly how our "convenience samples" were recruited, screened for eligibility, and enrolled into the experiments in question (Barnes, 1999; Barnes et al., 2010).
4. The full experiment took nearly five years to reach the desired sample size in all four RCTs.
5. While not applicable to the intoxicated driving experiment, victim interviews were also performed in two of the four RISE experiments.
6. A preliminary report, based on official arrest data (Sherman et al., 2000), found far more encouraging results among young violent offenders.
7. Low risk, in this case, meant that the offenders' forecasts indicated that they would either receive no charges for new offenses committed over the subsequent two years or would only incur charges for nonserious offenses. Serious charges were defined as those for murder, attempted murder, robbery, aggravated violence, and sexual offenses. Note that the Philadelphia probation and parole agency later defined these nonserious offenders as "moderate risk."
8. While offender interviews are not mentioned in the cited source (Sherman et al., 1992b), other writings (Sherman et al., 1992a; Paternoster et al., 1997) show that interviews were conducted with offenders in some, but not all, of the randomly assigned treatment groups.
9. Although there is little discussion of theory in the cited source (Mills et al., 2002), the article itself cites a number of other sources as the theoretical foundation for both of the experimental treatments.

Bibliography

Abrahamse, A. F., P. A. Ebener, P. W. Greenwood, N. Fitzgerald, and T. E. Kosin. "An Experimental Evaluation of the Phoenix Repeat Offender Program." *Justice Quarterly* 8, no. 2 (1991): 141–268.

Ahmed, E., N. Harris, J. Briathwaite, and V. Braithwaite. *Shame Management Through Reintegration.* Cambridge, UK: Cambridge University Press, 2001.

Armstrong, T. A. "The Effect of Moral Reconation Therapy on the Recidivism of Youthful Offenders: A Randomized Experiment." *Criminal Justice and Behavior* 30 (2003): 668.

Bandura, A. "Self-Efficacy: Toward a Unifying Theory of Behavioral Change." *Psychological* 94 (1977): 191–215.

Barnes, G. C. "Procedural Justice in Two Contexts: Testing the Fairness of Diversionary Conferencing for Intoxicated Drivers." Unpublished doctoral dissertation, University of Maryland at College Park, 1999.

Barnes, G. C., L. Ahlman, C. Gill, L. W. Sherman, E. Kurtz, and R. Malvestuto. "Low-Intensity Community Supervision for Low-Risk Offenders: A Randomized, Controlled Trial." *Journal of Experimental Criminology* 6, no. 2 (2010): 159–89.

Barton, W. H. "Viable Options: Intensive Supervision Programs for Juvenile Delinquents." *Crime and Delinquency* 36 (1990): 238–56.

Bennett, T. *Evaluating Neighbourhood Watch.* Aldershot, UK: Gower, 1990.

Bennett, T., K. Holloway, and D. P. Farrington. "Does Neighborhood Watch Reduce Crime? A Systematic Review." *Journal of Experimental Criminology* 2 (2006): 437–58.

Berk, R. A. *Regression Analysis: A Constructive Critique.* Newbury Park: Sage, 2003.

————. "Randomized Experiments as the Bronze Standard." *Journal of Experimental Criminology* 1, no. 4 (2005): 417–33.

Berk, R. A., G. C. Barnes, L. Ahlman, and E. Kurtz. "When Second Best Is Good Enough: A Comparison between a True Experiment and a Regression Discontinuity Quasi-Experiment." *Journal of Experimental Criminology* 6 (2010): 191–208.

Berk, R. A., A. Campbell, R. Klap, and B. Western. "A Bayesian Analysis of the Colorado Springs Spouse Abuse Experiment." *Journal of Criminal Law and Criminology* 83, no. 1 (1992): 170–200.

Berk, R. A. and J. de Leeuw. "An Evaluation of California's Inmate Classification System Using a Generalized Regression Discontinuity Design." *Journal of the American Statistical Association* 94 (1999): 1045–52.

Berk, R. A., L. W. Sherman, G. C. Barnes, E. Kurtz, and L. Ahlman. "Forecasting Murder within a Population of Probationers and Parolees: A High Stakes Application of Statistical Learning." *Journal of the Royal Statistical Society, Seriese A: Statistics in Society* 172, no. 1 (2009): 191–211.

Borduin, C. M., B. J. Mann, L. T. Cone, S. W. Henggeler, B. R. Fucci, D. M. Blaske, and R. A. Williams. "Multisystemic Treatment of Serious Juvenile Offenders: Long-Term Prevention of Criminality and Violence." *Journal of Consulting and Clinical Psychology* 63, no. 4 (1995): 569–78.

Braithwaite, J. *Crime, Shame and Reintegration.* Cambridge, UK: Cambridge University Press, 1989.

Campbell, F. A., C. T. Ramey, E. Pungello, J. Sparling, and S. Miller-Johnson. "Early Childhood Education: Young Adult Outcomes from the Abecedarian Project." *Applied Developmental Science* 6, no. 1 (2002): 42–57.

Carr, P. J. "The Problem with Experimental Criminology: A Response to Sherman's 'Evidence and Liberty'." *Criminology and Criminal Justice* 9, no. 2 (2010): 3–10.

Clampet-Lundquist, S. and D. S. Massey. "Neighborhood Effects on Exonomic Self-Sufficience: A Reconsideration of the Moving to Opportunity Experiment." *American Journal of Sociology* 114 (2008): 107–43.

Davis, R. C. *Does Batterer Treatment Reduce Violence? A Randomized Experiment in Brooklyn.* Washington, DC: National Institute of Justice, 2000.

Deschenes, E. P. "Drug Court or Probation? An Experimental Evaluation of Maricopa County's Drug Court." *Justice System Journal* 18 (1995a): 55–73.

————. "A Dual Experiment in Intensive Community Supervision: Minnesota's Prison Diversion and Enhanced Supervised Release Programs." *Prison Journal* 75 (1995b): 330–56.

Dugan, J. R. and R. S. Everett. "An Experimental Test of Chemical Dependency Therapy for Jail Inmates." *International Journal of Offender Therapy and Comparative Criminology* 42 (1998): 360.

Dunford, F. W. "System-Initiated Warrants for Suspects of Misdemeanor Domestic Assault: A Pilot Study." *Justice Quarterly* 7, no. 4 (1990): 631–53.

Dunford, F. W., D. Huizinga, and D. S. Elliott. "The Role of Arrest in Domestic Assault: The Omaha Police Experiment." *Criminology* 28, no. 2 (1990): 183–206.

Eck, J. "Learning from Experience in Problem-Oriented Policing and Crime Prevention: The Positive Functions of Weak Evaluations and the Negative Functions of Strong Ones." In *Evaluation for Crime Prevention. Crime Prevention Studies*, edited by N. Tilley, vol. 14, 93–117. Monsey: Criminal Justice Press, 2002.

Ellis, A. *Humanistic Psychotherapy.* New York: Julian, 1973.

Fagan, J. A. "Treatment and Reintegration of Violent Juvenile Offenders: Experimental Results." *Justice Quarterly* 7 (1990): 233–63.

Farrington, D. P. "Age and Crime." In *Crime and Justice: An Annual Review of Research*, edited by M. Tonry and N. Morris, vol. 7, 189–250. Chicago, IL: University of Chicago Press, 1986.

————. "A Short History of Randomized Experiments in Criminology: A Meager Feast." *Evaluation Review* 27, no. 3 (2003): 218–27.

Farrington, D. P. and B. C. Welsh. "Randomized Experiments in Criminology: What Have We Learned in the Last Two Decades." *Journal of Experimental Criminology* 1, no. 1 (2005): 9–38.

Feder, L. and L. Dugan. "A Test of the Efficacy of Court-Mandated Counselling for Domestic Violence Offenders: The Broward Experiment." *Justice Quarterly* 19 (2002): 343–75.

Feder, L., A. Jolin, and W. Feyerherm. "Lessons from Two Randomized Experiments in Criminal Justice Settings." *Crime and Delinquency* 46, no. 3 (2000): 380–400.

Garner, J. and C. Visher. "The Production of Criminological Experiments." *Evaluation Review* 27 (2003): 316.

Goldkamp, J. S. "Pretrial Drug-Testing Experiments in Milwaukee and Prince Georges County: The Context of Implementation." *Journal of Research in Crime and Delinquency* 29 (1992): 430–65.

Gottfredson, D. C. "Effectiveness of Drug Treatment Courts: Evidence from a Randomized Trial." *Criminology and Public Policy* 2 (2003): 171–96.

Greenwood, P. W. and S. Turner. "Evaluation of the Paint Creek Youth Center: A Residential Program for Serious Delinquents." *Criminology* 31 (1993): 263–79.

Harrell, A., S. Cavanagh, and S. Sridharan. *Evaluation of the Children at Risk Program: Results 1 Year After the End of the Program.* Washington, DC: National Institute of Justice; Research in Brief, 1999.

Heckman, J. J. "The Scientific Model of Causality." *Sociological Methodology* 35 (2005): 1–97.

Henggeler, S. W., W. G. Clingempeel, M. J. Brondino, and S. G. Pickrel. "Four-Year Follow-Up of Multisystemic Therapy with Substance-Abusing and Substance-Dependent Juvenile Offenders." *Journal of the American Academy of Child and Adolescent Psychiatry* 41, no. 7 (2002): 868–74. DOI: 10.1097/00004583-200207000-00021.

Henggeler, S. W., G. B. Melton, M. J. Brondino, D. G. Scherer, and J. H. Hanley. "Multisystemic Therapy with Violent and Chronic Juvenile Offenders and Their Families: The Role of Treatment Fidelity in Successful Dissemination." *Journal of Consulting and Clinical Psychology* 65, no. 5 (1997): 821–33.

Hirschel, J. D., I. W. Hutchison, and C. W. Dean. "The Failure of Arrest ot Deter Spouse Abuse." *Journal of Research in Crime and Delinquecy* 29, no. 1 (1992): 7–33.

Hope, T. "Pretend It Doesn't Work: The 'Anti-social' Bias in the Maryland Scientific Methods Scale." *European Journal of Criminal Policy and Research* 11 (2005): 275–96.

———. "The Illusion of Control: A Response to Professor Sherman." *Criminology and Criminal Justice* 9 (2009): 125–34.

Hope, T. and A. Trickett. "Angst Essen Seele Auf . . . But It Keeps Away the Burglers! Private Security, Neighbourhood Watch and the Social Reaction to Crime." *Kölner Zeitschrift für Soziologie und Sozialpsychologie, Sonderheft* 43 (2004): 441–68.

Hough, M. "Gold Standard or Fool's Gold? The Pursuit of Certainty in Experimental Criminology." *Criminology and Criminal Justice* 10 (2010): 11–22.

Inciardi, J. A. "An Effective Model of Prison-Based Treatment for Drug-Involved Offenders." *Journal of Drug Issues* 27 (1997): 261–78.

Killias, M. A. "Does Community Service Rehabilitate Better Than Short-Term Imprisonment? Results of a Controlled Experiment." *Howard Journal* 27 (2000): 40–57.

Klein, M. "Labeling Theory and Delinquency Policy: An Experimental Test." *Criminal Justice and Behavior* 13 (1986): 47–79.

Kling, J. R. "Neighborhood Effects on Crime for Female and Male Youth: Evidence from a Randomized Housing Voucher Experiment." *Quarterly Journal of Economics* 120 (2005): 87–130.

Latessa, E. J. "The Effectiveness of Acupuncture in an Outpatient Drug Treatment Program." *Journal of Contemporary Criminal Justice* 8 (1992): 317–31.

Leschied, A. and A. Cunningham. *Seeking Effective Interventions for Serious Young Offenders.* London, ON: Centre for Children and Families in the Justice System of the London Family Court Clinic, 2002.

Lewis, R. V. "Scared Straight—California Style: Evaluation of the San Quentin SQUIRES Program." *Criminal Justice and Behavior* 10 (1983): 209–26.

Ludwig, J., J. B. Liebman, J. R. Kling, G. J. Duncan, L. F. Katz, R. C. Kessler, and L. Sanbonmatsu. "What Can We Learn about Neighborhood Effects from the Moving to Opportunity Experiment?" *American Journal of Sociology* 114 (2008): 144–88.

Lum, C. and S.-M. Yang. "Why Do Evaluation Researchers in Crime and Justice Choose Non-experimental Methods?" *Journal of Experimental Criminology* 1 (2005): 191–213.

Marlowe, D. B. "Are Judicial Status Hearings a Key Component of Drug Court? During-Treatment Data from a Randomized Trial." *Criminal Justice and Behavior* 30 (2003): 141–62.

Marques, J. K. "Effects of Cognitive-Behavioral Treatment on Sex Offender Recidivism: Preliminary Results from a Longitudinal Study." *Criminal Justice and Behavior* 20 (1994): 28–54.

McCold, P. and B. Wachtel. *Restorative Policing Experiment: The Bethlehem Pennsylvania Police Family Group Conferencing Project.* Pipersville, PA: Community Service Foundation, 1998.

McGarrell, E. O. *Returning Justice to the Community: The Indianapolis Restorative Justice Experiment.* Indianapolis: Hudson Institute Crime Control Policy Center, 2000.

Meldrum, M. "A Brief History of the Randomized Controlled Trial: From Oranges and Lemons to the Gold Standard." *Hematology/Oncology Clinics of North America* 14 (2000): 745–60.

Mills, P. E., K. N. Cole, J. R. Jenkins, and P. S. Dale. "Early Exposure to Direct Instruction and Subsequent Juvenile Delinquency: A Prospective Examination." *Exceptional Children* 69, no. 1 (2002): 85–96.

Mosteller, F. A. *Evidence Matters: Randomized Trials in Education Research.* Washington, DC: Brookings Institution Press, 2002.

Olds, D., C. R. Henderson, R. Cole, J. Eckenrode, H. Kitzman, D. Luckey, L. Pettitt, K. Sidora, P. Morris, and J. Powers. "Long-Term Effects of Nurse Home Visitation on Children's Criminal and Antisocial Behavior." *Journal of the American Medical Association* 280, no. 14 (1998): 1238–44.

Ortmann, R. "The Effectiveness of Social Therapy in Prison: A Randomized Experiment." *Crime and Delinquency* 46 (2000): 214–32.

Pate, A. M. and E. E. Hamilton. "Formal and Informal Deterrents to Domestic Violence." *American Sociological Review* 57, no. 5 (1992): 691–97.

Paternoster, R., R. Brame, R. Bachman, and L. W. Sherman. "Do Fair Procedures Matter? The Effect of Procedural Justice on Spouse Assault." *Law and Society Review* 31, no. 1 (1997): 163–204.

Peters, M. T. *Boot Camps for Juvenile Offenders.* Washington, DC: Office of Juvenile Justice and Delinquency Prevention (Program Summary), 1997.

Petersilia, J. and S. Turner. "Intensive Probation and Parole." In *Crime and Justice*, edited by M. Tonry, vol. 17, 281–335. Chicago, IL: University of Chicago Press, 1993.

Robinson, D. *The Impact of Cognitive Skills Training on Post-release Recidivism among Canadian Federal Offenders*. Ottowa: Correctional Service of Canada, 1995.

Rosenbaum, D. P. "The Theory and Research Behind Neighbourhood Watch: Is It a Sound Fear and Crime Reduction Strategy?" *Crime and Delinquency* 33, no. 1 (1987): 103–34.

Rosenbaum, P. R. *Observational Studies*. 2nd ed. New York: Springer, 2002.

Rothwell, P. M. "Subgroup Analysis in Randomised Controlled Trials: Importance, Indications, and Interpretation." *Lancet* 365 (2005): 176–86.

Sampson, R. J. "Moving to Inequality: Neighborhood Effects and Experiments Meet Social Structure." *American Journal of Sociology* 114 (2008): 189–231.

———. "Gold Standard Myths: Observations on the Experimental Turn in Quantitative Criminology." *Journal of Quantitative Criminology* 26 (2010): 489–500.

Sampson, R. J. and J. H. Laub. *Crime in the Making: Pathways and Turning Points through Life*. Cambridge, MA: Harvard University Press, 1993.

Schneider, A. L. "Restitution and Recidivism Rates of Juvenile Offenders: Results from Four Experimental Studies." *Criminology* 24 (1986): 533–52.

Schochet, P. Z., J. Burghardt, and S. McConnell. "Does Job Corps Work? Impact Findings from the National Job Corps Study." *American Economic Review* 98, no. 5 (2008): 1864–86.

Shadish, W. R., T. D. Cook, and D. T. Campbell. *Experimental and Quasi-Experimental Designs for Generalized Causal Inference*. Boston, MA: Houghton-Mifflin, 2002.

Sherman, L. W. "Evidence and Liberty: The Promise of Experimental Criminology." *Criminology and Criminal Justice* 9 (2009): 5–28.

Sherman, L. W. and R. A. Berk. "The Specific Deterrent Effects of Arrest for Domestic Assault." *American Sociological Review* 49, no. 2 (1984): 261–72.

Sherman, L. W., D. Gottfredson, D. MacKenzie, J. Eck, P. Reuter, and S. Bushway. *Preventing Crime: What Works, What Doesn't, What's Promising*. Washington, DC: U.S. National Institute of Justice, 1998.

Sherman, L. W. and D. P. Rogan. "Deterrent Effects of Police Raids on Crack Houses: A Randomized, Controlled Experiment." *Justice Quarterly* 12, no. 4 (1995): 755–81.

Sherman, L. W., J. D. Schmidt, and D. P. Rogan. *Policing Domestic Violence: Experiments and Dilemmas*. New York: Free Press, 1992a.

Sherman, L. W., J. D. Schmidt, D. P. Rogan, D. A. Smith, P. R. Gartin, E. G. Cohn, D. J. Collins, and A. R. Bacich. "The Variable Effects of Arrest on Criminal Careers: The Milwaukee Domestic Violence Experiment." *Journal of Criminal Law and Criminology* 83, no. 1 (1992b): 137–69.

Sherman, L. W., H. Strang, and D. J. Woods. *Recidivism Patterns in the Canbera Reintegrative Shaming Experiments (RISE).* Canberra, Australia: Centre for Restorative Justice, Research School of Social Sciences, Australian National University, 2000.

Sherman, L. W. and D. Weisburd. "General Deterrent Effects of Police Patorl in Crim 'Hot Spots': A Randomized, Controlled Trial." *Justice Quarterly* 12, no. 2 (1995): 625–48.

Sontheimer, H. and L. Goodstein. "An Evaluation of Juvenile Intensive Aftercare Probation: Aftercare versus System Response Effects." *Justice Quarterly* 10 (1993): 197–227.

Strang, H. *Repair or Revenge: Victims and Restorative Justice.* Oxford, UK: Oxford University Press, 2002.

Strang, H., G. C. Barnes, J. Braithwaite, and L. W. Sherman. *Experiments in Restorative Policing: A Progress Report on the Canberra Reintegrative Shaming Experiments.* Canberra, Australia: Law Program, Research School of Social Sciences, Australian National University, 1999.

Strang, H. and L. W. Sherman. "Restorative Justice to Reduce Victimization." In *Preventing Crime: What Works for Children, Offenders,* 147. New York: Springer, 2005.

Strang, H., L. W. Sherman, C. M. Angel, D. J. Woods, S. Bennett, D. Newbury-Birch, et al. "Victim Evaluations of Face-to-Face Restorative Justice Conferences: A Quasi-Experimental Analysis." *Journal of Social Issues* 62, no. 2 (2006): 281–306.

Swanson, J. W. "Can Involuntary Outpatient Commitment Reduce Arrests among Persons with Severe Mental Illness?" *Criminal Justice and Behavior* 28 (2001): 156–89.

Tilley, N. "Sherman vs Sherma: Realism vs Rhetoric." *Criminology and Criminal Justice* 9, no. 2 (2009): 135–44.

Tyler, T. R., L. W. Sherman, H. Strang, G. C. Barnes, and D. J. Woods. "Reintegrative Shaming, Procedural Justice, and Recidivism: The Engagement of Offenders' Psychological Mechanisms in the Canberra RISE Drinking-and-Driving Experiment." *Law and Society Review* 41, no. 3 (2007): 533–85.

van Voorhis, P. S. "The Georgia Cognitive Skills Experiment: A Replication of Reasoning and Rehabilitation." *Criminal Justice and Behavior* 31 (2004): 282–305.

Visher, J. H. "The Production of Criminological Experiments." *Evaluation Review* 27 (2003): 316.

Weisburd, D. "Randomized Experiments in Criminal Justice Policy: Prospects and Problems." *Crime and Delinquency* 46, no. 2 (2000): 181–93.

————. "Justifying the Use of Non-experimental Methods and Disqualifying the Use of Randomized Controlled Trials: Challenging Folklore in Evaluation Research in Crime and Justice." *Journal of Experimental Criminology* 6 (2010): 209–27.

Weisburd, D., A. Petorsino, and G. Mason. "Design Sensitivity in Criminal Justice Experiments." In *Crime and Justice: A Review of Research*, edited by M. Tonry, vol. 17, 337–79). Chicago, IL: University of Chicago Press, 1993.

Wexler, H. K. "Three-Year Reincarceration Outcomes for Amity In-Prison Therapeutic Community and Aftercare in California." *Prison Journal* 36 (1999): 321–36.

Wickström, P.-O. and R. J. Sampson. *The Explanation of Crime: Context, Mechanisms, and Development.* Cambridge, UK: Cambridge University Press, 2006.

Wilson, J. Q. "Crime and the Criminologists." *Commentary*, July 1974.

Woods, D. J. *Unpacking the Impact of Restorative Justice in the RISE Experiments: Facilitators, Offenders, and Conference Non-delivery.* Philadelphia, PA: Publicly Accessible Penn Dissertations, Paper 73, 2009.

Yochelson, S. S. *The Criminal Personality: Vol 1. A Profile for Change.* New York: Jason Aronson, 1976.

9

Causal Inference via Natural Experiments and Instrumental Variables: The Effect of "Knifing Off" from the Past

David S. Kirk

According to Laub and Sampson (2003), desistance from crime is made possible by "knifing off"—"offenders desist in response to structurally induced turning points that serve as the catalyst for sustaining long-term behavioral change" (p. 149). What turning points create are new situations that allow individuals to knife off the past, in part, by changing those routine activity patterns that led to trouble with the law prior to incarceration (Sampson and Laub, 2005). This idea is straightforward, but the corresponding intervention is extraordinarily complex, as the crippling expenditures on imprisonment and parole and the alarming recidivism rates in the United States clearly reveal.[1]

How is knifing off achieved? Laub and Sampson (2003) examine the importance of marriage and military service as turning points in the life course that enabled men in their sample to knife off from their past and then desist from crime. Marriage, in part, promotes desistance from crime because it produces changes in individual's routine activities, including reduction of time spent in unstructured activities and in association with criminal peers (see also Warr, 1998). Yet the marriage–crime association may be spurious. For instance, Gottfredson and Hirschi (1990) offer a competing explanation for the observed negative relationship between marriage and crime found in countless studies. They contend that criminals are shortsighted and that the low level of self-control associated with criminality also causes individuals to discount the long-term benefits of commitments like marriage in favor of short-term gratifications. Ultimately, the marriage–crime association may be spurious, with each explained by self-control. Failing to account for self-control may lead to biased inferences about the effect of marriage on desistance from crime.

Military service is a striking example of knifing off from the past. Military service in World War II afforded many of the formerly institutionalized individuals in Laub and Sampson's study (2003; see also Sampson and Laub, 1996) the opportunity to desist from crime. The G.I. Bill provided opportunities for education and socioeconomic advancement following the war, and military service also facilitated desistance by separating individuals from the criminogenic contexts and stigmas associated with their earlier juvenile delinquency. Here again, though, there may be unmeasured characteristics that are related to both crime and military service, particularly voluntary service, that create a spurious association between the two. These characteristics may include education and socioeconomic status as well as impulsivity and risk-seeking behavior (Wright et al., 2005).

The challenge then to estimate the causal effects of knifing off from past criminogenic influences is to either understand and measure the mechanisms by which individuals select into certain environments and institutions (e.g., marriage, military service, work, place of residence), or design away such confounding influences through an approach like experimentation where equivalent individuals are randomly assigned into contrasting contexts. The goal of this chapter is to highlight the challenges of testing Laub and Sampson's (2001, 2003) theory of desistance—and of testing criminological theories more generally—and to offer one framework for estimating causal effects in criminological research net of selection effects. I confront the issue of selection bias through research design, by means of instrumental variables (IVs). IV techniques are a standard tool in the economics literature, yet have seen limited (although growing) application in criminology. This chapter will demonstrate the utility of IV techniques for testing criminological theory.

This chapter proceeds as follows. First I provide a brief introduction to IVs, focusing attention on the use of IVs to resolve the issue of omitted variable bias. In the interest of brevity, I do not offer a full technical explication of IV methods and its many uses or a detailed literature review of the use of IVs in criminological research. Econometric textbooks and several recent publications already do this (Angrist, 2006; Angrist and Pischke, 2009; Bushway and Apel, 2010). Rather my focus is on explicating the main conceptual and methodological rationale for employing IV methods to test theory. IVs provide a remedy to the issue of selection bias by using only that portion of the variability in an independent variable (e.g., marriage or military service) that is uncorrelated with omitted variables (e.g., self-control) to estimate the causal relationship between the independent variable and the dependent variable. With an introduction to IV methods in hand, in the second part of the chapter I turn to an empirical application of IV methods. I use IVs to estimate the causal effect of an underexplored form of knifing off—residential change—on the likelihood of recidivism.

A Primer on IVs

Estimating the causal effect of a correlate of crime such as place of residence on the likelihood of criminal behavior is complicated by the issue of selection bias—that is, the possibility that some unmeasured characteristic of individuals influences both where they live and their criminal behavior, and may therefore account for any relation between place of residence and recidivism. The same logic can be applied to other commonly recognized correlates of crime. For instance, unobserved characteristics of individuals may be related to the acquisition of criminal peers as well as individual's behavior, thus rendering the relationship between criminal peers and crime spurious (see, e.g., Glueck and Glueck (1950) and Kornhauser (1978) for critiques of the peer influence hypothesis). Put simply, it may be the case that individuals with a high propensity toward criminal offending self-select into certain geographic contexts (or certain peer groups) and that the characteristics of these contexts have little causal bearing on individual's behavior.

More technically, a key assumption of standard regression models is that a given treatment or independent variable is uncorrelated with the model's error term. This is known as the exogeneity assumption. By contrast, the problem of endogeneity occurs when an independent variable is correlated with the error term in a regression model. Why might they be correlated? Two key reasons are simultaneity and measurement error (Angrist and Krueger, 2001; Bushway and Apel, 2010).[2] A third reason in accord with the discussion above is omitted variables. Omitted variables will be captured in the error term of a model. Making valid causal inferences becomes problematic *if that error term and the treatment variable are correlated* because of an omitted variable. This can be seen in Figure 9.1, in which T denotes the observed treatment variable and X_O denotes the unobserved (omitted) variable that is correlated with T. If the model was specified correctly to include the omitted variable, it would look as follows:

$$Y_i = \beta_0 + \beta_1 T_i + \beta_2 X_i + \varepsilon_i. \quad (9.1)$$

If we omit the confounding variable X, however, then the coefficient for the treatment effect ultimately yields the following:

$$\beta_1^* = \beta_1 + \beta_2 \gamma_1 \quad (9.2)$$

The difference between β_1^* and β_1 (i.e., $\beta_2 \gamma_1$) is the omitted variable bias. The estimated coefficient for the treatment variable T absorbs the effect of the omitted variable X_O. There are two scenarios where $\beta_1^* = \beta_1$, thus meaning there is no omitted variable bias. If there is no association between the dependent variable and the unobserved variable (i.e., $\beta_2 = 0$), or no association between the treatment variable and the unobserved variable (i.e., $\gamma_1 = 0$), then the unobserved variable is not a confounding covariate. If the unobserved variable is related to the dependent and treatment variables, however, then the estimated effect of the treatment variable on the dependent variable will be biased.

The omitted variable bias can be positive or negative; positive bias results in an overestimation of the treatment effect (β_1) and negative bias leads to an underestimation. If both the effect of the omitted variable on the outcome (i.e., β_2) and the correlation between the omitted variable and treatment are positive (i.e., ρ_{XT}), then the bias will be positive,

9.1A   **9.1B**

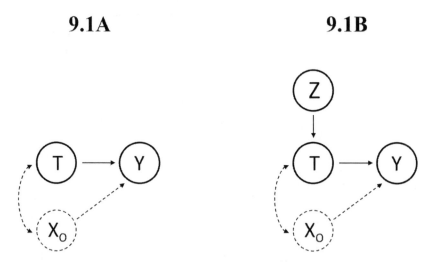

Figure 9.1   Visualizing omitted variable bias

resulting in an overestimation of the treatment effect. The same is true if the effect of the omitted variable is negative and the correlation with the treatment variable is negative. If, however, either the effect of the omitted variable or the correlation with the treatment variable is positive whereas the other is negative, then the bias will be negative, and the coefficient estimate of the treatment effect will be underestimated. For instance, in an analysis of the effect of a criminal record on wages, omission of a variable on education may lead to an underestimation of the effect of a criminal record—because the correlation between a criminal record and education is likely negative whereas the effect of education on wages is positive. By contrast, omission of a variable measuring the immigration status of an individual may lead to an overestimation of the effect of a criminal record—because both the correlation between a criminal record and immigrant status and the effect of immigrant status on wages are negative (see Kirk and Laub (2010) for a review of research on the effect of immigration on crime).

Suppose we can find a variable that is (1) correlated with the treatment variable yet is (2) uncorrelated with the dependent variable Y except through the treatment variable. Such a variable can be used as an instrument (denoted by Z in Figure 9.1B). An IV (Z) for T is one solution to the problem of omitted variable bias. With an IV approach, a variable that satisfies the two conditions above is used as a predictor (i.e., instrument) of the key explanatory variable (i.e., the treatment), and then the outcome variable is regressed on the *predicted* treatment measure. This approach removes the spurious correlation between the treatment variable and omitted variables.[3] As noted previously, an IV remedies the issue of omitted variables by using only that portion of the variability in the treatment variable that is uncorrelated with omitted variables to estimate the causal relation between the treatment and the outcome.

One central challenge to using IVs to resolve the issue of omitted variable bias is uncovering an observed variable that is correlated with the treatment variable yet unrelated to the outcome variable (except indirectly through the treatment variable). Despite the challenge of meeting these conditions, there are plenty of examples in the research literature. In a study of the effect of incarceration length on subsequent labor market outcomes, Kling (2006) argues that the random assignment of criminal cases to judges serves as an IV for incarceration length. In this case, Kling capitalizes on the fact that some judges are more lenient in their sentencing decisions than others. It is assumed that the judge doing the sentencing (Z) affects incarceration length (T), yet is uncorrelated with subsequent labor market outcomes (Y) except indirectly through the treatment variable. Lochner and Moretti (2004) use changes in state compulsory school attendance laws as an IV for testing the effect of years of schooling on arrest and incarceration, assuming that the timing of the changes in law is unrelated to the outcome variables. In a noncriminological example, Angrist (1990) uses Vietnam-era draft lotteries as an instrument to assess the effect of military service on future earnings. In all these examples, the authors make convincing cases that the respective IVs are related to the treatment effect but are unrelated to the outcome variable except indirectly through the treatment variable.

Note that in all three examples the instrument is derived from some form of a natural experiment. This does not always have to be the case, but again, a key challenge with the use of IVs is finding a variable that is only indirectly related to the outcome (through the treatment). However, the use of an instrument derived from a natural experiment obviates this issue. We can have more confidence that the instrument and the outcome variable are unrelated (except through the treatment condition) if that instrument derives from a random assignment process (Angrist and Krueger, 2001). This assumption is known as the exclusion restriction—that is, $\text{cov}(Z_i, u_i) = 0$. Random assignment of cases to judges creates an exogenous source of variation, which ultimately influences sentence length. Change in policy, as in the Lochner and Moretti (2004) study, is a common example of a natural experiment. Randomized lotteries, whether related to military drafts, school choice, housing programs, or some other kind of assignment process, are useful as instruments because a convincing case can be made that the random lottery is unrelated to the outcome variable (earnings in the case of Angrist's (1990) study) except through the treatment variable. In the empirical example presented in the next section, I truly capitalize on the "natural" part of natural experiments by using a random force of nature—a hurricane—as an instrument that affects where people live.

There are several methods to implement an IV analysis, the most common being a two-step estimator (e.g., two-stage least squares).[4] The first stage models the treatment variable T_i as a function of an IV Z_i and a vector of control variables X_i used to account for observed differences between the treatment and control groups:

$$T_i = Z_i\theta_1 + X_i\pi + \xi_i \quad (9.3)$$

The second stage of the two-stage estimation process models the dependent variable Y_i as a function of the predicted treatment variable from the first stage and a vector of control variables X_i. Including statistical controls leads to greater statistical efficiency (i.e., a smaller standard error for the treatment effect). The coefficient α represents the treatment effect.

$$Y_i = \alpha \hat{T}_i + X_i \beta + u_i \quad (9.4)$$

A common concern with the IV approach is what is known as the weak instruments problem. If a treatment variable and the instrument used in analyses are only weakly correlated (or completely unrelated), then the two-step estimator just described will produce inconsistent IV estimates (Bound et al., 1995). In other words, the IV estimate of the causal effect will not be close to the true causal effect (Angrist and Pischke, 2009). Additionally, a weak instrument increases standard errors of the IV estimates and therefore affects hypothesis testing. Generally, a strong correlation between the treatment and instrument and a large sample size will measurably improve consistency. Because of the potential for weak instruments, it is imperative to examine the first stage of the results to determine the extent to which the instrument and treatment variable are correlated. In the empirical example reported to follow, I present the results from the first stage of the estimation to examine the explanatory power of the instrument.

Rhodes (2010) suggests an alternative to the two-step estimator in order to ensure consistency of the causal estimate when using *censored* data (see also Abbring and van den Berg, 2005; Abbring and Heckman, 2008). Censored data are common in the study of recidivism because the observation period often ends before some of the study participants recidivate. In Rhodes's strategy, first, the probability of treatment is estimated as a function of an IV Z_i and a vector of control variables X_i as in equation (9.3). The predicted probability of treatment for each group is then computed from model coefficients and a user-specified value for predictor variables (e.g., the sample mean). This predicted probability is used in subsequent analysis. Second, the dependent variable Y_i is modeled as a function of the IV Z_i and the vector of control variables X_i (by contrast, in the two-step estimation, Y_i is modeled as a function of the predicted treatment variable T_i). The predicted probability of the outcome, in this case for re-incarceration, is computed with model coefficients and user-specified values of predictor variables. Third, the predicted probability of re-incarceration is regressed on the predicted probability of treatment using a least-squares regression model. If there are different sample sizes per group, particularly if the samples are small, then it is advantageous to use a weighted least-squares regression in this step (i.e., weight by the sample size of the treatment and control groups). The estimated treatment effect is inferred from the parameter estimate from this final model. In the empirical example below, I employ both the two-step and Rhodes's IV estimation strategies.

Estimating the Causal Effect of Knifing Off

Ex-prisoners often return to the same criminogenic neighborhoods where they resided prior to incarceration (La Vigne et al., 2003). Not surprisingly, a majority of former prisoners are back in confinement within three years (Langan and Levin, 2002). If Laub and Sampson's (2003) theory of desistance is correct, then it reasons that those ex-prisoners who knife off from their past by moving some distance from where they used to live should have a reduced likelihood of recidivism. Yet estimating the causal effect of place of residence on the likelihood of recidivism is extraordinarily difficult because of selection bias. Differences in recidivism between individuals who moved to new neighborhoods versus individuals who moved back to their former neighborhoods following incarceration may not result from residential mobility; rather, recidivism differences may simply be due to the fact that individuals who moved are different from individuals who did not. Movers may have fewer familial bonds that tie them to former places of residence, or they may have the savings and income necessary to relocate. Presumably these factors are also correlated with recidivism. Thus, an observed correlation between place of residence and recidivism may be biased because of omitted variables that influence both where someone lives and his criminal behavior.

In this empirical example, I utilize an exogenous source of variation from a natural experiment as an IV to provide a consistent estimate of the effect of residential change on the likelihood of recidivism. In August 2005, Hurricane Katrina and the associated flooding and property damage devastated the Gulf Coasts of Louisiana and Mississippi. In New Orleans, more than 70 percent of housing units suffered some damage following Hurricane Katrina, and 56 percent of housing units suffered significant damage (U.S. Department of Housing and Urban Development, 2006). The residential destruction resulting from Hurricane Katrina is an exogenous source of variation that influences *where* a parolee will reside upon release from prison. In the absence of complete data on why an ex-prisoner moves to one geographic area versus another, to estimate the causal effect of residential migration on recidivism it is advantageous to have an exogenous source of variation that induced residential mobility (i.e., the treatment) and which can then be used as an IV. The research question this empirical example attempts to answer is whether knifing off, in the form of residential change, lessens a parolee's likelihood of recidivism. I expect that induced residential change due to Hurricane Katrina allows for a separation between parolees and their criminal past, thus reducing the likelihood of re-incarceration. To test this argument, I compare the monthly hazard of re-incarceration during the first six months following prison release for parolees who resided in the same parish upon release as where they were originally convicted versus parolees who moved to a different parish.

Data and Research Design

The analytic sample is drawn from male prisoners released from Louisiana correctional facilities who were originally convicted of their crime in New Orleans (i.e., Orleans Parish).[5] For those prisoners released soon after Hurricane Katrina, their residential choices were significantly different than if they had been released prior to the hurricane, resulting in geographic displacement.

In analyses, I include three cohorts of prison releasees, two of which were released from prison prior to Hurricane Katrina and one released afterward. I use two pre-Katrina cohorts to more fully establish that Hurricane Katrina altered prior geographic patterns of parolee residence. The first cohort comprises males released from a Louisiana prison to parole supervision anytime from September 2001 to February 2002. The second cohort similarly consists of releases between September 2003 and February 2004, and the third cohort consists of releases onto parole supervision between September 2005 and February 2006 (the post-Katrina cohort). Sample sizes equal 711, 768, and 495 for the 2001–2, 2003–4, and post-Katrina cohorts, respectively.

Data utilized in this study are of three types: (1) individual-level data on parolees from the Louisiana Department of Public Safety & Corrections (DPS&C) and the Division of Probation and Parole (DPP), (2) zip code and parish-level characteristics from the U.S. Department of Housing and Urban Development, the Louisiana Department of Labor, and ESRI, and (3) Louisiana criminal justice system data from the Supreme Court of Louisiana, DPS&C, DPP, and the Uniform Crime Reports.

Given that macrolevel social and economic conditions in Louisiana changed drastically immediately following Hurricane Katrina, it is necessary to control for such temporal changes to isolate the effect of residential change on recidivism. Controls included in statistical models include segregation, average household income, the unemployment rate, average weekly wages, and fair market rents. Similar to the effect on social and economic conditions, the implications of Hurricane Katrina for temporal changes in the criminal justice system in Louisiana are many (Garrett and Tetlow, 2006; Roman et al., 2007). Given the effect of Katrina on the criminal justice system, it is vital to account for temporal variation in the operation of the justice system to draw causal inferences about the effect of residential change on recidivism. Thus, I include control variables in analyses related to parole practices, court operations, and the probability of arrest given the commission of a crime.

My dependent variable, *re-incarceration*, measures whether a parolee returned to a Louisiana prison for a new criminal conviction or a parole violation within a given month during the first six months following the release from prison. As will be described in greater detail below, analyses will utilize survival analysis, so the dependent variable represents the hazard of re-incarceration at each month from one to six. Simply, it is the probability of re-incarceration in a given month conditional on the fact that the parolee had not yet been re-incarcerated.

The treatment variable used in analyses is labeled *different parish as conviction*. This is a binary variable indicating whether the parolee moved to a different parish following incarceration relative to where he was originally convicted. This variable equals zero if the parolee returned to the same parish as where he was convicted and one if he moved to a different parish.

The instrument used in analyses is *post-Katrina release*, which is a binary variable indicating whether the parolee was released from prison following Hurricane Katrina (equals one) or before (zero).

In addition to the contextual and criminal justice system controls already described, the analyses employ five individual-level control variables: race (black equals one, otherwise zero), age at the time of release, marital status, time served in prison, and first release.[6] *Time served* refers to the amount of time a parolee served in prison (in years or fraction thereof) until release.[7] Controlling for time served is necessary to account for any differences between cohorts in the average severity of prior offending. *First release* is a binary variable indicating whether the parolee was released from his first term of incarceration (equals one) or from his second or greater term (zero).

In prior work examining the effects of residential migration on recidivism (Kirk, 2009), I estimated the likelihood of re-incarceration at any point during the first year following release from prison. Yet in addition to examining the prevalence of re-incarceration, it is also informative to estimate the time to re-incarceration. With recidivism rates so high in the United States, we know that most released offenders will end up back in confinement within just a few years (Langan and Levin, 2002). Just as it is important to investigate *whether* an individual will recidivate, it is useful for understanding the path to recidivism to examine why some individuals recidivate soon after their release from prison whereas others may not recidivate for some time. *When* recidivism occurs is an interesting question in its own right. Thus, in this empirical example, I use an IV in a survival analysis to estimate the effect of moving on the monthly hazard of recidivism. My data file is structured as a person–period data set with up to six observations for each parolee. In this case, the estimation outlined in equations (9.3) and (9.4) would simply be augmented to include a notation for month, with binary variables added to the model to represent each month from one to six. Data will be right-censored if an individual was never re-incarcerated, or if they were re-incarcerated sometime after the six-month observation period used in this study.

Before turning to the results, it is necessary to confront one final methodological issue. Why is the use of IVs advantageous even in the presence of a natural experiment? Why doesn't a simple comparison of recidivism outcomes for pre- versus post-Katrina parolees yield a valid causal effect of residential migration on recidivism? The answer is related to treatment noncompliance and to the causal mechanism of interest. As noted, the treatment of interest in this example is the effect of moving to a different parish upon release from prison relative to where an offender was convicted. Perfect treatment compliance would represent the situation where all parolees released post-Katrina moved to a different parish, and all parolees released pre-Katrina moved to the same parish as where they were originally convicted. By contrast, in the sample of male parolees used in the analyses below, 38 percent of parolees released post-Katrina returned to the same parish and 17 percent of parolees from the two pre-Katrina cohorts moved to a different parish. As in many natural and social experiments, the treatment was diluted in the sense that some individuals released post-Katrina moved back to their old parishes (see Angrist, 2006).

Why is the issue of noncompliance consequential? Although it is adequate to assume that the *assignment* to treatment is ignorable, a consequence of noncompliance is that the *receipt* of treatment is nonignorable

(Angrist et al., 1996). If this is the case, simply computing the difference between the pre- and post-Katrina cohorts on recidivism will not provide an unbiased or consistent estimate of the *average causal effect* of migrating to a different parish on recidivism.[8] Put simply, because of noncompliance, the group receiving treatment (i.e., those who moved) may not be equivalent to the control group (i.e., those who did not move). Yet through the use of IV methods, I can compute a consistent estimate of the effect of migrating to a different parish on re-incarceration for those parolees who otherwise would not have moved had it not been for Hurricane Katrina. This effect is known as the local average treatment effect (LATE) (see Angrist (2006) for a more extensive discussion).

Results

In terms of descriptive evidence, during the six-month follow-up of male parolees post-incarceration, 9 percent of ex-offenders who migrated to a different parish from where they were originally convicted (i.e., movers) were re-incarcerated, whereas 13 percent of parolees who returned to the same parish where they were convicted (i.e., stayers) were re-incarcerated. Clearly, there is some initial evidence that residential change leads to lower rates of recidivism, yet these descriptive results do not account for selection bias. Thus, I turn to the IV estimates to examine the effect of residential migration net of selection effects.

Table 9.1 shows the first-stage IV results (i.e., equation (9.3)), which regresses the binary treatment indicator of residential change on the IV and a vector of control variables. The coefficient for *post-Katrina release* is positive and highly significant, indicating that the time period during which a prisoner was released from prison in Louisiana (i.e., pre- versus post-Katrina) substantially influences whether they returned to the same parish where they were originally convicted or moved to a different parish. An F-test can be used to assess the fit of the model and to assess the instrument's explanatory power.[9] An F-statistic below ten is indicative of a weak instrument (Staiger and Stock, 1997). Results reveal that the instrument, *post-Katrina release*, is significantly correlated with the treatment variable ($F = 56.30$; df = 1, 43; $p < 0.001$). Given the strong association between the instrument and the treatment variable, I now proceed to results from the second stage of the two-step estimation (i.e., equation (9.4)).

Table 9.2 presents the IV probit results of the duration until re-incarceration. Results show that those individuals who migrated to a different parish are significantly and substantially *less* likely to be re-incarcerated.

Table 9.1   First Stage of the IV Probit Estimates, Predicting Residential Migration

	Robust	
	Coef.	**Std. Err.**
Post-Katrina Release	0.531	(0.071) ***
Individual-Level		
Black	-0.117	(0.025) ***
Married	0.014	(0.024)
Age at Release	-0.001	(0.001)
Time Served	0.005	(0.001) ***
First Release	0.004	(0.012)
Context and Crim. Justice System		
Unemployment Rate	0.196	(0.037) ***
Avg. Weekly Wage	-0.031	(0.010) **
Avg. Household Income	0.013	(0.007) *
Dissimilarity	0.089	(0.037) *
Fair Market Rent	-0.007	(0.007)
Avg. Parole Contacts	-0.026	(0.014)
Judge Caseloads	0.002	(0.001)
UCR Arrests per Crime (Parish)	-0.031	(0.031)
Month following Release (versus 1)		
Month 2	0.000	(0.001)
Month 3	0.001	(0.001)
Month 4	0.002	(0.001) *
Month 5	0.003	(0.001)
Month 6	0.003	(0.002)
Intercept	2.127	(0.495) ***

Notes: * $p \leq 0.05$ ** $p \leq 0.01$ *** $p \leq 0.001$
The instrument Zi is a binary indicator of the release period (pre-hurricane versus post-hurricane). The coefficient and standard error for *Avg. Household Income* is multiplied by 1,000. Coefficients and standard errors for all other Context and Criminal Justice System measures except *UCR Arrests per Crime* are multiplied by 10. Significance tests are calculated from robust standard errors.

Table 9.2 Second Stage of the IV Probit Estimates of the Hazard of Re-Incarceration

	Robust	
	Coef.	**Std. Err.**
Different Parish as Conviction	-0.615	(0.184) ***
Individual-Level		
Black	-0.241	(0.081) **
Married	-0.397	(0.351)
Age at Release	-0.001	(0.002)
Time Served	-0.063	(0.019) ***
First Release	-0.210	(0.035) ***
Context and Crim. Justice System		
Unemployment Rate	0.060	(0.241)
Avg. Weekly Wage	-0.019	(0.011)
Avg. Household Income	0.011	(0.007)
Dissimilarity	0.046	(0.059)
Fair Market Rent	-0.008	(0.007)
Avg. Parole Contacts	0.000	(0.013)
Judge Caseloads	-0.005	(0.002)
UCR Arrests per Crime (Parish)	-0.007	(0.122)
Month following Release (versus 1)		
Month 2	0.677	(0.114) ***
Month 3	0.788	(0.090) ***
Month 4	0.873	(0.091) ***
Month 5	0.876	(0.109) ***
Month 6	0.997	(0.086) ***
Intercept	-0.627	(0.579)

Notes: * $p \leq 0.05$ ** $p \leq 0.01$ *** $p \leq 0.001$
The instrument Z_i is a binary indicator of the release period (pre-hurricane versus post-hurricane). The coefficient and standard error for *Avg. Household Income* is multiplied by 1,000. Coefficients and standard errors for all other Context and Criminal Justice System measures except *UCR Arrests per Crime* are multiplied by 10. Significance tests are calculated from robust standard errors.

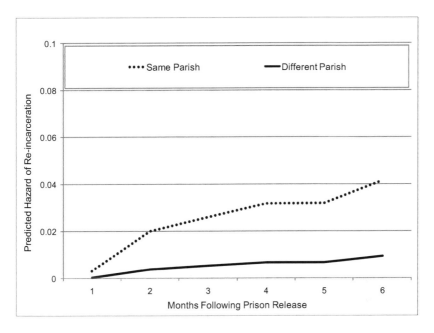

Figure 9.2   Estimated hazard of re-incarceration, by place of residence following incarceration

The coefficients for the month indicators (added to the intercept) can be used to assess the hazard of recidivism within each given month following incarceration. For instance, as depicted in Figure 9.2, in the first month following incarceration, the hazard of re-incarceration for the average male offender who moved (holding the control variables at their means) is roughly 0.001. For those parolees who returned to the same parish following incarceration, the probability of re-incarceration is 0.003. In the second month, the likelihood of re-incarceration given that the parolee was not re-incarcerated in the first month is 0.004 for the treated group and 0.020 for the control group. Following the second month, the gap between the two groups stabilizes to a difference of around 0.025–0.030. This gap represents the treatment effect of moving to a different parish. After six months, an estimated 4 percent of movers were back in prison versus 14 percent of stayers (net of control variables). Whether the size of the gap between the two hazard functions remains stable is a research question worthy of investigation. The treatment effect may dissipate over time as those parolees who moved

Table 9.3   Estimated Treatment Effect

	IVProbit	Rhodes's method
Month 1	0.003	0.002
Month 2	0.016	0.015
Month 3	0.021	0.020
Month 4	0.025	0.024
Month 5	0.025	0.024
Month 6	0.032	0.031

Notes: * p<=0.05   ** p<=0.01   *** p<=0.001
The treatment effect refers to the estimated difference in the
hazard of re-incarceration between stayers and movers.

establish new criminal networks and become readily more aware of criminal opportunities in their new neighborhoods. The gap could also shrink because the police in the mover's new place of residence become relatively more aware of his behavior and reputation and therefore scrutinize his behavior to a similar degree as would police in the mover's old neighborhood (see Kirk (2011) for further discussion and analysis of the longer term effects of moving).

Table 9.3 compares the monthly hazard rates from the two-step *ivprobit* model with Rhodes's (2010) method. This table reveals that the estimated gap between the hazard functions displayed in Figure 9.2, which was produced based on *ivprobit* results in Stata, is virtually the same using Rhodes's estimation strategy.[10] Findings are robust to how the IV survival model is estimated. The hazard of re-incarceration for each month during the first six months post-incarceration is significantly and substantially lower for movers.

Concluding Thoughts

Estimation of treatment or causal effects in criminological research is routinely hindered by the issue of selection bias. There are several methods available to researchers to parse out selection effects when attempting to estimate the causal effect of a treatment on an outcome (see Gangl (2010) for an extended review of the various approaches for addressing selection bias). One common approach, using the selection of place of residence as an example, is to introduce individual and family characteristics as control variables in regression models to account for the nonrandom process by which individuals select where to live. However, even with extensive measurement of characteristics known to be related to residential choice, unobserved factors may still create omitted variable bias. Another potential solution to selection bias is the use of propensity-score matching. With this approach, control and treatment cases are matched according to a propensity score. The propensity score is defined as the probability that a given individual receives the treatment (e.g., moves to a new neighborhood) given all that we observe about them. In essence, matching via propensity scores is a data-reduction strategy that turns a multidimensional matching problem (i.e., because of numerous statistical controls in a regression model) into a match based on a single variable (i.e., dimension). This statistical adjustment is used to account for differences between treatment and control groups, and matched cases are then compared on the outcome variable to produce an estimated treatment effect. The logic of propensity-score matching is akin to a case-control design in which control subjects are selected with similar observable features to those that received the treatment. Yet because cases in the treatment and control groups are matched only on observed characteristics, there is still the potential for omitted variable bias in the estimation of the effect of a treatment. Both of these approaches to selection—statistical controls and propensity scores—may help minimize selection bias, but the extent depends upon the measurement of confounding variables.

IV methods take a different approach to addressing selection. With an IV approach, a variable (or variables) that is unrelated to the outcome is used as an independent variable to predict the treatment variable, and then the outcome variable is regressed on the predicted treatment variable. Conceptually, this approach removes the spurious correlation between the treatment variable and omitted variables. Rather than trying to eliminate omitted variable bias by attempting to measure all potential omitted variables, the IV approach provides an estimate of a treatment effect by using only that portion of the variability in the treatment variable that is uncorrelated with the omitted variables.

In the empirical example above and in related work on the same project (Kirk, 2009, 2011), I have used IVs to address whether separating individuals from their former residential environment reduces their likelihood of recidivism. Findings strongly suggest that it does. Thus, "knifing off"—independent of selection effects—does appear to lower the likelihood of recidivism among those individuals who moved.

This research has exploited a natural disaster to construct an IV. As noted, use of an instrument from a natural occurrence provides justification that the instrument is exogenous—that is, it is uncorrelated with the model's error term. Such an exogenous source of variation does not necessarily have to come from a natural disaster. The relationship between residential change and recidivism could also be studied through other natural experiments. For instance, one could identify states that changed the residency restrictions imposed upon released prisoners. In this case, the timing of the change in residency restrictions could serve as an IV for residential migration. Similarly, one could contrast recidivism rates of states that require prisoners to return to their county of last residence versus those states that do not, using differences in state residency restrictions for parolees as an instrument for residential change (see Apel et al. (2008) for a criminological application that uses differences in state laws as an IV).

As way of conclusion, let me emphasize that IV methods are no panacea. They crucially rely upon two conditions: that the instrument is correlated with the treatment variable, yet it is uncorrelated with the dependent variable except indirectly through the treatment variable. When these conditions can be met, IVs provide a powerful remedy for the issue of selection bias that plagues so many tests of criminological theory.

Notes

1. Two-thirds of returning prisoners in the United States are rearrested within three years of prison release and half are re-incarcerated (Langan and Levin, 2002).
2. For example, there is likely to be simultaneous causation between the size of the prison population and crime rates, in which the prison population size influences the crime rate while at the same time crime rates influence the size of the prison population. To resolve this simultaneity issue in an investigation of the effect of changes in the prison population on crime, Levitt (1996) uses prison overcrowding litigation as an IV for changes in the prison population. Tita and colleagues (2006) use IVs to alleviate the issue of measurement error in an investigation of the causal effect of crime on housing values. Because crime is typically underreported to the police, there will be measurement error in such an analysis. As a remedy, Tita et al. (2006) use murder, which is generally measured with accuracy, as an IV for the violent crime rate.
3. Conceptually, suppose we wish to determine what would happen to the criminal behavior of the same individual under two different circumstances (e.g., they moved to a new neighborhood or they stayed in the same neighborhood). Yet in reality we observe only one of these two potential outcomes for an individual at a given point in time (i.e., either they moved or did not). Given that only one outcome is observed, randomization is one strategy to estimate an average causal effect of moving, by comparing the likelihood of criminal behavior across equivalent groups

where one group receives an experimental treatment (i.e., moves). In the absence of an experiment, we can capitalize on an exogenous source of variation (i.e., an IV) to induce treatment.

4. The commands *ivreg* and *ivprobit* can be used to implement a two-step estimator in Stata, and the *mfx* command can be used to calculate the marginal (i.e., treatment) effect based on the *ivreg* or *ivprobit* results. IV models can be estimated in SAS using the *Proc Syslin* command. The two stages can be estimated separately by the analyst if desired (i.e., the analyst can manually save the predicted values from stage one and insert these values into stage two). However, if the two stages are estimated separately, the standard errors from the second stage will be incorrect, unless they are manually adjusted (see Gelman and Hill (2007) for a procedure). If unadjusted, the standard errors from the second stage do not reflect uncertainty present at the first stage of the model. The need for some kind of manual adjustment to the standard errors can be eliminated by using one of the standard IV commands in Stata or SAS that automatically calculates the correct standard errors for the user.

5. The sample excludes sex offenders.

6. Analyses are restricted to male parolees, so there is no control for gender.

7. Time served is highly associated with the offense of conviction (e.g., prisoners convicted of violent offenses serve more time in Louisiana relative to other offenses). Thus, in the interest of minimizing collinearity, I use *time served* as a control in analyses but not indicators of offense of conviction.

8. In a similar vein, the widely lauded Moving to Opportunity (MTO) housing mobility program suffered from considerable treatment noncompliance (see, e.g., Ludwig et al., 2001; see also Clampet-Lundquist and Massey, 2008). Research results may be biased by selection because of unobserved characteristics of families that led them to drop out of the program or to never "take up" entry into the program once randomly assigned. Part of the reason why some families did not or could not move is because of the difficulty of finding housing in low-poverty neighborhoods (e.g., finding landlords who would accept housing vouchers). With MTO, assignment to treatment is ignorable (i.e., assignment to control and treatment groups is random), but the receipt of treatment is not. Given this, MTO researchers have, in some instances, examined intention-to-treat estimates, which provide information on the effect of being *offered* the opportunity to move with an MTO voucher regardless of whether this *offer* is ever utilized (e.g., Ludwig et al., 2001). For the purposes of evaluating public policy, determining the effect of the offer to move is useful, yet it does not demonstrate the actual effect of mobility (as would estimation of the LATE).

9. I used the *ivreg2* function in Stata to perform this test for a weak instrument.

10. Again, the potential issue that Rhodes (2010) describes is that IV estimates provided by a two-step estimator may be inconsistent because of the complexities of working with censored data. The data used in this analysis are censored because the event (i.e., re-incarceration) is observed only for a portion of the sample.

Bibliography

Abbring, Jaap H. and Gerard J. van den Berg. "Social Experiments and Instrumental Variables with Duration Outcomes." Tinbergen Institute discussion paper 2005-047/3, 2005. http://www.tinbergen.nl/discussionpapers/05047.pdf (accessed June 15, 2010).

Abbring, Jaap H. and James J. Heckman. "Dynamic Policy Analysis." In *The Econometrics of Panel Data: Fundamentals and Recent*

Developments in Theory and Practice, edited by L. Matyas and P. Sevestre, 3rd ed., 795–863. Berlin: Springer Verlag, 2008.

Angrist, Joshua D. "Lifetime Earnings and the Vietnam Era Draft Lottery: Evidence from Social Security Administration Records." *American Economic Review* 88 (1990): 450–77.

———. "Instrumental Variables Methods in Experimental Criminological Research: What, Why and How." *Journal of Experimental Criminology* 2 (2006): 23–44.

Angrist, Joshua D., Guido W. Imbens, and Donald B. Rubin. "Identification of Causal Effects Using Instrumental Variables." *Journal of the American Statistical Association* 91 (1996): 444–55.

Angrist, Joshua D. and Alan B. Krueger. "Instrumental Variables and the Search of Identification: From Supply and Demand to Natural Experiments." *Journal of Economic Perspectives* 15 (2001): 69–85.

Angrist, Joshua D. and Jorn-Steffen Pischke. *Mostly Harmless Econometrics: An Empiricist's Companion.* Princeton, NJ: Princeton University Press, 2009.

Apel, Robert, Shawn D. Bushway, Raymond Paternoster, Robert Brame, and Gary Sweeten. "Using State Child Labor Laws to Identify the Causal Effect of Youth Employment on Deviant Behavior and Academic Achievement." *Journal of Quantitative Criminology* 24 (2008): 337–62.

Bound, John, David A. Jaeger, and Regina M. Baker. "Problems with Instrumental Variables Estimation When the Correlation between the Instruments and the Endogenous Explanatory Variable Is Weak." *Journal of the American Statistical Association* 90 (1995): 443–50.

Bushway, Shawn D. and Robert J. Apel. "Instrumental Variables in Criminology and Criminal Justice." In *Handbook of Quantitative Criminology*, edited by Alex R. Piquero and David Weisburd, 595–612. New York: Springer, 2010.

Clampet-Lundquist, Susan and Douglas S. Massey. "Neighborhood Effects on Economic Self-Sufficiency: A Reconsideration of the Moving to Opportunity Experiment." *American Journal of Sociology* 114 (2008): 107–43.

Gangl, Markus. "Causal Inference in Sociological Research." *Annual Review of Sociology* 36 (2010): 21–47.

Garrett, Brandon L. and Tania Tetlow. "Criminal Justice Collapse: The Constitution after Hurricane Katrina." *Duke Law Journal* 56 (2006): 127–78.

Gelman, Andrew and Jennifer Hill. *Data Analysis Using Regression and Multilevel/Hierarchical Models.* New York: Cambridge University Press, 2007.

Glueck, Sheldon and Eleanor Glueck. *Unraveling Juvenile Delinquency.* New York: The Commonwealth Fund, 1950.

Gottfredson, Michael and Travis Hirschi. *A General Theory of Crime.* Stanford, CA: Stanford University Press, 1990.

Kirk, David S. "A Natural Experiment on Residential Change and Recidivism: Lessons from Hurricane Katrina." *American Sociological Review* 74 (2009): 484–505.

———. "Residential Change as a Turning Point in the Life Course of Crime: Desistance or Temporary Cessation?" Working paper. Austin, TX: Department of Sociology, University of Texas at Austin, 2011.

Kirk, David S. and John H. Laub. "Neighborhood Change and Crime in the Modern Metropolis." *Crime and Justice: A Review of Research*, edited by Michael Tonry, vol. 39. Chicago: University of Chicago Press, 2010.

Kling, Jeffrey R. "Incarceration Length, Employment, and Earnings." *American Economic Review* 96 (2006): 863–76.

Kornhauser, Ruth R. *Social Sources of Delinquency*. Chicago: University of Chicago Press, 1978.

La Vigne, Nancy G., Cynthia A. Mamalian, Jeremy Travis, and Christy Visher. *A Portrait of Prisoner Reentry in Illinois*. Washington, DC: Urban Institute, 2003.

Langan, Patrick A. and David J. Levin. *Recidivism of Prisoners Released in 1994*. Washington, DC: Bureau of Justice Statistics, 2002.

Laub, John H. and Robert J. Sampson. "Understanding Desistance from Crime." In *Crime and Justice*, edited by Michael Tonry, vol. 28. Chicago: University of Chicago Press, 2001.

———. *Shared Beginnings, Divergent Lives: Delinquent Boys to Age 70*. Cambridge, MA: Harvard University Press, 2003.

Levitt, Steven D. "The Effect of Prison Population Size on Crime Rates: Evidence from Prison Overcrowding Litigation." *Quarterly Journal of Economics* 111 (1996): 319–51.

Lochner, Lance and Enrico Moretti. "The Effect of Education on Crime: Evidence from Prison Inmates, Arrests, and Self-Reports." *American Economic Review* 94 (2004): 155–89.

Ludwig, Jens, Greg J. Duncan, and Paul Hirschfield. "Urban Poverty and Juvenile Crime: Evidence of a Randomized Housing Mobility Experiment." *Quarterly Journal of Economics* 116 (2001): 655–80.

Rhodes, William. "Estimating Treatment Effects and Predicting Recidivism for Community Supervision Using Survival Analysis with Instrumental Variables." *Journal of Quantitative Criminology* 26 (2010): 391–413.

Roman, Caterina Gouvis, Seri Irazola, and Jenny W. L. Osborne. *After Katrina: Washed Away? Justice in New Orleans*. Washington, DC: Urban Institute, 2007.

Sampson, Robert J. and John H. Laub. "Socioeconomic Achievement in the Life Course of Disadvantaged Men: Military Service as a Turning Point, Circa 1940–1965." *American Sociological Review* 61 (1996): 347–67.

———. "A General Age-Graded Theory of Crime: Lessons Learned and the Future of Life-Course Criminology." In *Testing Integrated*

Developmental/Life Course Theories of Offending, Advances in Criminological Theory, edited by D. Farrington, vol. 14, 161–85. Piscataway, NJ: Transaction Publishers, 2005.

Staiger, Douglas and James H. Stock. "Instrumental Variables Regression with Weak Instruments." *Econometrica* 65 (1997): 557–86.

Tita, George E., Tricia L. Petras, and Robert T. Greenbaum. "Crime and Residential Choice: A Neighborhood Level Analysis of the Impact of Crime on Housing Prices." *Journal of Quantitative Criminology* 22 (2006): 299–317.

U.S. Department of Housing and Urban Development. "Current Housing Unit Damage Estimates: Hurricanes Katrina, Rita, and Wilma." Washington, DC: U.S. Department of Housing and Urban Development. http://www.huduser.org/publications/destech/GulfCoast_HsngDmgEst.html (Retrieved December 8, 2006).

Warr, Mark. "Life-Course Transitions and Desistance from Crime." *Criminology* 36 (1998): 183–216.

Wright, John Paul, David E. Carter, and Francis T. Cullen. "A Life-Course Analysis of Military Service in Vietnam." *Journal of Research in Crime and Delinquency* 42 (2005): 55–83.

10

Criminal Career Research: A Statistical and Substantive Comparison of Growth Modeling Approaches

Christopher J. Sullivan and Alex R. Piquero

Developmental, life course (DLC) criminology has become a prominent paradigm in the study of crime, and with its emergence has come advances in estimation methods intended to answer research on questions of interest in this area (Piquero et al., 2003). For instance, researchers may be interested in the onset of offending, its continuance, and its cessation. Each of these questions can be considered in the context of more general longitudinal "growth" in offending behavior. Multiple alternative approaches to studying longitudinal trajectories of criminal behavior have been utilized. This study investigates three alternatives in order to extend recent work on the relative merits of these models for estimating criminal career trajectories. In particular, we examine model performance in two important cohort studies as a conduit to considering model results in terms of theoretical implications, subsequent refinement, and future research.

This study has two specific objectives: (1) assess and compare the dominant analytic model in the study of criminal careers (latent class growth analysis (LCGA)) to alternatives (latent growth curve (LGC) models and growth mixture models (GMM)) and (2) determine the degree to which these models converge and/or diverge in terms of their substantive conclusions for theory and empirical findings. These aims are pursued through (1) systematic specification and testing of model fit

Financial support for this project was provided by the University of South Florida, Division of Sponsored Research.

with a classic longitudinal cohort study and (2) subsequent examination of results as they relate to extant literature in the study of criminal careers (e.g., does the best fitting model also comport with existing theoretical frameworks?). Considering these points together maintains important connections between theory and methods. A guiding theme of this work is that these models are of limited use without theoretical grounding, so the specification and assessment of different models must account for both fit to data and correspondence with basic expectations from relevant theories.

Conceptual Framework

The Study of Criminal Careers

Beginning in the mid-1980s, many criminologists started to view the study of delinquency and crime through a "career" lens (Blumstein et al., 1986). This descriptive line of empirical inquiry led, eventually, to the emergence of DLC criminology, which has aided in framing and understanding continuance and desistance from criminal activity on the part of individual offenders (Farrington, 2003). The study of components of criminal careers such as onset, persistence, escalation, and desistance is now commonplace, and their explanation is a key object of criminological theory today (D'Unger et al., 1998; Piquero et al., 2003; Farrington, 2005a). In pursuing such aims, empirical investigations provide information relevant to the assessment and planning of prevention activities (Loeber and Farrington, 1998, 2000). They also may aid in providing a better understanding of the processes that lead to the termination of offending behavior during adolescence and early adulthood (Laub and Sampson, 2001). As DLC criminology has reached a greater level of prominence, parallel methodological innovation has been spurred. Longitudinal research has permeated the field, allowing for a more complete examination of the development of antisocial behavior across the life course (Farrington, 1979; Blumstein et al., 1988a, 1988b; Piquero et al., 2003).

A number of latent variable–based analytic models have emerged for the analysis of these longitudinal data (McCardle and Epstein, 1987; Nagin, 1999, 2005; Muthén, 2004).[1] These approaches are, in part, predicated on the fact that there is a good deal of heterogeneity in longitudinal patterns of behavior more generally and in offending careers specifically (D'Unger et al., 1998). Cohen and Vila (1996), in reviewing an important debate in the study of criminal careers, suggest that understanding distinctions in offender types is a key to elaboration in the study of criminal careers. The extent of variation among and within offender career trajectories is now a common and contentious issue in criminology.

Gottfredson and Hirschi (1990) contend that offenders differ more in degree than kind and that distinctions among low-, medium-, and high-rate offenders introduce more complexity than necessary because offenders simply differ along a continuum of criminal propensity. Osgood (2005) argues that this perspective best reflects the reality that there are "shades of gray" in offending careers (p. 203). On the opposite end lie those theories that argue for the importance of offender types. Foremost among those are the models advanced by Moffitt (1993), Loeber and Hay (1994), and Patterson et al. (1989). As an example, Moffitt's developmental taxonomy anticipates three distinct sets of individuals: non-offenders, adolescence-limited offenders, and life-course-persistent offenders. Adolescence-limited offenders engage in offending primarily in adolescence during a maturity gap and within the context of peer networks. For those who limit their offending to adolescence, offending wanes as adulthood approaches. Life-course-persistent offenders are expected to engage in criminal activity at steady rates over much of their lives. Thus, the latter two groups should evince age–crime curves that are wholly distinct from one another. Adjudicating between the merits of these two competing perspectives has become part of contemporary criminological research. Farrington (2006) describes the matter of whether there are discrete types or a continuum of offenders with different career properties as a key research question in DLC criminology.

Broadly speaking, there are three statistical modeling approaches commonly used to model offending trajectories: LCGA, LGC modeling, and GMM. These models typically estimate parameters reflecting a starting point and an average trend over time. They all rely on growth modeling approaches to estimating crime trajectory parameters, but with different assumptions about the process generating the estimates. These three contemporary approaches, and their relative strengths and weaknesses, are discussed in the section that follows. As the goal of the present study is to clarify the utility of different available modeling approaches as they fall in line with established insight on crime over the life span, a basic understanding of the analytic properties is a first step toward assessing their correspondence with substantive understanding of offending over time.

Latent Class Growth Analysis

In criminology, a good deal of expansion in understanding criminal behavior longitudinally has involved the use of group-based trajectory modeling, or LCGA (Muthén, 2004). This group-based approach has been applied in general population and offender samples, focused on adolescence and adulthood, has been linked to covariates, and has been adapted to various outcome variable distributions (e.g., counts, dichotomies) (Nagin, 1999, 2005). The application of LCGA to estimating criminal offending trajectories was developed by Nagin and Land (1993). To date, there are more than eighty published applications of the LCGA approach to estimating offending trajectories (Piquero, 2008).

The LCGA estimation approach is particularly useful for DLC criminology because it can aid in evaluating theoretical positions that call for specific taxonomies of offending (e.g., Moffitt, 1993). This approach does not rely on a priori categorization of trajectories; hence, a good deal of the subjectivity regarding the class, or type, that an individual belongs to is removed (Nagin, 1999, 2005). It is a flexible tool for modeling criminal offending trajectories in that it relaxes assumptions about the distribution of unobserved heterogeneity in offending patterns and approximates that continuum using discrete points of support (Nagin and Land, 1993). In simple terms, this approach estimates the number of unique trajectory patterns that most closely fits the observed data. The approach also permits the sorting of offenders into the group to which they are most likely to belong based on probabilities of class membership as derived from model-based estimates and observed data.

Of the three described here, the LCGA approach has been the most frequently applied modeling strategy for the study of longitudinal offending data. Over the last fifteen years, a number of prominent works have utilized the LCGA technique to understand key characteristics of criminal behavior (Piquero, 2008). For instance, Nagin and Land (1993) and Land et al. (1996) found that four trajectory groups most closely approximates the observed offending patterns in longitudinal cohort data from Cambridge, UK, and Philadelphia, Pennsylvania. Specifically, in the initial study applying the LCGA approach, Nagin and Land (1993) identified the following trajectory groups in the Cambridge criminal conviction data: (1) non-offenders, 2) adolescence-limited offenders, and (3) high- and (4) low-level chronic offenders who continued their criminal activity into adulthood. With the same data set, Nagin et al. (1995)

used both self-report and conviction measures, and likewise identified four offender trajectory groups. Laub et al. (1998) used official arrest data from the Glueck sample of five hundred Boston-area boys to examine offense trajectories and relevant correlates. The authors identified four distinct classes of offenders. Again using the Glueck data set, but with a longer follow-up (to age seventy), Laub and Sampson (2003) found seven distinct trajectories comprising some high- and low-rate chronic offenders as well as three groups that peaked in mid-adolescence, late adolescence, and early adulthood, respectively.

Using data from Shannon's (1988, 1991) Racine, Wisconsin, cohort study, D'Unger et al. (1998) found good fit for five offending trajectory groups in the earlier cohort (1942) and four in the later cohort (1949). Although empirically estimated trajectories seem to be data dependent, with more groups identified using self-report rather than official record data (Piquero, 2008), D'Unger et al. found that the empirical results of these models were fairly similar across major cohort studies. The authors do suggest that studies of this type are likely to identify an adolescence-peaked trajectory pattern and also a chronic offender group that drops far more slowly in its criminal offending over time. In comparing the Racine findings to those from other major cohort studies, the authors suggest that the number of identified groups tended to be similar, but the offending-by-age patterns showed some variability.

Overall, researchers tend to find approximately three to four offending groups in most previous studies utilizing the LCGA approach (Piquero, 2008). Typically, studies are clear in identifying serious chronic offending trajectories that are distinguishable from the other offending patterns in a sample. These studies of latent trajectory groups have also demonstrated a fair degree of variety in offending patterns and have provided some basic support for taxonomic explanations of criminal behavior (e.g., chronic and adolescence-peaked groups). At the same time, in general, the data used in these studies of criminal careers tend to suggest more complexity than that captured in the theoretical frameworks that have been advanced to date (Laub and Sampson, 2003; Osgood, 2005).[2] As a result, the explanatory utility of LCGA results has become a matter of some concern (Raudenbush, 2005; Sampson and Laub, 2005a, 2005b). So while the group-based method has made substantial contributions to the understanding of criminal behavior (Nagin and Tremblay, 2005a, 2005b), there have been criticisms of the approach that require continued examination (Raudenbush, 2001, 2005; Muthén, 2004, Eggleston et al., 2004; Osgood, 2005).

Kreuter and Muthén (2008) review three potential issues that may materialize in the application of these models. First, they discuss the question of whether latent classes really represent distinct groupings or are merely a statistical approach to capture heterogeneity. Second, the question of whether a single trajectory with no variation fully captures everyone's growth within a given class is a matter requiring further consideration. This speaks to the issue of whether a key assumption of the model fits with what would be expected in reality. Muthén (2004) and Raudenbush (2005), for example, have recently raised this question in considering the utility of these models and whether we really would expect individuals within a class to follow the same longitudinal offending pattern. Raudenbush (2005), for instance, questions the magnitude of variation that exists around the pooled average trajectories defining latent subgroups and suggests that a continuous approximation may be more appropriate. Lastly, there is a question around the selection of the optimal number of classes. Recent analytic work has examined the properties of different fit measures in an attempt to sort out these issues (e.g., Brame et al., 2006; Nylund et al., 2007), but some uncertainty remains with respect to assessing model fit and classification quality. The selection of the appropriate number of classes is especially important in that it may have implications for particular theoretical perspectives, most notably Moffitt's developmental taxonomy. In sum, while this approach has a great deal to offer, it is important to consider its weaknesses and potential alternatives to estimating offending trajectories. Examination of the LCGA approach and consideration of other relevant alternatives are particularly important because of the manner in which the results of this approach may impact the resolution of discussion regarding key theoretically informed hypotheses (e.g., existence of qualitative distinctions among offenders and how key theoretical covariates distinguish between trajectory patterns). In particular, it is important to consider the bottom-line question of the yield in terms of substantive understanding of crime over the life course.

Alternatives to LCGA

Two main alternatives to LCGA are available. The first approach, LGC modeling, assesses the average starting point and growth in the target variable over time, along with variation around the mean growth patterns (McCardle and Epstein, 1987; Lawrence and Hancock, 1998). Raudenbush (2001) suggests that there are certain developmental processes that are likely to reflect a similar growth trend across a given population, and he uses the case of early vocabulary development to exemplify such a process. In such situations, the LGC model would be most relevant, because it is expected that almost everyone will show some linear growth pattern over time, but the slope and intercept will vary. This type of modeling approach has been utilized to some benefit in the investigation of developmental patterns in crime as well. For instance, Jang (1999) used a nested analytic structure to estimate an LGC model to assess the time-varying effects of parental attachment, school commitment, and deviant peers on delinquent behavior. Also Horney et al. (1995) used a similar approach to investigate the effects of short-term changes in local life circumstances, such as marital relationships and employment, on individual shifts in the frequency of offending. The LGC model, as applied in a hierarchical nested manner, is also believed to allow greater flexibility in terms of incorporating time-varying influences on offending trajectories (Raudenbush and Bryk, 2002).[3] This can provide greater insight into theoretical mechanisms that underlie stability and change in offending over time (Osgood, 2005).

As applied here, the LGC model captures five key parameters: latent growth factors for the initial level (intercept) and growth trend (slope) and their respective variance estimates. Their covariance, which assesses the relationship between the initial level and growth over time, is the final model-estimated parameter. Two key assumptions of the models are the parameters to be estimated are drawn from a normal distribution (i.e., vary continuously across subjects) and subjects share a common growth process (i.e., it can be expressed with a single mean and variance for each growth factor) (Nagin and Land, 1993). Substantively, this model builds on a foundation suggesting that the true distribution of individual criminal behavior over time is continuous and that specifications including latent subgroups are unnecessary. LGC models also reflect the notion that all individuals in the sample have similar expected crime trajectories and that the individual variation around that trajectory has a symmetric distribution in terms of intercepts and slopes. In other words, the variation in offending trajectories can be captured with a normally distributed variance term. Nagin and colleagues challenged this assumption and subsequently developed the LCGA or semiparametric mixture model to allow for different variance structures (Nagin and Land, 1993; Land et al., 1996; Nagin, 1999, 2005). Their approach estimates a model comprising distinct latent subgroups with their own trajectories as a means of capturing the variation in individual offending curves.

Although the analyst must appropriately specify the model regarding the observed outcome measures (e.g., Logit, Poisson), distributional assumptions with respect to the variance of the estimated latent growth factors are relaxed.

The second alternative technique, GMM, can be viewed as a generalization of both the LGC and LCGA models (Muthén, 2004; Kreuter and Muthén, 2008; cf., Nagin, 2005). This group-based approach has been applied with less frequency in the study of criminal careers (Nagin, 2005). Like LCGA, it identifies latent classes in the distribution, but extends those capabilities by allowing variation around the average growth within groups (i.e., relaxes the assumption of zero variance in intercepts and slopes). As in LGC, there are means and variances to summarize the growth parameters, but the model can also identify latent classes. Thus, an argument can be made that GMM addresses the problem of the "zero-variance restriction" raised in some critiques of LCGA (Muthén, 2004; Raudenbush, 2005) while also preserving its most important feature: the extraction of empirically identified trajectory groups. Further, a nonparametric or generalized GMM allows for the variation in extracted groups to take on a form other than a normal distribution.[4] Simply put, GMM allows for both the estimation of latent classes with distinct trajectories and also the variation within those classes (i.e., deviation around the class average). Although an analyst can specify nonparametric subclasses, GMM, like LGC, does make a normality assumption regarding that within-class variance.

Comparing the Models

There have been few attempts to compare how the various models perform and fit with respect to longitudinal patterns of criminal activity. Muthén (2004) suggests the use of GMM as a technique that draws on the important features of LCGA and LGC. Applying the three approaches just discussed to data from the Cambridge study, Kreuter and Muthén (2008) found that LCGA and GMM resulted in similar statistical fit and substantive conclusions on the distribution of criminal convictions from ages ten to thirty. Further, both models were superior to the LGC model in terms of statistical fit values. Specifically, the authors found that a two-class GMM provided superior fit to the LGCM, suggesting that some latent classes are necessary to capture the pattern of longitudinal offending in the data. For GMM, they found that the three-class iteration best fit the Cambridge data. Although the authors suggest investigating all three approaches within a given data set, they appear to settle on the GMM specification. The LCGA specification required five classes to capture heterogeneity in offending patterns. In that same study, the authors took a similar approach to the analysis of a cohort of Philadelphia youth and, in that case, found greater substantive and statistical differentiation in results across models.

That study, while clarifying and elaborating a number of issues related to empirical research on criminal careers, requires replication and extension, particularly since the results varied across the two data sets. It is also important to further consider this group of models, in particular GMM, in relation to potentially relevant theoretical propositions about criminal careers. Given continued growth in the use of these models in the study of criminal careers, the current work informs the substantive understanding of criminal careers by examining their features in relation to existing theory and empirical knowledge of criminal careers. Maintaining this substantive grounding in comparing models is essential as varied specifications of longitudinal growth in offending either inherently carry implications for particular theories or may be prohibited from assessing certain propositions based on their properties. For example, key debates in criminology deal explicitly with whether there are distinct groups of (serious) offenders and whether they can be distinguished by theoretically derived risk and protective factors at different stages of the life span. As a result, this work can also speak further to the relative utility of these commonly used methods in the longitudinal analysis of offending.

Methods

In this section of the chapter, we apply LGC model, LCGA, and GMM to data from the Racine, Wisconsin, cohort study (Shannon, 1988, 1991). The models are then assessed for their statistical adequacy and fit as well as the meaningfulness of their substantive results (i.e., are considered in the context of existing DLC theory and prior research findings). The data include two cohorts of white and black, general population youth in Racine, Wisconsin. The current analyses are based on the 1942 cohort, comprising 337 cases, and the 1949 cohort, which is made up of 561 individuals.

Data comprise police contacts from youth through early adulthood and a retrospective interview conducted in adulthood. Police contact data were collected for all youth born in Racine during 1942–49. Subjects were identified based on school records and consisted of individuals who had lived in Racine throughout the observation period (with a maximum allowable absence of three years). Subsequently, a random subsample, which is used here, was selected for interviews. Outcome measures are drawn from the police contacts for delinquent and criminal behavior of subjects at each age. The main dependent variable in the estimation of the three longitudinal models is the number of serious police contacts (felonies, misdemeanors). Overall, for the 1942 cohort, 69.2 percent of the sample had at least one police contact—with a mean of 3.71 offenses (SD = 6.52). For those individuals who did offend, the mean offense count over the years studied was 5.43. Similarly, 69.4 percent of the 1949 cohort had a police contact. The average number of offenses was slightly greater in that sample (4.12, SD = 8.88). For offenders only, the average number of police contacts was 6.03. These figures are comparable to those reported in the D'Unger et al. (1998) study. There were twenty-two years of observation period (aged eight to thirty) in the observation window for the 1942 cohort and seventeen (aged eight to twenty-five) for the 1949 cohort.

Analytic Plan

LCGA has previously been utilized with these data (D'Unger et al., 1998), but the current study extends and elaborates on that work by applying the comparative GMM and LGC models to the Racine data. The models were estimated in MPlus using maximum likelihood. Due to the descriptive patterns of offending across the years in question, and in keeping with evidence suggesting that criminal careers are often described with such curves, all models were specified with quadratic growth parameters.

Assessing fit and determining the appropriate latent class solution have been identified as difficult aspects of working with mixture models. Consequently, we used several commonly applied statistics to make such decisions. These statistics included the Bayesian information criterion (BIC) (Brame et al., 2006; Nylund et al., 2007), Lo–Mendell–Rubin (LMR) test (Lo et al., 2001), and bootstrapped likelihood ratio test (BLRT) (Nylund et al., 2007; Kreuter and Muthén, 2008). The quality of classification and substantive considerations were also utilized in making choices about the models. The standardized residuals for particular response patterns were used as further indicators of the degree of misfit between the specified model and the response patterns observed in the data. These values are assessed like critical ratio tests with values above 2.0 viewed as statistically significant (Kreuter and Muthén, 2008). Finally, for the models drawing on probabilistic assignment to latent classes, we examined the degree of overlap in assignment between the LCGA and GMM specifications with simple cross-tabs. This allows for a comparison of the relative correspondence or differences in class assignment based on the two model specifications.

Selection of the appropriate number of classes or trajectory groups is based on a number of key benchmarks: the BIC, the entropy value, and the LMR adjusted test. The BIC is calculated from the log-likelihood of the fitted model and assesses penalties based on the number of estimated parameters and cases included in the analysis (Brame et al., 2006; Nylund et al., 2007). Lower values on information criteria indicate better fit. The "entropy" statistic ranges from "0" to "1" with values closer to "1" demonstrating clear placement of subjects into the model-estimated classes (Muthén, 1998–2004; Vermunt and Magidson, 2003). Finally, the LMR test is utilized in assessing a given "k" class model relative to one with "$k-1$" classes. Lower observed probability values associated with this test indicate that the "$k-1$" class model can be rejected in favor of the "k" class model (Muthén and Muthén, 1998–2004; Lo et al., 2001). The BLRT is utilized with the LCGA models in situations where the other tests gave mixed conclusions and is assessed in a manner similar to that of the LMR.

The latent classes associated with the selected models are presented in figures as a means of illustrating longitudinal patterns of offending. The values in the figures demonstrate the mean level of observed offenses for each class. Models are benchmarked against theory and previous empirical findings to determine whether they provide similar or different answers to substantive questions of interest. Specifically, this involves taking the results from the previous step and comparing them to extant research. For instance, selection of a model including offender subgroups fits with some existing theoretical and empirical literature, making it a reasonable solution on both statistical and substantive grounds. On the other hand, a conclusion supporting the fit of the LGCM would contradict some existing theory and empirical findings, suggesting a need for further reconciliation of the two. This aspect of the process will allow for greater focus on substantive considerations associated with the GMM findings. This is important as these models have not been frequently applied in criminology, and Kreuter and Muthén's (2008) recent work did not go into detail on this issue as it relates to GMM.

Results

Table 10.1 shows the various fit measures for the estimated models: LGC, LCGA, and GMM. We present the results for an unconditional model. These iterative model specifications relied on a number of random starts and utilized a Poisson distribution. LGC models for the respective cohorts led to similar substantive conclusions. In both cases, the average intercept, slope, and quadratic term were statistically significant. The linear slope was positive and the quadratic term was negative in both cases. Importantly, the results suggested significant sample variation around those latent growth factors. This indicates that individuals varied in terms of their initial levels of offending and its growth over the observed time period. Variation around the quadratic term was modest, however. For LCGA and GMM, we first present the results for the 1942 cohort and then the 1949 cohort. The figures show the results for each latent class across the LCGA and GMM specifications to generally describe the findings as pertains to observed trajectories and facilitate greater understanding of where they converge and disagree.

1942 Cohort

The LCGA model specification results in reasonable fit for the four- and five-class models. The four-class LCGA model shows low probability values on the LMR (114.2, p .00) and BLRTs (119.1, p = .04). This suggests that the three-class model can be rejected in favor of one with four classes. Still, the five-class LCGA specification has a lower BIC value than that associated with four classes and also has a BLRT with a probability value of .00. Two of the descriptive curves for the five-class model appeared redundant in that their shapes were similar but with only slightly different levels of offending. For that reason, the four-class model was selected as more parsimonious. This specification also had reasonable entropy (0.83) and solid correct classification probability values across the identified latent classes (0.88–0.97).

In the case of the GMM and LGC models, the four-class GMM had a similar BIC to that of the growth curve model (5,981.4 versus 5,968.0), suggesting comparable fit. The LMR test indicated that the three-class model could be rejected in favor of the four-class GMM. Comparing the BIC to that of the five-class LCGA, this GMM specification had a lower value (5,981.4 versus 6,069.4). It had a lower BIC value than the four-class LCGA as well (6,131.9), so the GMM was preferable on that basis. An examination of the four-class GMM and LCGA models show that they had similar numbers of significant standardized residuals, indicating that there were only small differences in terms of how well each model fit particular response patterns. Importantly, the LGC specification

Table 10.1   Iterative model fit results for longitudinal analysis of offending
in Racine cohort (Poisson Distribution)

					Avg. correct class
Model	BIC	LMR test	BLR test	Entropy	placement
			1942 cohort		
LGC	5,968.0	–	–	–	–
LCGA-2	6,475.0	1,649.4 (.00)	–	0.97	.97, .99
LCGA-3	6,227.8	259.4 (.16)	–	0.95	.98, .99, .95
LCGA-4	6,131.9	114.2 (.00)	119.1 (.04)	0.83	.88, .96, .97, .95
LCGA-5	6,069.4	82.2 (.14)	102.7 (.00)	0.85	.92, .87, .96, .96, .99
LCGA-6	6,051.5	39.5 (.19)	–	0.80	.97, .99, .83, .98, .90, .85
GMM-2	5,991.4	159.4 (.001)	–	0.79	.95, .94
GMM-3	5,973.1	39.8 (.11)	–	0.81	.86, .86, .95
GMM-4	5,981.4	74.1 (.02)	–	0.80	.85, .93, .82, .94
GMM-5	5,989.8	1,300.7 (.00)	–	0.80	.86, .92, .94, .79, .74
			1949 cohort		
LGC	9,511.6	–	–	–	–
LCGA-2	10,593.5	3,026.3 (.03)	–	0.97	.99, .98
LCGA-3	9,967.9	626.2 (.41)	–	0.92	.97, .97, .95
LCGA-4	9,777.2	207.8 (.01)	216.0 (.00)	0.87	.99, .94, .90, .95
LCGA-5	9,714.8	84.4 (.22)	87.7 (.00)	0.89	.99, .95, .90, .92, 1.0
LCGA-6	9,676.7	61.1 (.51)	–	0.85	.85, .79, 1.0, .93, .97, .92
GMM-2	9,577.0	263.5 (.001)	–	0.75	.89, .95
GMM-3	9,524.6	67.1 (.21)	–	0.69	.89, .81, .95
GMM-4	9,495.2	52.64 (.05)	–	0.69	.94, .83, .81, .90
GMM-5	9,509.0	26.36 (.05)	–	0.68	.81, .81, .80, 1.0, .85

did perform better than GMM and LCGA on the BIC, which is the most frequently used measure of fit in extant criminological studies.

Model fit notwithstanding, it is important to consider the substantive implications of each set of results as well. Specifically, how do these model estimates and trajectory representations equate with theoretical prediction of heterogeneous offending trajectories with different shapes, levels, and time trends? The top panel of Figure 10.1 shows the descriptive mean growth trajectories for the four-class LCGA in the 1942 cohort. Two classes showed "no" (44.2 percent) and very low (38.1 percent) levels of offending across the longitudinal time window. A class comprising 12 percent of the sample peaks at age seventeen and begins to decline steadily through the rest of the observed years. Lastly, 5 percent of offenders had a mean curve that is greater than the others for the majority of the time period in question. Members of that class had relatively high

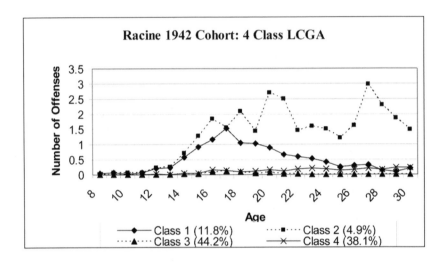

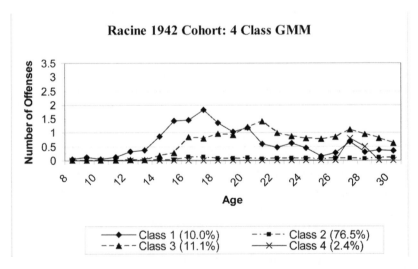

Figure 10.1   Racine 1942 cohort: LCGA and GMM results

levels of offending in their twenties, although their offending tended to ebb and flow a fair deal during those years.

The bottom panel of Figure 10.1 portrays the descriptive curves associated with the GMM specification. One group comprising 77 percent of the sample had a very low level of offending throughout the study period. A second class (2.4 percent) showed a fairly low level of offending, but had a sharp uptick at age twenty-seven before dropping off just as sharply in the latter years. This likely reflects the magnification of a large change among one member of a very small group. A third class (10.0 percent) roughly mirrors one seen in the LCGA specification in that it peaked around age seventeen and then declined for the balance of the observation period. A final class comprising 11 percent of subjects followed a trend where offending rose steadily to age twenty-two and, while generally declining, remained above the other trajectory groups for the balance of the time window.

Overall, both approaches suggest considerable "low" and "no" offense classes. Interestingly, in the GMM specification, which allows within-class variation on growth parameters, the "low offense" group was the most prevalent (77 percent) and the "no" offending group was fairly small, representing only 2.4 percent of the estimated offending sample. The latter group, however, had a rather large offense increase at age twenty-eight. As noted above, this is due to a large change for a single person in such a small class. The LCGA specification extracts a clear adolescence-peaked trajectory, whereas in the GMM, a comparable group peaked in the early twenties and did not drop off as consistently across those years. The LCGA specification extracts a group that is relatively more persistent across the time period of interest. There was a larger group in the GMM specification that has elevated offense patterns as well. Overall, it appears that the GMM classes were more volatile than their LCGA counterparts in this case. For the less restrictive GMM specification, the within-class variance estimates associated with the growth factors were significant only for the quadratic slope. This suggests that, despite somewhat better fit for the GMM overall, a model that fixes the variance within each class may be tenable.[5] Substantively, this raises the question of whether an approximate, but simpler, model is suitable for assessing the propositions about offending groups that have been raised by extant theories.

The comparison of classes across models (LCGA, GMM) discussed above is not standardized and may be somewhat tenuous as a result. Cross-tabulation of each individual's class membership for the GMM and LCGA models was undertaken in an attempt to attain more information about the relative implications of the two models. The most likely class membership values, based on posterior probabilities, were utilized to assess whether the LCGA and GMM viewed the same individuals similarly. Although this is an imperfect comparison and the probabilistic nature of categorization must be held in mind, we can look at the extent to which individuals would fall into similar, albeit nonidentical, trajectory groups. Since GMM is held to be the more general model, we examine how well classes from the LCGA model comport with its results. For the 1942 cohort trajectory groups, overall there are clear differences between placement in given GMM classes and placement in like LCGA classes. There was full compatibility between GMM placement and placement in a like LCGA class in only one instance (class 4). That GMM class comprised the lowest prevalence of the four. There was 80 percent overlap for the late adolescence-peaked classes for GMM and LCGA. The overlap in classification for the other pairs of like classes is a good bit lower (e.g., 61 percent for the group that persists further into adulthood).

1949 Cohort

For the 1949 cohort, the four-class LCGA was selected as the best fitting model. It shows a pronounced decline in BIC from the three-class iteration (9,967.9 versus 9,777.2), low p values for the LMR (207.8, $p = .01$) and BLRT (216.0, $p = .00$), a solid entropy value of 0.87, and strong average correct classification values (.90–.99). Looking at the GMM results, the BIC for the four-class model (9,495.2) was lower than the values associated with the relevant LCGA-4 class model and also the LGC model (9,511.6). The four-class model was also superior to the other GMM specifications in terms of its BIC. The LMR (52.6, $p = .05$), entropy (.69), and average correct classification values (.94, .83, .81, .90) were sound, relative to the other models, as well. It appears that in both cases four classes are optimal. The GMM, however, looked to fit better than the LCGA and also captures within-class variation. It also had 15 percent fewer significant standardized residuals for observed data patterns compared to LCGA.

The LCGA portrayed in the top panel of Figure 10.2 shows one class with virtually no offending during this time window (60.8 percent) and another with a very low level of offending from ages eight to twenty-five (29.3 percent). A third class, comprising approximately 8 percent of the

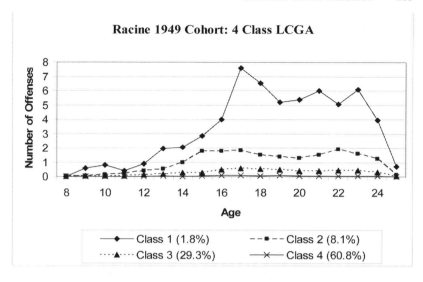

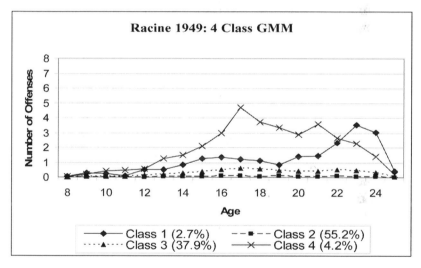

Figure 10.2   Racine 1949 cohort: LCGA and GMM results

sample, had modest mean offense counts throughout their teens and early twenties before they dropped from age twenty-two onward. The final latent class (2 percent) had offense counts that were consistently higher than the others, gradually rising to a peak in the mid to late teens before dropping off in their twenties. Still, this group had higher levels of offending than the other classes throughout the observation window.

For the most part, the descriptive results for the GMM model show similar patterns as those identified in the top panel of this figure. The "no" and "low" offending classes made up 55 and 38 percent of the sample, respectively. The high offending class made up 4 percent of the sample. It shows the same general pattern as in the LCGA specification, but evidenced a steady decline from age twenty-one onward. This demonstrates a contrast from the LCGA cases where there was a slight uptick followed by a decline at that age. The moderate offending class (2.7 percent) now shows a slightly different pattern than that in the LCGA. In the GMM, the number of offenses increased from ages nineteen to twenty-three before declining from age twenty-three to the end of the observation period. For the GMM, the within-class variance estimates associated with the growth factors were significant in all cases, suggesting the need to estimate a model that captures such variance. This indicates that the theoretical frameworks focused on groups may have to provide explanatory accounts for some individual variation among aggregated types of offenders that they hypothesize.

As in the 1942 cohort, the match between GMM and LCGA posterior class membership was examined for the 1949 cohort. Again, this required cross-tabulation of like groupings across the results for the two models. In this case, there was less agreement in terms of group overlap. Specifically, the highest degree of overlap in the GMM and LCGA classes was 70 percent, which was observed for the offending classes with trajectories that extend into the twenties (i.e., more serious offenders). Otherwise, there was more instability across the two models within the offending classes with lower frequencies. For instance, in the classes with near-zero offenses throughout the observation period (GMM-2, LCGA-4), there was less than 40 percent overlap. Thus, there appears to be less correspondence between the models in situations where there are fewer offenses identified.

This suggests two important substantive conclusions. First, the inherent properties of the data (e.g., offense frequency) should be borne in mind when considering different model specifications. The discrepancy in the less frequent offending groups is not surprising—given the different manner in which the two models treat variance within classes. Second, this assessment of overlap may have useful implications for understanding the degree to which the assumptions of these models fit with empirical findings. If the two models converge (substantively) in terms of classification, this suggests that the streamlined LCGA approach maintains a good correspondence with the essence of the data—despite a simplifying assumption. With that comes a broader message about the fact that some gap between data and the model is to be expected in testing and then refining (parsimonious) theories of offending.

Discussion

The intent of this study was to extend the understanding of latent variable models used in criminal career research and what results from these models may indicate about potential offender heterogeneity and how it comports with extant DLC theories. In this regard, we undertook a comparison of three statistical models that attempt to describe and portray the variation in offending careers. It is important to consider the sensitivity of variants of latent growth models as they are increasingly being applied in the field. The fit measures and classification criteria triangulated around four class specifications for LCGA and GMM. In general, we found that the GMM specification resulted in lower BIC values compared to the LGC and LCGA models. This suggests the importance of assessing within-class variation in situations where it is substantively relevant. In this case, within-class variance in the growth parameters of the models was significant across the board in one case, but not in the other. This suggests some inconsistency in whether a model that simplifies and treats all cases within a group as having the same growth patterns offers parity in fitting the observed data. Theoretically, this is important as disagreements about the utility of results from trajectory models sometimes hinge on whether they engender a strong oversimplification of reality and whether their ability to capture variation approximates the actual longitudinal patterns of criminal activity. At the same time, it is important to note that the LGC fit values were comparable to those for the GMM (and lower than that in the LCGA). This suggests that specification of growth models with latent classes to capture heterogeneity in longitudinal offense patterns may be unnecessary. At the very least, those specifications should be motivated by some consideration of substantive issues (e.g., the relative knowledge about latent class subgroups they might yield and the impact of that knowledge).

Theoretically, the results suggest that typical taxonomic frameworks for viewing the criminal career take on more complexity in the face of changing analytic specifications (e.g., within-class variation). The GMM extracted latent classes, while corresponding to better fitting models statistically, did not take on the same patterns as those from comparable LCGA specifications. Empirically, this demonstrates that the underlying simplifying assumption of zero variance may aid in identifying cleaner latent classes, as indicated by their better entropy values, but this might have a cost in terms of fitting the model to the data. So more flexible models may generally provide better fit to the data, but, theoretically speaking, consideration of the propositions outlined by extant theories may be obscured by the additional parameters.

The ancillary analysis demonstrates that class placements are likely to be divergent across the LCGA and GMM specifications. Consequently, it is imperative that appropriate choices regarding model specifications are made to ensure that the classes derived from their estimates are substantively worthwhile. As has been pointed out in the discussion of these models (Nagin, 2005; Nagin and Tremblay, 2005a, 2005b), the membership of a latent class is probabilistically derived, and it is essential that the basis of those classifications is examined in depth. This is particularly salient because the number, size, and composition of latent classes are often theoretically relevant. For example, prior theory and knowledge suggest that high-level chronic offenders will make up a small proportion of a general population sample. There are also held theoretical positions with respect to the likely composition of those groups—beyond offending patterns (e.g., Bartusch et al., 1997; Moffitt and Caspi, 2001).

The "zero-variance" assumption also presents an important point for further consideration because its treatment raises the question of whether the variance within theoretically posited and/or empirically derived offending classes holds substantive meaning or is mere noise. To the extent that variance within classes is allowed, there is a need for further assessment of its properties. It may be useful to differentiate and test the relative variance between and within classes in GMM to get a sense of the added value of that specification and/or incorporate theoretically meaningful covariates to determine how the variance in growth trends is affected. The question of whether the magnitude of variation for a given class around its curve can distinguish it from other trajectory groups in any meaningful way raises a key point about explanatory utility and precision. Also it is important to consider whether there is a significant benefit in creating a taxonomy that contains within-group variation—beyond what might be learned from initially specifying a continuous distribution or extracting simplified latent classes. While incorporation of within-group variation may better capture the data, it is important to establish a clear rationale for the utility of understanding such variability from a theoretical perspective or at least offer that its estimation is necessary to obtain an accurate picture of those aspects of the model that are more substantively relevant. Further consideration of this statistical modeling issue in a substantive framework reflects Maltz's (1994) statement regarding the importance of understanding "deviation" as well as the typical case (see also Von Eye, 2010). It also suggests the importance of considering the sensitivity of variants of latent growth models in the same data set to get a comparative sense of how well they operationalize theoretical propositions and capture observed data (Bushway et al., 1999; Nagin and Paternoster, 2000).

Overall, it is clear that, given the current availability of longitudinal data and the fertile DLC questions that still require analysis and resolution, these models will continue to be utilized frequently in the study of developmental perspectives on criminal behavior. Consequently, it is important that they continue to be assessed in terms of their theoretical implications and the questions that they can and cannot answer. For example, all of the approaches discussed here provide summaries of longitudinal patterns of change, but, in many instances, studies using these methods stop at providing a sense of the pattern of stability or change in offending. Incorporating theoretically relevant predictors in order to study developmental theories like the social development model (Catalano and Hawkins, 1996), and emerging integrated perspectives such as those recently presented by Farrington (2005b) and Wikström (2005) is necessary in furthering the development of these models. Clearly, some of this work requires further consideration of data collection plans and instruments to capture key predictors at relevant time intervals. These models must be considered in light of their ability to provide answers to mechanistic questions about behavioral trajectories as opposed to their ability to capture past events without imparting explanatory insight (Raudenbush, 2005). This will facilitate greater understanding of the factors leading to the "production of outcomes" in criminal behavior over time (Wikström, 2008: 122).

Although we have tried to highlight the implications of these models in broad scope, the key theoretical debate that seems to emanate from work is the consideration of models that capture offending trajectory groups (Moffitt, 1993) versus those that suggest a continuous distribution (Gottfredson and Hirschi, 1990). The findings here have some connotations for that discussion both in terms of the overall comparative fit of these models and the within-model class makeup and trajectory patterns. Taxonomic explanations of any behavior are inherently based on simplification of the true underlying reality. Given the results presented here, two problems arise for taxonomic perspectives in terms of adequately describing the empirical data. First, the continuous LGC model seems to capture the data better than a taxonomically informed specification based on the BIC. As a result, specification of underlying classes may be superfluous in considering longitudinal offending processes. Thus, the foundation inherent in Gottfredson and Hirschi's (1990) theory and Osgood's (2005) commentary has some credence. Second, in the present case, even if one were to draw on the better fitting taxonomic model, it would be the GMM, which generally suggests that there is within-class variance around the growth curve. This result is not an inherent misfit with taxonomic perspectives, but would require greater elaboration in terms of explaining observed within-class heterogeneity. Overall, in light of the emerging latent class model without a zero-variance restriction, the intent behind taxonomic approaches should be revisited to determine the relative trade-off between providing an intuitive simplification and capturing a complicated underlying reality. At the same time, in considering differences in both degree and kind (Meehl, 1992), the field might consider whether the two perspectives may be used in concert and assess whether such a model might provide an opportunity to further theoretical development on how potential quantitative variation within qualitatively distinct offending groups can be explained.

Future Research

Given the controversy surrounding the use of these models in criminological applications, it is essential that future studies expand the consideration of the statistical–substantive fit inherent in their application. Researchers should attempt to simultaneously specify all three of these models within the same study whenever possible. Kreuter and Muthén (2008) provide a sense of how this might be done in the case of latent growth models. As Bushway et al. (1999) have pointed out, such an approach can aid in triangulating key findings and reconciling questions with respect to the fit between model and data. They might also allow for a more nuanced understanding of the number and form of extracted trajectory groups and their concomitant implications for theory. For instance, contrasting these models might provide a sense of what the variation captured in the GMM suggests in terms of similarities within and across particular theoretically relevant latent classes. All the same, it is essential that a clear statement as to the potential theoretical implications of each model is made.

Although we did not estimate the nonparametric version of the GMM proposed by Kreuter and Muthén (2008) in the current study, we suggest that such a specification should be critically examined in future research. Researchers might focus on the implication of the "subclasses" that are utilized in place of the normality assumption for within-group variance. Clearly, this is an issue that might have implications for the discussion of longitudinal mixture models as pertains to the substantive meaning of model-extracted latent classes (Sampson and Laub, 2005a, 2005b). As a result, it is important that the application of this model proceed with an eye toward the substantive conclusions that might emerge from its results. Specifically, researchers must be clear on what the nonparametric points of support within model-extracted classes would mean for theory. This is an issue that requires considerable unpacking in tying the statistical model to underlying substantive conclusions.

Kreuter and Muthén (2008) suggest the importance of exercising caution in assuming that an "unconditional" model, without covariates or outcome measures, best describes the data. They also indicate that it can be useful to assess the utility of latent classes by predicting distal outcomes. It is important that the model is properly specified in terms of predictive covariates and potential outcomes that may be influenced by latent classes. A key question in this area, for instance, is what factors account for the intermittency observed in the GMM results when individuals are placed in latent classes, but can vary around the average offending pattern. This is associated with a substantive need for better understanding of short-term changes in life circumstances (job, family) that might influence offending trajectories (Horney et al., 1995; Piquero et al., 2002; McGloin et al., 2007). As Osgood (2005) has discussed, it is essential that these modeling approaches be attached to theory, and, in order to fully understand the mechanisms at work in shaping ongoing behavioral trajectories, relevant time-stable and time-varying influences should be included as much as possible (Raudenbush, 2005). It is also important that the complex interactive processes that are believed to undergird and actively impact individual development can be incorporated into a given model (Sterba and Bauer, 2010a). In that sense, the utility of longitudinal growth models to provide a concise summary of a career must be weighed against their ability to incorporate covariates that are specified in a manner that allows for estimates that follow closely from substantive questions (Sullivan and Piquero, 2010). For example, Horney and colleagues (1995) considered the impact of shifts in local life circumstances on short-term changes in offending trends, and Piquero and colleagues (2001) utilized "street time" as a covariate to understand how conditioning on "time at risk" affected estimates and characterization of trajectory groups.

Similarly, distal outcomes might be drawn into such models in a way that allows for the assessment of theoretical questions regarding the effects of distinct offending patterns on relevant outcomes. For instance, adolescent trajectory groups might be assessed in relation to adult outcomes as a means of assessing the "snares" question embedded in Moffitt's developmental taxonomy, or those included in "adolescence-limited" offending classes might be assessed with respect to adult behaviors to determine whether they have fully curtailed offending behaviors or they have been displaced to other deviant, but legal, activities (Massoglia, 2006).

Future research should also make use of emerging approaches to testing fit and classification quality in these analyses to ensure the selection of the most appropriate model. For instance, the comparative examination of standardized residuals suggested by Kreuter and Muthén (2008) is important to understanding both whether a model fits and the potential sources of misfit. This is important because, while a particular model specification may fit in a broad sense, it may not best capture the response patterns that are of most interest to criminologists (i.e., those that might reflect key theoretical propositions). For example, a response pattern with high offense counts in the teens that then declines precipitously reflects an adolescence-limited trajectory, and the relative ability of two alternatives to capture such a class is a relevant consideration in the choice of an optimal model. Presently, applications of trajectory models in criminology tend to rely mainly on the BIC in assessing fit, which, while possessing sound qualities (Brame et al., 2006), may not be as useful as other potential fit indices (Nylund et al., 2007). In the future, the use of multiple models and sources of support for fit and classification quality would aid in demonstrating the most appropriate model in a given data set. It might then be more fruitful to engage in a discussion of substantive conclusions with a better sense that all things are equal in terms of statistical fit criteria and the viability of the resulting classification.

Conclusion

This study sought to contribute further empirical and substantive information to the discussion around growth modeling of criminal careers. Overall, analyses of two different Racine cohorts indicated that models considering within-class variance (GMM) seemed to better capture these data than those relying on LCGA, albeit they tended to result in more complex class distributions that moved away from previous substantive conclusions and theoretical propositions. At the same time, the fit values for the LGC model suggest that explicit modeling of underlying latent classes may not be necessary to capture the heterogeneity in these data. This indicates that more flexible models do not necessarily imply more elegant solutions. The importance of studies such as the one presented here is enhanced by the fact that disagreements over the use of these modeling approaches appear to be as much a function of the theoretical framework that each calls to mind as they are a reflection of their statistical properties.

None of these approaches is inherently correct or incorrect, but rather, they may have differing uses depending on the substantive context. As a result, it is essential that both statistical and substantive issues are considered in assessing their relative utility. It is also important that the sensitivity of the chosen model (s) is tested in each particular data set to ensure appropriate statistical inference (Bushway et al., 1999; Nagin and Paternoster, 2000; Kreuter and Muthén, 2008). Still, this should be done with explicit consideration of the relative theoretical implications of a particular set of findings. In general, it appears that the models that have fewer simplifying assumptions are likely to fit the data better. Given this, it is essential to thoroughly consider what heterogeneity implies in terms of understanding criminal careers. In that manner, if one wishes to consider such variation in terms of possible latent classes, an informed strategy for considering particular groups must be developed. Without that, the models will not provide any clear insight into the longitudinal patterning of criminal careers nor be able to assess general and developmental theories of crime.

Applications of these models generate statements that influence conclusions about theory and policy. Recently, this has precipitated debate on both substantive and methodological grounds (Nagin and Tremblay 2005a, 2005b; Raudenbush, 2005; Sampson and Laub, 2005b; Skardhamer, 2010). As these techniques are still growing in their application, it is imperative that more work is done in evaluating their properties— particularly as pertains to understanding the processes underlying criminal careers. Avoidance of the "seduction of method" requires that efforts be made to (1) fully consider strengths and weaknesses of available methodological tools and (2) understand how those factors relate to substantive research questions to produce sound or inadequate answers (Sampson and Laub, 2005b). It is also important that developments in methodology are used to enhance theory without the former overtaking the latter—to the exclusion of certain approaches that may prove equally or more useful in a given situation (Sterba and Bauer, 2010b).

In the spirit of developing the most complete theoretical model of crime over the life span, we must remember that both the theory and statistical models designed to assess its predictions are imperfect and will always approximate the true reality of criminal career trajectories. In that regard, there may be compromises with theory, and with the methods used for their assessment, that must be made if we are to advance as a science that is built on describing and explaining criminal activity. In part, these compromises stem from the recognition that all models are meant to act as explanatory tools and merely capture a portion of an underlying reality (Lave and March, 1993). Consequently, it may make sense to acknowledge that, while there are dangers in the process, people have a propensity to group things in an attempt to enhance their understanding of a complex reality. Given that, it is important that we have tools for evaluating such classifications as rigorously as possible (Meehl, 1992) and consider the implications of these strategies from a broader risk/reward perspective in terms of the meaning of groups (Mun et al., 2010).

Statistical models will be rendered useless absent a theory that is being tested. Results emerging from requisite analyses should, then, have relevance for theory and its modification, re-specification, and refutation. Statistical models are merely tools that aid in the process of evaluating information in order to describe, test, and refine theory. This study and the accompanying review sought to add some useful information to the discussion of how we might integrate emerging methods and extant theory in the study of offending over the life course.

Notes

1. Although the focus here is on the criminal career, these modeling approaches are prominent in other disciplines as well. See Lawrence and Hancock (1998), Nagin (2005), and Muthén (2004) for discussion of some examples.
2. Additionally, it is possible that alterations in model specification (exclusion/inclusion of covariates) or available data may lead to different observations regarding offending trajectory groups (e.g., Eggleston et al., 2004).
3. The LGC model may be applied in a structural equation modeling or hierarchical linear modeling framework. The former allows for a broader array of covariance structures, while the latter allows for incorporation of time-varying influences and unbalanced data (Raudenbush and Bryk, 2002).
4. Although Kreuter and Muthén (2008) recommend specification of the nonparametric GMM as another aspect of the analysis of criminal career data, we focus only on GMM in the current study. We provide some general comments on the potential application of this model to criminal career questions in the discussion.

5. The fixing or freeing of within-group variance has potential implications for theo-
    retical accounts and explanations of longitudinal offending patterns. For example,
    a question around the precision with which individuals may be seen to "belong"
    to a particular group arises with such a shift. If the assumption of no within-group
    variance holds, that would speak more readily to the view of these groups as rela-
    tively pure types. Conversely, with uncertainty around that assumption, there may
    be questions with respect to the demarcation points surrounding the nature of the
    behavior that would lead to placement in a given group. So for instance, if there is
    a great deal of within-group variance in a class labeled as "adolescence-limited"
    offenders, the theory's ability to fully account for the behavior of those assigned
    to that latent subgroup may require further consideration.

Bibliography

Bartusch, D. R. J., D. R. Lynam, T. E. Moffitt, and P. A. Silva. "Is Age
    Important? Testing a General versus a Developmental Theory of
    Antisocial Behavior." *Criminology* 35 (1997): 13–48.
Blumstein, A., J. Cohen., and D. P. Farrington. "Criminal Career Re-
    search: Its Value for Criminology." *Criminology* 26 (1988a): 1–35.
———. "Longitudinal and Criminal Career Research: Further Clarifica-
    tions." *Criminology* 26 (1988b): 57–74.
Blumstein, A., J. Cohen, J. Roth, and C. A. Visher, eds. *Criminal Ca-
    reers and "Career Criminals."* Washington, DC: National Academy
    Press, 1986.
Brame, R., D. S. Nagin, and L. Wasserman. "Exploring Some Analytic
    Characteristics of Finite Mixture Models." *Journal of Quantitative
    Criminology* 22 (2006): 31–59.
Bushway, S., R. Brame, and R. Paternoster. "Assessing Stability and
    Change in Criminal Offending: A Comparison of Random Effects,
    Semiparametric, and Fixed Effects Modeling Strategies." *Journal of
    Quantitative Criminology* 15 (1999): 23–61.
Catalano, R. and J. D. Hawkins. "The Social Development Model: A
    Theory of Anti-social Behavior." In *Delinquency and Crime: Current
    Theories*, edited by J. D. Hawkins. New York: Cambridge University
    Press, 1996.
Cohen, L. E. and B. J. Vila. "Self-Control and Social Control: An Ex-
    position of the Gottfredson–Hirschi/Sampson–Laub Debate." *Studies
    on Crime and Crime Prevention* 5 (1996): 125–50.
D'Unger, A., K. Land, P. McCall, and D. Nagin. "How Many Latent
    Classes of Delinquent/Criminal Careers? Results from Mixed Poisson
    Regression Analyses of the London, Philadelphia, and Racine Cohort
    Studies." *American Journal of Sociology* 103 (1998): 1593–630.
Eggleston, E. P., J. H. Laub, and R. J. Sampson. "Methodological Sensi-
    tivities to Latent Class Analysis of Long-Term Criminal Trajectories."
    Journal of Quantitative Criminology 20 (2004): 1–26.
Farrington, D. P. "Longitudinal Research on Crime and Delinquency."
    In *Crime and Justice: An Annual Review of Research*, edited by
    N. Morris and M. Tonry, vol. 1. Chicago, IL: University of Chicago
    Press, 1979.

———. "Developmental and Life-Course Criminology: Key Theoretical and Empirical Issues, the 2002 Sutherland Award Address." *Criminology* 41 (2003): 221–25.

———. "Introduction to Integrated Developmental and Life-Course Theories of Offending." In *Integrated Developmental and Life-Course Theories of Offending*. Advances in Criminological Theory, edited by D. P. Farrington, vol. 14. New Brunswick, NJ: Transaction, 2005a.

———. "The Integrated Cognitive Antisocial Potential (ICAP) Theory." In *Integrated Developmental and Life-Course Theories of Offending*. Advances in Criminological Theory, edited by D. P. Farrington, vol. 14. New Brunswick, NJ: Transaction, 2005b.

———. "Building Developmental and Life-Course Theories of Offending." In *Taking Stock, The Status of Criminological Theory*. Advances in Criminological Theory, edited by F. T. Cullen, J. P. Wright, and K. R. Blevins, vol. 15. New Brunswick, NJ: Transaction, 2006.

Gottfredson, M. R. and T. Hirschi. *A General Theory of Crime*. Stanford, CA: Stanford University Press, 1990.

Horney, J., D. W. Osgood, and I. H. Marshall. "Criminal Careers in the Short-Term: Intra-individual Variability in Crime and Its Relation to Local Life Circumstances." *American Sociological Review* 60 (1995): 655–73.

Jang, S. J. "Age-Varying Effects on Family, School, and Peers on Delinquency: A Multilevel Modeling Test of Interactional Theory." *Criminology* 37 (1999): 643–85.

Kreuter, F. and B. Muthén. "Analyzing Criminal Trajectory Profiles: Bridging Multilevel and Group-Based Approaches Using Growth Mixture Modeling." *Journal of Quantitative Criminology* 24 (2008): 1–31.

Land, K. C., P. L. McCall, and D. S. Nagin. "A Comparison of Poisson, Negative Binomial, and Semiparametric Mixed Poisson Regression Models, with Empirical Applications to Criminal Careers Data." *Sociological Methods and Research* 24 (1996): 387–442.

Laub, J. H., D. S. Nagin, and R. J. Sampson. "Trajectories of Change in Criminal Offending: Good Marriages and the Desistance Process." *American Sociological Review* 63 (1998): 225–38.

Laub, J. H. and R. J. Sampson. "Understanding Desistance from Crime." In *Crime and Justice: A Review of Research*, edited by M. Tonry, vol. 28. Chicago, IL: University of Chicago, 2001.

———. *Shared Beginnings, Divergent Lives: Delinquent Boys to Age 70*. Cambridge, MA: Harvard University Press, 2003.

Lave, C. A. and J. G. March. *An Introduction to Models in the Social Sciences*. Lanham, MD: University Press of America, 1993.

Lawrence, F. and G. Hancock. "Assessing Change over Time Using Latent Growth Modeling." *Measurement and Evaluation in Counseling and Development* 30 (1998): 211–24.

Lo, Y., N. Mendell, and D. Rubin. "Testing the Number of Components in a Normal Mixture." *Biometrika* 88 (2001): 767–78.

Loeber, R. and D. P. Farrington. "Never Too Early, Never Too Late: Risk Factors and Successful Interventions for Serious and Violent Juvenile Offenders." *Studies on Crime and Crime Prevention* 7 (1998): 7–30.

———. "Young Children Who Commit Crimes: Epidemiology, Developmental Origins, Risk Factors, Early Interventions, and Policy Implications." *Development and Psychopathology* 12 (2000): 737–62.

Loeber, R. and D. F. Hay. "Developmental Approaches to Aggression and Conduct Problems." In *Development Through Life: A Handbook for Clinicians*, edited by M. Rutter and D. F. Hay. Oxford: Blackwell, 1994.

Maltz, M. D. "Deviating from the Mean: The Declining Significance of Significance." *Journal of Research in Crime and Delinquency* 31 (1994): 434–63.

Massoglia, M. "Desistance or Displacement? The Changing Patterns of Criminal Offending from Adolescence to Adulthood." *The Journal of Quantitative Criminology* 22 (2006): 215–39.

McCardle, J. J. and D. Epstein. "Latent Growth Curves within Developmental Structural Equation Models." *Child Development* 58 (1987): 110–33.

McGloin, J. M., C. J. Sullivan, A. R. Piquero, and T. C. Pratt. "Explaining Qualitative Change in Offending: Revisiting Specialization in the Short-Term." *Journal of Research in Crime and Delinquency* 44 (2007): 321–46.

Meehl, P. E. "Factors and Taxa, Traits and Types, Differences of Degree and Differences in Kind." *Journal of Personality* 60 (1992): 117–74.

Moffitt, T. E. "Adolescence-Limited and Life-Course-Persistent Antisocial Behavior: A Developmental Taxonomy." *Psychological Review* 100 (1993): 674–701.

Moffitt, T. E. and A. Caspi. "Childhood Predictors Differentiate Life-Course Persistent and Adolescent-Limited Antisocial Pathways among Males and Females." *Development and Psychopathology* 13 (2001): 355–75.

Mun, E. Y., M. E. Bates, and E. Vaschillo. "Closing the Gap between Person-Oriented Theory and Methods." *Development and Psychopathology* 22 (2010): 261–71.

Muthén, B. O. *MPlus Technical Appendices.* Los Angeles, CA: Muthén & Muthén, 1998–2004.

———. "Latent Variable Analysis: Growth Mixture Modeling and Related Techniques for Longitudinal Data." In *Handbook of Quantitative Methodology for the Social Sciences*, edited by D. Kaplan. Newbury Park, CA: Sage Publications, 2004.

Muthén, B. O. and L. K. Muthén. *MPlus User's Guide.* 3rd ed. Los Angeles, CA: Muthén & Muthén, 1998–2004.

Nagin, D. S. "Analyzing Developmental Trajectories: A Semi-Parametric, Group-Based Approach." *Psychological Methods* 4 (1999): 139–57.

————. *Group-Based Modeling of Development.* Cambridge, MA: Harvard, 2005.

Nagin, D. S., D. P. Farrington, and T. E. Moffitt. "Life-Course Trajectories of Different Types of Offenders." *Criminology* 33 (1995): 111–40.

Nagin, D. S. and K. Land. "Age, Criminal Careers, and Population Heterogeneity: Specification and Estimation of a Nonparametric, Mixed Poisson Model." *Criminology* 31 (1993): 327–62.

Nagin, D. S. and R. Paternoster. "Population Heterogeneity and State Dependence: State of the Evidence and Directions for Future Research." *Journal of Quantitative Criminology* 16 (2000): 117–44.

Nagin, D. S. and R. E. Tremblay. "What Has Been Learned from Group-Based Trajectory Modeling? Examples from Physical Aggression and Other Problem Behaviors." *The Annals of the American Academy of Political and Social Science* 602 (2005a): 82–117.

————. "Developmental Trajectory Groups: Fact or a Useful Statistical Fiction?" *Criminology* 43 (2005b): 873–903.

Nylund, K. L., T. Asparouhov, and B. O. Muthén. "Deciding on the Number of Classes in Latent Class Analysis and Growth Mixture Modeling: A Monte Carlo Simulation Study." *Structural Equation Modeling* 14 (2007): 535–69.

Osgood, D. W. "Making Sense of Crime and the Life-Course." *The Annals of the American Academy of Political and Social Science* 602 (2005): 196–211.

Patterson, G. R., B. D. DeBaryshe, and E. Ramsey. "A Developmental Perspective on Antisocial Behavior." *American Psychologist* 44 (1989): 329–35.

Piquero, A. R. "Taking Stock of Developmental Trajectories of Criminal Activity over the Life Course." In *Longitudinal Research on Crime and Delinquency,* edited by A. Liberman. New York: Springer, 2008.

Piquero, A. R., A. Blumstein, R. Brame, R. Haapanen, E. P. Mulvey, and D. S. Nagin. "Assessing the Impact of Exposure Time and Incapacitation on Longitudinal Trajectories of Criminal Offending." *Journal of Adolescent Research* 16 (2001): 54–74.

Piquero, A. R., A. Blumstein, and D. P. Farrington. "The Criminal Career Paradigm." In *Crime and Justice: A Review of Research,* edited by M. Tonry, vol. 30. Chicago, IL: University of Chicago Press, 2003.

Piquero, A. R., R. Brame, P. Mazerolle, and R. Haapanen. "Crime in Emerging Adulthood." *Criminology* 40 (2002): 137–69.

Raudenbush, S. W. "Comparing Personal Trajectories and Drawing Causal Inferences from Longitudinal Data." *Annual Review of Psychology* 52 (2001): 501–25.

————. "How Do We Study 'What Happens Next'?" *The Annals of the American Academy of Political and Social Science* 602 (2005): 131–44.

Raudenbush, S. W. and A. Bryk. *Hierarchical Linear Models*. 2nd ed. Thousand Oaks, CA: Sage, 2002.

Sampson, R. J. and J. H. Laub. "A Life-Course View of the Development of Crime." *The Annals of the American Academy of Political and Social Science* 602 (2005a): 12–45.

———. "Seductions of Method: Rejoinder to Nagin and Tremblay." *Criminology* 43 (2005b): 905–13.

Shannon, L. W. *Criminal Career Continuity: Its Social Context*. New York: Human Sciences Press, 1988.

———. *Changing Patterns of Delinquency and Crime: A Longitudinal Study in Racine*. Boulder, CO: Westview, 1991.

Skardhamer, T. "Distinguishing Facts and Artifacts in Group-Based Modeling." *Criminology* 48 (2010): 295–320.

Sterba, S. K. and D. J. Bauer. "Matching Method with Theory in Person-Oriented Developmental Psychopathology Research." *Development and Psychopathology* 22 (2010a): 239–54.

———. "Statistically Evaluating Person-Oriented Principles Revisited." *Development and Psychopathology* 22 (2010b): 287–94.

Sullivan, C. J. and A. R. Piquero. "Investigating Stability and Change in Substance Use and Criminal Activity Using a Synthesized Longitudinal Modeling Approach." *Journal of Drug Issues* 40 (2010): 63–91.

Vermunt, J. K. and J. Magidson. "Latent Class Analysis." In *The Sage Encyclopedia of Social Science Research Methods*, edited by M. Lewis-Beck, A. E. Bryman, and T. F. Liao. Newbury Park, CA: Sage, 2003.

Von Eye, A. "Developing the Person-Oriented Approach: Theory and Methods of Analysis." *Development and Psychopathology* 22 (2010): 277–85.

Wikström, P.-O. H. "The Social Origins of Pathways in Crime: Towards a Developmental Ecological Action Theory of Crime Involvement and Its Changes." In *Integrated Developmental and Life-Course Theories of Offending*. Advances in Criminological Theory, edited by D. P. Farrington, vol. 14. New Brunswick, NJ: Transaction Publishers, 2005.

———. "In Search of Causes and Explanations of Crime." In *Doing Research on Crime and Justice*, edited by R. D. King and E. Wincup. New York: Oxford University, 2008.

11

Understanding Desistance: Theory Testing with Formal Empirical Models

Shawn D. Bushway and Raymond Paternoster

Interest in the "career criminal" in the early 1980s forced criminologists to become more concerned about dimensions of criminal offending other than onset—including duration, persistence of offending over time, escalation from less serious to more serious offending, and the eventual termination or desistance from crime. Desistance has received perhaps the most attention, with propositions and theories abounding about why people quit crime. Early understandings conceptualized desistance as a somewhat static event, the event of moving from a state of committing crime to a state of not committing crime. Gradually, however, scholars have begun to understand desistance not as an event but as a more dynamic process or evolution. Fagan (1989) was perhaps the first to recognize this, differentiating the process of desistance, defined as the reduction in the frequency and severity of offending, from the event of quitting crime. LeBlanc and Fréchette (1989) also referred to desistance as a set of processes that lead to the cessation of crime. They use the term "deceleration" to refer to a reduction in the frequency of offending prior to its cessation. More recently, Laub and Sampson (2001) explicitly separated the process of desistance from the termination of offending, which they viewed as the outcome of desistance.

Gottfredson and Hirschi (1990) argued that desistance too was best thought of as a process, but a much more uniform process than what others had conceived, where offenders desist from criminal acts over time from roughly a similarly starting point and at roughly the same rate. Unlike theorists like Laub and Sampson (2003) and others, Gottfredson and Hirschi (1990: 141) thought that desistance need not and indeed could not be explained by any set of criminological or sociological variables but that its uniformity suggested that desistance was simply due to age—"the inexorable aging of the organism."

Once desistance was reconceptualized as a process that unfolded over time, many scholars needed special tools to capture the movement from offending to much less or virtually no offending. Given their understanding both of the origins of offending, a time-stable difference in the propensity to commit crime, and of the uniformity of the desistance process, Gottfredson and Hirschi's theoretical position required no special methodology and no special analytical tools. For them, entry both into and out of crime could be studied with cross-sectional research designs and standard analytical methods. For other desistance scholars, however, the desistance process was not thought to be uniform at all, but was characterized as having great heterogeneity as some offenders quit crime early, some very late, and others somewhere between the two. In addition, the rate at which desistance could occur over time could be fundamentally different for different persons or groups of persons. Given this great heterogeneity in the process of desistance, it is unlikely to be due to a uniform process like the biological aging of the organism and, therefore, is unlikely to be captured with cross-sectional data. When desistance is conceptualized as occurring at different times and with different speeds or rates, long-term patterns of individual offending are needed to empirically understand it. As a result, theoretical and conceptual refinement of the process of desistance became intricately aligned with the search for new analytical tools that could best capture that longitudinal process.

Coinciding with this new conceptualization of desistance as a process, then, was the development of new methodologies and analytic strategies to study it. For example, Bushway et al. (2001) proposed using growth curve models that describe the change in something like the latent propensity to commit crime over time to identify desisters. These methods, particularly the group-based trajectory models developed by Nagin and Land (1993), can identify long-term changes in offending propensity over time. Using this approach, Bushway et al. (2003) demonstrated that these methods identify different people as desisters than more traditional static methods (those that use an analogue to clinical cut-points such as not committing a crime in three successive measurement periods). This more dynamic approach does not allow people with very low levels of offending to be included in the group of people who are eligible to desist because their initial rates of offending are not high enough to be considered "offenders," something that happens routinely when using the static method. As a result, static methods were concentrating on explaining the behavior of low-level offenders, who, from a statistical perspective, had experienced little or no real change in offending.

The group-based trajectory method is now a fairly standard statistical tool to describe offending over the life course (Piquero, 2008), and Sampson and Laub (2003) and Blokland et al. (2005) (see also Blokland and Nieuwbeerta, 2005) have used this method to describe the latent propensity to offend over the entire life course (roughly age twelve to age seventy). While each set of analyses identifies some people who have a relatively flat long-term pattern of offending indicative of persistence in crime, the more typical pattern is a period of increasing propensity of offending followed by a long-term decline in offending that usually reaches very low or nonexistent levels of offending propensity by the end of the period. Offenders who follow this pattern are typically referred to in the literature as desisters.

In this chapter, we hope to contribute to desistance scholarship by offering both a different theory of desistance and different analytical strategies to study desistance than has been suggested thus far in the literature (for a more complete theoretical description, see Paternoster and Bushway, 2009). We begin by laying out the facts that any theory of desistance must address, and we argue that current theories are suspect in the face of these facts. We then briefly outline a theory that we think is more consistent with these facts, a theory that argues that desistance from crime is due to both an intentional change in one's identity from a criminal offender to a non-offender and simultaneous work toward a desired future identity or possible self while avoiding an undesired future identity or feared self. We do not argue in our theory that the kinds of structural factors such as good jobs and marriages that have been identified by other theorists are unimportant. Rather, our position is that involvement in these conventional institutions comes later, only after an offender has begun to change their identity. We further suggest a process through which offenders become dissatisfied with their lives as offenders, the *crystallization of discontent*, as a result of which they begin to think of a new identity as both a possibility and a necessity.

After briefly describing our theory of desistance, we offer an outline of a two-pronged methodological strategy to study identity change and desistance from crime. The first prong involves thinking of life-course data as a type of individual time series. Analysis of time series data is a separate and rich area of statistics that is more commonly associated with the study of aggregate time trends in criminology. There is nothing inherent in individual-level data, however, which precludes the use of time series statistical tools. The fact that there are many individual time series represented in any set of panel data adds to the richness of the data, but it does not negate the need to take the basic time series character of the data into account.

A second strategy is to think about how different theories of desistance translate in hazard models. Kurlychek et al. (2010) have tested different models of desistance using parametric hazard models. They find substantial support for the idea of instantaneous desistance, with little evidence for declining hazards, at least in the short term. This is much more consistent with models of desistance that allow for a dramatic change in offending rather than a more gradual change. An understanding of these facts suggest to us that desistance could not simply be due to the inexorable aging of the organism, nor be due at least initially to the structural roles that people are in (worker, marriage partner), but that the offender must first change and change themselves in a rather dramatic way. These models of dramatic or instantaneous desistance are still processes and still need to be thought about in dynamic rather than static ways.

What We Currently Know about Desistance

There has been much discussion in the literature about what desistance from crime is, how to recognize it when it occurs, and who desists (Fagan, 1989; Loeber and LeBlanc, 1990; Shover, 1996; Bushway et al., 2001; Laub and Sampson, 2001; Maruna, 2001; Giordano et al., 2002, 2007). Our own view is that desistance is characterized by the decline in offending from some nontrivial level to an observed rate that is not significantly different from zero. This implies three things: (1) desistance is a process and not a state, (2) there must be some prior level of criminal offending that is substantial or at least nontrivial, and (3) crime does not have to decline to zero, but does need to decline to a level that is not significantly different from zero. To distinguish desistance from the temporary suspension of offending or "false desistance," the nonoccurrence of criminal acts must also be demonstrated over a nontrivial length of time.

Aggregate arrest data provide a good starting point for a discussion of the facts of desistance from crime. Figure 11.1 comes from U.S. Uniform Crime Report data in 2007. As can be seen, 77 percent of all arrests are of people of age forty and below, which suggests that crime is primarily a young person's game. However, we also see nontrivial involvement

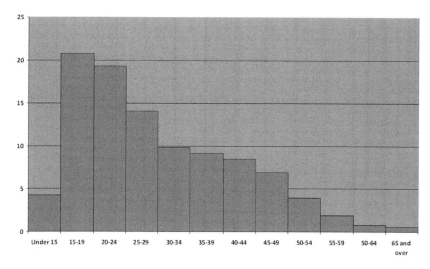

Figure 11.1   Arrest distribution by age in U.S. uniform crime reports 2007

in crime among quite elderly individuals. Seven percent of the arrestees are fifty years old or older, and 1.4 percent of all arrestees are sixty years of age or older. Moreover, these percentages may understate the actual involvement of the non-young in crime. Those sixty years of age or older accounted for over 150,000 arrests that year. The arrest data therefore tell a two-part story—crime is mostly committed by the young but not all people desist by age forty, or even age fifty.

Perhaps a more comprehensive picture about desistance comes from the follow-up to the Glueck data reported by Sampson and Laub in their most recent publications (Laub and Sampson, 2003; Sampson and Laub, 2003, 2005a, 2005b, 2005c). Their data show a decline in offending behavior even among this group of formerly high-rate delinquent offenders. Figure 11.2 is reprinted from their data. It shows the number of total crimes committed from ages seven to seventy for the Glueck delinquent sample. Within this group of high-rate adolescent offenders, the commission of criminal acts declines consistently after adolescence and drops to a low but not zero rate by age fifty. This declining offending rate is consistent with the aggregate arrest rate data in Figure 11.1. But, as in Figure 11.1, there is substantial offending in the Glueck data after age fifty. Sampson and Laub report that 23 percent of the delinquent boys were arrested in their fifties, 12 percent were arrested in their sixties, and that the average career length for these boys was 25.6 years!

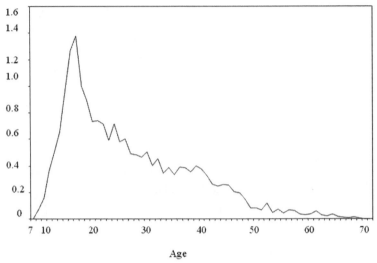

Source: Sampson and Laub (2003) Figure 1 p. 566.

Figure 11.2   Actual mean number of offenses for total crime: ages seven to seventy

Sampson and Laub argue that even these adolescent high-risk individuals ultimately desist from crime if they survive to age seventy.
Their estimated offending trajectories show a group of what they call
"high-rate chronic" offenders who began offending when children and
commit crimes well into their fifties and sixties (Sampson and Laub,
2003: 328–29). Figure 11.3 reports the identified offending trajectories
(total crime) for different groups of offenders within the Glueck data.
Again, while there is substantial heterogeneity within the full sample
(compare Figure 11.3 with Figure 11.2), Sampson and Laub concluded
that desistance was normative—all previously active offenders eventually desist. These findings are consistent with other data suggesting that
criminal offending and other analogous behaviors decline to zero with
increasing age for those who survive (Hirschi and Gottfredson, 1983;
Gottfredson and Hirschi, 1990; Piquero et al., 2001).

Blokland et al. (2005) used data from the Netherlands to also follow
individual offending through age seventy. They found a similar pattern of
declining offending with age, yet with a meaningful number of convictions after age fifty. Moreover, they found the existence of a subset of
offenders who both live to age seventy and do not desist. The existence
of this life-course-persistent group could be theoretically meaningful,
depending on how one chooses to define persistence in this context. For

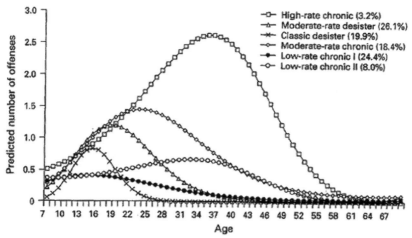

Source: Sampson and Laub (2003) Figure 11 p. 582.

Figure 11.3   Estimated trajectory groups of offenders based on total crimes from the Glueck data

our purposes, what is important is that (1) people who do not die tend to decrease in their offending over time and (2) this decline does not follow a similar trajectory for all people. The level of offending for some people declines by age thirty, while others keep offending through their fifties and some into their sixties.

This heterogeneity leads us to be somewhat skeptical of Gottfredson and Hirschi's theory (1990: 141) that attributes desistance from crime to the direct effect of age—"the inexorable aging of the organism."[1] When the Glueck sample of former delinquents was looked at as a whole and for total crimes, desistance generally occurred around age fifty. This might suggest that desistance is a process that comes to fruition in later life with the implication that it may be sparked by the type of purely physical decline alluded to by Gottfredson and Hirschi (1990) and Robins (2005). If desistance from crime is due simply to the biological aging of the organism, then there is no need for other variables to explain the decline in crime with age, and no need for a theory of desistance based on cognitive transformations, identity, or any other social or psychological process.

While it is undoubtedly true that sometimes desistance does occur because former offenders are, or at least feel, old and no longer physically capable of crime, we are skeptical that the direct-effect-of-age explanation is sufficient. The kinds of offenses, either property or violent, most frequently committed by offenders do not require the physical deftness of a "cat burglar" or great physical strength. If routine activities theory has taught us anything, it reminds us that crime is ordinary and staggeringly mundane (Felson, 2002). It does not take a great deal of physical prowess or intellectual cunning to walk into an unoccupied dwelling and steal things, to open an unlocked car door and either steal it or the contents, to pilfer some of the contents of a cash register, or to sell narcotics. A difference in physical strength between disputants is easily neutralized with the help of a well-placed swing from a Louisville Slugger, knife, or other available object. In addition, "softer" targets for one's physical violence (a spouse, partner, or child) can be found easily if one is so inclined. Even granting the fact that a life involving crime is arduous and that those who commit crimes live in environments where life is generally harsh and more physically demanding, we think there is little evidence to suggest that individuals are physically or mentally unable to commit crime beyond age fifty. This fact is supported by the consistent evidence that a nontrivial number of people actually do offend in their fifties and sixties.[2] Figure 11.3 above, Figures 5.11–5.14 in Laub and Sampson (2003: 104–6), and Figures 12 and 13 in Sampson and Laub (2003) show quite clearly that some former delinquents desist by their mid-twenties, some by the mid-thirties to forty, and some not until age fifty or even later. Steffensmeier and Ulmer's (2005) detailed qualitative description of the criminal career of a lifelong thief make it abundantly clear that offenders have access to numerous criminal opportunities even as they age. Moreover, work by Dabney et al. (2004) show that older offenders may actually have an advantage for activities such as shoplifting, at least in part because defenders of a space will be less suspicious of them than of someone younger.

We further illustrate our skepticism about the aging of the organism argument with Figure 11.4, which contains the age distribution of current rosters of Major League Baseball teams in the United States. As avid fans of the other "beautiful game," we needed little motivation to delve into baseball statistics, but we asked ourselves, "What would a desistance process driven by the aging of the organism look like?" The data in Figure 11.4 suggest an answer to that question; it shows quite clearly that virtually all players "desist" from participation in major league baseball by age forty (and by implication clearly not by age fifty or sixty). Anecdotal evidence suggests that few players (in any sport, think of Bret Favre) voluntarily retire in their prime—instead, most retire due to degradation in their physical skills, what we might refer to as the "inexorable aging of the organism." In the context of major league baseball, we find the

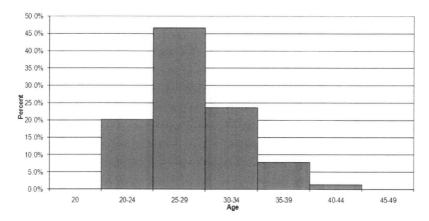

Figure 11.4   Age distribution of major league baseball, active rosters 2007

aging argument convincing. Baseball at that level is a highly skilled sport that requires a great deal of physical stamina, strength, and dexterity. The biological consequences of aging affect everyone who plays and involuntarily leads to a short, sometimes very short, career length and a relatively homogenous age of desistance. The image of the major league ballplayer "burning out," then, is consistent with the biological process of aging and the physical deterioration of skills.

By contrast, consider Figure 11.5, which includes a condensed version of the arrest distribution shown earlier, along with the age distribution of U.S. workers more broadly, and farmworkers specifically. Farmworkers, like arrestees, are more than 75 percent male. We find it telling that the age distribution of farmwork mimics so closely the age distribution of arrestees. Although individuals exit farmwork at earlier ages than they exit the larger labor market, that exit is clearly heterogeneous, with the majority of individuals leaving by age forty, but with a substantial minority working past the age of fifty well into their sixties. We believe that individuals stop working as low-paid farm laborers not simply because they cannot get hired or are physically unable to do it anymore, but *because they choose not to*. By the same token, we believe the evidence suggests that individuals stop committing crime not because they physically or biologically cannot commit crime anymore, but because they choose not to. Some choose to exit before others who wait until much later in their lives before deciding to quit crime, and as a result we have a long right-hand tail in the age distribution of offending.

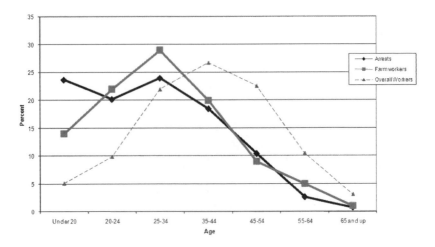

Figure 11.5   Farmwork and arrest age distributions

This long right-hand tail also casts doubt on a strictly structural version of desistance that attributes the initial thrust into conformity to an acquiring of pro-social roles like jobs and marriages. While there is a convincing body of research that documents the ability of marriage and work to decrease crime, this work frequently does not speak to the *causal mechanism* by which this effect occurs (Sampson et al., 2006). If the explanation is entirely or immediately structural, we would expect that desistance would be highly correlated with the arrival rates of first marriages and stable employment during the twenties and into the thirties as people move into adulthood. And indeed, a large portion of desistance clearly occurs between twenty and forty (see Figure 11.3). But employment and marriage have been the available states for twenty years by age forty. A simple matching or sorting story in which people desist when matched to jobs and spouses should not require more than twenty years to reveal itself.

Of course, it is possible that work (and potentially marriage) has a differential impact depending on age (Uggen, 2000) such that work is involved in the desistance process but only when offenders reach a certain age in their lives. But this explanation would imply that something about the individual or their set of circumstances has changed with age, their identity and preferences, or tastes, for example, and it is these changes that in turn lead to different choices by the individual. The typical interpretation of this is that the effect of these variables is age-graded (without a clear conceptual or theoretical explanation as to precisely what this means). However, another interpretation is that these factors have a different impact on *different kinds of people*, and different kinds of people select into marriage and employment at different ages. Research on employment and crime now increasingly shows that the established "fact" that employment is bad for youth (but good for adults) is entirely an artifact of selection. Strong controls for selection show that employment has the same modest negative impact on crime for youth as it does for adults (Apel et al., 2008). Entering into pro-social roles may have a role to play in desistance but perhaps the acquisition of conventional roles such as worker or spouse is only part of the picture and comes later in the desistance process when other obstacles have first been overcome.

In sum, we think that the facts of desistance state loudly and clearly that desistance cannot be explained by either strictly biological or structural explanations. But if not biology and if not the immediate acquisition of pro-social roles, what then? We believe the explanation lies in a person's identity and the corresponding changes this brings in how they weigh the inputs of their decision-making, their preferences and tastes, and how they make choices. In the pages that follow, we outline the framework of a theory of desistance that relies on the change in identity a person must undergo *before* entering into pro-social roles that over time will solidify their leaving crime.

An Identity Theory of Desistance from Crime

Identity Theory: The Working Self and the Possible Self

There is a long intellectual tradition in sociology and social psychology that emphasizes the importance of one's identity (James, 1890; Cooley, 1902; Mead, 1934; Stryker, 1968, 1980). Identity is important for numerous reasons; the most important for our concerns is that it motivates and provides a direction for behavior (Foote, 1950; Stryker, 1968; Burke, 1980; Burke and Reitzes, 1981, 1991; Stryker and Burke, 2000). A person's actions are seen as expressions of their self-identity— we intentionally behave in ways that are consistent with who we think we are. In interaction with others, therefore, people project an identity of who they are, and a primary vehicle for communicating to others what "one is" is through one's behavior.

Identities or selves vary in terms of their temporal orientation. Some selves are oriented toward the present as the *working self* (Markus, 1977, 1983; Markus and Wurf, 1987). The working self is that component of the self that can be accessed at the moment and is based upon the individual's here-and-now experience (Markus and Kunda, 1986; Markus and Wurf, 1987). In addition to a sense of who and what one is at the moment, or a self that is fixed on the present, we also have a sense of self that is directed toward the future. This future-oriented self is defined positively as the self we would like to become and negatively as the self we would not want to become or fear that we might become. Markus and Nurius (1986, 1987) have defined this future orientation of the self as a *possible self*.[3] The possible selves "are conceptions of the self in future states" (Markus and Nurius, 1987: 157) and consist of goals, aspirations, anxieties, and fears that the individual has as to what she could become or what she might become. While the working self is aware of what skills we have and do not have and what we can and cannot do in the present, the possible self is directed toward the future and what it is possible for us to be and what we would not like to be. I may, for example, see myself currently (my working self) as a thief, drug user, poor father, or unskilled worker, but may see myself in the future as working in a job (though perhaps for minimum wage), legitimately buying things for my family, owning a used car, and ceasing my life of drug use and crime. I may, however, also fear that I may turn out to be a burned-out addict, riddled with disease, homeless, childless, and jobless and destined to die alone. Both of these self-conceptions might lead me at some point to critically evaluate my participation in crime and drugs.

An important consequence of a possible self is that it provides directed motivation for one's behavior (Markus and Nurius, 1986, 1987). Possible selves, both positive and negative, therefore, not only contain images of what the person would like to be or desperately fears becoming, but can also provide a specific and realistic set of instructions or a "road map," directing what one can do to achieve the positive future self and avoid the negative possible self (Hoyle et al., 1999; Oyserman et al., 2004; Hoyle and Sherril, 2006). This is referred to as the self-regulating component of the possible self. The self is self-regulating because, among other things, it compares the past and current working self with the possible self and provides specific directions, strategies, or plans for narrowing any discrepancy between the two, thereby connecting the present with the future. Motivation is generated and is more likely to be successful, then, when we not only have a goal of self-improvement but specific and realistic means to reach that goal. In fact, at least initially, movement out of a deviant or "spoiled identity" is more likely to be based on a motivation to avoid a feared self than it is desired to achieve a positive self (Goffman, 1963).

The fact that possible selves contain both a sense of what one wants to be and fears being in the future and a specific and realistic sense of what one must do to make that self a reality implies that the possible self guides, directs, and regulates behavior toward a more or less specific and desired end. The vision of the possible self one wants to become and other possible selves that one wants to avoid becoming provides the motivation and goal for behavior and links the past and present to the future. Action in the service of a possible self is, therefore, planful, intentional, and purposeful action. The possible self provides incentives and motivation for specific actions and links present behavior with some future state: "Possible selves are represented in the same way as the here-and-now self . . . and can be viewed as cognitive bridges between the present and future, specifying how individuals may change from how they are now to what they will become" (Markus and Nurius, 1986: 961).

Though stable, identities clearly can and do change. We are arguing that a working identity as a criminal offender can change to a more conventional identity when the person thinks of a conventional identity as a positive possible self and an identity of a burned-out ex-con with no friends or possessions as a negative possible self or feared self. Contemplation of a possible self that does not include criminal offending in turn occurs when the working identity of criminal is perceived to be unsatisfying or disappointing. Just as a criminal identity emerges in response to perceived successes so does a break from that identity. As one begins to find less success and satisfaction with the criminal identity, it is likely to conjure up negative possible selves—long terms in prison with young hoodlums, the possibility of a violent death, small payoffs from criminal enterprises, and the loss of family and friends. These negative possible selves and the activation of positive selves—a working person, a person with a good spouse, a giving father, a law abider—can provide both the motivation and the direction for change. Before one is willing to give up his/her working identity as a law breaker, then, one must begin to perceive it as unsatisfying, thus weakening one's commitment to it. This weakening of one's commitment to a criminal identity does not come about quickly, nor does it come about in response to one or two failures, but only gradually and to the linking of many failures and the attribution of those linked failures to one's identity and life as a criminal. However, once the dissatisfaction with crime has settled in, the break from crime may be swift and dramatic.

The process of desisting from crime first requires an offender to recognize that their working identity of offender is no longer satisfactory and their attachment to this identity must be weakened. We believe that the weakening of a criminal identity comes about gradually and comes about as a result of a growing sense of dissatisfaction with crime and a criminal lifestyle. The dissatisfaction with crime is more likely to lead to a conventional possible self when failures or dissatisfactions with many aspects of one's life are linked together and attributed to the criminal identity itself. It is not just that one has experienced failures but that diverse kinds of failures in one's life become interconnected as part of a coherent whole that leads the person to feel a more general kind of life dissatisfaction, the kind of life dissatisfaction that can lead to identity change, or what Kiecolt (1994) has termed "intentional self-change."

Baumeister (1991, 1994) has referred to the linking of previously isolated dissatisfactions and senses of failure in one's life as the "crystallization of discontent." While no one single complaint or dissatisfaction may be enough to motivate someone to question their life, the linking together of numerous previously isolated complaints may be sufficiently strong to undermine a person's commitment to a role or identity. When understood as single unrelated events, failures, complaints, or misgivings can be more easily dismissed as simply isolated difficulties to be expected and ignored as part of ordinary life. Assisting us in this process is a self-serving attribution bias whereby we consistently attribute our success to our own abilities but attribute failures to external sources or chance (Miller and Ross, 1975; Fiske and Taylor, 2007). At the very least, the significance of setbacks and failures can be ignored, and seen singly and isolated, they do not lead the person to make major life considerations or reevaluations and do not lead them to weaken their commitment to an identity. Once linked, however, once made part of a pattern that might not easily be fixed or ignored it requires a revaluation or reassessment of one's current situation.

Commitments to criminal identities are, then, maintained in part because of the ability to keep many failures isolated and unconnected while successes are interrelated and seen as a typical outcome. That is, I am able to keep my criminal identity intact, in spite of the low financial reward, physical risk, and turmoil with social relationships because I am successful in both exaggerating the benefits and minimizing the costs of my actions as well as attributing successes to my abilities but failures to the workings of bad luck. One's commitment to an identity becomes reevaluated when this changes—when successes begin to be seen as isolated while failures become to be seen as part of a whole—discontent becomes crystallized. In order for this questioning of commitment to identity to occur, there does not have to be an increase in either the frequency or magnitude of one's failures or dissatisfactions. Rather, there reaches a point, a subjective perceptual "tipping point" (Gladwell, 2000), where previous dissatisfactions with isolated events now become seen as a pattern of connected events. What changes, then, is how contents and discontents in one's life are perceived and evaluated. Dissatisfaction with a few unpleasant outcomes becomes dissatisfaction with one's life and with the kind of person one is.

It is such a new understanding of one's life that leads to the effort to intentionally change it, or as Shover (1996: 132) put it: "[t]his new perspective symbolizes a watershed in their lives . . . [t]hey decide that their earlier identity and behavior are of limited value for constructing the future." After this occurs, the dissatisfactions that one has experienced has implications for the future. Events that seemed atypical and isolated are now seen as interrelated and are therefore both less easily dismissed, more characteristic of who we are, and are therefore seen as likely to continue to occur in the future. It is this projection into the future of continued life dissatisfaction that initially motivates the person to begin to seek changes.

A possible self provides the foundation for a change in one's identity. What has to occur now is for one to begin to change their behavior, to begin acting in ways that disconfirm the old identity and tentatively present the new one. If one is to make these behavioral changes permanent rather than whimsical and temporary, he/she need to have structural support for the new identity. In other words, successful self-change cannot be done alone, with just positive selves. Whether motivation for self-change and tentative indications or behavioral cues that one's identity has changed is turned into actual identity change depends upon social and structural features in one's environment.

Kiecolt (1994: 56) has argued that intentional self-change is unlikely to be successful without what she calls "structural supports" for change.[4] These supports "provide individuals with means and opportunities for effecting self-change" and include self-help groups, and professional changers such as psychiatrists and social workers. As a separate condition for successful self-change, Kiecolt includes the assistance of social supports such as friends, family members, and spouses and partners. To this list of structural supports for positive self-change, particularly for criminal offenders, we would add legitimate means of support—a conventional job. Obviously if successful self-change is going to occur, the benefits of a new identity must outweigh the costs of leaving the old one. However economically marginal a life of crime is, criminal offenders, particularly those with official records of arrest, conviction, and incarceration, find legitimate employment opportunities, even in the secondary labor market, very restricted (Bushway and Reuter, 2002). Some opportunity to secure a conventional job must be available for criminal offenders to desist, no matter how strong the motivation to change their identities and selves. Generally, anyone exiting one role or identity needs access to alternative sources of employment—nuns leaving religious orders (Ebaugh, 1988) no less than prostitutes leaving "the trade" must find outside employment, as do physicians wanting to leave their profession. Without these kinds of structural supports, identity change becomes difficult. Social supports, whether in the form of friends, spouses or partners, jobs, or professional help, are important in self-change because they provide the one in the throes of a crystallization of discontent with an alternative existence or identity.

In our theory of desistance, changes in friendship networks and the securing of alternative jobs and vocations are important because they help maintain or bolster a fledging changed identity. To be clear, securing jobs, attracting new partners, and involvement with new friends come about *after* a change in identity has occurred. The change in identity has already occurred in the mind of the person; they have weighed the costs and benefits of the exiting identity and alternatives, and are behaving in ways that conform to the new possible self.

With respect to persons changing their identities of alcoholic or married person, Ebaugh (1988: 168–69) noted that "at the point at which an alcoholic stopped drinking and became an ex-alcoholic, many considered it mandatory to stop associating with other alcoholics and to make friends with people who would discourage drinking ... divorced people likewise tended to shift friendship patterns dramatically *after* divorce" (emphasis added). For those leaving a marriage, alcoholics ceasing to drink, or opiate addicts ceasing drug use, and those desisting from crime a change in identity must later be maintained by changes in behavior that are consistent with that possible self. Those wanting to leave a life of crime must at some point find more conventional partners or spouses, secure legitimate forms of employment, and seek after and affiliate with non-offending peers and friends. All of these changes are in accordance with their possible self as non-offender and all, therefore, are behaviors deliberately enacted after the change in identity has been decided. When a changed identity is followed by a change in other dimensions of one's life (social network, job), movement toward desistance is more likely and will be manifested in a break from the past in terms of one's participation in crime.

An empirical question remains: How do researchers test this idea by identifying breaks with past criminal behavior? In the following section we suggest two possible analytic strategies: (1) the analysis of individual-level time series of offending, and (2) the analysis of hazard rates.

An Analytical Framework for Desistance as an Identity Change—Time Series

The starting point for an analysis of an individual time series of offending revolves around thinking about the stochastic process that is generating the data. In its most basic form, any time series can be described (not explained) by the following autoregressive time series[5]:

$$Y_t = \alpha + \rho Y_{t-1} + e_t \quad (11.1)$$

where e_t is a time series of uncorrelated shocks. A key assumption of time series analysis is that the process is *stationary*, which simply means that the parameters of the model—in this case, α, ρ, and $var(e)$—are stable throughout the time period. This kind of process, with time-constant parameters and $-1 < \rho < 1$, cannot create a long-term path of desistance as described by Sampson and Laub (2003), Blokland and Nieuwbeerta (2005), or Blokland et al. (2005). The kind of path described by equation (11.1) will move to its equilibrium level and then stay flat with short-term variation around the equilibrium line. Laub and Sampson (2003) are right—state dependence and individual heterogeneity as captured in the lagged Y term in equation (11.1) *cannot* explain desistance. We restate this important observation in time series language—desistance is inherently a nonstationary process.

Practitioners of time series analysis recognize that the first step of any time series analysis involves a test for stationarity. This is logical because if the parameters are inconstant, and we use regression models, which assume time-constant parameters, then our estimates will be biased. Typically, the researcher can make a nonstationary time series stationary by taking differences or detrending the data. The researcher then focuses on explaining the resulting stationary time series. In this case, however, we are not interested in the stationary part of the time series. Rather, we are interested in first characterizing and then explaining the nonstationary part of the time series, the long-term path or trajectory over time (Osgood, 2005).

In the time series literature, there are four broad classes of nonstationary time series. The first is a series with a trend. This trend is based on time (in this case, age). The trend predetermines the path. With a trend, equation (11.1) becomes equation (11.2):

$$Y_t = \alpha_t + \rho Y_{t-1} + e_t \quad (11.2)$$

This model does not try to explain the existence of the trend, except in the most basic or general terms. The best example in criminology of a desistance theory that appeals to a basic trend is Gottfredson and Hirschi's theory of self-control. Any change in an individual's time series trend in offending over time is attributed to the "inexorable aging of the organism" (1990: 141). Since age is the time marker in this time series, saying age explains desistance is simply the same thing as saying that there is an undefined trend (Bushway et al., 2001). Glueck and Glueck's (1974) maturational theory is but one small step removed from Gottfredson and Hirschi's (1990). They are careful to explicitly distinguish age from maturation—which means that the maturational process need not occur at the same age for everyone. However, this simply extends equation (11.2) to say that there is some distribution of time trends in the population—everyone does not have the same time trend over time. This claim leaves open the possibility that this maturational process is preprogrammed and deterministic. Laub and Sampson (2003) characterize these kinds of preprogrammed processes—essentially fixed trends—as compatible with developmental theories of crime. Moffitt's (1993) typological theory involving life-course-persistent and adolescence-limited offenders is a classic example of this kind of preprogrammed trend.

The second type of time series, a cointegrated time series, captures the counterargument to Sampson and Laub's characterization of the developmental path. Here, equation (11.3) is developed by adding a time-varying covariate X_t. The coefficient on X_t is time constant. This variable trends in the same way as criminal propensity, such that the residual time series is stationary. In other words, the time-varying covariate X detrends the time series (α no longer varies over time) and makes the error stationary.

$$Y_t = \alpha + \rho Y_{t-1} + \delta X_t + e_t \quad (11.3)$$

This basic model in which time-varying covariates can explain the long-term pattern of desistance fits with the class of theoretical models in which theorists simply extended existing theories to account for desistance. Agnew (2005) argued that the bulk of offenders desist from crime simply because the strains that they experienced as adolescents that launched them into crime in the first place (school, relationship, and job strains) diminish over time, and the ability to adapt in a conventional way to existing strains increases as they enter adulthood. The movement into adulthood, then, comes with both fewer and/or less intense strains and an increased capability to adapt to strain in a nondeviant way. Similarly, Akers (1998: 164) argued that the most important predictor of all dimensions of offending, including desistance, is involvement with delinquent peers: ". . . the single best predictor of the onset, continuation, or desistance of delinquency is differential association with law-violating or norm-violating peers." Existing theories of crime responded to the new conceptual and empirical terrain brought about by the criminal career perspective, then, by simply insisting that they could as easily explain desistance as they could the onset or other dimensions of offending.

Developmental or maturational theories of crime can also be thought of as describing a cointegrated time series rather than a deterministic trend to the extent to which the theorist describes a variable or process that explains the change in propensity over the life course. For example, Gove (1985) posits that there are biological and psychological factors over time that peak and decline in the same manner as offending propensity. These factors are plausibly cointegrated with offending propensity.

Although the statistical idea of cointegration has not been previously applied to desistance, this framework is consistent with Gottfredson and Hirschi's (1990) challenge to "positivistic" theories to explain the age–crime curve with sociological or psychological variables. Although they are skeptical about whether this can be done, Gottfredson and Hirschi (1990) acknowledge the possibility that time-varying covariates can explain long-term change. On the empirical side, Osgood (2005) advocates inserting time-varying covariates with time-constant parameters into growth curve models in an attempt to explain the age–crime curve. Within the growth curve framework, Osgood (2005) suggests testing to see if the time-varying covariates can detrend the data. This basic approach has been applied by Blokland and Nieuwbeerta (2005) where they look to see how much marriage and employment can explain the age–crime curve. It is also seen in Thornberry et al. (2008) in which they look to see how much a set of time-varying covariates can explain the divergence between those who desist from and those who persist in crime. In each case, the researchers are looking to see if the time-varying covariates can make a nonstationary time series stationary—with time-constant parameters, the only way this is possible is if the covariates themselves trend or track in the same manner as offending propensity.

The third type of time series that can explain or accommodate non-stationarity is a time series with a structural break. A structural break implies that there are two or more sets or parameters, meaning that the causal process is different across periods.

$$Y_t = \begin{cases} \alpha_a + \rho_a Y_{t-1} + e_{at} & \text{if } t < T \\ \alpha_b + \rho_b Y_{t-1} + e_{bt} & \text{if } t >= T \end{cases} \quad (11.4)$$

There can be more than one structural break. Again, theorists have not formally discussed structural breaks, but we see elements of structural breaks in some desistance theories. For example, the notion of age-graded causal factors is consistent with the idea that the value of coefficients on some time-varying variables vary over time. For example, if peers matter more during adolescence than during adulthood, we have time-varying coefficients, which could generate time-varying α or ρ in equation (11.4).

A more general way of thinking about structural breaks is that a relatively time-stable component of an individual, such as self-control, changes over time. This is relevant only if life events and social context interact with self-control to affect behavior. In Thornberry's interactional model, for example, the exact nature of state dependence depends in meaningful ways on the individual's relatively stable characteristics (Thornberry, 1987; see also Moffitt, 1993). Those individuals who are heavily embedded in crime are less "dynamic," in that they are less responsive to changes in their environment and, therefore, are also less state dependent. Nagin and Paternoster build on this idea in their own version of an interactional theory when they posited that the impact of sanctions depended in meaningful ways on the person's level of self-control (Nagin and Paternoster, 1994). Although not developed further by Nagin and Paternoster, subsequent empirical work by Wright and colleagues (2001, 2004), as well as Hay and Forrest (2008) and Ousey and Wilcox (2007), have all found evidence for an interaction between life events and stable individual characteristics such as self-control.[6] If this basic preference function shifts over time in purposeful ways, as suggested by Hay and Forrest (2008), we can have a situation where the same inputs and opportunities lead to different behaviors—and state-dependent processes can start to head people in a different direction.

This situation, where a person experiences different causal processes depending on changes in their underlying personal preferences, extends interactional theories to accommodate a structural break and strengthens the ability of these types of theories to explain long-term changes in offending propensity. The identity theory of desistance we have described can be described as a structural break.

The importance of identity theories from this perspective is that they provide an explanation for how fundamental individual characteristics such as self-control can change from one time period to another. Changes in identity can trigger fundamental shifts in how people value the future (time discounting) or value their social contacts. Simply saying that preferences change is easy—explaining the mechanism by which they change is both important and difficult. Identity theorists like Giordano and colleagues (2002, 2007) and Maruna and Farrall (Maruna, 2001; Farrall and Maruna, 2004; Maruna, 2004; Farrall, 2005; Maruna and Roy, 2007) offer social psychological theories of desistance that revolve around structural breaks in the process that generates crime. Basing their views on a symbolic interactionist foundation, Giordano et al. (2002) argue that desistance requires substantial cognitive transformations or "up-front" work such as the development of a general openness to change, receptivity to "hooks for change," and consistent support from social others. In a later revisiting of this view, Giordano et al. (2007) developed a desistance theory that relies on the regulation of emotions and the emotional identity (an "anger identity") of ex-offenders as they struggle with getting out of crime. Maruna also adopts a theory of desistance that relies on notions of the actor's identity. For Maruna (2001), "making good," however, does not so much involve a change in the desister's identity from bad to good as it does a reinterpretation of one's criminal past to make it consistent with their current pro-social identity.

The fourth major type of nonstationary time series is a random walk, a well-known form that has been found occurring in many contexts, including the stock market price of a company and the financial status of a gambler. Random walks have a unit root, which means the parameter ρ is equal to one, or to be more specific,

$$Y_t = \alpha + Y_{t-1} + e_t \quad (11.5)$$

According to equation (11.5), behavior during this period is simply where you were in the last period, plus a constant and a shock. The series has an infinite memory, since any shock is permanently incorporated into the time series. Random walks do not, therefore, return to any mean. The same formula can generate flat, increasing, decreasing, or U-shaped curves, depending entirely on the time series of uncorrelated shocks e_t.

This description of a random walk is consistent with Laub and Sampson's (2003: 34) characterization of life-course theories of desistance as the result of a series of random events or "macrolevel shocks largely beyond the pale of individual choice (e.g., war, depression, natural disasters, revolutions, plant closings, industrial restructuring)." Random walks are inherently unpredictable, and as described by Laub and Sampson (2003), this lack of predictability is the key factor that distinguishes life-course trajectories from predetermined or preprogrammed trajectories that characterize developmental theories of crime.

Another way to discuss the time series properties of life-course theories is to consider the key life-course assertion that the impact of life events depends on when they occur in a person's life. This is the notion that "timing matters" (Elder, 2000; Abbott, 2001). To the extent to which this timing dependence is predictable, it is consistent with time series models with structural breaks. There are simply different models for different time periods. If there are a small number of changes, and these changes are tied to observable changes in identity, then this age-gradedness should be both predictable and identifiable. But if there are many structural breaks, and these breaks are tied to malleable social context, the age-gradedness becomes much more unpredictable. Indeed, a random walk can be characterized as a time series with N structural breaks, where N converges to the total number of periods in the time series (Hansen, 2001).

The main difference between life-course theories (random walks) and identity theories (structural breaks) is the number of breaks. In a world with many breaks, we can no longer predict long-term change and therefore need to focus on explaining change in any given period, which is driven by these relatively exogenous life events. This conclusion is consistent with empirical practice—if a time series is a true random walk, with no trend and no cointegrated time series, the only feasible strategy is to explain period-to-period change. It is simply not possible to explain any long-term pattern because that long-term pattern is driven by random shocks. Ironically, this interpretation of life-course theory implies that it is neither possible nor even interesting to study a life-course "trajectory" since only period-to-period change contains interesting information.

In summary, we believe that all theories of desistance fit into one of four basic categories of nonstationary time series models—trends, cointegrated series, series with a structural break (our own identity theory), and random walks. Given the distinct empirical character of each of these four basic types of time series, a serious examination of individual time series characteristics should be a fruitful avenue for future research and how it may inform desistance theory in criminology. For example, there are numerous techniques available to identify cointegrated time series and to distinguish random walks from models with structural breaks. Moreover, there are many techniques available for indentifying the nature of trends and the timing of structural breaks (Hansen, 2001). Further explication of theories within the framework provided by the extensive literature on time series processes should also help to clarify and delineate theories of desistance by making explicit the empirical implications of those theories for times series offending. Readers interested in seeing empirical examples of this approach should reference Paternoster and Bushway (2009), where some basic illustrations are provided using data from the Cambridge Study in Delinquency Development (Farrington et al., 2006). Another productive source for people interested in studying individual time series or trajectories of offending is Bushway et al. (2009), where separate time series trajectories are estimated for every member of the Criminal Career and Life course Study in the Netherlands.

An Analytical Framework for Studying Desistance Using Hazard Models

A reasonable critique of the time series approach described in the preceding section is that the very nature of the data—a dichotomous measure of relatively rare events—makes any estimate rather imprecise. As a result, the confidence intervals around the individual time series trajectories will be large, and we have only a limited ability to test some of the models described above. We acknowledge this reality, but we are nonetheless intrigued by the notion, discussed at length in Bushway et al. (2009), that there is substantially more change in these individual trajectories than what we would expect if we look only at growth curve models (semi-parametric trajectory or HLM-like models). Bushway et al. (2009) show convincingly that the major growth curve models largely discard as noise valuable information about change from the individual trajectories. This finding should be particularly troubling for desistance scholars, who are fundamentally interested in studying change.

But how can we study change if individual trajectories are too imprecise and long-term trajectory models essentially ignore the very change
we are interested in studying? Another possibility would be to turn to a
study of recidivism. Thirty years ago, recidivism and desistance were
complementary measures. Those who failed after a certain period were
recidivists, and those who did not were desisters. But as we reviewed
above, this static approach to thinking about recidivism and desistance
has been effectively rejected. It may be time now, however, to revisit
that conclusion since cutting-edge recidivism studies focus on hazard
rates of offending over time and cutting-edge desistance studies focus on
measuring trajectories of offending rates over time. It is a well-known
fact in statistics and quantitative criminology that hazard rates and trajectory models are actually measuring the same concept, with hazard
rate models focusing on *short-term* change in the propensity to offend
and trajectory models focusing on *long-term* change in the propensity
to offend. For example, having noted that the hazard rate focuses on the
hazard of involvement in a given criminal event,[7] Hagan and Palloni
(1988) observe that

> [T]he expected number of criminal events during the age interval being examined
> is a unique function of these hazards. This expected number of criminal events is
> what Blumstein et al. are estimating when they calculate lambda (offending rate). So,
> lambda is a summary of the combined hazards of criminal events of various orders
> over a period time. (p. 97)

As a result, the use of trajectories of rates to study desistance has
brought the study of desistance conceptually very close to the study of
recidivism. In their article, Hagan and Palloni (1988) present arguments
for focusing on the causal nature of the events, rather than on the rate
of offending. At the time they made their argument, however, empirical
methods allowed only for the estimation of time-stable rates for individuals. The ability to capture time variation in offending rates while controlling for individual heterogeneity, combined with the new emphasis on
the *process* of desistance, provides a persuasive counterargument for a
focus on the more long-term perspective. But once we focus on more
long term, we can still learn much from returning to a discussion of the
short-term change captured by hazard models.

The potential productivity of this approach was highlighted by Barnett
et al. (1989), who applied their insight about desistance and trajectories
of offending into an analysis of recidivism using a hazard model. Barnett
et al. (1989) examined the risk of recidivism until the thirtieth birthday
among a small group of eighty-eight offenders who had at least two

convictions before their twenty-fifth birthday. Each offender was given a probability of a new offense as well as a desistance parameter that indicated the probability of instantaneous desisting after each event. Thus after each criminal event, the offender had the choice of continuing to offend at the given rate (λ), or desisting. By dividing the offenders into two groups, "frequents" (annual $\mu = 1.14$ or a 1 in 320 daily chance of offending) and "occasionals" (annual $\mu = 0.4$ or a one in 913 daily chance of offending), they were able to quite reliably predict future patterns of recidivism. The only complication in their models was a small group of "frequent" offenders who had appeared to desist from crime according to their predictions, but actually resumed a criminal career later in life. It was this small group of offenders they deemed "intermittent" and for which their basic models were not adequate. They therefore called for "more elaborate models to incorporate the concept of intermittency, whereby offenders go into remission for several years and then resume their criminal careers" (p. 384).

Unfortunately, from our perspective, their analysis was based on a very small sample and has never been replicated or extended in the last twenty years. Recently, however, Kurlychek et al. (2010) have attempted to learn about desistance in the short term by using survival models that can be tied to different models of desistance. Research on survival starts with a group (g) of active offenders and then follows them for a period of time to model the risk of recidivism as well as time (t) to recidivism. A hazard ratio is then estimated for each time period (t) as follows:

$$H(tg) = \frac{\text{Number of arrested time } t}{\text{Number of survived through time } t_{-1}}. \quad (11.6)$$

Those who have not failed by the end of the follow-up period may be assumed to have desisted from crime; however, it is also possible that they would recidivate if followed for a longer period of time, meaning that the observation was merely right censored. While much current recidivism research utilizes the semi-parametric Cox regression strategy, which does not force a functional form on the data over time (e.g., the models are more interested in explaining the effect of covariates over time), Kurlychek et al. (2010) suggest that the use of parametric methods might be more informative if one is attempting, as we are here, to explain the actual form or time pattern of offending.

This approach to the study of recidivism was first introduced to criminology by Maltz (1984) and extended by Schmidt and Witte (1988). For example, Schmidt and Witte (1988) applied a variety of functional forms to two cohorts of releasees from the North Carolina prison system and were unsatisfied with the fit of any of the basic hazard models. They identified the problem to be the basic assumption that everybody will fail. To address this issue, the authors then turned to what is known as a "split-population" or mixture model (Maltz and McCleary, 1977) that allows for the fact that everyone does not fail. That is, some people do desist.

Split-population models therefore include an extra parameter, often referred to by biostatisticians as the "cure" factor, which estimates the portion of the risk set that will never experience a failure (will be "cured"). We interpret the cure factor as evidence of instantaneous desistance, or a structural break, particularly for individuals who had substantial rates of offending before the current offense. When applying the split-population models to their data, Schmidt and Witte found that all split-population models outperformed their non-split model counterparts. This particular study is notable in that it was the first systematic exploration of parametric survival models to recidivism data. The authors lay important groundwork for future endeavors and provide useful summaries of the various distributions available. However, Schmidt and Witte (1988) do not attempt to interpret what these distributions might mean regarding the nature of the underlying desistance process. Further, they follow their subjects only for five to seven years, not necessarily long enough to fully conclude that there has been desistance.

Kurlychek et al. (2010) repeat the analysis with data that have an eighteen year follow-up and were able to largely replicate Schmidt and Witte's results. Even for individuals who are high-level offenders, their hazard analysis finds convincing and compelling evidence for substantial instantaneous desistance. They also find no evidence in favor of intermittency and only a small amount of evidence in favor of short-term gradual changes in the hazard rates. Although desistance can still occur slowly over the long term, the finding of Kurlychek et al. (2010) does seem to support theories of desistance that feature stark structural breaks in the crime generation process. And more generally, it highlights the ability of short-term recidivism models to shed light on the longer term question about the desistance process. Future work that could link multiple-event hazards together could eventually be both the short-term hazard perspective and the long-term trajectory perspective (Bushway et al., 2004).

Conclusions

We have outlined a theory of criminal desistance that is anchored in notions of social identity. In this theory, what we think about ourselves—our social identities—is an important source of our motivation, including the motivation to do crime and to desist from crime. The self is a complex entity, however, made up of multiple identities arranged in a hierarchy and includes different temporal orientations. The self that both links us to the past and guides our conduct in the present is our working self—who we now are. In addition to this present self, we have in our self-schema a representation of our selves in the future—both who we would like to be and who we fear we might become—our possible selves. The possible self contains not only our hopes and aspirations, but a detailed and realistic strategy or road map to reach that goal as well. Possible selves are constructed in large part when the benefits and satisfactions of our old selves are outweighed by the dissatisfactions, a consequence hastened when difficulties and failures in life become linked through a crystallization of discontent. There is a tipping point at which we surrender our commitment to an old self and begin the process of constructing both a new self and a new set of social supports for that self.

At some point in their "careers," criminal offenders realize that the benefits of committing crimes and being a criminal are outweighed by the costs. For those affected by this tipping point and for those who have a possible self in their schema of self-knowledge, a new, more conventional life can be created. The possible self need have both a detailed and a realistic plan for attaining the conventional future self—a life as a construction worker, for example, and not as an accountant or brain surgeon—and there are many points at which the search for a new self can be thwarted.[8] In addition, while a new identity as a non-offender is necessary for desistance from crime to occur, it is not by itself sufficient. There must be deliberate behavioral changes in the direction of non-offending, and there must be social or structural supports to bolster and maintain that change in identity.

We have outlined only the beginning of our theory, and there is a great deal more work to be done. For instance, we have only alluded to the kinds of changes in preferences that are integral to changes in identity. Part of the identity change to a non-offender, we think, is a change in the preference one has for crime—in essence, crime has much less appeal. We have left the content of these changes in preferences for the moment unspecified.[9] In addition, much work needs to be done in understanding the link between changes in identity and behavioral attempts to support that new identity. While we think we have offered a reasonable outline for a new theory of desistance, only time will tell how useful our efforts have been.

We have also presented two new approaches to studying desistance, which could shed light on the nature of the desistance process. The first approach involves applying basic time series models to long ($\geq$40 years) time series of data on individuals. In what we believe is a useful contribution, we outline how different statistical forms map to different theories of desistance. The second approach involves using hazard models on panel data to explain short-term changes in behavior. In particular, hazard models can be used to compare instantaneous desistance with gradual declines in behavior over time. This approach, presented more fully in Kurlychek et al. (2010), appears to show strong support for sudden, sharp changes in behavior consistent with a time series model of structural breaks and our identity theory of desistance.

In both time series models and hazard models we specify parametric statistical models with parameters and assumptions that can then be "fit" to the data to see which models best explain the data. This approach is a radical break from an approach that focuses on distinguishing between key explanatory variables to differentiate between competing theoretical models. While time will tell whether we are right, we believe this approach of using formal statistical models with identifiable features will lead to more productive theory testing and building. Although only limited work has been done so far, the work that has been done suggests that theories of desistance need to account for sudden and sharp changes in behavior. We are hopeful that future work in this area will shed light on the validity of this insight.

Notes

1.　Sampson and Laub (2005b) come close to agreeing with Gottfredson and Hirschi's aging conclusion themselves after examining their data showing how regular the decline in crime with age was: "Although we were critical of Gottfredson and Hirschi (1990) in our earlier work (Sampson and Laub, 1993), and still do maintain an age-graded theory, like them we are now inclined to see in the data from Figures 1 through 7 the overwhelming power of age in predicting desistance from crime." Further, when they do provide an account of desistance by the strengthening of informal controls, they come very close to accepting Gottfredson and Hirschi's position that what changes with age is crime (opportunity) and not criminality (propensity).

2.　This is yet another example of the observation that controversies are more often about the interpretation of facts than they are about the existence of facts. Someone else might look at the same figures and be more impressed with the uniformity in desistance from offending over time and unimpressed with the age-heterogeneity. If you think the uniformity is impressive, you might be inclined to believe it is the work of biology overlaid with uninteresting variation. If you think the heterogeneity is impressive, you might be inclined to wonder what might be causing it.

3. Along similar lines, Schlenker (1985: 74) speaks of a "desired self." A desired self is "what the person would like to be and thinks they can really be." A desired self then emphasizes a positive identity that a person would like to have and is realistic to have.

4. Giordano et al. (2002: 992) calls these supports "hooks for change."

5. The following is the simplest possible dynamic model. It can be generalized by including more lags. However, the basic concepts apply.

6. Wright et al. (2004) find, in contrast to Nagin and Paternoster's prediction, that those with the most self-control are the least responsive to structural events. Doherty (2006) finds no evidence of an interaction between social bonds and social control. This latter result could be explained by Doherty's use of a sample of serious juvenile delinquents rather than a more heterogeneous general population sample.

7. People who have no offenses are at hazard for a first criminal event, those who offend once are at hazard for a second criminal event, etc.

8. There are numerous points at which things can go wrong for someone trying to create a new identity and desist from crime: (1) they have only a self-enhancing possible self and not the one that includes self-regulation, (2) the discontent in their life as offender does not get crystallized or linked to their identity but remains isolated and part of the present and not a projection into the future as well, (3) the alternatives to a criminal identity are found to be insufficient to create a desire for change, and (4) social supports to maintain and bolster an identity change are either not available or are misplayed. An important avenue of future theoretical development and future empirical research is to determine where these pitfalls to change occur and what their effects are.

9. There is ample evidence in the ethnographic literature to indicate that something like a change in the discount rate occurs among offenders (Shover, 1996), and while the discount rate may generally diminish with age, it likely occurs at different ages for different offenders. Further, Giordano et al. (2007) have argued that one's preferences for peers and the "party life" it offers greatly diminish among those seeking or maintaining a way out of crime.

Bibliography

Abbott, Andrew. *Time Matters: On Theory and Method.* Chicago: University of Chicago Press, 2001.

Agnew, Robert. *Why Do Criminals Offend? A General Theory of Crime and Delinquency.* Los Angeles: Roxbury Publishing, 2005.

Akers, Ronald L. *Social Learning and Social Structure: A General Theory of Crime and Deviance.* Boston: Northeastern University Press, 1998.

Apel, Robert, Shawn Bushway, Raymond Paternoster, Robert Brame, and Gary Sweeten. "Using State Child Labor Laws to Identify the Causal Effect of Youth Employment on Deviant Behavior and Academic Achievement." *Journal of Quantitative Criminology* 24 (2008): 337–62.

Barnett, Arnold, Alfred Blumstein, and David P. Farrington. "A Prospective Test of a Criminal Career Model." *Criminology* 27 (1989): 373–88.

Baumeister, Roy F. "The Crystallization of Discontent." In *Can Personality Change?*, edited by T. F. Heatherton and J. L. Weinberger, 281–97. Washington, DC: American Psychological Association, 1991.

———. *Meanings of Life*. New York: Guilford Press, 1994.

Blokland, Arjan, Daniel Nagin, and Paul Nieuwbeerta "Life Span Offending Trajectories of a Dutch Conviction Cohort." *Criminology* 43 (2005): 919–54.

Blokland, Arjan and Paul Nieuwbeerta. "The Effects of Life Circumstances on Longitudinal Trajectories of Offending." *Criminology* 43 (2005): 1203–40.

Burke, Peter J. "The Self: Measurement Requirements from an Interactionist Perspective." *Social Psychology Quarterly* 43 (1980): 18–29.

Burke, Peter J. and Donald C. Reitzes. "The Link between Identity and Role Performance." *Social Psychology Quarterly* 44 (1981): 83–92.

———. "An Identity Theory Approach to Commitment." *Social Psychology Quarterly* 54 (1991): 239–51.

Bushway, Shawn D., Robert Brame, and Raymond Paternoster. "Connecting Desistance and Recidivism: Measuring Changes in Criminality over the Lifespan." In *After Crime and Punishment: Pathways to Offender Reintegration*, edited by Shadd Maruna and Russ Immarigeon. Devon, UK: Willan Publishing, 2004.

Bushway, Shawn D., Alex Piquero, Lisa Broidy, Elizabeth Cauffman, and Paul Mazerolle. "An Empirical Framework for Studying Desistance as a Process." *Criminology* 39 (2001): 491–516.

Bushway, Shawn D. and Peter Reuter. "Labor Markets and Crime." In *Crime*, edited by James Q. Wilson and Joan Petersilia, 191–224. Oakland: ICS Press, 2002.

Bushway, Shawn D., Gary Sweeten, and Paul Nieuwbeerta. "Measuring Long Term Individual Trajectories of Offending Using Multiple Methods." *Journal of Quantitative Criminology* 25, no. 3 (2009): 259–86.

Bushway, Shawn D., Terence P. Thornberry, and Marvin D. Krohn. "Desistance as a Developmental Process: A Comparison of Static and Dynamic Approaches." *Journal of Quantitative Criminology* 19 (2003): 129–53.

Cooley, Charles H. *Human Nature and the Social Order*. New York: Scribners, 1902.

Dabney, Dean A., Richard C. Hollinger, and Laura Dugan. "Who Actually Steals? A Study of Covertly Observed Shoplifters." *Justice Quarterly* 21 (2004): 693–725.

Doherty, Elaine Eggleston. "Self-Control, Social Bonds, and Desistance: A Test of Life-Course Interdependence." *Criminology* 44 (2006): 807–34.

Ebaugh, Helen Rose Fuchs. *Becoming an Ex: The Process of Role Exit.* Chicago: University of Chicago Press, 1988.

Elder, Glen H. "The Life Course as Developmental Theory." *Child Development* 69 (2000): 1–12.

Fagan, Jeffrey. "Cessation of Family Violence: Deterrence and Dissuasion." In *Crime and Justice: An Annual Review of Research*, edited by Lloyd Ohlin and Michael Tonry, vol. 11, 377–425. Chicago: University of Chicago Press, 1989.

Farrall, Stephen. "On the Existential Aspects of Desistance from Crime." *Symbolic Interaction* 28 (2005): 367–86.

Farrall, Stephen and Shadd Maruna. "Desistance-Focused Criminal Justice Policy Research." *Howard Journal of Criminal Justice* 43 (2004): 358–67.

Farrington, David P., Jeremy W. Coid, Louise Harnett, Darrick Jolliffe, Nadine Soteriou, Richard Turner, and Donald J. West. *Criminal Careers Up to Age 50 and Life Success Up to Age 48: New Findings from the Cambridge Study in Delinquency Development.* London: Home Office, 2006.

Felson, Marcus. *Crime and Everyday Life.* 3rd ed. Thousand Oaks, CA: Sage, 2002.

Fiske, Susan T. and Shelley E. Taylor. *Social Cognition.* New York: McGraw-Hill, 2007.

Foote, Nelson N. "Identification as the Basis for a Theory of Motivation." *American Sociological Review* 16 (1950): 14–21.

Giordano, Peggy C., Stephen A. Cernkovich, and Jennifer L. Rudolph. "Gender, Crime, and Desistance: Toward a Theory of Cognitive Transformation." *American Journal of Sociology* 107 (2002): 990–1064.

Giordano, Peggy C., Stephen A. Cernkovich, and Ryan D. Schroeder. "Emotions and Crime over the Life Course: A Neo-Median Perspective on Criminal Continuity and Change." *American Journal of Sociology* 112 (2007): 1603–61.

Gladwell, Malcolm. *The Tipping Point: How Little Things Can Make a Big Difference.* Boston: Little Brown, 2000.

Glueck, Sheldon and Eleanor Glueck. *Of Delinquency and Crime.* Springfield, IL: Charles C. Thomas, 1974.

Goffman, Erving. *Stigma: Notes on the Management of Spoiled Identity.* New York: Simon and Schuester, 1963.

Gottfredson, Michael R. and Travis Hirschi. *A General Theory of Crime.* Stanford, CA: Stanford University Press, 1990.

Gove, Walter R. "The Effect of Age and Gender on Deviant Behavior: A Biopsychosocial Perspective." In *Gender and the Life Course*, edited by Alice S. Rossi, 115–44. New York: Aldine de Gruyter, 1985.

Hagan, John and Alberto Palloni. "Crimes as Social Events in the Life Course: Reconceiving a Criminological Controversy." *Criminology* 26 (1988): 87–100.

Hansen, Bruce E. "The New Economics of Structural Change: Dating Breaks in U.S. Labor Productivity." *Journal of Economic Perspectives* 15 (2001): 117–28.

Hay, Carter and Walter Forrest. "Self-Control Theory and the Concept of Opportunity: Making the Case for a More Systematic Union." *Criminology* 46 (2008): 1039–72.

Hirschi, Travis and Michael R. Gottfredson. "Age and the Explanation of Crime." *American Journal of Sociology* 89 (1983): 552–84.

Hoyle, Rick H., Michael H. Kernis, Mark R. Leary, and Mark W. Baldwin. *Selfhood: Identity, Esteem and Regulation*. Boulder, CO: Westview Press, 1999.

Hoyle, Rick H. and Michele R. Sherrill. "Future Orientation in the Self-System: Possible Selves, Self-Regulation, and Behavior." *Journal of Personality* 74 (2006): 1673–96.

James, William. *The Principles of Psychology*. New York: H. Holt, 1890.

Kiecolt, K. Jill. "Stress and the Decision to Change Oneself: A Theoretical Model." *Social Psychology Quarterly* 57 (1994): 49–63.

Kurlychek, Megan, Shawn Bushway, and Robert Brame. "Testing Theories of Desistance and Intermittency by Studying Long-Term Survival Models." Working paper, State University of New York at Albany, 2010.

Laub, John H. and Robert J. Sampson. "Understanding Desistance from Crime." In *Crime and Justice: A Review of Research*, edited by Michael Tonry, vol. 28, 1–69. Chicago: University of Chicago Press, 2001.

———. *Shared Beginnings, Divergent Lives: Delinquent Boys to Age 70*. Cambridge: Harvard University Press, 2003.

LeBlanc, Marc and Marcel Fréchette. *Male Criminal Activity from Childhood Through Youth*. New York: Springer-Verlag, 1989.

Loeber, Rolf and Marc LeBlanc. "Toward a Developmental Criminology." In *Crime and Justice: A Review of Research*, edited by Michael Tonry and Norval Morris, vol. 12, 375–473. Chicago: University of Chicago Press, 1990.

Maltz, Michael. *Recidivism*. Orlando, FL: Academic Press, 1984.

Maltz, Michael and Richard McCleary. "The Mathematics of Behavioral Change: Recidivism and Construct Validity." *Evaluation Quarterly* 1 (1977): 421–38.

Markus, Hazel. "Self-Schemata and Processing Information about the Self." *Journal of Personality and Social Psychology* 35 (1977): 63–78.

———. "Self-Knowledge: An Expanded View." *Journal of Personality* 51 (1983): 543–65.

Markus, Hazel and Paula Nurius. "Possible Selves." *American Psychologist* 41 (1986): 954–69.

———. "Possible Selves: The Interface between Motivation and the Self-Concept." In *Self and Identity: Psychological Perspectives*, edited by K. Yardley and T. Honess. New York: Wiley, 1987.

Markus, Hazel and Z. Kunda. "Stability and Malleability of the Self-Concept." *Journal of Personality and Social Psychology* 51 (1986): 858–66.

Markus, Hazel and Elissa Wurf. "The Dynamic Self-Concept: A Social Psychological Perspective." *Annual Review of Psychology* 38 (1987): 299–337.

Maruna, Shadd. *Making Good: How Ex-convicts Reform and Build Their Lives.* Washington, DC: American Psychological Association Books, 2001.

———. "Desistance and Explanatory Style: A New Direction in the Psychology of Reform." *Journal of Contemporary Criminal Justice* 20 (2004): 184–200.

Maruna, Shadd and Kevin Roy. "Amputation or Reconstruction? Notes on the Concept of 'Knifing Off' and Desistance from Crime." *Journal of Contemporary Criminal Justice* 23 (2007): 104–24.

Mead, George H. *Mind, Self, and Society.* Chicago: University of Chicago Press, 1934.

Miller, Dale T. and Michael Ross. "Self-Serving Biases in Attribution of Causality: Fact or Fiction?" *Psychological Bulletin* 82 (1975): 213–25.

Moffitt, Terrie. "Adolescence-Limited and Life-Course-Persistent Antisocial Behavior: A Developmental Taxonomy." *Psychological Review* 100 (1993): 674–701.

Nagin, Daniel S. and Kenneth C. Land. "Age, Criminal Careers, and Population Heterogeneity: Specification and Estimation of a Nonparametric Mixed Poisson Model." *Criminology* 31 (1993): 327–62.

Nagin, Daniel S. and Raymond Paternoster. "Personal Capital and Social Control: The Deterrence Implications of a Theory of Individual Differences in Offending." *Criminology* 32 (1994): 581–606.

Osgood, Wayne. "Making Sense of Crime and the Life Course." *The Annals of the American Academy of Political and Social Science* 602 (2005): 196–211.

Ousey, Graham C. and Pamela Wilcox. "Interactions between Antisocial Propensity and Life-Course Varying Correlates of Delinquent Behavior: Differences by Method of Estimation and Implications for Theory." *Criminology* 45 (2007): 401–42.

Oyserman, Daphna, Deborah Bybee, Kathy Terry, and Tamera Hart-Johnson. "Possible Selves as Roadmaps." *Journal of Research in Personality* 38 (2004): 130–49.

Paternoster, Raymond and Shawn Bushway. "Desistance and the 'Feared Self': Toward an Identity Theory of Criminal Desistance." *Journal of Criminal Law and Criminology* 99 (2009): 1103–56.

Piquero, Alex R. "Taking Stock of Developmental Trajectories of Criminal Activity over the Life Course." In *The Long View of Crime: A Synthesis of Longitudinal Research*, edited by A. Lieberman, 23–78. New York: Springer-Verlag, 2008.

Piquero, Alex R., Alfred Blumstein, Robert Brame, Rudy Haapanen, Edward P. Mulvey, and Daniel S. Nagin. "Assessing the Impact of Exposure Time and Incarceration on Longitudinal Trajectories of Criminal Offending." *Journal of Adolescent Research* 16 (2001): 54–74.

Robins, Lee N. "Explaining When Arrests End for Serious Juvenile Offenders: Comments on the Sampson and Laub Study." *The Annals* 602 (2005): 57–72.

Sampson, Robert J. and John H. Laub. *Crime in the Making: Pathways and Turning Points through Life.* Cambridge, MA: Harvard University Press, 1993.

———. "Life-Course Desisters? Trajectories of Crime among Delinquent Boys Followed to Age 70." *Criminology* 41 (2003): 301–39.

———. "A General Age-Graded Theory of Crime: Lessons Learned and the Future of Life-Course Criminology." In *Integrated Developmental and Life Course Theories of Offending*, edited by David P. Farrington, 165–81. New Brunswick, NJ: Transaction, 2005a.

———. "A Life-Course View of the Development of Crime." *The Annals* 602 (2005b): 12–45.

———. "When Prediction Fails: From Crime-Prone Boys to Heterogeneity in Adulthood." *The Annals* 602 (2005c): 73–79.

Sampson, Robert J., John H. Laub, and Christopher Wimer. "Does Marriage Reduce Crime? A Counter-Factual Approach to within-Individual Causal Effects." *Criminology* 44 (2006): 465–508.

Schlenker, Barry R. "Identity and Self-Identification." In *The Self and Social Life*, edited by Barry R. Schlenker, 65–100. New York: McGraw-Hill, 1985.

Schmidt, Peter and Ann D. Witte. *Predicting Recidivism Using Survival Models*. New York: Springer-Verlag, 1988.

Shover, Neal. *Great Pretenders: Pursuits and Careers of Persistent Thieves*. Boulder, CO: Westview Press, 1996.

Steffensmeier, Darrell and Jeffery T. Ulmer. *Confessions of a Dying Thief: Understanding Criminal Careers and Criminal Enterprise*. New Brunswick, NJ: Transaction Aldine, 2005.

Stryker, Sheldon. "Identity Salience and Role Performance: The Relevance of Symbolic Interaction Theory for Family Research." *Journal of Marriage and the Family* 4 (1968): 558–64.

———. *Symbolic Interactionism: A Social Structural Version*. Menlo Park, CA: Benjamin Cummings, 1980.

Stryker, Sheldon and Peter J. Burke. "The Past, Present, and Future of an Identity Theory." *Social Psychology Quarterly* 63 (2000): 284–97.

Thornberry, Terence P. "Toward an Interactional Theory of Delinquency." *Criminology* 25 (1987): 863–91.

Thornberry, Terence P., Shawn D. Bushway, Alan J. Lizotte, and Marvin D. Krohn. "Accounting for Behavioral Change." Working paper, University of Colorado, Boulder, 2008.

Uggen, Christopher. "Work as a Turning Point in the Life Course of Criminals: A Duration Model of Age, Employment, and Recidivism." *American Sociological Review* 65 (2000): 529–46.

Wright, Bradley R. E., Avshalom Caspi, Terrie E. Moffitt, and Ray Paternoster. "Does the Perceived Risk of Punishment Deter Criminally-Prone Individuals? Rational Choice, Self-Control, and Crime."

Journal of Research in Crime and Delinquency 41, no. 2 (2004): 180–213.

Wright, Bradley R. E., Avshalom Caspi, Terrie E. Moffitt, and Phil Silva. "The Effects of Social Ties on Crime Vary by Criminal Propensity: A Life-Course Model of Interdependence." *Criminology* 39, no. 2 (2001): 321–48.

12

Meta-Analysis and the Relative Support for Various Criminological Theories

Ojmarrh Mitchell

Introduction

Criminologists have developed numerous theories to explain criminal behavior, crime rates, and other phenomena of interest. The literature testing hypotheses derived from the field's major theories is vast and continues to grow. A fundamental question concerns the strength of empirical support for these various hypotheses, in absolute and relative terms. One of the most common ways of addressing this question is by conducting narrative, qualitative literature reviews. Narrative reviews typically summarize the results of a group of selected studies examining the relationship (or hypothesis) of interest, while neglecting many other available studies. Further, narrative reviews often focus on the statistical significance of individual study findings—if a high proportion of the reviewed studies find that the relationship of interest is statistically significant, then the hypothesis is considered empirically corroborated. The popularity of narrative reviews is evident from a recent volume of *Advances in Criminological Theory* that attempted to "take stock" of the empirical status of various criminological theories (Cullen et al., 2008); it included fifteen chapters, and all but one of these chapters employed narrative reviews.[1]

Despite narrative reviews' popularity, they exhibit several major flaws that undermine their utility. First, qualitative reviews are typically *noncomprehensive* as many apparently relevant studies are omitted. Second, narrative reviews most often are *unsystematic* in that the authors provide no guidelines or criteria in deciding which studies to discuss. Third, narrative reviews are *unreplicable* as the reviewers fail to adequately describe their search strategy (and other key decisions) necessary to replicate the researchers' work. Fourth, narrative reviews' focus on the statistical significance of each individual study's findings is *myopic*, as statistical significance is heavily influenced by sample size; in small samples, strong relationships may not be statistically significant at conventional levels of statistical significance, but in very large samples weak relationships may be statistically significant.

In recent years, the use of meta-analysis in criminology has become increasingly popular as criminologists attempt to remedy the shortcomings of narrative reviews. Meta-analysis is a quantitative literature review methodology that involves searching for research addressing a specific research question (or more broadly, examining relationships among a particular set of variables), carefully coding the findings of these studies, and then analyzing the information coded from the studies. Unlike narrative reviews, meta-analysis is *systematic* as it relies on explicit eligibility criteria for study inclusion, *comprehensive* as standard meta-analytic practice requires extensive literature searches for published and unpublished studies, and *replicable* as standard meta-analytic practice requires carefully detailed searches, coding procedures, and analyses. Most importantly, meta-analysis shifts the attention of research synthesis away from the myopic focus on statistical significance of individual findings to a measure of "effect size" to standardize study findings. Effect sizes are quantitative measures that capture the magnitude and direction of the relationship between two variables and thus are a broader gauge of the strength of the relationship between the variables of interest than that of statistical significance. The use of objective eligibility criteria, explicit search strategy, and effect size–coding procedures imposes "a useful discipline" (Lipsey and Wilson, 2001) on meta-analytic reviews that makes them more transparent, replicable, and systematic than narrative reviews. Simply put, meta-analysis is more scientific than narrative reviews.

Meta-analytic syntheses of program evaluations are numerous in the criminal justice literature (e.g., Lipsey, 1992; Lipsey et al., 2001; MacKenzie et al., 2001; Mitchell et al., 2007). Recently, the use of meta-analysis has spread to the synthesis of tests of criminological theories. Currently, a small but growing number of such meta-analytic syntheses exist (see, e.g., Pratt and Cullen, 2000, 2005; Baier and Wright, 2001; Pratt et al., 2008, for examples of meta-analysis of criminological theory tests). Some view the application of meta-analysis to theory tests as beneficial (see, e.g., Cullen et al., 2008). Others, however, consider the application of meta-analysis to theoretical research as "inappropriate" (Chow, 1987). In theory, meta-analytic synthesis of theory tests is no different than meta-analytic synthesis of program evaluations; in practice, however, there are several standard meta-analytic issues that appear to be more problematic in the integration of criminological theory tests.

This chapter discusses the potential strengths and weaknesses of meta-analytic reviews, as well as its problems, in integrating tests of criminological theories. The thesis of this chapter is that while applying meta-analysis to criminological theory tests is *not* without significant problems, meta-analysis is still an improvement over qualitative, narrative reviews. Further, the problems encountered in meta-analysis of criminological research could be reduced and the utility of such meta-analyses is increased by adhering more closely to current meta-analytic *practices* and, perhaps more importantly, by adhering more closely to the *philosophy* of meta-analysis.

This chapter is organized into four parts. The first section discusses narrative reviews and their flaws. The second section describes meta-analysis in some depth, including current standard meta-analytic practices, the strengths and weaknesses of meta-analysis, as well as the implicit philosophy underlying meta-analysis. The third section discusses challenges in applying standard meta-analytic techniques to empirical tests of theoretical research in criminology. The fourth and final section discusses recurring flaws in existing meta-analysis of theory tests and offers suggestions for improving future meta-analyses of this sort.

Narrative Reviews and Their Flaws

Criminologists have proven to be prolific theorists and theory testers. The proof of their productivity can be found in the sheer number of theories generated and the subsequent tests of these theories' hypotheses. Scores of studies have tested the validity of hypotheses central to criminology's most prominent theories (e.g., Agnew's General Strain Theory, Aker's Social Learning Theory, Gottfredson and Hirschi's General Theory of Crime). The volume of empirical research testing criminological theories is both a blessing and a curse. Criminology is fortunate to have this body of empirical research as it serves as a rich and strong foundation for criminological knowledge. On the other hand, many view the development of knowledge as a cumulative endeavor based on past research, replication, extension, and ultimately integration of research findings. If this perspective of knowledge development is correct, then the size of this body of research complicates that task of extracting *knowledge* from all of the *information* provided by these studies.

A large part of the difficulty in extracting scientific knowledge from criminology's research base stems from the unscientific manner in which prior research is typically summarized. Prior research is commonly summarized using a qualitative, narrative approach in which reviewers describe the results of some relevant research and use subjective judgment to integrate the findings of these studies. Narrative reviews often focus on describing statistically significant results and/or tally the number of studies finding statistically significant relationships as a measure of support for a particular hypothesis. Reviewing research in this manner is deeply problematic.

Perhaps the most important flaw in such reviews is that they overemphasize statistical significance of individual findings. This focus on statistical significance is flawed for two fundamental reasons. First, statistical significance is intimately related to statistical power, which in turn is heavily influenced by sample size. Studies with very large samples typically have ample statistical power, and, as a result, even substantively weak relationships often are statistically significant in these studies. Conversely, studies with small samples have low statistical power, and in these studies, even strong relationships may not be statistically significant. Second, the focus on statistical significance shifts attention away from the most salient research questions toward conceptually flawed ones. For instance, narrative reviews do not ask: How strong is the relationship between the variables under scrutiny? Or is this relationship between these variables stronger than that of other theoretically relevant variables? Instead of addressing these questions, narrative reviews essentially ask: What proportion of studies found a statistically significant relationship between the variables of interest? In the extreme, this question is tantamount to asking: How many studies used large samples?

Above and beyond the overemphasis of statistical significance of individual findings, narrative reviews often require reviewers to use complex "mental algebra" to integrate findings (Wang and Bushman, 1999). Given the size of the empirical knowledge base, its often divergent findings, as well as methodological and sample differences between studies, it becomes difficult for reviewers to accurately summarize research findings and discern systematic patterns in research findings. The amount of mental algebra necessary to accomplish this task is simply too daunting.

Another problem in narrative reviews is that they typically are unsystematic and noncomprehensive. In essence, narrative reviews use convenience samples of available studies. Like all research relying on convenience samples, the findings of such reviews run a substantial risk of being distorted by selection bias of two forms. Narrative reviews are unsystematic in that they fail to delineate a set of *eligibility criteria* that had to be met in order for the study to be included in the review. As a result, it is unclear why one study examining the relationship of interest was included but another was not. Further, instead of reviewing all studies that meet a well-defined set of eligibility criteria, narrative reviews typically focus on the findings of published articles. Yet research that compares the findings of *published* (e.g., books, journal articles, book chapter) and less formally published "gray" research (e.g., corporate or governmental technical reports, dissertations, conference papers) consistently finds that published research is more likely to find statistical significant results than gray research (Greenwald, 1975; Smith, 1980; Callaham et al., 1998; Wilson, 2009a). This phenomenon is so prevalent that it has been termed "publication bias" (Wilson, 2009a).

There is evidence that the shortcomings of narrative reviews make their conclusions susceptible to being inconsistent with the research they intend to synthesize. As evidence of this, consider Cooper and Rosenthal (1980). These authors tested researchers' ability to synthesize research findings with and without relying on meta-analytic thinking. Specifically, Cooper and Rosenthal randomly assigned researchers unfamiliar with meta-analysis to two groups. The control group was asked to review and synthesize the findings of seven studies assessing gender differences in task persistence using whatever methods they typically use. The experimental group was given a tutorial on meta-analysis and then asked to synthesize the same seven studies. Cooper and Rosenthal found that the group introduced to meta-analysis was approximately three times more likely to reject the null hypothesis, which was the correct conclusion. Another more practical example of narrative reviews' susceptibility to bias is offered by Mann (1994). Mann contrasted the findings of narrative and meta-analytic reviews of interventions in five areas of research, including delinquency prevention. Mann found that narrative reviews in comparison to meta-analyses understated the magnitude of the interventions' effects in all five research areas. Such research findings suggest that the mental algebra employed by narrative reviewers often produces miscalculations. Further, it stands to reason that the required mental algebra increases in difficulty as the number of studies and/or the variability in study findings increases. Given the sheer number of criminological theory tests available, and these tests' variability in results, the mental algebra required to accurately summarize these findings would appear to be a Herculean chore.

The Rise of Meta-analysis

What Is Meta-analysis? And Is Meta-analysis the Solution to Narrative Reviews' Flaws?

Glass (1976) categorizes research into three types: primary, secondary, and meta-analysis. Primary research concerns the analysis of original data. Secondary research is the reanalysis of data for the purpose of answering the original research question with more advanced analytic techniques or addressing new questions with previously analyzed data. Glass refers to meta-analysis as "the analysis of analyses . . . [T]he statistical analysis of a large collection of analysis results from individual studies for the purpose of integrating the findings" (p. 3). Glass argues that meta-analysis provides a method for summarizing the results from a large body of research in a manner that permits *knowledge* to be extracted from a mass of *information* provided by individual studies.

The key to summarizing the results from a quantitative body of research is to standardize results from each study in a manner that facilitates comparisons across studies. Meta-analysis accomplishes this important task by utilizing "effect sizes." While there are many different types of effect sizes (e.g., standardized mean difference, Pearson's *r*, odds ratio), the goal of these various measures is to create a common, quantitative scale capable of capturing variation in the direction and magnitude of the relation between the variables of interest across heterogeneous studies (Wang and Bushman, 1999; Borenstein, 2009; Fleiss and Berlin, 2009; Lipsey and Wilson, 2001).

Lipsey and Wilson (2001) explain the method of meta-analysis by comparing it to survey research:

> Meta-analysis can be understood as a form of survey research in which research reports, rather than people, are surveyed. A coding form (survey protocol) is developed, a sample or population of research reports is gathered, and each research study is "interviewed" by a coder who reads it carefully and codes the appropriate information about its characteristics and quantitative findings. The resulting data are then analyzed using special adaptations of conventional statistical techniques to investigate and describe the pattern of findings in the selected set of studies. (pp. 1–2)

Thus, one way to think of meta-analysis is as a survey of the existing research, where each study's empirical results are treated as scores on the dependent variable, and features of the study are coded as independent (or moderator) variables. Once a database containing scores on the dependent and independent variables has been constructed, these data are analyzed to describe variables' distributions, especially the dependent variable's distribution, and to describe relations between the dependent variable (effect size) and independent variables (i.e., do the independent variables "explain" variation in effect size).

Standard Meta-analytic Practices

The definitive how-to manual and reference guide for meta-analysis is Cooper and Hedges's *The Handbook of Research Synthesis* (1994), which was recently updated and re-titled *The Handbook of Research Synthesis and Meta-analysis* (Cooper et al., 2009). According to Cooper and Hedges (2009), conducting a meta-analysis involves six steps. The first step is to formulate the research problem or question (and hypotheses). As Hall and colleagues note, meta-analysis "can accomplish two fundamental tasks: learning from combining studies and learning from comparing studies" (Hall et al., 1994: 18). These tasks lead to three common types of research questions: How large (and varied) is the body of empirical research examining the relationship of interest? What is the average effect size? And what factors (moderator variables) are systematically associated with variations in effect size?

The second step is to search for relevant literature. Standard meta-analytic practice calls for the meta-analyst to specify a set of eligibility criteria that delineate the study features required for inclusion in the meta-analysis. Once these criteria are developed, the meta-analyst conducts an exhaustive search for all literature meeting the eligibility criteria, while carefully documenting the search process (e.g., listing databases searched, keywords used in the search) (see, e.g., White, 1994; Wilson, 2009a).

The third step is to evaluate and code relevant studies. Eligible studies are coded using a preformulated coding forms (i.e., a "coding protocol"). Not only are the empirical findings of each study coded via effect sizes, but also important methodological, sample, and less often contextual features are coded. These coded study features are used to describe the extant literature and as potential moderator variables "explaining" variation in study findings (see Lipsey and Wilson, 2001; Lipsey, 2009; Wilson, 2009b).

The fourth step is to analyze the data (see, e.g., Shadish and Haddock, 2009). Data analysis involves using meta-analytic analogues to standard data analytic techniques (descriptive statistics, t-test, ANOVA, linear regression) that weigh study findings based on each study's precision. The inverse of standard error is often used to down-weight the importance of studies in which there is significant error around the estimate due to low sample sizes or measurement problems. Studies with more precision (smaller standard errors typically accompanied by larger sample sizes) typically receive more weight. One analytic issue that is more prominent in meta-analytic research than primary research is the issue of random- or fixed-effects estimation. Essentially, fixed-effects analyses assume that effect size variation is due to *just* sampling error and identified (i.e., coded) factors. By contrast, random-effects analyses assume that effect size variation is due to such factors and other unidentifiable factors (i.e., random factors). These two different approaches have important conceptual and statistical implications. The fixed-effects approach has fewer sources of variation, and therefore this approach has smaller standard errors and is more likely to reject the null hypothesis than random-effects specifications. The extra variability in the random-effects approach often is a more accurate depiction of the sources of effect size variation and allows for greater generalizability. For more discussion of these two approaches, see Hedges (1994) Overton (1998) and Raudenbush (1994). For examples of these two approaches in criminal justice research, see Prendergast et al. (2002). It is important to note that if the less conservative fixed-effects approach is applied when there are unidentified sources of variation (i.e., there are random effects), then standard errors and confidence intervals will be artificially narrower than they should, and as a result, the probability of type I error increases. Fortunately, it is possible to test which of these two analytic approaches is most tenable; specifically, the homogeneity of variance (Q) test examines the null hypothesis that the only source of effect size variation is sampling variation. The retention of this null hypothesis supports fixed-effects analyses, and its rejection supports random-effects analyses. Thus, this test is an important component of effect size analysis.

The fifth and sixth steps in meta-analysis are comparable to the corresponding steps in primary research. In particular, the fifth step concerns proper interpretation of meta-analytic results; these interpretations should be based on what the data support, qualified by limitations of the data and analysis and tested for sensitivity to alternative specifications. Last, in the sixth step, findings are presented using charts, graphs, tables, and text to summarize and explain the meta-analysis's key results.

Meta-analysis is sometimes described as a set of statistical procedures for research synthesis, but it should be apparent from these six steps that meta-analysis is much more than a set of statistical procedures. Implicit in these six steps is a *philosophy of research synthesis* that intimates how knowledge is generated and how knowledge should be extracted from empirical research. Perhaps most important, underlying these steps is the notion that scientific knowledge formation is a cumulative, collaborative, and self-correcting endeavor. This orientation implies that any individual study, by itself, has great difficulty in fully addressing a particular research question. Hunter and Schmidt (2004) make this point more strongly when they state the following: "One of the contributions of meta-analysis has been to show that no single study is adequate by itself to answer a scientific question. Therefore, each study should be considered as a data point to be contributed to a later meta-analysis" (p. 12). Another implication is that while no one study conclusively addresses a research question, nearly all studies contain some information that may be useful; this being the case, research synthesis should consider including a broad set of studies, regardless of statistical significance of individual findings, sample size, or publication status.

Moreover, research syntheses should be as transparent as possible; this philosophical goal requires that meta-analysts explicitly state eligibility criteria, outline key features of the search strategy, provide details concerning effect size and moderator variable coding, discuss strategies used to handle statistically dependent effect sizes, and describe the techniques used to analyze the data. The goal of transparency facilitates reader's understanding of meta-analytic results and aids other researchers' efforts to replicate the meta-analytic synthesis.

Meta-analyses that closely adhere to the philosophy of research synthesis and current meta-analytic statistical procedures offer a number of *potential* advantages over narrative reviews. The systematic, comprehensive, and well-documented searches that are the standard for meta-analytic reviews make meta-analytic synthesis transparent and replicable. The coding of effect sizes eliminates the focus on statistical significance of individual study findings, and effect size analyses reduce the amount of "the mental algebra" required to synthesize numerous studies. Likewise, the use of coded moderator variables facilitates the search for and testing of study features systematically related to effect size. In sum, meta-analysis has become the preferred method for synthesizing empirical research because it addresses many of the problems commonly encountered by narrative literature reviews and offers a more consistent approach to research synthesis.

General Weaknesses and Problems in Meta-analysis

Meta-analysis has several shortcomings and persistent problems that need acknowledgment. Perhaps most abstractly, some critics of meta-analysis argue that meta-analysis is based on the false premise that scientific knowledge develops out of an accumulation of research findings. Instead, these critics argue that scientific knowledge develops from an evolutionary process. Chow (1987), for example, contends that "accumulation of changes is *not* a numerical exercise; it is a conceptual one. It is more appropriate and less misleading to say 'knowledge evolves,' rather than 'knowledge accumulates'" (emphasis in original, p. 267). The implication of such arguments is that meta-analysis, which focuses on integrating the cumulative results of empirical research, potentially obscures this evolutionary process. Take, for example, strain theory, which has evolved considerably over time (especially individual-level versions); meta-analytically synthesizing tests of strain theory without regard to this evolutionary process would run a substantial risk of distorting what we have learned about the validity of strain theory.

Another, more concrete, weakness in meta-analysis is that this offers no formal way of integrating qualitative research—only quantitative research can be meta-analytically synthesized. Here, all is not lost. To this point, I've discussed meta-analytic and narrative reviews as competing methods for pedagogical purposes. Yet in reality, narrative and meta-analytic reviews can be conducted jointly as complementary methods, particularly, when the research base includes a sizable body of qualitative research.

The biggest practical weakness of meta-analysis is the time and resource intensity of meta-analytic reviews. High-quality meta-analytic reviews require reviewers to develop eligibility criteria, search relevant databases, record which databases were searched and which keywords were used, track down studies that appear to be eligible, code studies found to be eligible, and analyze coded information. All of these tasks consume considerable time and resources—much more so than the typical narrative review.

Still another problem with meta-analysis is that it is limited by the quality and quantity of the primary research. Meta-analysis is largely incapable of remedying problems in the primary research upon which it is based. For example, if the primary research uniformly consists of studies with poor internal validity, then a synthesis of this research will also have weak internal validity. One hundred poorly constructed studies will yield a point estimate in a meta-analysis, but the number of studies doesn't remedy basic problems with the science behind these studies. Likewise, if a body of research consistently has low construct validity, then meta-analytic synthesis of this research will be negatively influenced by this problem.[2] With that having been said, *variation* in terms of internal validity and construct validity can be substantively interesting and explain inconsistent findings in the research (i.e., this variation can be coded as moderator variables). Further, meta-analysis is limited by the number of studies addressing a particular relationship. Areas of research that have only a few relevant studies can do little more than estimating the average effect size of the relationship of interest; moderator analyses seeking to examine relevant variation in research findings are crippled by small research bases. For some theories in criminology that are currently less popular (e.g., labeling theory), this means that there won't be a sufficient number of studies to conduct a meta-analysis.

One of the criticisms most often levied against meta-analysis is that it synthesizes studies that differ in too many important ways to be meaningful. For instance, relevant studies may measure the key concepts differently, use different research designs, measure the dependent variable on different scales, use different analytic techniques, and so forth. Integrating studies regardless of such differences potentially mixes "apples and oranges" and, thus, all but the narrowest meta-analyses are potentially flawed. Meta-analysis of large bodies of research, the very context in which meta-analysis is most useful, run the greatest risk of encountering this criticism.

Meta-analysis has also been criticized on a number of statistical grounds. First, Berk (2007) challenges the notion that effect sizes yield measures of study findings that are truly comparable across studies. Berk argues that the comparability of effect sizes is undermined by the use of different dependent variables. In Berk's words, "In many social science applications of meta-analysis, what is being measured is arguably quite different in different studies" (p. 256). According to Berk, these conceptual differences undermine the assumption implicit in standardization that the "only systematic difference across studies is a difference in scale" (p. 255). Berk's criticism may not go far enough, as not only do studies utilize varying dependent variables, but they also utilize varying analytic strategies (even when the dependent variables are identical). These differences in analytic strategies present another source of variability that complicates effect size comparability.

Second, Berk demonstrates that standard meta-analytic practice is statistically flawed and breaks several important statistical assumptions necessary for statistical inference. Berk notes that accurate statistical inference in meta-analysis requires the twin assumptions of randomly sampled studies from a well-defined population and statistically independent effect sizes. The former assumption is consistently broken, as meta-analysts almost uniformly *attempt* to synthesize all available meeting the stated eligibility criteria. In regard to the latter assumption, some meta-analysts include multiple effect sizes from the same data set and thereby create dependencies among effect sizes. Berk argues that without these twin assumptions holding, all statistical inference in meta-analysis is deeply flawed.[3] Because of these issues, Berk recommends the use of narrative reviews instead of meta-analytic reviews, and when meta-analysis is used, its analyses should be strictly descriptive, not inferential (i.e., statistical significance tests should not be conducted).

Problems in the Synthesis of Theory Tests

Applying meta-analysis to integrate the results of theory tests is no different in process or procedure than the synthesis of evaluation research where meta-analysis is much more common; however, *meta-analytic integration of theoretical research presents several problems that potentially are more severe than that in evaluation research*. First, conceptualizing a meta-analysis of theoretical research requires considerably more thought than that in evaluation research where the realm of potentially eligible studies is usually well-defined by the type of intervention being evaluated. By contrast, the volume of potential relevant theory tests requires meta-analysts to carefully craft a set of eligibility criteria that include relevant studies and exclude irrelevant studies. Delineating such a set of eligibility criteria can appear deceptively straightforward, but the development of such criteria must confront several important issues, such as the following: Must studies focus primarily on testing the same theory as the meta-analyst? Or will eligible studies include studies that focus primarily on other theories but include variables relevant to the theory of interest to the meta-analyst? Must all eligible studies measure the key constructs *identically*? If not, which kinds of measures will be permitted? Must studies include a set of control variables (e.g., demographic factors, key measures from rival theories)? If so, which controls must be included? Must studies employ particular types of data analyses? (Perhaps, studies utilizing ordinary least-squares regression will be included but not studies using structural equation modeling.)

Meta-analyst may be tempted to adopt broad eligibility criteria but doing so often comes at considerable cost. Obviously, the broader the eligibility criteria, the more onerous and resource intensive the study search becomes. Further, broad eligibility criteria considerably complicate study coding and therefore necessitate the creation of thoughtful, thorough coding protocols (i.e., coding forms) that are capable of capturing important methodological and sample variation. These variations if coded properly may explain apparent inconsistent findings in research findings (one of the most valuable functions of meta-analysis). Last, the broader the eligibility criteria, the more susceptible the meta-analysis becomes to the "apples and oranges" criticism.

Second, the issues of effect size noncomparability and statistical dependencies between effect sizes are potentially more pronounced in meta-analysis of theory tests. The potential problem of noncomparability of effect sizes increases as the variability in the measurement of the dependent variable increases. Likewise, the comparability of effect sizes is potentially weakened by large variability in the types of data analytic strategies employed by primary authors. Broad reviews may encounter studies utilizing analyses ranging from simple cross-tabulations to complex structural equation models. Moreover, criminologists repeatedly have used several data sets (e.g., the National Youth Survey, the Causes and Correlates of Delinquency, the National Longitudinal Survey of Youth) to test hypotheses from various criminological theories. The inclusion of multiple effect sizes coded from the same data violates the assumption of statistical independence crucial for standard statistical inference.

To illustrate the difficulties likely to occur in the meta-analysis of theory tests, consider Kempf's (1993) review of the research testing Hirschi's control theory. I focus on Kempf's review because this narrative review was unusually systematic and relatively comprehensive. In many regards, Kempf's review approximates the meta-analytic standards for literature searches; in fact, Kempf refers to her research as a "quasi-meta-analysis" (p. 147). I also chose to focus on this review because it examines a very well-known theory, and it describes in detail methodological variation in this body of research.

Kempf's search strategy was usually systematic as it explicitly listed the eligibility criteria necessary for inclusion in the review. Specifically, eligible studies had to be as follows: (1) published between 1970 and 1991, (2) self-acknowledged tests of Hirschi's control theory, (3) cite Hirschi (1969) to ensure that each study was a test of Hirschi's version of control theory, and (4) must be published (although several dissertations were included)—Kempf argues that these criteria ensure methodological quality. Kempf listed the databases searched and the keywords used, which allow researchers to replicate her review's search.

Kempf's review was relatively narrowly crafted as it focused only on studies primarily testing Hirschi's control theory (instead of all research including measures of Hirschi's theory) and because only published studies were deemed eligible for inclusion. Despite this relatively narrow search strategy, seventy-one eligible studies were identified. Twenty-eight of these studies were classified as replications of Hirschi's test (i.e., examined the validity of theory when applied to various demographic groups, geographic contexts, or crime types). Sixteen were theoretical competitions that pitted Hirschi's theory against other theories. Sixteen more were theoretical integrations that included elements of Hirschi's theory, and eleven were classified by Kempf as "theory developments" that attempted to improve Hirschi's theory in various ways.

Kempf's review found relatively modest variation in sample characteristics and data collection strategies. Studies overwhelmingly collected data by using cross-sectional surveys of students. These student samples were largely comprising whites and males, but rarely included adults. Another interesting finding regarding the data used to test Hirschi's theory is that many authors analyzed the same data sets. For example, six studies used Hirschi's Richmond Youth Survey data and five studies used the Youth in Transition data. Further, several primary authors collected their own data and published multiple tests of Hirschi's theory using these data.

Perhaps the most striking revelation from Kempf's review is the great diversity in the measurement of key constructs in Hirschi's theory. Relatively few (24 percent) of the included studies measured all four bonds, and no one bond was measured in every study. The actual measurement of each bond also varied considerably. Outside of attachment to parents, which commonly used measures identical to Hirschi's (1969), the other concepts often utilized measures that were similar but not identical to Hirschi's. More interestingly, in a sizable proportion of studies, variables used by Hirschi to assess social bonding were used as measures of other theories. Further, these tests of social bonding also used a multitude of crime and delinquency measures as the dependent variable including measures focused on both minor and serious delinquency/crime, adolescent sexual behavior, school infractions, and even mental health disorders.

Kempf's review also reveals that primary authors used a multitude of analytic techniques to analyze these data. Some primary authors used bivariate analyses, like Hirschi (1969); others used multivariate analyses. Still other authors used path analyses with observed variables or latent variables (i.e., structural equation modeling). Last, while most analyses were cross-sectional, some were longitudinal.

In short, Kempf's thorough review of tests of Hirschi's social control theory revealed marked variation. Studies used various measures of key concepts, outcomes of interest, and analytic techniques. Given all the observed variation in study methodology, Kempf's conclusion that "different, and sometimes contrary, results were found" (p. 164) should come as no surprise.

Kempf's review illustrates the problems likely to confront meta-analysts conducting reviews of theory tests. First, even a narrowly crafted review like Kempf's is likely to encounter a large number of eligible studies and a very large number of potentially eligible studies. Thus, meta-analysis of theory tests has the potential to become very resource intensive. Second, the repeated use of publicly accessible data sets creates potential dependency problems between effect sizes—violating a key assumption for valid statistical inference. Third, eligible studies are likely to vary considerably in terms of the nature of the test (e.g., replication, theoretical integration, theory competition), measurement of key constructs, and analytic techniques. A major challenge for meta-analysts in this area is developing coding forms capable of capturing important variation between studies. Fourth, variability in the measurement of the dependent variable and the techniques used to analyze them complicate meta-analysis. The results from these different types of analyses may require the use of different effect sizes that are measured on different scales (see, e.g., Hasselblad and Hedges, 1995; Lipsey and Wilson, 2001). Converting these effect sizes onto a common scale adds an additional layer of complexity. Above and beyond this issue, different dependent variables may produce different average effect sizes. These two issues taken together potentially undermine the comparability of effect sizes.

Problems in Existing Meta-analyses of Theory Tests and Their Potential Solutions

Despite the serious problems that confront meta-analysts of criminological theory tests and calls for the abandonment of meta-analysis (see Berk, 2007), undoubtedly meta-analysis of theoretical research will continue. Given this reality, I offer several suggestions below, which I believe will serve to strengthen future meta-analyses of this sort. In a nutshell, I suggest that meta-analysts adhere more closely to the philosophy of meta-analysis and its *current* standards.[4] In some situations, however, the challenges to meta-analytic synthesis may be too daunting; in these situations I suggest the use of a middle-ground approach that blends meta-analysis and narrative review.

Above I argued that meta-analytic synthesis is a more systematic, comprehensive, objective, and scientific approach to research synthesis than narrative reviews. The many potential benefits of meta-analysis, however, are most likely to be realized when meta-analysts adhere to the standards of meta-analysis (as discussed above). Namely, meta-analytic synthesis should be

- systematic and replicable by delineating eligibility criteria, noting which databases were searched, and listing keywords used (including combinations of keywords);
- comprehensive by searching for all eligible research, regardless of publication status;
- potentially illuminating by coding relevant study variation (e.g., methodological variation, sample variation) that may explain inconsistent findings in the research; and
- statistically defensible by avoiding known violations of meta-analytic statistics.

Unfortunately, existing meta-analytic syntheses of theory tests fall short of these admittedly lofty goals. Below I review collectively existing meta-analyses of theory tests and highlight recurring issues in this growing body of research.

One recurring flaw in the existing meta-analyses of theory tests is that they often are noncomprehensive and unreplicable—just like the narrative reviews, they are designed to replace. Most often, meta-analysts in this area violate the philosophy of meta-analysis by reviewing only published studies. As stated above, this is problematic because meta-analyses in other areas of research consistently find that published studies are a biased subset of available research. Further, despite the assertions to the contrary, publication status is a poor indicator of methodological quality as many unpublished studies are comparable in methodological rigor as published studies (Wilson, 2009a). Existing meta-analyses also are unreplicable, as they fail to adequately describe their search strategy and the coding of moderator variables. As an example, one often cited that meta-analysis published in a criminology/criminal justice journal inadequately describes the search strategy used, as the authors to describe the databases searched but not the keywords used in their search. Another meta-analysis of theory tests published in a criminology/criminal justice journal codes many moderator variables, but most of these moderators are not described in enough detail to permit replication.

Existing meta-analyses of theory tests also exhibit significant short-comings in terms of effect size coding and analysis. Extant meta-analyses often fail to adequately discuss effect size coding. For example, commonly meta-analysts state that standardized regression coefficients (OLS) were converted into Pearson's r effect size, yet these authors fail to address analytic strategies besides OLS regression. What was done to studies that employed other data analytic strategies? Were these studies/outcomes excluded? Or were these studies' results converted onto the r effect size scale? If so, how was this accomplished? These unaddressed issues go against meta-analysis' philosophy of transparency and replicability. Further, failing to address such issues inhibits the reader's understanding and ability to interpret meta-analytic results.

In regard to the analysis of effect sizes, another recurring flaw concerns the use of fixed-effects analyses without establishing that the homogeneity of variance assumption is tenable. Authors typically fail to report results of the homogeneity of variance assumption. The use of fixed effects without proof of this assumption's validity is highly questionable and leads to concerns about elevated probabilities of type I errors, given fixed-effects small standard errors and confidence intervals.

Another analytic concern is that meta-analysts have adopted questionable practices for handling dependent effect sizes. Standard meta-analytic practice dictates that each data set contribute one and only one effect size to any analysis. To meet this standard, meta-analysts often develop criteria for the selection of this one effect size when multiple effect sizes from the same study are available. For instance, perhaps the effect size from the study employing the largest number of control variables is selected for inclusion. Another, more controversial, practice is to calculate the weighted average of the effect sizes coded from a common data set, and this mean effect size becomes the "selected" effect size. A third approach utilizes techniques specifically designed for meta-analysis that adjust for the covariance between dependent effect sizes (e.g., Kalaian and Raudenbush, 1996; Gleser, L. J. and Olkin, I. 2009). Contrary to these standard practices, meta-analysts in this area commonly include multiple effect sizes from the same data set and then attempting to model and adjust for statistical dependencies using techniques that were not specifically designed for meta-analysis. For example, several meta-analyses have employed methods similar to those used in multiple regression to deal with serial correlation as a means adjust for statistical dependencies. These techniques are unproven in the meta-analytic context, and their use has unknown implications for hypothesis testing.

The solutions to these issues are straightforward. For clarity, future meta-analyses of theory tests should adhere more closely to the philosophy and current practices of meta-analysis by (1) searching comprehensively for both published and unpublished research,[5] (2) carefully documenting the search strategy (e.g., keywords used, databases searches), (3) making available the coding forms used, (4) detailing how effect sizes were coded, particularly results from nonstandard outcomes/analyses, (5) following standard practices for maintaining statistical independence of effect sizes, and (6) testing the homogeneity of variance assumption before using fixed-effect analyses.

While I think Berk's (2007) suggestion that meta-analysis should be abandoned is unreasonable, I do believe that Berk's suggestion for meta-analysts to adopt a descriptive approach deserves consideration. The above discussion clearly shows that the most serious threats to meta-analytic results concern statistical inference via statistical significance testing. As Berk points out, conventional tests of statistical significance require several assumptions that are difficult to meet in meta-analysis. Thus statistical inference via significance testing is deeply troublesome in meta-analysis. *Rather than abandon meta-analysis because it has difficulty in meeting the assumptions for statistical significance testing, meta-analysts should consider abandoning tests of statistical significance!* Tests of statistical significance in meta-analysis are unnecessary, because the mean effect size and the width of its confidence interval are more meaningful gauges of a relationship's importance than the statistical significance. Simply put, the mean effect size and its variability contain more information than any test of statistical significance: large mean effect sizes with narrow confidence intervals affirmatively indicate that a relationship is of *substantive significance*, and, conversely, small mean effect sizes, especially those with narrow confidence intervals, affirmatively indicate that a relationship is negligible. No tests of statistical significance need to be conducted! This proposal for a descriptive approach to meta-analysis may sound radical but it is actually quite modest and has been proposed for years by meta-analysts such Frank Schmidt and John Hunter (see, e.g., Schmidt, 1992, 1996; Schmidt and

Hunter, 1997). Thus, Berk's suggestion of abandoning meta-analysis because of its difficulties in meaning the assumptions necessary for significance tests is unreasonable; instead, researchers should strongly consider Berk's other suggestion and abandon significance testing in the realm of meta-analysis (and perhaps more generally as well).

Another suggestion is that researchers take a "middle-ground" approach to research synthesis. Specifically, given the problems confronting meta-analysis of theory tests and the shortcomings of meta-analysis, especially its statistical difficulties and inability to integrate findings from qualitative research, conducting "systematic review" of theory tests—much like Kempf's view of Hirschi's social control theory—may be less problematic than a purely meta-analytic approach. Systematic review, like meta-analysis, systematically and comprehensively reviews research by developing explicit eligibility criteria and searching extensively for eligible studies (for a more detailed discussion of systematic reviews, see Farrington and Petrosino, 2001). Unlike meta-analysis, however, systematic reviews do not necessarily rely on effect sizes. Kempf's systematic review discussed above shows just how powerful this systematic review approach can be as a descriptive tool for synthesizing theoretical research. The benefits of this middle-ground approach embodied by systematic review are that it is not weighed down with the statistical difficulties likely to be encountered in meta-analytic synthesis, and systematic review is able to integrate qualitative research. On the other hand, a deficiency of systematic reviews is that they are incapable of quantitatively estimating the average relationship between the variables of interest; systematic reviews mitigate this deficiency by being able to qualitatively judge the magnitude of such relationships.

Conclusion

Meta-analytic synthesis of theory tests potentially produces findings that more accurately describe the empirical tests of extant theories and can better explain inconsistencies in it than narrative reviews. Applying meta-analysis to such research is potentially problematic because the volume of potentially relevant research is vast, research has tested the same theories in a multitude of ways, and the same data sets are repeatedly used to test various theories (causing statistical dependencies). These problems are daunting but not usually insurmountable. Fortunately, the solutions to these problems are largely already available—meta-analysts merely need to make better use of currently available techniques and more importantly the philosophy of meta-analysis.

Notes

1. Much to their credit, the editors of this volume advocate "the use of meta-analysis to organize the empirical literature for every theory of crime" (Cullen et al., 2008: 29).
2. It should be noted that some methods have been developed to fix particular errors in primary research (see Hunter and Schmidt, 2004).
3. See Shadish (1997) and Lipsey (2007) for a defense of meta-analysis's statistical procedures.
4. It is important to emphasize that meta-analysis is a relatively young approach to research synthesis and as such it is developing rapidly. Thus relying on meta-analytic practices and standards from the mid-1980s (e.g., Wolf, 1986) may be outdated.
5. If researchers are concerned about differences in methodological quality by publication status, then they should develop explicit methodological standards and integrate these standards into the eligibility criteria, rather than utilizing publication status as a (flawed) proxy for methodological quality.

Bibliography

Baier, Colin J. and Bradley R. E. Wright. "'If You Love Me, Keep My Commandments': A Meta-analysis of the Effect of Religion on Crime." *Journal of Research in Crime and Delinquency* 38, no. 1 (2001): 3–21.

Berk, Richard. "Statistical Inference and Meta-analysis." *Journal of Experimental Criminology* 3, no. 3 (2007): 247–70.

Borenstein, Michael. "Effect Sizes for Continuous Data." In *The Handbook of Research Synthesis and Meta-analysis*, edited by Harris M. Cooper, Larry V. Hedges, and Jeffrey C. Valentine, 2nd ed., 221–36. New York: Russell Sage Foundation, 2009.

Callaham, Michael L., Robert L. Wears, Ellen J. Weber, Christopher Barton, and Gary Young. "Positive-Outcome Bias and Other Limitations in the Outcome of Research Abstracts Submitted to a Scientific Meeting." *Journal of the American Medical Association* 280, no. 3 (1998): 254–57.

Chow, Siu L. "Meta-analysis of Pragmatic and Theoretical Research: A Critique." *Journal of Psychology* 121, no. 3 (1987): 259–71.

Cooper, Harris M. and Larry V. Hedges. "Research Synthesis As a Scientific Process." In *The Handbook of Research Synthesis and Meta-analysis*, edited by Harris Cooper, Larry V. Hedges, and Jeffrey C. Valentine, 2nd ed., 3–16. New York: Russell Sage Foundation, 2009.

Cooper, Harris M., Larry V. Hedges, and Jeffrey C. Valentine. *The Handbook of Research Synthesis and Meta-analysis*. New York: Russell Sage Foundation, 2009.

Cooper, Harris M. and Robert Rosenthal. "Statistical versus Traditional Procedures for Summarizing Research Findings." *Psychological Bulletin* 87, no. 3 (1980): 442–49.

Cullen, Francis T., John P. Wright, and Kristie R. Blevins, eds. *Taking Stock: The Status of Criminological Theory*. Advances in

Criminological Theory, vol. 15. New Brunswick, NJ: Transaction Publishers, 2008.

Farrington, David P. and Anthony Petrosino. "The Campbell Collaboration Crime and Justice Group." *The Annals of the American Academy of Political and Social Science* 578 (2001): 35–49.

Fleiss, Joseph L. and Jesse A. Berlin. "Effect Sizes for Dichotomous Data." In *The Handbook of Research Synthesis and Meta-analysis*, edited by Harris M. Cooper, Larry V. Hedges, and Jeffrey C. Valentine, 237–54. New York: Russell Sage Foundation, 2009.

Glass, Gene V. "Primary, Secondary, and Meta-analysis of Research." *Educational Researcher* 5, no. 10 (1976): 3–8.

Greenwald, Anthony G. "Consequences of Prejudice against the Null Hypothesis." *Psychological Bulletin* 82, no. 1 (1975): 1–20.

Hall, Judith A., Linda Tickle-Degnen, Robert Rosenthal, and Frederick Mosteller. "Hypotheses and Problems in Research Synthesis." In *The Handbook of Research Synthesis*, edited by Harris Cooper and Larry V. Hedges, 17–28. New York: Russell Sage Foundation, 1994.

Hasselblad, Vic and Larry V. Hedges. "Meta-analysis of Screening and Diagnostic Tests." *Psychological Bulletin* 117, no. 1 (1995): 167–78.

Hedges, Larry V. "Fixed Effects Models." In *The Handbook of Research Synthesis*, edited by Harris Cooper and Larry V. Hedges, 285–99. New York: Russell Sage Foundation, 1994.

Hirschi, Travis. *Causes of Delinquency*. Berkeley, CA: University of California Press, 1969.

Hunter, John E. and Frank L. Schmidt. *Methods of Meta-analysis: Correcting Error and Bias in Research Findings*. 2nd ed. Thousand Oaks, CA: Sage, 2004.

Kalaian, H. A. and S. W. Raudenbush. "A Multivariate Linear Model for Meta-Analysis." *Psychological Methods* 1, no. 3 (1996): 227–35.

Kempf, Kimberly L. "The Empirical Status of Hirschi's Control Theory." In *New Directions in Criminological Theory*. Advances in Criminological Theory, edited by Freda Adler and William S. Laufer, vol. 4, 143–85. New Brunswick, NJ: Transaction Publishers, 1993.

Lipsey, Mark W. "Juvenile Delinquency Treatment: A Meta-analytic Inquiry into the Variability of Effects." In *Meta-analysis for Explanation: A Casebook*, edited by Thomas D. Cook, Harris Cooper, David S. Cordray, Heidi Hartman, Larry V. Hedges, Richard J. Light, Thomas A. Louis, and Frederick Mosteller, 83–128. New York: Russell Sage Foundation, 1992.

———. "Unjustified Inferences about Meta-analysis." *Journal of Experimental Criminology* 3, no. 3 (2007): 271–79.

———. "Identifying Interesting Variables and Analysis Opportunities." In *The Handbook of Research Synthesis and Meta-analysis*, edited by Harris Cooper, Larry V. Hedges, and Jeffrey C. Valentine, 147–58. New York: Russell Sage Foundation, 2009.

Lipsey, Mark W., Gabrielle Chapman, and Nana Landenberger. "Cognitive-Behavioral Programs for Offenders: A Synthesis of the

Research on Their Effectiveness for Reducing Recidivism." *The 2001 Jerry Lee Crime Prevention Symposium*, Washington, DC. Nashville, TN: Institute for Public Policy Studies, Vanderbilt University, 2001.

Lipsey, Mark W. and David B. Wilson. *Practical Meta-analysis*. Thousand Oaks, CA: Sage Publications, 2001.

MacKenzie, Doris L., David B. Wilson, and Suzanne B. Kider. "Effects of Correctional Boot Camps on Offending." *The Annals of the American Academy of Political and Social Sciences* 578, no. 1 (2001): 126–43.

Mann, Charles C. "Can Meta-analysis Make Policy?" *Science* 266, no. 5187 (1994): 960–62.

Mitchell, Ojmarrh, David B. Wilson, and Doris L. MacKenzie. "Does Incarceration-Based Drug Treatment Reduce Recidivism? A Meta-analytic Synthesis of the Research." *Journal of Experimental Criminology* 3, no. 4 (2007): 353–75.

Overton, Randall C. "A Comparison of Fixed-Effects and Mixed (Random-Effects) Models for Meta-analysis of Moderator Variable Effects." *Psychological Methods* 3, no. 3 (1998): 354–79.

Pratt, Travis C. and Francis T. Cullen. "The Empirical Status of Gottfredson and Hirschi's General Theory of Crime: A Meta-analysis." *Criminology* 38, no. 3 (2000): 931–64.

———. "Assessing Macro-Level Predictors and Theories of Crime: A Meta-analysis." In *Crime and Justice: A Review of Research* 32, edited by Michael Tonry, 373–450. Chicago, IL: University of Chicago, 2005.

Pratt, Travis C., Francis T. Cullen, Kristie R. Blevins, Leah E. Daigle, and Tamara D. Madensen. "The Empirical Status of Deterrence Theory: A Meta-analysis." *Taking Stock: The Status of Criminological Theory*. Advances in Criminological Theory, edited by Francis T. Cullen, John P. Wright, and Kristie R. Blevins, vol. 15. New Brunswick, NJ: Transaction Publishers, 2008.

Prendergast, Michael L., Deborah Podus, Eunice Chang, and Darren Urada. "The Effectiveness of Drug Abuse Treatment: A Meta-analysis of Comparison Group Studies." *Drug and Alcohol Dependence* 84, no. 1 (2002): 53–72.

Raudenbush, Stephen W. "Random Effects Models." In *The Handbook of Research Synthesis*, edited by Harris Cooper and Larry V. Hedges, 302–21. New York: Russell Sage Foundation, 1994.

Schmidt, Frank L. "What Do Data Really Mean? Research Findings, Meta-analysis, and Cumulative Knowledge in Psychology." *American Psychologist* 47 (1992): 1173–81.

———. "Statistical Significance Testing and Cumulative Knowledge in Psychology: Implications for Training of Researchers." *Psychological Methods* 1 (1996): 115–29.

Schmidt, Frank L. and John E. Hunter. "Eight Common But False Objections to the Discontinuation of Significance Testing in the Analysis of

Research Data." In *What If There Were No Significance Tests?*, edited by Lisa L. Harlow, Stanley A. Mulaik, and James H. Steiger, 37–64. Mahwah, NJ: Lawrence Erlbaum Associates, Inc., 1997.

Shadish, William R. "A World without Meta-analysis." *Journal of Experimental Criminology* 3, no. 3 (1997): 281–91.

Shadish, William R. and C. K. Haddock. "Combining Estimates of Effect Size." In *The Handbook of Research Synthesis and Meta-analysis*, edited by Harris Cooper, Larry V. Hedges, and Jeffrey C. Valentine, 257–78. New York: Russell Sage Foundation, 2009.

Smith, Mary L. "Publication Bias and Meta-analysis." *Evaluation in Education* 4, no. 1 (1980): 22–24.

Wang, Morgan C. and Brad J. Bushman. *Integrating Results through Meta-analytic Review Using SAS Software*. Cary, NC: SAS Institute, Inc., 1999.

White, Howard D. "Scientific Communication and Literature Retrieval." In *The Handbook of Research Synthesis*, edited by Harris Cooper and Larry V. Hedges, 41–56. New York: Russell Sage Foundation, 1994.

Wilson, David B. "Missing a Critical Piece of the Pie: Simple Document Search Strategies Inadequate for Systematic Reviews." *Journal of Experimental Criminology* 5 (2009a): 429–40.

———. "Systematic Coding." In *The Handbook of Research Synthesis and Meta-analysis*, edited by Harris Cooper, Larry V. Hedges, and Jeffrey C. Valentine, 2nd ed., 159–76. New York: Russell Sage Foundation, 2009b.

Wolf, Frederic M. *Meta-analysis: Quantitative Methods of Research Synthesis*. Beverly Hills, CA: Sage, 1986.

Contributors

Geoffrey C. Barnes (gbarnes@sas.upenn.edu), University of Pennsylvania

Shawn P. Bushway (SBushway@uamail.albany.edu), University of Albany

Jordan M. Hyatt (jhyatt@sas.upenn.edu), University of Pennsylvania

David S. Kirk (dkirk@prc.utexas.edu), University of Texas

Marvin D. Krohn (mkrohn@crim.ufl.edu), University of Florida

John M. MacDonald (johnmm@sas.upenn.edu), University of Pennsylvania

Charles F. Manski (cfmanski@northwestern.edu), Northwestern University

Ojmarrh Mitchell (ojmarrh@gmail.com), University of South Florida

Andrew Morral (morral@rand.org), RAND Corporation

Daniel S. Nagin (dn03@andrew.cmu.edu), Carnegie Mellon University

Candice L. Odgers (codgers@uci.edu), University of California Irvine

Andrew V. Papachristos (apapachr@hsph.harvard.edu), Harvard University

Raymond Paternoster (rpaternoster@crim.umd.edu), University of Maryland

Alex R. Piquero (apiquero@fsu.edu), Florida State University

John K. Roman (JRoman@urban.org), Urban Institute

Michael A. Russell (m.a.russell@uci.edu), University of California Irvine

Christopher J. Sullivan (sullivc6@ucmail.uc.edu), University of Cincinnati

Ralph B. Taylor (rbrecken@temple.edu), Temple University

Terence P. Thornberry (tthornberry@crim.umd.edu), University of Maryland

Index

Abbott, Andrew, 72, 75, 91, 106, 320
Abbring, Jaap H., 251
Abrahamse, A. F., 232
Achenbach, T. M., 7
Action, theory of, 91
Adaptive diversification, 195
Add Health (National Longitudinal
	Survey of Adolescent Health), 113,
	117, 118, 120, 128
Administrative data, viii, 38–39
Adoption studies, 143–145
Advances in Criminological Theory, 335
Adversity, 148
African-Americans, 11, 12, 23
Age
	of crime victim, and price of crime,
		39–40
	descriptive statistics for, 28, 31
	desistance and, 299–300, 302–309,
		303, 305, 318, 326n1
	distribution in major league baseball,
		307
	farm work and arrests, *308*
	influence on crime, 29
	total crimes committed by, *304*
	trajectory groups of offenders, *305*
Ageton, S.S., 5, 6
Aggravated assaults, 57
Agnew, R., 85, 92n4, 317, 337
Ahmed, E., 225, 226
Ahn, Hyungtaik, 162
Akers, Robert L., 3, 33, 317, 337
Albonetti, Celesta A., 182
Alcohol consumption, 28, 29, 30, 31, 32
American Journal of Epidemiology,
	130n1
American Journal of Public Health,
	130n1
American Journal of Sociology, 130n1
American Sociological Review, 130n1
Analytic data sets, 40

Anderson, Linda S., 4
Anderson, Michelle Chernikoff, 47
Angrist, J. D., 41, 162, 246, 247, 250,
	251, 255, 256
Anomie theory, 3
Anonymity and response bias, 25
Anticrime intervention strategies, 41, 42.
	See also Crime prevention
Antisocial behavior
	genes in, 146, 149–150
	genes-to-brain-to-behavior pathways
		in, 152
	genetic and environmental effects on,
		141–142, 142–143, 151
	heritability of, 143–145
	mechanisms for, 148–149
	prenatal smoking, 147–148
Apel, Robert J., 246, 247, 262, 309
Applied economics studies of crime,
	41–42
Arkin, R., 24
Armstrong, T. A., 233
Arrest data, 49, 129, 236n6, 271,
	302–303, *303*
Arrests
	DUI's, 216, 219, 221
	UCR data, 253, 257, 258, *303*
Arrow, K., 44
Assaults
	direct and indirect costs, 57
	estimated price of victimization, 61,
		62
	price of aggravated, 60
	ranking of crimes by severity, 58
Attitudinal measures, 9
Attitudinal scales, 22
Australia, 220
Australian Capital Territory, 217
Australian Reintegrative Shaming
	Experiments (RISE). *See* Reintegra-
	tive Shaming Experiments